M7 N 1. 3985

MW01487627

PHANTOMS OF THE SOUTH FORK

CIVIL WAR SOLDIERS AND STRATEGIES
Brian S. Wills, Series Editor

Phantoms

of the

South Fork

CAPTAIN MCNEILL AND
HIS RANGERS

STEVE FRENCH

The Kent State University Press
Kent, Ohio

© 2017 by The Kent State University Press, Kent, Ohio 44242

Library of Congress Catalog Card Number 2017016117
ISBN 978-1-60635-309-7
Manufactured in the United States of America

Library of Congress Cataloging-in-Publication Data
Names: French, Steve, author.
Title: Phantoms of the South Fork : Captain McNeill and his Rangers / Steve French.
Description: Kent, Ohio : The Kent State University Press, 2017. | Series: Civil War soldiers
    and strategies | Includes bibliographical references and index.
Identifiers: LCCN 2017016117 (print) | LCCN 2017025154 (ebook) | ISBN 9781631012662
    (ePub) | ISBN 9781631012679 (ePDF) | ISBN 9781606353097 (hardcover : alk. paper)
Subjects: LCSH: McNeill, John Hanson, 1815-1864. | Confederate States of America. Army.
    McNeill Partisan Rangers. | United States--History--Civil War, 1861-1865--Underground
    movements. | Potomac River, South Branch (Va.-W. Va.)--History, Military--19th century.
    | United States--History--Civil War, 1861-1865--Campaigns. | Guerrillas--Confederate
    States of America--Biography. | Soldiers--Confederate States of America--Biography. |
    Moorefield (W. Va.)--Biography.
Classification: LCC E581.6.M36 (ebook) | LCC E581.6.M36 F74 2017 (print) | DDC
    973.7/42--dc23
LC record available at https://lccn.loc.gov/2017016117

21 20 19 18 17   5 4 3 2 1

This book is dedicated to my mother,

Donna Jean Baker French, for always encouraging me

in the study of history.

Contents

—❦—

Acknowledgments

I would like to thank a number of individuals who greatly assisted the author in the research and preparation of the manuscript.

Ted Alexander read and commented on the manuscript and gave the author many helpful suggestions and much encouragement. Richard Armstrong provided the author with Private James Vallandingham's recollections and answered questions about Company F, 7th Virginia Cavalry, and Jeff Brown gave the author a number of books from his vast library, along with valuable research assistance. Clyde Cale Jr. furnished the author with many little-known *Ranger* magazine and newspaper articles; an accomplished author and dedicated researcher, Clyde's help was crucial to the completion of this manuscript. Marshall Coiner took the author on a guided tour of the Piedmont Battlefield in Virginia, and Jim Creed, 23rd Illinois Infantry expert, answered the author's questions about Colonel James Mulligan's time in Missouri and West Virginia. Jim Droegemeyer gave the author a number of period newspaper articles and provided valuable research and technical assistance. George Fletcher took the author on guided tours of the Folck's Mill and Old Town, Maryland, battlefields, McNeill Ranger skirmish sites in Green Spring and Springfield, West Virginia, and sites in Cresaptown and Cumberland in Maryland, associated with the kidnapping of Generals Crook and Kelley; George also provided rare documents on the kidnapping of the generals and the aftermath of the March 30, 1865, Dan's Run, West Virginia, train robbery.

Joe Geiger of the West Virginia Archives assisted the author in locating hard-to-find information on Mountain State Civil War soldiers. Joyce Harrison, former Kent State University Press acquiring editor, helped to shepherd the author through the publishing process. Mark Jones answered the author's questions about Cresaptown, Cumberland, and Wiley Ford and also provided some rare photographs. Dr. Robert Keller, a noted McNeill Ranger aficionado, answered many of the author's questions about partisan activities in the Shenandoah Valley and elsewhere; Bob also volunteered much information on the Ringgold Battalion and provided the story of Private Joseph M. Womack. Aaron Kilmer located many important documents and provided research assistance, and George Martin, of the Civil War Message Board Portal, answered a number of the author's questions. Rex Miller graciously provided the author with a number of important contacts and gave great encouragement in the completion of this project. Bob Mohr was not only extremely helpful in answering the author's many questions on ranger skirmishes against federal cavalry and West Virginia Home Guards in the Petersburg, West Virginia, area but also gave me a guided tour of Ranger sites throughout present-day Grant County, and he read and commented on a portion of the manuscript.

Ben Ritter of Winchester, Virginia, allowed the author to examine and copy period newspaper articles and obituaries from his McNeill Ranger collection and also provided a number of period photos. Royce Saville, who was a great help answering the author's questions about Civil War activities in Hampshire and Hardy Counties, also took me on a guided tour of important Ranger sites in Romney, Keyser, and Piedmont, West Virginia, and in Bloomington, Maryland. Donna Shrum read and commented on the manuscript, and besides providing editorial assistance, she shared her wealth of knowledge on the Rangers. Woodrow "Jay" Simmons helped the author in ways too numerous to mention; from answering my many questions on old roads and skirmish locations in the Moorefield area, guiding me on tours of Grant and Hardy Counties, and providing obscure newspaper articles and pictures, I could always count on Jay to lend a hand. Tim Snyder gave the author a copy of his Potomac River fords manuscript, a number of period newspaper articles, and period maps. Allan Tischler, Union cavalry historian and first-class researcher, who gave the author tremendous help by providing portions of his research on Sheridan's Scouts, also read and commented on a few chapters of the manuscript and provided much encouragement. Civil War author Dan Toomey provided information on the B&O Railroad, and Dr. Brian S. Wills read the manuscript and offered many helpful suggestions. Rick Wolfe answered a number of the author's questions, contributed pictures, and accompanied me on a visit to Ranger sites along Trough Road. Rob Wolford also answered a number of the author's questions, these on Ranger actions in and around Romney, and identified a number of local skirmish sites.

The following individuals also assisted the author in this project:

Kellee Blake, Bob Boal, Jeff Bowers, Dennis Brooke, Sam Buterbaugh, John Chapman, Don Corbett, Ray Cox, Roger Delauter, Peggy Dillard, Shaun

Dorsey, Tim Doyle, Vernall Doyle, Will Ford, John Frye, Scott Fullerton, Alice Gayley, Marian Golden, Keith Hammersla, Eph Herriott, Kermit Hoffman, Mike Hogbin, Elizabeth Howe, Carey Johnson, Eileen Johnson, Kenny Johnson, David Judy, Rudi Keller, Rita Knox, Carol Koontz, Jim McGhee, Ryan McPherson, Horace Mewborn Jr., Brian Monahan, Mike Musick, Dave Pancake, Doug Perks, Fred Price, Chris Rankin, Richard Rankin, Dr. John Rathgeb, Mollie Rebuck, Tommie Rebuck, Frank Roleff, Bill Root, Wayne Shilling, Martin Shobe, Nancy Grandstaff Shrum, Rick Snowden, Tim Sullivan, Tommy Swain, Kelley Taylor, Sherry Uhl, Rodney Walburn, Kyle Wichtendahl, Kelley Williams, and Tim Williams.

In closing, the author would like to thank Kent State University Press acquiring editor Will Underwood, managing editor Mary Young, marketing manager Susan Cash, and design and production manager Christine Brooks, for their help with this project. Last but not least, copyeditor Margery Tippie did a fantastic job of smoothing out the manuscript's rough edges.

The following institutions gave the author valuable assistance:

Allegany County (Md.) Public Library, Antietam National Battlefield Library, C&O Canal NHP Cumberland Visitors Center Library, Baltimore and Ohio Railroad Museum Library, Enoch Pratt Free Library, Fulton County (Pa.) Historical Society, Grant County (W.Va.) Public Library, Hampshire County (W.Va.) Historical Society, Hampshire County Public Library, Hancock (Md.) Historical Society, Hardy County (W.Va.) Public Library, Jefferson County (W.Va.) Museum, Library of Congress, Martinsburg–Berkeley County (W.Va.) Public Library, Morgan County (W.Va.) Historical Society, National Archives, National Museum of Civil War Medicine, New Hampshire Department of Cultural Resources, New York State Military Museum and Veterans Research Center, Rosenberg Library, Sharpsburg (Md.) Historical Society, and Washington County (Md.) Free Library–John Clinton Frye Western Maryland Room.

Prologue

Partisan Rangers

"Let no one, then, be deterred from enlisting with the partisans."

On April 21, 1862, the Confederate Congress voted to pass the Partisan Ranger Act, a law that in due course became one of that legislative body's most controversial and divisive measures. Although the act had its opponents in both Congress and the military, its supporters argued that partisan service would attract more men into the Southern forces, allow for more cooperation between irregular fighters and the army, and give these guerrillas the same legal protection when captured that enlisted soldiers had.

Two days later the adjutant and inspector general's Office of the War Department issued General Order No. 30. Made up of three parts, it authorized President Jefferson Davis to commission officers who would in turn "form bands of partisan rangers." These new units could be companies, battalions, or regiments of cavalry or infantry. Second, rangers would "be entitled to rations and quarters . . . and be subject to the same regulations as other soldiers." Finally, unlike a regular, the partisan could sell captured war supplies "to any quartermaster" and be "paid their full value."[1]

Over the next two years, ranger outfits performed countless military feats that benefited the Confederate cause, but by the winter of 1864 numerous incidents of banditry and murder, and the irritating penchant of some partisan chieftains to ignore orders issued by army officers, enraged many important Southern civilian and military leaders. On top of this, the siren's call of the carefree, profitable partisan life had lured numerous deserters, and many facing conscription, to enlist in these bands, thereby depriving the army of men needed to replenish its fast-dwindling ranks.

On February 17, 1864, Congress rescinded the act, and in April, following General Robert E. Lee's recommendation, current Secretary of War James

Captain John Hanson McNeill. Courtesy Ben Ritter.

Seddon ordered all partisan units disbanded and their soldiers enrolled in army or cavalry commands. Seddon, though, did make two exceptions: the famed Mosby's Rangers and McNeill's Rangers, a much smaller unit than the former but one whose star was just as bright.[2]

Almost as soon as General Order No. 30 went into effect, former army officers and private citizens throughout the South, especially from areas now occupied by federal troops, began applying to the War Department for permission to form partisan commands. Soon various self-proclaimed captains, who may have envisioned themselves as following in the giant footsteps of South Carolinian Francis Marion, the "Swamp Fox" of Revolutionary War fame, posted broadsides and advertisements in local newspapers calling for volunteers.

A good example is a military notice that appeared in the May 7 *Richmond Daily Dispatch*. Fauquier County native Captain John Scott called for "enterprising men to join me, who are not engaged in the military service . . . whether animated by a simple love of country, or a hatred of the public enemy; whether they have a wrong to redress, a vengeance to slake, or a home to protect."[3]

In the North many believed that Richmond had given these "guerrilla bands, or bushwhackers," the authority "to steal and rob to their hearts content." With this in mind, no doubt some men were reluctant to enlist, fearing summary execution if captured by the enemy. In fact, on June 2 the *Macon Telegraph* reported that "two Confederate partisan rangers have been hung in Northwestern Virginia."[4]

To bolster the spirits of the unwilling and encourage them to enlist, on June 5 a writer who identified himself only as "Whig" penned a fervent defense of this type of unconventional warfare in the *Daily Dispatch*. He wrote that although some thought "that Partisan Rangers are nothing more or less than guerrillas . . . and as such are not entitled to the protection of the code of civilized warfare," he differed. Noting that a congressional act had established the partisans, Whig added:

> If the enemy shall attempt to deprive our partisan warriors of those advantages of which other prisoners are guaranteed by the civilized code, not only may the partisans themselves retaliate upon the enemy, but President Davis himself would doubt feel called upon to in later pose for their protection. Let no one, then, be deterred from enlisting with the partisans under the apprehension that they will be treated as brigands or pirates. They stand upon as high a ground, nay, upon the same ground, as do the regular and provisional armies.[5]

John D. Imboden. Courtesy Ben Ritter.

Recruiting in the Shenandoah Valley, Potomac Highlands, and the Allegheny Mountains of Virginia, Colonel John D. Imboden, former captain of the Staunton Artillery, had no trouble filling the ranks of his 1st Virginia Partisan Rangers with men looking for excitement, plunder, and a chance to settle scores with the Northern invaders. By June 23 Imboden had already organized eight companies. Many of his recruits hailed from counties in the northwestern portion of the "Old Dominion" that were under federal occupation or other areas that were often menaced by bands of pillaging bluecoats and marauding local Unionists.[6]

It was in this climate that on July 24, 1862, a battle-scarred veteran from Missouri arrived in Richmond, seeking then Secretary of War George W. Randolph's permission to form a ranger company for service in northwestern Virginia. The next day that veteran was identified by a *Richmond Whig* reporter, who noted that "Capt. John H. McNeill, of the Missouri State Guard, who was taken prisoner by the enemy last February and confined in St. Louis, . . . succeeded in escaping about the middle of June and after a series of adventures reached this city." And was on his way toward founding the company that was to be known as "McNeill's Rangers."[7]

CHAPTER I

The Missouri State Guard

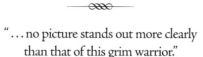

"…no picture stands out more clearly
than that of this grim warrior."

John Hanson McNeill, the son of Strother and Amy Pugh McNeill, was born near Moorefield, Virginia, on June 12, 1815. John's father, a well-off Hardy County farmer, died some three and a half years later. Like most of the boys who lived in the rich farmlands that bordered the South Branch River, young John Hanson soon learned the value of honest labor and grew into a self-reliant young man.

On January 19, 1837, McNeill, now twenty-one, married seventeen-year-old Jemima Cunningham, and the couple soon moved onto their own farm. Just eleven months later Jemima gave birth to William Strother, the couple's first son. Not long afterward, according to historian Maud Pugh, the family packed up and moved "to Bourbon County, Kentucky, where they lived until 1844."[1]

While the family lived in the Bluegrass State, two other sons, George and Jesse, were born, but by 1844 McNeill, with his wife in ill health, had sold his Kentucky property and moved back to Moorefield, and on July 18 of that year Sarah Emily, their only daughter, was born. Some four years later, however, wanderlust struck again, and the McNeill family, along with a handful of slaves, migrated to Boone County, Missouri, settling on the "Johnston place," a farm not far from Columbia.

In Missouri McNeill, known by his friends as Hanson or "Hanse," continued a long family tradition of raising Shorthorn cattle, a venture that not only proved lucrative but won him prizes at the local county fair as well. According to W. D. Vandiver, who as a boy knew the Virginian, "he replenished his herd with the finest stock that he could find in Kentucky and Ohio and continued to win blue ribbons and awards." In 1855 the McNeills moved again, this time northwest to a farm in Daviess County. There, on October 7, 1859, Jemima gave birth to John Hanson McNeill Jr., the couple's last child.[2]

While the McNeills lived in Missouri, their friends and relatives back in Virginia corresponded with the family. On September 21, 1855, fifty-six-year-old spinster Rebecca Van Meter, who lived with her two sisters at "Traveler's Rest," in Old Fields, jotted a few lines in her diary about a letter a neighbor had just received from Jemima. After commenting that her husband "was powerfully Blest at Camp M.," Jemima added that it had been hard to get him there: "He had been thrown from his Mule broke his collarbone just able to get to the meeting with it bandaged up tight." The family would also make an occasional trip home. On March 5, 1858, Hanse stopped at "Traveler's Rest" and visited with the sisters for "an hour or two."[3]

When the war began, McNeill promptly formed a cavalry company that included his three oldest sons and various neighbors. His recruits signed up for six months' duty. Once organized, McNeill's troop joined the pro-Southern Missourians then rallying around Governor Claiborne Fox Jackson, a man who was determined to take his state into the Confederacy despite overwhelmingly strong opposition from thousands of Missouri Unionists. McNeill's company eventually became Company B, 1st Cavalry, 4th Division, Missouri State Guard. Colonel Benjamin A. Rives commanded the regiment, and Brigadier General William Y. Slack commanded the division, in Major General Sterling Price's army.[4]

The company's first taste of action came on June 17, 1861, in a skirmish at Boonville. There 1,700 federal troops commanded by Brigadier General Nathaniel Lyon attacked Colonel John S. Marmaduke's 450 barely trained recruits. In a June 18 message to Colonel Chester Harding Jr., Lyon wrote, "We met their advance[d] pickets and soon after their whole force. At first the secessionists made a weak effort, which doubtless was to lead us to their stronghold, where they held on with considerable resolution, and gave us check for a short time and made some havoc." Moving forward slowly, Lyon reported that by two o'clock that afternoon his men had taken the town.[5]

On July 5, though, the State Guard rebounded with a victory over Colonel Franz Sigel's force in the Battle of Carthage. Commanded by Governor Jackson in person, his four thousand troops pushed the heavily outnumbered federals back ten miles to Carthage, where some street fighting then took place. As the enemy retreated from the town, daring horsemen dashed off after the federal wagons. In his after-action report, Colonel Rives mentioned McNeill, the first of many official commendations he would receive during the war: "Captain McNeil of Company B, being separated from my command, succeeded in capturing a portion of the transportation and baggage of the enemy."[6]

Seven months later, in a February 13, 1862, letter to Department of Missouri commander Major General Henry Halleck, Brigadier General John M. Schofield, soon to be commanding the District of Saint Louis, commented on the dubious military merits of Sigel, whom McNeill was destined to harass farther east in the spring of 1864. The brigadier noted Sigel's mediocre performance at Carthage:

> Sigel had about two regiments of infantry, well-armed and equipped, most of the men old German soldiers, and two good batteries of artillery. Price had about twice Sigel's number of men, but most of them mounted, armed with shot-guns and common rifles, and entirely without organization and discipline, and a few pieces of almost worthless artillery. Sigel retreated all day before this miserable rabble, contenting himself with repelling their irregular attacks, which he did with perfect ease whenever they ventured to make them.[7]

Over the next three weeks after Carthage, Price's officers trained their "miserable rabble" at Cowskin Prairie, a remote spot in the state's far southwestern corner. Soon they had organized a fighting force of some 7,000 men, including about 2,000 without weapons. On July 25 the State Guard marched northeast toward Springfield. Four days later at Cassville, Brigadier General Ben McCulloch's Confederate Brigade, a 2,700-man contingent that included troops from Texas, Arkansas, and Louisiana, joined the Missourians. General Nicolas "Bart" Pearce's Arkansas Brigade, nominally under McCulloch's command, also coupled with Price, bringing Southern numbers up to 12,125. Although Price outranked McCulloch, "Old Pap" met with him and turned over command of the so-called Western Army to the celebrated former Texas Ranger.[8]

In the subsequent Battle of Wilson's Creek on August 10, the Confederates defeated General Lyon's 5,200-man Army of the West, inflicting over 1,300 casualties on the federals. The unfortunate Lyon was among the federal dead, wounded twice before going down with a bullet through his heart. But the victory was inconclusive. Just like the July 21, 1861, Battle of Bull Run in Virginia, the graybacks had suffered substantial losses—1,232—and could not pursue the federals and follow up their victory. Rives's command, numbering 284 troopers, suffered 4 killed and 8 wounded. Luckily, all the McNeills came through the bitter fight unscathed.[9]

On August 25 the State Guard marched out of Springfield. Eight days later Price's men defeated some Kansas bluecoats in a sharp skirmish at Drywood Creek before moving on to Lexington. There on September 13, General Price, now with additional recruits swelling his ranks to 15,000, attacked Colonel James Mulligan's 3,500-man force consisting of the colonel's own 23rd Illinois

Infantry, the 1st Illinois Cavalry, and miscellaneous troops from Kansas, Iowa, and Missouri. Sporadic skirmishing and sometimes heavy fighting continued in and around the town for the next eight days. Finally, with his men heavily outnumbered and out of water, Mulligan surrendered.[10]

Today historians of the battle and other interested persons remember the fight for the strange tactic the Missourians used in their final attack. The night before the assault on Mulligan's trenches, the men soaked hemp bales in river water and the next day used them to form a movable breastwork two hundred yards long that proved to be almost impervious to cannon and rifle fire. Upon nearing the trenches, Price's troops rushed the fortifications and carried the day.[11]

But the Battle of Lexington had been very costly to the McNeill men and proved to be their last combat as members of the State Guard. On September 16 a Union marksman shot twenty-one-year-old George while he was on picket duty, and the young sergeant died about an hour later. Two days later, Hanse suffered a serious wound to his right shoulder.[12]

After the surrender, an ironic incident occurred between Colonel Mulligan and Captain McNeill. The two men, who in 1863 and 1864 would constantly match wits against one another in West Virginia, reportedly rode out of Lexington in the same carriage. Unlike the enlisted men and most officers in his command, the thirty-two-year-old commander refused to sign a parole and therefore remained a prisoner, destined to travel with the Missourians for some time before being exchanged. Governor Jackson later offered the use of his personal carriage to the wounded Mulligan, disabled "the last day of the fight by a ball that passed through the calf of his leg." The colonel accepted, and the injured McNeill accompanied Mulligan and his young wife, Marian, when they left Lexington.[13]

Much of the information we have about McNeill in the following months comes from the pen of the aforementioned W. D. Vandiver. According to Vandiver, William S. McNeill returned home not long after the battle. Meanwhile, his father and Jesse continued with the State Guard as Price withdrew from Lexington. Later, though, the pair stopped at Neosho to give the older man's wound some time to heal. Then, taking a furlough, they visited relatives at Arrow Rock before crossing the Missouri River and stopping at the Vandiver house, located "a few miles southwest of Columbia," where Mrs. McNeill was staying temporarily. Along with Jemima was "Uncle Sam," the family servant. Sam, who back on the farm had two wives, was determined to go along with the men when they returned to the army. He told W. D. and others that he "could get another wife but might never get another good master."[14]

The time spent with the McNeills forever impressed the young boy. Over fifty years later, W. D. reminisced: "In my childhood recollections of Civil War times in Missouri no picture stands out more clearly than that of this grim warrior in well-worn Confederate uniform and heavy dark whiskers extending almost down to his waist, and his son Jesse, a beardless and long-legged young man just grown, as they came back from Price's army in the fall of 1861."[15]

Soon the pair moved on to stay with David B. Cunningham, Jemima's brother. Early on the morning of January 18, 1862, Hanse and Jesse were fast asleep at the farmhouse when troopers from Colonel Lewis Merrill's 2nd Missouri Cavalry, also

James Mulligan. Library of Congress.

known as "Merrill's Horse," surrounded the dwelling and called for them to come out. With nowhere to run, the pair surrendered. Once back in Columbia, their jailers quartered the men in the university.

Their stay in Columbia, however, proved to be very pleasant. Colonel William F. Switzler was a former acquaintance, and he arranged for the father and son to "visit their friends in town during the day, but return to prison at night." Referring to Hanse, Switzler once said to Merrill, "Let him go anywhere in the country and I guarantee he will return when he promises to do so." Later, the federal commander let the pair roam up to ten miles out from town.[16]

Surprisingly, Merrill even permitted Jesse to go back to his uncle's farm. When he returned, the young man swapped the colonel a fine mule in exchange for his captured horse. Merrill also allowed some local women to make the captain some clothes to replace his shabby outfit but was somewhat surprised when the ladies fashioned McNeill a Confederate uniform. Jesse later commented that their stay in Columbia "was more like an extended visit among friends than an enforced confinement."[17]

After a little over two months in Columbia, their captors transferred father and son to a military prison in St. Louis. According to Vandiver, their new jailers confined them with numerous other prisoners in an "old slave market." If correct, this would have been the Myrtle Street Prison, formally Bernard Lynch's Slave Market. Federal records, however, do not note this but show that on April 8 Hanse arrived at Gratiot Street Prison, the former McDowell Medical College. It is certainly possible that the federals first housed the men in the overcrowded slave market for a short time before transferring them to

Jesse McNeill. Author's collection.

Gratiot or separated the men, placing Jesse in the former and Hanse in the latter. The Unionists used Gratiot, like the slave market, to hold prisoners temporarily. It housed not only rebel soldiers, "but also Southern sympathizers, political prisoners, mail-runners, bridge burners, and even Union deserters."[18]

According to Vandiver, Jesse escaped first and set sail for Virginia. A news article that appeared over seventy years later added more to the story, relating that "in the course of several weeks he escaped during a change of guards." Upon passing through Tennessee, not long after the Battle of Shiloh, Jesse "assisted in caring for many of the wounded." In early June prison officials transferred Hanse across the Mississippi to the prison at Alton, Illinois. There, on June 8, the captain "escaped through Cook House in broad daylight." Once free, he made tracks for Moorefield.[19]

But there is another unofficial version of the captain's escape. According to the June 27, 1862, edition of the *Columbia Missouri Statesman*:

> Escaped from the Military prison in St. Louis, Capt. W. F. Petty, G. W. Pulliam, Mathew Thompson, Calvin Sartrain, Capt. John H. McNeil and 8 or 10 others whose names we have not learned. Petty and Pulliam were under sentences of death for bridge burning. Thompson for bridge burning and complicity with Cobb and his desperadoes; and Sartrain for firing into the steamer White Cloud in August 1861. Capt. McNeil was a prisoner of war, he having been engaged in the rebellion under Gen. Price. Escaping from the Military prison in St. Louis seems not to be a very difficult matter.[20]

Within a month or so, McNeill was back in Virginia with his kin and looking for a way to help the Southern cause. After resting up from his exhausting journey, he traveled to Richmond, on a mission to ask for the secretary of war's permission to raise a partisan company.[21]

CHAPTER 2

1st Virginia Partisan Rangers

∽∞∽

"…they came charging on,
yelling like fiends."

After meeting with and receiving Secretary of War Randolph's consent to organize a partisan ranger company, McNeill journeyed to Staunton and met with
Colonel Imboden. As Imboden remembered, McNeill, introducing himself as
"Captain John H. McNeill, late of Missouri," then said that Imboden's recent
proclamation had convinced him and Jesse to join up. During their one-hour
talk, Hanse added that he could enlist plenty of well-mounted men but would
need "doubled-barreled shotguns and Colt revolvers." Over the following weeks,
McNeill began filling the ranks of his "Hardy Rangers" with former neighbors,
relatives, and assorted young men from Hardy and Hampshire Counties, plus
a few Maryland secessionists. Some of his first recruits included Solomon Ar-
mentrout, Anthony Cosner, "Missouri John" Cunningham, Charles "Jim" Dailey,
Isaac Judy, Charles Miles, Charles Nicolas, Abel Seymour, Martin Shobe, Fred
Stewart, Harrison Taylor, and James Welch. Dailey and Stewart were the first
Marylanders to become members of the outfit.[1]

On either September 10 or 11, 1862, McNeill took twenty men on a mission that proved to be a most successful foray. At Ridgeville, a hamlet along
the Northwestern Turnpike just west of Burlington, the partisans captured
three Yankee pickets and eleven Virginia Unionists. Soon, however, Captain
William Firey and the troopers of Company B, 1st Maryland Potomac Home
Brigade Cavalry, saddled up and gave chase. Although the rebels had a good
head start, Firey's men, mostly farm boys hailing from Washington County,
Maryland, and Berkeley County, Virginia, were skilled riders who picked up
the raiders' trail quickly. Finally catching up to the graybacks, the bluecoats
collared three of them, along with five horses. McNeill and the rest, however,
escaped. According to the September 13 edition of the *Wheeling Intelligencer*,

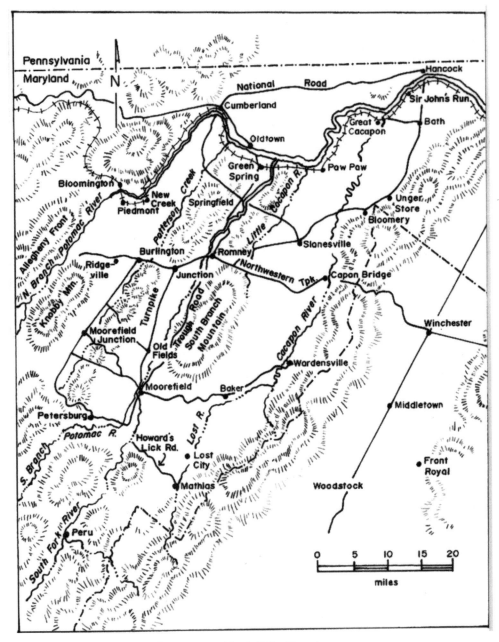

South Branch Valley and Potomac Highlands (John Heiser).

one of the Southerners captured "was Smoot, ex postmaster at New Creek, a rebel and a defaulter to the government."[2]

James Trout, a Hampshire County delegate to Unionist Governor Francis H. Pierpont's Restored Government of Virginia, was the most politically prominent of McNeill's captives. The *Point Pleasant Daily Register* reported that the notorious guerrilla "Sam High . . . captured Mr. Trout." High, who it seems never formally enlisted in McNeill's company, later lost his life in an October 29 skirmish. On September 19 the *Rockingham Register*, in trumpeting the captain's feat, said that Trout "will arrive in Richmond as soon as Captain McNeill can spare men to guard him to this place." The paper also noted that the captain "turned auctioneer, and sold off, to the highest bidder, the lot of horses, carbines, and pistols captured when he went to New Creek." According to one of his men, McNeill kept for himself "a swift and tough little roan" he captured on Knobly Mountain.[3]

On September 24 at Camp Lee, Imboden's remote outpost located along the banks of the narrow, meandering South Fork River five miles upstream from its junction with the South Branch at Moorefield, McNeill's company joined the 1st Regiment Virginia Partisan Rangers. Before riding to Camp Lee, McNeill's recruits had met in nearby Petersburg and elected Hanse as their captain and Jesse first lieutenant. The colonel assigned his new Company L to the command's cavalry battalion, bringing its numbers to four companies of approximately three hundred troopers. Another six hundred or so soldiers, three hundred of whom were unarmed, made up Imboden's infantry contingent. The colonel's so-called "jackass artillery" consisted of some mountain howitzers, small, lightweight cannons that soldiers could disassemble easily and transport on the backs of mules.[4]

In an earlier incident, McNeill had captured a band of Union irregulars from nearby Pendleton County. Led by Captain John Bond, these men were among the many mountain folk who deeply opposed Virginia's secession from the United States, and in the months following Virginia's breakaway, they formed local home guard organizations to protect their lives and property. Dubbed "Swamp Dragons" or "Swamp Dragoons" by their Southern counterparts, over the course of the war these mountaineers proved to be quite effective in thwarting various Southern incursions into the Alleghenies.

But from time to time the Swamp Dragons also terrorized the friends and relatives of Confederate soldiers. Their depredations against these people ranged from burning barns and houses and stealing livestock to vicious beatings, as well as an occasional murder. Unionist Bond and his followers had attracted McNeill's attention, Imboden later wrote, by "perpetrating their

Benjamin F. Kelley.
Author's collection.

outrages upon the loyal citizens of Hardy and Pendleton." Along with Bond and six of his men, the rebels also captured "two other Yankees, belonging to a company commanded by Capt. Dyke." McNeill soon sent the prisoners on their way to Staunton. Somewhere along the trail, however, four of Bond's privates slipped into the heavily wooded, rocky terrain and escaped. The rest arrived at Staunton on September 23.[5]

In a September 27 report to his commander, Major General Thomas J. "Stonewall" Jackson, Imboden commented on the capture of Bond and his efforts to capture or disperse other Union guerrilla fighters:

> We have sent off Captain Bond, the bandit leader of this county, and four or five of his gang to Staunton, having been fortunate enough to "bag" them. Most of these desperadoes will be captured, killed or driven off by us. In Pendleton and the eastern part of Randolph, I have restored order in the community, have broken up horse-thieving and plundering by arresting those engaged in it and sending them to Staunton.[6]

Previously, Imboden had completed an expedition in which he occupied Romney for a few days before marching up Trough (or River) Road to Moorefield and on to Camp Lee. Imboden reported that his Romney raid had kept Brigadier General Benjamin F. Kelley "running up and down the railroad with troops for ten days."[7]

From Cumberland, "Queen City of the Alleghenies," Kelley commanded the Railroad Division, and it was his responsibility to keep the B&O line open from Cumberland to Wheeling. The general's troops also protected the B&O's Northwestern Virginia line from Grafton to Parkersburg. The fifty-five-year-old brigadier was widely known as the "Hero of Philippi," due to his success and almost fatal wounding in the June 3, 1861, one-sided rout of Colonel George A. Porterfield's six hundred–man force, now known as the Philippi Races.[8]

East of the Allegheny Front, Kelley had plenty of infantry to guard the rail towns of Cumberland, New Creek, Piedmont, and Bloomington, but his few cavalry companies allowed only nominal offensive actions against Imboden's partisans and the numerous small guerrilla bands that infested the area. On September 27, however, all that changed when a small brigade of troopers rode into New Creek. Led by Mexican War veteran Colonel Andrew T. McReynolds, it consisted of his 1st New York (Lincoln) Cavalry and a few companies of the 12th Pennsylvania Cavalry.

Two days later Kelley telegraphed Army of the Potomac commander Major General George B. McClellan and asked the general about keeping McReynolds's horsemen. "If you could spare them," he wrote, "I would gladly have them remain here for a time." McClellan agreed, and soon McReynolds set up his headquarters along the railroad at Green Spring Run, just across the Potomac from Old Town, Maryland. The colonel also stationed a squadron under Captain William Boyd at Springfield, a village seven miles south of Green Spring and about halfway between it and Romney. McReynolds ordered Boyd to "establish . . . pickets on the roads leading from the town, and scouts were to be sent out to keep watch on Imboden's mounted rangers."[9]

Besides the New Yorkers, Kelley had some other help. Just east of Green Spring, Company A, 54th Pennsylvania Infantry guarded the B&O's span over the South Branch River. From there on down the track fifty-six miles to Back Creek Bridge, other companies protected bridges and important depots along the line. Colonel Jacob Campbell, the commander of the 54th, had his headquarters at Sir John's Run, near Bath (Berkeley Springs). The regiment did not belong to Kelley's command but had previously been part of Colonel Dixon Miles's Railroad Brigade, headquartered in Harpers Ferry. On September 15 Stonewall Jackson captured Harpers Ferry, effectively cutting off Campbell's soldiers from their command. Eventually McClellan transferred the 54th to Major General William Franklin's VI Corps, but the Pennsylvanians remained in the highlands on their own hook.[10]

Toward the end of September, Imboden moved his men from Camp Lee north to Capon Bridge, a small town along the Northwestern Turnpike about halfway between Romney and Winchester. The village, which got its name from the turnpike's covered bridge across the Cacapon River, put the colonel in an excellent position to strike federal camps at Little Cacapon and Paw Paw, two isolated outposts on the nearby railroad.[11]

On October 2, McNeill's company was guarding Blue's Gap, a hamlet on the turnpike, approximately fourteen miles east of Romney and eight miles west from Capon Bridge. Hanse had also posted vedettes on the pike near Pleasant Dale, a few miles to the west. The gap had an interesting past. On January 7, 1862, the steep pass over North River Mountain had been the location of a brief skirmish between woefully trained Virginia militia forces and veteran Union troops that had marched out of Romney early that morning. The Yankees had won easily, but their needless depredations there and subsequent burning of houses, stealing all sorts of private property, and wantonly shooting domestic animals and livestock on their way back to camp had forever infuriated the helpless locals.[12]

Around midday on October 2, McNeill's pickets noticed four blue riders headed their way. The men mounted quickly, spurred their horses, and took off for the gap. The Yankees chased after them and soon were close behind. But when the federals got within sight of the pass, they spotted trouble and let their prey go. There, just across the North River, were too many graybacks for them to handle. For a short while the enemies just stared at one another, but presently the Northerners, now joined by a few of their friends, turned tail and galloped away. The rebels followed cautiously at a distance.[13]

That morning Captain Jenyns Battersby, 1st New York (Lincoln) Cavalry, had led a patrol from Springfield. The squadron, consisting of his own Company B and Company H, commanded by Lieutenant Eugene Lewis, proceeded to Romney. Arriving there, the captain ordered four soldiers to remain behind and then rode eastward toward Blue's Gap. After traveling some distance and reaching a village the Northerners called Burnt Mills (Frenchburg), the bluecoats presently came upon the pike's intersection with the Hampshire-Martinsburg Grade. There the captain ordered Lewis to take his company and scout northward. Meanwhile, Battersby continued following the pike. The officers decided that whichever company returned to the place first would spread pine branches across the road as a signal that they were back and would be waiting nearby to reunite.[14]

At first Battersby's scouts had a sizable lead on the graybacks. Upon arriving at the Northwestern Hotel, they found their commander, according to regimental historian Captain James H. Stevenson, "taking things easy." The men quickly reported the troop's precarious situation. Battersby, a former British cavalry officer, then ordered Sergeant Lem Evans and four others to form the rear guard; the captain and the rest rode off to find Lewis. Presently they heard the sound of sporadic gunfire to the rear. Hanse, not knowing the size of the opposing force and fearing an ambush, kept his twenty-four men back. Upon encountering Battersby's rear guard, though, fighting broke out. Once McNeill realized that only a handful of men opposed him, he ordered his riders forward. Stevenson wrote that "they came charging on, yelling like fiends, and swept Sergeant Evans little force before them like leaves of the forest." One of the Rangers added, "He charged them, and the frightened Yankees yelled like they were being murdered."[15]

Battersby knew that he still had plenty of time to reunite with Lewis and turn the tables on his pursuers. Upon reaching the intersection, the captain noticed that branches were across the pike. If he could just find Company H, all would be fine. Now, though, with the rebels fast closing in on his band, the chase was on, and unfortunately for the Yankees, their horses were tiring rapidly. To escape imminent capture, some soldiers decided to ditch their mounts and take to the brush. "On arriving at the point of the road where it made a double around the head of a gorge-like ravine," Stevenson said, "some of the men abandoned their horses and crossed the gorge on foot . . . thus saving themselves from capture."[16]

Private James Gleeson was one of fifteen New Yorkers who dismounted and sprinted for the woods, but when he hurried to get over a roadside fence, his scabbard caught between the rails and held him fast. When a Ranger demanded his surrender, Gleeson replied, "I don't see it just yet!" Quickly unbuckling his belt, the Irishman escaped amid a "shower of bullets."[17]

That day Battersby was riding a "large framed, long-geared, steep-rumped black horse" that he had picked out of a batch of "condemned animals." Carefully nursing the steed, over the next few months the captain had watched with fatherly pride as the worn-out charger gradually regained its health and strength. But this day the rapid pace of the troop's flight proved to be too much for the horse. Upon reaching the top of a long grade, Battersby, realizing his old friend was finished, pulled back on the reins, stopped, and dismounted.[18]

As the rest of his men disappeared in the distance, the captain awaited his fate. Soon Captain McNeill approached, and after engaging Battersby in some friendly banter, accepted his surrender. Stevenson added that "McNeill . . . was so overjoyed at his good fortune that he made a sort of hero of his captive, treating him to a good drink of apple jack as a starter."[19]

Besides capturing Battersby, the partisans had seized five soldiers, fifteen horses, and much-needed weapons and equipment. The rebels allowed the Yankees to ride their mounts as far as Capon Bridge. Then, after Imboden finished questioning them, their guards rode alongside as they walked another twenty miles to Jackson's Winchester headquarters. Once there, Battersby asked the general if he could keep his sword, a family heirloom that his ancestors had carried in countless battles. Jackson granted his request under the condition that the captain put it away for the rest of the war. Five days later the Confederates paroled Battersby, and he returned to Springfield to await exchange.[20]

The next day, October 3, Imboden began an expedition to destroy the railroad bridge across the Little Cacapon River and the line's tunnel through nearby Paw Paw Ridge. Except for Lieutenant Henderson Stone and a hundred unarmed soldiers, the colonel took the whole command. To give Stone's men some protection, Imboden left two mountain howitzers in place on the eastern side of the turnpike bridge.

Then the partisans, with the cavalry leading the way, marched northwest to the Forks of the Capon and continued over Sidling Hill and Spring Gap Mountain. Upon reaching a crossing of the Little Cacapon a few miles upstream from his objective, Imboden ordered some horsemen to scout along the B&O to South Branch Bridge. This detachment traveled from the ford to Levels Crossroads and then down the steep ridge to French's Depot before finding a spot to observe the troops guarding the bridge.[21]

Early on the morning of October 4, Imboden had his men in position near the mouth of the Little Cacapon to overrun the camp of Company K, 54th Pennsylvania Infantry. Fog coming off that river and the nearby Potomac blanketed the ground and made it easy for the Southerners to seize the pickets and sneak into some empty rifle pits. At six o'clock Captain Edward Newhard was calling the roll when a tremendous volley of musketry erupted, wounding seven Northerners and scattering the rest. Of these bluecoats, the rebels were able to catch fifty. Thirty-five others escaped into the woods or across the shallow Potomac.[22]

As some partisans got ready to burn the bridge and destroy other railroad property, the rest ransacked the camp, collecting clothing, firearms, and provisions. Meanwhile, three miles down the track at Paw Paw, the sound of distant gunfire had startled the soldiers of Company B. Sure that it signaled a rebel attack on their compatriots, assistant surgeon Andrew Matthews saddled up and went to investigate.

Matthews reached a point about four hundred yards from the camp and viewed the scene. Wary of getting any closer, the doctor forded the Potomac and rode upstream along the C&O Canal towpath to get a better look. Once certain that the Confederates had prevailed, he returned to Paw Paw and met with Captain John Hite and Lieutenants Harry Baer and John Cole. Not long afterward, two other scouts confirmed the doctor's assessment of the situation. With an attack on the post now probable, Hite ordered his soldiers into the rifle pits. The men had plenty of food and ammunition and were anxious for a fight. Hite's defenses were located in the floodplain some distance west of the tunnel.[23]

It took a little time before a portion of the partisan infantry, numbering between two and three hundred soldiers, arrived and formed into battle lines. Eventually, eighty to a hundred horsemen rode in and stopped atop a hill one-half mile from the federal left flank. As the Pennsylvanians looked across the way, a lone rider carrying a white flag rode between the lines, entered the camp, and stopped to talk with the officers. All three of the men followed him back to the Confederate line and met with Imboden. When they returned, Captain Hite told his incredulous soldiers he had surrendered the post.[24]

For a time a stunned Dr. Matthews watched from atop Paw Paw Ridge as his compatriots came out of their defenses and laid down their arms. The partisans then swarmed into the camp and began collecting prisoners and booty. But before Imboden could have his men wreck the tunnel, a scout rode in and reported two trains full of Yankees coming up the track. Presently, the rebels marched out on Winchester Road on their way back to Capon Bridge. Although Imboden had failed to destroy the tunnel, in the two actions his men had captured 152 Yankees, 175 new rifles, and 8,000 rounds of ammunition and had severely damaged the railroad line at Little Cacapon.[25]

When Imboden's mounted units arrived at Capon Bridge later that day, the troopers discovered a chaotic scene. Earlier a battalion of horsemen from the 1st New York Cavalry had attacked and overrun the camp, capturing Stone along with twenty-three soldiers and two civilians. By now most of the other partisans who had escaped by scampering off into the brush were back in camp, inspecting the damage. The New Yorkers had not only wrecked the place but had taken "40 horses and mules, 1,000 blankets, two wagons loaded with clothing, three wagons loaded with ammunition, 15 wagons, 100 new muskets, two fine brass rifled 4 pounder cannon mounted, a large amount of ammunition with cannon, and all of Col. Imboden's private papers and clothing." The riders soon gave chase and later, according to Imboden, recovered much plunder the Yankees had abandoned as they hurried back to Springfield.[26]

In the next day or two the colonel had his men on the march for Camp Lee. By this time General McClellan had ordered Brigadier General William W. Averell's cavalry into Hampshire County to help search for the partisans. Upon reaching Camp Lee, Imboden gave his soldiers time to rest and refit.

Later on he established another camp for his infantry at Peru, thirteen miles farther up the South Fork. There the soldiers began building winter quarters.[27]

On October 29 the sound of distant cannon fire signaled trouble along the Patterson Creek Valley Turnpike. McNeill's company and other rangers saddled up quickly and rode off to help some rebel cattle drovers. But the Virginians would be too late to aid their friends. After a long ride the would-be rescuers finally reached the skirmish site along the banks of Lanice Creek's north fork. They soon discovered that federal artillery and cavalry out of New Creek had surprised some of Brigadier General Fitz Lee's troopers driving cattle toward Petersburg. The Northerners escaped with some prisoners and a substantial portion of the herd. Diarist Van Meter recorded that "our cavalry saved more than half, went back and gathered up what was scattered."[28]

During this time, Imboden was planning another expedition into the high Alleghenies to take out the Cheat River Bridge, an important B&O viaduct at the town of Rowlesburg in Preston County. Since the beginning of the war, Confederate military leaders had advocated the destruction of the 312-foot-long, 27-foot-high structure. Located deep within the rugged Cheat River Canyon, its ruin would undoubtedly force a long delay in traffic along the line before work crews could repair the damage. That August the colonel had led a raiding party into the area but turned back after a young woman named Jane Snyder spotted his column and made a dangerous midnight ride to warn the Union troops posted at Parsons Mill, some distance south of the rail town.[29]

On the afternoon of November 7 Imboden and 310 troopers departed Camp Lee. At the head of the column rode Bill Harper, the renowned highland guide from Tucker County. Brother of the famed guerrilla fighter Captain Ezekiel Harper, most of the soldiers knew Bill from his reputation as one of the premier hunters of the Alleghenies. His days spent tracking game in the still-wild, still-untamed mountains had given him an unsurpassed knowledge of the backwoods trails.[30]

McNeill and his men were in the column as it traveled in the falling snow toward Petersburg, and after reaching their destination the men dismounted, fed their horses some field corn, and tried to keep warm. Within an hour the raiders were back on the trail, and by midnight they had passed through North Fork Gap. Once beyond the pass, the column turned north and continued until midnight before stopping to camp at the base of the Allegheny Front. It was hard going the next morning as the Virginians began their tough

Robert H. Milroy. Library of Congress.

ascent of the precipitous slope. As one of them later wrote, "Up, up stretches the long line of horses and men along the narrow path some leading, some driving their unwilling stock, with an occasional heels-over-head performance by some unfortunate trooper in the cool, refreshing snow."[31]

To keep Swamp Dragons from spotting them, Harper guided the men along a seldom-used track that skirted the southern edge of Dolly Sods and the Canaan wilderness. Imboden had planned on attacking and capturing the Union post at Saint George that evening. But the snow played havoc with his schedule, and he did not reach the town until daybreak on November 9. By that time, though, a local Southern sympathizer had met the colonel and informed Imboden that at least six hundred federals were now east of him at Seneca. Also, another four thousand troops under Brigadier General Robert H. Milroy, the formidable "Gray Eagle," were off to Imboden's south, marching from Beverly to Monterey.[32]

The Rangers surrounded Saint George that morning, and after some light skirmishing, they captured Captain William Hall and twenty-nine of his soldiers. Ironically, these men of Company F, 6th (West) Virginia Infantry, hailed from Rowlesburg. As Imboden's officers paroled the Yankees, other partisans gathered the plunder, which included "all the arms, oil-cloth blankets, overcoats, cooking utensils, 1 horse and bridle, and about 530 rations."[33]

Less than twenty miles now separated Imboden from the bridge, but the fear of Union forces trapping him on his return to camp forced the colonel to call off the advance. Now began a torturous retreat southward through "the wildest and ragged of the mountain districts." On November 10 another friendly local reached Imboden with intelligence that Milroy had parked his lightly defended baggage train at Camp Bartow. Presented with this tempting prize, the colonel decided upon heading cross-country the next morning and capturing the wagons.[34]

Although Camp Bartow was not too far away, the deep snow, icy rains, and rugged terrain proved to be too much for the men. After two days of struggling to get there, Imboden gave up. On November 13 he left camp at Upper Sinks and marched for home. Early the next morning, after narrowly slipping by Union forces trying to capture them, the partisans finally reached the headwaters of the South Fork. There Imboden learned the sad news that General Kelley had attacked and destroyed his Peru camp.[35]

CHAPTER 3

Early Exploits

" . . . they have got awfully afraid of Capt. McNeill."

During the following weeks in late 1862, Imboden moved his camp atop Shenandoah Mountain and once again put his soldiers to work preparing winter quarters. Although the cold weather should have brought the men much-needed rest from active campaigning, troubling news out of the northwest soon created great concern among the ranks.[1]

In response to the November attack on Saint George, Brigadier General Milroy, commanding the eight thousand–man Cheat Mountain Division had issued an order demanding that known secessionists pay individual assessments to compensate their loyal neighbors for any losses caused by the Confederates. Additionally, the order also stated that citizens who failed to notify Union soldiers of approaching raiders would have "their houses . . . burned and the men shot."[2]

Once word of Milroy's declaration reached Richmond, the Confederate government and local press both condemned him. The *Daily Dispatch* called on their "military leaders . . . to retaliate a hundredfold at once for every atrocity that hellhound, Milroy, may commit." Although Commanding General Henry Halleck eventually forced Milroy to rescind the order, the embattled Hoosier later defended his actions as necessary.[3]

In a February 1863 letter to Halleck, Milroy wrote:

I have been in command in West Virginia since 30th May, 1861. During that time, . . . I could not fail in my position to learn much of the views and feelings of the Union population, (largely in the majority) of that region, and of the atrocities which it has suffered at the hands of the rebel government at Richmond.

That government has viewed the Union citizens of West Virginia in the double aspect of rebels against the Confederate States of America, and of the State of Virginia, and for that reason has regarded and treated them as outlaws.... Influenced by this view, that government has encouraged and patronized organizations in that region variously known as mountain rangers, partisan rangers, bushwhackers and guerrilla bands of every description, composed of men enrolled in no regular army ... instigated to action solely by the motives of rapine and plunder.

To such an extent did these lawless bands conduct their depredations ... that the country in many localities was entirely denuded of ... horses, cattle and other livestock. Nor were their outrages confined to mere plundering. Murders of the most atrocious characters were of daily occurrences.[4]

In early December Brigadier General Benjamin F. Kelley not only had his cavalry out scouring the area farms for livestock and watching for Confederates, but he also took offensive actions to keep the rebels at bay. Late on the afternoon of December 2, Lieutenant Henry A. Myers rode out of New Creek, leading Ringgold Battalion troopers south to Moorefield, via Greenland Gap. About eight miles from camp, Captain Weston Rowand and Company K, 1st (West) Virginia Cavalry, joined the column. Sometime after daybreak Myers halted at Widow Solomon's Patterson Creek farmstead. Then, after caring for and feeding their mounts and eating breakfast, the troopers got back in the saddle and continued another fourteen miles to Moorefield, a town the *Boston Traveler* described as having "several stores and mills and about one hundred dwellings." Along the way, Myers picked up the news that two companies of rebel horsemen were in the town.[5]

That same morning, the folks at Old Fields sent some food to the Confederate camp, just across the South Branch. Not long after finishing their hearty meal, the soldiers rode into Moorefield to say good-bye to their friends and relatives. Neither Captain Edward H. McDonald nor any of the troopers in his squadron suspected that Yankees were about. Piloted skillfully by a spy, Myers completely surprised them. He later wrote, "When we came in sight of the town, a charge was ordered.... The rebels were dispersed in all directions." The bluecoats killed two Confederates and captured ten, including McDonald. Myers "had one man wounded and three horses killed."[6]

In a recent shake-up, General Halleck had transferred Kelley's Railroad Division from Brigadier General Jacob D. Cox's District of Western Virginia to Major General Robert "Fighting Bob" Schenck's 8th Corps Middle Military Department. Before this Kelley, who outranked Milroy by seniority, "had intended that Milroy should occupy Petersburg in Hardy County with a portion of his force for preventing a raid into Randolph and Tucker by guerrillas, but will now, of course, have to wait until I hear from General Halleck." In due course Milroy brought most of his command east of the Allegheny Front. But he left two regiments behind in the mountains to guard the railroad and patrol that area.[7]

By December 11 the "Gray Eagle's" troops had occupied Moorefield and Petersburg. Not long afterward, Milroy, knowing that presently there were few Confederate defenders in the Shenandoah Valley, wrote Kelley that he was anxious to combine his troops and march to Winchester. Meanwhile, in Moorefield on the eleventh, Colonel Thomas M. Harris, commanding the 10th (West) Virginia Infantry, ordered the townspeople to supply "a contribution of war as a punishment for the aid given to Captain MacDonald." The next day Harris demanded "1,200 pounds beef, 700 pounds pork, 1,000 pounds flour and 1,200 pounds of corn-meal." Local Aaron Canady told Rebecca Van Meter that Harris had quartered his troops in "the Hotel, new Courthouse, & the Presbyterian Church." The colonel also prohibited anyone going in or out of the town.[8]

As some Yankees began planting telegraph poles and stringing wire, others roamed the countryside, collecting food and livestock. Supply and forage wagons constantly traveled the Moorefield and North Branch Turnpike, the road connecting Moorefield with the Northwestern Turnpike at Junction. Watching from her home in Old Fields, Van Meter commented, "It is a gloomy time with us."[9]

But a week later the situation for the locals turned even darker. On December 20 Milroy issued General Order 39, calling on all Hardy County citizens "desiring the protection of the United States for their property and persons . . . to . . . take an oath of allegiance to the United States Government and the State of West Virginia." If a citizen failed to report to Union headquarters at either Moorefield or Petersburg, Northern officers could use his property "to quarter troops, for government store-rooms, &c." The person would also have to "furnish supplies of provisions and forage for the use of the U.S. Army."[10]

The *Rockingham Register* reported that "the army under Gen. Milroy is now stationed in and around Moorefield, and the people there are realizing some of the bitter fruits of the invasion of the sacred soil of Virginia by this horde of Vandal plunderers. All of the best citizens who can get off are leaving the county." When one old woman refused to take the oath of allegiance, a soldier told her, "*Take the oath or starve!*"[11]

On December 15 McNeill's troop became Company E of the 2nd Virginia Partisan Rangers, soon to become the 18th Virginia Cavalry. Colonel George Imboden, John's brother, commanded the "ten full, well-mounted companies."

For some time in Richmond there had been discussions among military and political leaders wanting to bring Imboden's large force into the regular service. On the twenty-third Adjutant and Inspector General Samuel Cooper contacted the partisan leader about the matter. Cooper insisted that "the consent of the men now enrolled as partisan rangers must be obtained before the desired change can be undertaken."[12]

Although so far the partisans had not initiated much offensive action against Milroy's occupation of Hardy, that was soon to change. On December 26 McNeill's company and Captain Frank Imboden's Company H drifted into the area to scout the Yankees. Once there, according to Captain Imboden's diary, he "sent to South Branch for provisions." The next day Imboden added, "Reconnoitered South Branch Valley and Old Fields, crossed at Van Meter's Mill and ambuscaded road." That evening a few local women showed up at Imboden's Clifford Hollow camp, east of Old Fields, with food for the men. On Sunday, the twenty-eighth, the partisans once again roamed the area.[13]

That same day Milroy and most of his command marched out of Moore-field headed for Romney. His force consisted of the 7th, 10th, and 11th (West) Virginia; 87th Pennsylvania; and the 110th and 122nd Ohio infantry regiments. Some cavalry, artillery, and over a hundred baggage and supply wagons accompanied the foot soldiers. At dusk the last of Milroy's wagons were rolling along through Old Fields when disaster struck. Just as they were passing Fox's Lane, McNeill's company attacked, capturing a number of horses, soldiers, teamsters, and wagons. Frank Imboden, who witnessed his compatriot's amazing exploit, called it a "magnificent charge."[14]

On January 8, 1863, the *Daily Dispatch* informed its readers of the intrepid partisan's amazing feat, noting that in just ten minutes the captain, with only thirty-seven men had captured seventeen Yankees and four dozen horses "in full sight of the marching column." The Rangers then galloped away into the nearby hills under a barrage of cannon fire. They suffered no casualties.[15]

From her house, about a mile from the scene, Rebecca Van Meter witnessed the incident. "The Rebel Cavalry dashed down Mr. Foxes lane & got (the Yankey's told us) 53 horses out of their last Waggons and dashed back in the woods." She said that once the cannons began firing at the Southerners, some cavalry and a company of infantry, "running back fast as School boys," turned around and went to the rescue, but they were too late to save their comrades.[16]

Years later, in a letter to author Benjamin F. Van Meter, Ranger veteran Lieutenant Isaac Welton reminisced:

I think the most daring thing we ever did was attacking Milroy's wagon train in the Old Fields. . . . with a road full of the enemy, not less than

10,000 of them.... Without firing a gun from our force and no shot from them until we were about a mile away with our booty, when they commenced to shell the woods on the mountainside.

The attack was so bold, sudden, and reckless, that they could not understand it. They saw us charging right at them and unhitch their horses from their wagons and did not seem to realize that sixty or seventy men would do such a thing until we had the men and horses in the brush and out of harm's way.[17]

Frank Imboden. Courtesy Ben Ritter.

The next day, December 29, Milroy had his men searching the countryside in a vain attempt to round up the partisans. Meanwhile, the general interrogated a number of the locals. That afternoon, Milroy determined that McNeill was long gone, and shortly the march to Romney resumed. By New Year's Day his troops had reached Winchester. Back in Hardy County, however, Colonel James Washburn's brigade of Milroy's division was still occupying Moorefield and Petersburg. Isolated as they were, these soldiers presented a tempting target not only for the partisans but also for the Valley District commander, Brigadier General William E. "Grumble" Jones.[18]

On the morning of Friday, January 2, 1863, Grumble's men marched out of New Market and headed for Brock's Gap on their way to Moorefield. His contingent of horse soldiers consisted of the 6th, 7th, and 12th Virginia regiments and the 17th Virginia and 1st Maryland battalions. The command also included the 1st Maryland Infantry, Chew's Battery of Horse Artillery, and the Baltimore Light Artillery. The graybacks made good time crossing the mountains, reaching the South Fork the next morning, at about one o'clock. After resting two hours, they continued another twelve miles downstream until nearing Moorefield at about seven. Once there, Jones gave local resident Captain William Harness the

William E. "Grumble" Jones.
Author's collection.

responsibility of placing the artillery. The brigadier then divided his force, sending Colonel Richard Dulany with the 6th and 7th regiments and Chew's three guns across Petersburg Road and the South Branch River to a hilltop almost two miles northwest of the federal defenses. With the infantry still not up, the rest of the troops took up positions along or near the South Fork. The Baltimore Light Artillery prepared to fire from a rise south of the town. Around this time, McNeill and Captain Imboden's riders arrived.[19]

Colonel Washburn's force—consisting of the 116th and 123rd Ohio Infantry regiments; Battery D, 1st (West) Virginia Artillery; and Company D, 3rd (West) Virginia Cavalry—numbered approximately fourteen hundred men. On December 17 Washburn's 2nd Brigade, Cheat Mountain Division, had marched from New Creek for Petersburg, arriving there the next day. Ten days later Washburn sent the 116th, a section of artillery, and thirty cavalrymen to Moorefield. When he got word of the rebel advance on the town, the colonel promptly started his baggage train rolling north toward New Creek. At about nine o'clock that morning, Washburn led the 123rd Ohio to the relief of the Moorefield garrison. Along the way, the soldiers heard cannon fire up ahead and increased their pace, covering eleven miles, as one wrote, "in two hours and ten minutes."[20]

The fighting, consisting mostly of long-range cannon fire and skirmishing, started around ten o'clock and lasted on and off most of the day. Unfortunately, Chew's gunners set up out of range and watched as their shells fell far short of the Union lines atop a hill on the southeastern edge of Moorefield. Defective ammunition plagued the Baltimore Light Artillery, and though closer to the Northerners, this unit accomplished little. According to Jones, however, the enemy's shots "either passed over or struck in our midst." When the soldiers marching from Petersburg drew near, they blocked Dulany's troopers and Chew's Battery from the ford. Then the colonel, hoping to escape capture, broke off the engagement and took his soldiers west over Old Morgantown Road to the Patterson Creek Valley Turnpike. During the long roundabout journey back to their previous camp along the South Fork, the rebels eventually arrived in Petersburg and added forty-six Yankee prisoners to the twenty unlucky skirmishers they had captured around Moorefield. After Dulany retreated, Jones held his positions for another two hours before retiring upriver. Meanwhile, northwest of Moorefield, McNeill's band and some troopers from Company F, 7th Virginia Cavalry, kept watch for Union reinforcements marching from New Creek or Romney. Jones's men reached camp first, and at about ten the next morning, Dulany's dog-tired troopers and their exhausted horses finally got back.[21]

After resting in camp all day on Sunday, January 4, Jones once again prepared to attack Moorefield. Overnight the general placed his infantry and Frank Imboden's company within striking distance of the town. But he soon received word from McNeill's scouts that Colonel James Mulligan's 23rd Illinois Infantry, the Ringgold Battalion, and a battery of six cannons—a force of over five hundred men—was on the way. After hearing this bad news, Jones called off the attack and prepared to return to the Shenandoah Valley. McNeill, however, kept looking for a chance to strike a blow.[22]

Just before eleven Monday morning, the captain spotted a small wagon train and its guard of Union horsemen traveling north from Moorefield. While waiting for the federals to ford the South Branch, McNeill's company and a handful of 7th Virginia Cavalry troopers, some fifty men, lay hidden in the trees and brush. When the train reached Fox's Lane, they charged. In the short but fierce melee that followed, Hanse shot and killed a Union soldier, while the rest of the men captured all but one of the wagons, along with a number of bluecoats and their arms and equipment.[23]

In its January 14 edition, the *Richmond Examiner* trumpeted another McNeill success. Besides killing one Yankee and capturing thirty-three others, the partisans had also taken sixty-three horses. The men's big haul of booty included "9 sets of harness, saddles and bridles, 34 Burnside rifles and 20 sabres." Before riding off, the troopers set the wagons on fire.[24]

Van Meter recalled that as his soldiers rifled through the wagons and then began torching them, McNeill called out to a mob of curious African American bystanders to "run & get what they could." Although a lady who had been riding in one of the wagons protested vigorously, the blacks, mostly children, hurriedly gathered up armfuls of plunder. Later, when Lieutenant Henry Myers and his troopers arrived on the scene, the woman told Myers what had happened and pointed out Jim Plunket as being one of the scavengers. According to Van Meter, a soldier told the slave "they would blow him through if everything was not brought back." In a little while the disappointed children returned with their loot.[25]

At one-thirty on the morning of January 6, Mulligan advanced his command up South Fork Road, hoping to surprise Jones and his troops. But upon reaching the rebel campsite, the half-frozen bluecoats found it empty. A soldier in the 123rd Ohio later recorded "that they had left in a great hurry for a more Southern clime." He also recalled that on the way back "Gen. Mulligan compelled the men to throw down captured turkeys and chickens, which otherwise would have made many a good breakfast on our arrival in camp." Over the next few days locals noticed that many of the Yankees were especially nervous and became easily spooked by the sound of random gunshots. Van Meter noted that "they have got awfully afraid of Capt. McNeill." Nevertheless, the Yankees kept beating the bushes, hoping to flush out the gray phantoms. Sergeant S. G. Rogers, a Pennsylvania cavalryman, scribbled in his journal, "We remained in Moorefield for about a week, scouring the mountains and skirmishing with squads of McNeill's men almost daily."[26]

Finally, the federals gave up on their Moorefield outpost. On January 8 Mulligan's command began the forty-two–mile march back to Camp Jessie at New Creek; Washburn retired to Romney two days later. For the time being, Hardy County was back in Confederate hands.[27]

CHAPTER 4

Capture of a Hay Train

———— ∞∞∞ ————

"Throw down your arms,
and we will parole you."

News of McNeill's recent exploits spread throughout the South and even caught the attention of General Robert E. Lee. On January 10 Lee, responding to a report from Colonel Imboden that noted the December 28 attack on Milroy's wagons, wrote, "I am much gratified to hear of the gallant conduct of Captains McNeill and Imboden, and hope they will continue to harass the enemy as much as possible." Ten days later, after learning of McNeill's January 5 victory, the commander once again praised the veteran partisan, writing, "The success of Captain McNeill is very gratifying, and, I hope, may be often repeated."[1]

In a vote held in early January, a majority of Imboden's men had chosen to give up their partisan status and follow him into the regular service. But he did lose a substantial number of soldiers. Of the 167 of his followers who had voted no, many enlisted in other regiments; a number just drifted back home. Although some of his troopers elected to remain in Company E, soon to be under the command of Captain Abel S. Scott, Hanse and Jesse declined. Another seventeen men from the old company left the regiment with them, thus forming the nucleus of McNeill's Rangers. According to Ranger John B. Fay, the young Cumberland native who joined the outfit the following August, "The parent company then reorganized with McNeill captain and his son Jesse C. McNeill, Isaac S. Welton, and Bernard J. Dolan, first, second, and junior second lieutenants, respectively."[2]

In an article published in the August 7, 1906, edition of the *Baltimore Sun*, Fay recalled his charismatic captain:

McNeill was a born partisan leader and, like Mosby, could accomplish more with a handful of men than many officers could with a regiment.

Always on the alert, perfectly familiar with the country in which he operated, ever taking his foe unawares, striking swift and sudden blows when and where least expected, resourceful in the face of greatest danger and never caught a-napping. McNeill was a veritable wizard of the saddle and well deserved the title of the Marion of the South Branch Valley; the fairest land beneath the sun and his favorite rendezvous.[3]

On January 28 Secretary of War Seddon promoted Imboden to brigadier general of the newly formed Northwestern Virginia Brigade. As indicated by the brigade's title, its theater of operation would be in the counties of northwestern Virginia, an area that was then mostly under Union control. Imboden would report directly to General Lee. His command, in reality a legion, consisted of Colonel George Imboden's 18th Virginia Cavalry, Colonel George H. Smith's 62nd Virginia Infantry, and the six guns of Captain John McClanahan's battery of horse artillery. By March 6 recruitment efforts and the 62nd's addition of four companies that were formerly part of the 25th Virginia Infantry brought the brigade's numbers up to 1,592 men. That winter, while Imboden and his officers reorganized and trained the command, McNeill also looked for new recruits and, above all, opportunities to harass the federals.[4]

On the bright, pleasant morning of February 16, a twenty-two–wagon foraging expedition traveled from near Romney westward to a farm in the lower Patterson Creek Valley. Captain Matthew Brown commanded the guard of approximately seventy-five foot soldiers from the 116th and 123rd Ohio and eight or nine troopers from Company A, Ringgold Battalion. After loading the wagons with hay and taking two male slaves with them, the Yankees headed back to the Northwestern Turnpike and camp. Some distance out in front, Sergeant Hopkins Moffitt led the outriders, who kept a sharp lookout for any signs of trouble. Farther back, Captain Brown and Second Lieutenant Wilson S. Martin rode just in front of the train; most of the soldiers relaxed atop the hay, enjoying the ride.[5]

As the federals neared Junction, the intersection with the Moorefield and North Branch Turnpike seven miles from Romney, a twenty-seven–man force made up of Rangers and Captain George Stump and a few of his men from Company B, 18th Virginia Cavalry, watched the procession from atop a hill, just south of the pike. For most of the day the men had been hiding in the woods there, hoping to swoop down and capture stray Yankee troopers for their arms and equipment, and they could not believe their luck when they spotted the wagons in the distance. The rebels let the handful of blue horsemen ride by and then anxiously awaited their prize. Just beyond Junction, the teamsters in the lead wagons stopped to water their animals in Mill Creek. Hanse then led nineteen riders forward and left seven in reserve.[6]

Suddenly a few surprised bluecoats noticed the rebels just four hundred yards away. They immediately called out to Captain Brown and asked him what to do. According to a soldier-correspondent for the *Pittsburg Chronicle*, "He muttered that the news must be taken to Romney, and immediately himself and the second lieutenant . . . put spurs to their horses and off they went, leaving his men to take care of themselves as best they could." A few of the foot soldiers jumped down and scattered into the brush, but the majority of the terrified Buckeyes froze, unable to defend the wagons or themselves. Then, unexpectedly, a rebel cried out, "Throw down your arms, and we will parole you."[7]

As the partisans approached the train, the soldiers complied cheerfully and got busy unhitching the four- and six-horse teams. When they finished, the Virginians set the hay on fire. Soon some loaded guns that the bluecoats had left atop the wagons started going off. On up ahead, Captain Brown shouted to Moffitt's squad as he galloped by, "Don't go back for God's sake. The road is full of them." Nevertheless, the small band of daring Pennsylvanians ignored the captain's advice, turned, and rode to the rescue. Upon seeing they were outnumbered, the riders halted, and Sergeant Moffitt and Private John Yohe opened fire on the graybacks. Captain McNeill, eager to get the valuable livestock to Moorefield, promptly signaled for his men to retreat.[8]

"After the wagons had been fired by the Rebels," the *Chronicle* correspondent continued, "they made our men mount the team horses and mules, and quite a number they made carry their guns, and off they went towards Moorefield in full gallop." That evening, Rebecca Van Meter saw the Rangers riding past her farm, "with a considerable number of captured yankees & leading a number of horses." Upon reaching his South Fork camp, Hanse honored his promise and paroled the prisoners. As the regimental historian for the 123rd Ohio, Lieutenant Charles M. Keyes, remembered, "Our men were treated well by Capt. McNeil who gave them money to buy their dinner, and taking their parole, sent them back to camp."[9]

By three o'clock that afternoon, word of the embarrassing incident had reached Romney. Almost immediately, Captain Harvey Young led most of the cavalry back to the scene. Upon arrival, they found nineteen burned wagons and three others still piled with hay and unharmed. After following McNeill's trail for a few miles, Young, convinced the graybacks were now long gone, gave up the chase. The next day Colonel Washburn sent Captain Horace Kellogg and Company B, 123rd Ohio, to investigate the scene. On the way back, one of the foot soldiers remembered "accidently shooting several of the feathered family, who carelessly strayed across the road." In the meantime, Washburn arrested Captain Brown and Lieutenant Martin.[10]

Not long afterward, even the cavalry came under harsh scrutiny. In the February 20 edition of the *Wheeling Intelligencer,* a citizen identifying himself only as "Hampshire" started a row with battalion commander Captain John Keys when he expressed his disgust over the recent wagon train debacle. "When will our men learn wisdom?" he asked. Noting that most of the Ringgold Battalion was in camp when the incident occurred, "Hampshire" then told the readers that "only last week, . . . McNeill threatened them near this same point. . . . and is doing his party vastly more service with fifty men than the whole Key's Battalion is doing the government." Not stopping there, he added, "Verily at this rate, we shall keep the Rebels supplied with horses for some time."[11]

In a subsequent letter to the editor, Captain Keyes replied to what he called the "foul breath of slander broadcast through the *Intelligencer* over the land against the soldiers of Pennsylvania." After stating the facts of the incident and defending his horsemen guarding the wagons, Keyes turned his wrath on "Hampshire":

> Who is this director of wisdom, who advised decent well-bred men and soldiers . . . to take pattern by and learn from the wisdom of McNeill, the robber and highwayman who lies skulking in the pine bushes or on the hilltops—waiting like a beast of prey for his victims—who never attacks unless he is first informed that the party he is about to fight have declared they won't fight—or are so few as to be able to resist him. Then, and then only, he pounces on them from his hiding place, grasps his prey and runs off with it, as he did in this case, to hide in some mountain fastness where the uninitiated can never come—Devil's Hole. . . . God help us if "Hampshire" is the kind of counsel that in the future, we must follow.[12]

On February 23 in Harrisonburg, McNeill auctioned off the 104 captured horses and mules and other booty. According to the *Staunton Spectator,* he collected $36,000 to divide among the men. "The horse and mules sold for $30,000, the harness $3,000, and the pistols $1,000, and other things $2,000." The scribe continued, "This was emphatically a dash which paid. It paid in money, as well as glory, which does not often happen." The Rangers gave Jesse McNeill "a splendid horse taken in the late capture, as an evidence of appreciation of his gallant conduct in the attack upon the Yankee train near Romney. The company have also presented their leader with a very fine riding animal."[13]

Once again, Lee praised McNeill. On February 26 the commander wrote President Davis about recent cavalry actions, most notably McNeill's bloodless victory, noting, "These successes show the vigilance of the cavalry and do credit to their officers." On the federal side, a military tribunal eventually tried Captain Brown and found him guilty of "basely deserting his command in the face of the enemy." That April, however, General Milroy rejected the court's verdict and returned Brown to his company. About the same time, Second Lieutenant Martin was released from arrest, promoted to first lieutenant, and sent back to Company F.[14]

Constantly on the move, Captain McNeill appreciated the help many Southern sympathizers provided. Some, according to local lore, he provided with signed paroles to hand out to homesick Union soldiers. It was about this time that the Rangers presented one of the saddles taken in the raid to James Crawford, "as," the *Rockingham Register* reported, "a slight evidence of their appreciation of his open-hearted hospitality." The paper also praised the man's generosity noting that "Mr. Crawford's house has been kept open and his table spread for soldiers and refugees ever since the war commenced. . . . And he never charges . . . a cent."[15]

As the winter dragged on, Captain McNeill and General Imboden began making their final adjustments on a plan to cripple the B&O Railroad by destroying bridges and trestles from Oakland, Maryland, to Grafton, Virginia, including the three imposing structures in the Cheat River Canyon in and near Rowlesburg. But for the raid to be successful, they needed much help. In early March McNeill traveled to Richmond to discuss the scheme with Secretary of War Seddon. In the meantime, Imboden sent General Robert E. Lee an outline of the proposal.[16]

CHAPTER 5

The Jones-Imboden Raid

———∞∞∞———

"The charge in the rear of the town was led by
Capt. McNeill in person."

On March 2, 1863, while the Army of the Potomac and Army of Northern Virginia were still in their winter camps on opposite sides of the Rappahannock River in Central Virginia, Imboden and McNeill's audacious plan for a strike into the Union-held Alleghenies reached the desk of General Robert E. Lee. Not only did it promise to inflict great damage on the B&O, but the proposal also offered the rebels the hope of regaining the initiative in the area that, in the summer and fall of 1861, Union forces had taken from them.

Above all, the chance to wreak havoc on three large B&O bridges on the stretch of the line through the Cheat River Canyon, a natural choke point, greatly intrigued the commander. Since the beginning of the conflict, the large size of the structures had made them prime targets for annihilation by Southern raiders. Found in Rowlesburg, the two-span, 312-foot-long wood and iron bridge across the Cheat stood 27 feet above the shallow, rocky mountain stream. A mile up the track along the side of a steep ridge, the Buckeye Hollow Viaduct spanned a deep ravine. Resting on a stone wall base, this sturdy cast-iron structure was 340 feet long and 46 feet high, its track supported by heavy wooden beams. Situated on the side of another precipitous ridge approximately six-tenths of a mile farther on was the Trey Run Viaduct, a colossal structure that many railroad aficionados considered the company's masterpiece. Noted engineer Albert Fink had designed the edifice that construction crews built of the same materials as its nearby sister. This magnificent viaduct towered 57 feet above the rugged chasm and was 440 feet long.[1]

As explained to Lee, the plan called for a fast-moving mounted column to destroy all bridges and trestling from Oakland westward to the line's junction with the Northwestern Virginia Railroad at Grafton. Meanwhile, Imboden would be leading a diversionary force from Shenandoah Mountain northward toward the federal posts at Beverly, Philippi, and Buckhannon.[2]

Imboden also told Lee that, as part of his strategy, Grumble Jones's cavalry brigade would march north from its camps in the upper Shenandoah Valley to Moorefield. Once there, Jones's troopers would provide another diversion for the force moving against the railroad by continuing north and attracting the attention of federal troops stationed at Romney, Cumberland, and New Creek. In the meantime, late on the afternoon of the day Jones left Moorefield, a picked force of five hundred men from the 18th Virginia Cavalry and McNeill's Rangers would leave that town and, using back roads, ride overnight until they reached the Northwestern Turnpike. Later the graybacks would leave the pike, ride to Oakland, and burn the nearby railroad bridge over the Youghiogheny River. The destruction of the bridge was vital to the raid's success, since it would stymie any later federal attempt to convey soldiers west by rail to aid Rowlesburg's defenders.[3]

With the bridge at Oakland destroyed, the raiders would then descend on Rowlesburg either by way of the Northwestern Turnpike, crossing the Cheat River four miles south of the town, "or take the Kingwood Road, . . . crossing the Cheat River north of the railroad." Imboden also suggested that the strike force might divide in Oakland and come into Rowlesburg from both directions. To hinder pursuit by Union cavalry, once across the river the rebels would burn the road bridges behind them. With that accomplished, Imboden figured that the soldiers would have plenty of time to complete their work.[4]

Imboden then explained that if both wings were successful they would unite at either Buckhannon or Weston and then attack and destroy portions of the Northwestern Virginia Railroad, a B&O branch line that ran from Grafton to the Ohio River at Parkersburg. He believed that the damage to the two lines "will end . . . the occupation of the northwest by the enemy, at least for some months to come." Imboden also emphasized to Lee the huge herds of cattle and horses that the raiders could gather for the general's livestock-poor army, the likelihood that many new recruits would flock to the Confederate banners, and the chance to capture important local Unionist leaders. Before the raid could start, however, Imboden needed reinforcements for his column marching on Beverly. He asked the general to send him the 25th and 31st Virginia infantry regiments, then with the Army of Northern Virginia. He believed that these soldiers, hailing from the northwest, would not only be able to replenish their ranks with new recruits but would "fight like tigers the vandals who had so long domineered over their helpless families."[5]

After studying the brigadier's bold proposal for over a week, on March 11 the commander approved the plan, adding, "I think if carried out with your energy and promptness it should succeed." Lee added that if he could not send the two regiments Imboden requested, he would try to get him reinforcements from Major General Samuel Jones, then commanding the Department of Western Virginia.[6]

In the meantime, Captain McNeill had already met with Secretary of War Seddon and got his wholehearted support for the upcoming mission. On March 10 Seddon wrote McNeill a letter of introduction and sent him off to meet with Grumble and explain to the general his role in the proposed operation. In the letter, Seddon emphasized to Jones that the destruction of the railroad bridges "are objects of great importance and long engaged the attention and special interest of the President." Although other rebel forays had previously failed to reach the vicinity of Rowlesburg, the secretary believed that "the sudden dash of a small force" might succeed. Seddon told Jones that he hoped that the plan would have his "approval and cooperation." He added, "You will be expected to afford a portion . . . of the forces required for the enterprise."[7]

Over the next few weeks the Confederates went about getting ready for the expedition. Imboden convinced Sam Jones to lend him some troops and made repeated requests for General Lee to send him the 25th and 31st regiments. In the meantime, the decision to include Grumble Jones's cavalry in the initial part of the raid would eventually lead to Lee relegating Captain McNeill to a secondary role.[8]

Although its planners originally scheduled the incursion to begin in late arch, heavy rain and snow in the mountains disrupted their timetable. This delay allowed Grumble, who was not pleased with his auxiliary role in the endeavor, the time to craft a major change to the plan and send it to Lee for his consideration. In Grumble's version, the thirty-eight-year-old West Point graduate and former U.S. Army cavalry officer would replace McNeill as leader of the eastern wing. On April 8 Lee telegraphed both Imboden and Grumble that he approved the change.[9]

While this was going on, on April 5 the Rangers and Captain Isaac Kuykendall's 7th Virginia Cavalry squadron were camped at the Harness farm just upstream and across the South Branch from Old Fields. The next morning Lieutenant William F. Speer, Company G, Ringgold Battalion, led five hay wagons from the cavalry camp near Mechanicsburg Gap west to the Patterson Creek Valley. Near Burlington, Speer and his forty-five troopers ran into a Ranger ambush and scattered. The rebels captured Speer, fifteen soldiers, and the wagons and their teams. Soon McNeill was leading the caravan back over Patterson Creek Mountain to Old Fields.[10]

That same morning, Colonel Jacob Campbell, 54th Pennsylvania Infantry, now commanding the recently built fort at Mechanicsburg Gap, ordered Lieutenant Henry Myers to take fifty horsemen on a scout to Moorefield. Myers reached Old Fields shortly after two thirty that afternoon and observed, from a high point, the rebel camp across the river. After estimating the size of the enemy force to be at least five hundred, Myers started back to the fort. Rebecca Van Meter noticed the bluecoats riding past her place and figured they had only been gone about twenty minutes As the federals moved along, most of Kuykendall's riders and some Rangers got on their trail, and just past Reynolds Gap the Southerners finally caught up with the Pennsylvanians and a running fight started.[11]

Earlier, back at headquarters Campbell had received word of the wagon train's capture and sent Captain George Work and the rest of the battalion, between 200 to 250 troopers, out after McNeill. Work, figuring that the cunning fighter would make for Moorefield, turned off the "beautiful mud pike" at Junction and rode south for a time before stopping at Purgitsville. Following at a distance, Lieutenant Colonel John Linton led 600 foot soldiers from the 54th Pennsylvania and the 1st (West) Virginia, "and one section of the Upshur Battery."[12]

Upon finally reaching the hamlet of Purgitsville, some seven miles from Old Fields, Myers's hard-pressed band was relieved to find their comrades waiting for them. Work took command and quickly set up an ambush. He posted most of his men behind a nearby ridge, and according to Private Samuel C. Farrar, ordered "Lieutenant Welch to go forward, raise the enemy and then retreat, leading their pursuers past the reserve, when the latter would charge after them and cut off their escape."[13]

Upon nearing the village, Kuykendall had halted the pursuit to give all of his horse soldiers time to catch up. Now the Virginians were some distance back, "just out of view" of the federals. When Kuykendall saw a few Yankees advancing his way and then suddenly open fire, he became suspicious of a trap and warned his riders not to follow, but "they seemed to think it was a Yankee bluff"—and in an instant the impatient rebels took the bait and charged. They soon closed upon Welch's men and began fighting them.[14]

So far Work's tactics were sound. But just as the foremost rebels entered the trap, "unfortunately," as Farrar remembered, "a drunken soldier in Work's command fired on them." Suddenly the rest of the Pennsylvanians descended on the Southerners, who fought fiercely to escape.[15]

Farrar continued:

There was a short and sharp hand-to-hand pistol and sabre conflict, the Confederates fighting desperately, but only waiting until they could extricate themselves from the tangle, when they broke away in great disorder. In the first minute or two of the clash all revolvers and guns were emptied, and the "Johnnies," aware of this, ignored the demand to surrender, but spurred their horses and dashed away; then it became a question of the faster horse and sabre.[16]

Yankee casualties were light—only three wounded. Colonel Campbell later reported that his men had killed three rebels, wounded fourteen, and captured three. According to John Fay, Ranger losses included "a few men slightly wounded and Private A. A. Boggs taken prisoner."[17]

After stopping at the Van Meter place so the women could patch up the wounded, the Southerners returned to the Harness farm. The next morning Colonel Linton led the artillery, infantry, and about a hundred horse soldiers to Old Fields, arriving there about ten o'clock. Linton promptly posted his artillery atop the river bluffs and ordered the gunners to shell the enemy camp. The men fired twenty or more rounds. The surprised graybacks evacuated quickly, Campbell wrote, "leaving behind a quantity of stores, grain, and forage, with the wagons they had captured from Lieutenant Speer." Then, with the cavalry fording the river and infantry crossing in boats, the federals marched to the farm, destroyed the rebels' supplies, and burned the captured wagons.[18]

By mid-April the weather had improved, the road surfaces were finally firm, and it was time for the long-anticipated expedition to begin. On April 21 Imboden's brigade, reinforced by the 25th and 31st Virginia Infantry regiments rendezvoused with units from Sam Jones's command at Hightown. In all, Imboden's western wing, including 700 cavalry, numbered 3,365 men.[19]

Almost as soon as the soldiers started marching up the Staunton-Parkersburg Turnpike, though, the weather turned bad. But despite numerous delays in crossing the Alleghenies in heavy rain, sleet, and even snow, on April 24 Imboden's men arrived south of Beverly. That afternoon the Confederates attacked federal defenses, forcing Colonel George Latham and his 878-man contingent, mostly from his own 2nd (West) Virginia Infantry, to retreat toward Philippi. Latham would eventually join his brigade commander, Brigadier General Benjamin F. Roberts, at Buckhannon. In the meantime, word of Imboden's attack on Beverly caused General Kelley to rush Mulligan's 23rd Illinois by rail from New Creek to Grafton. So far, except for Mulligan being able to reach Grafton, Imboden's plan had worked perfectly and opened up an excellent opportunity for Jones to strike the railroad. But the same storms that had slowed down Imboden's march poured torrential rain on the eastern wing as it slogged its way up and down the steep mountain roads toward Moorefield.[20]

On April 21 Jones's command left its camps in the valley. Besides his cavalry, the 6th, 7th, 11th, and 12th Virginia regiments; 34th and 35th Virginia battalions; the 1st Maryland Battalion; and Captain McNeill's 40 Rangers, his forces, approximately 2,900 soldiers, also included the 1st Maryland Infantry Battalion, the Baltimore Light Artillery, and Chew's Battery. The march, which normally took little more than a day, ended up taking three. Upon arriving in Moorefield on the afternoon of the twenty-third, Jones discovered that high, rushing waters made it impossible to cross the South Branch. The next morning the general took his command upriver to the Petersburg ford. There, in a difficult crossing, he lost one man drowned, along with a number of horses. More important to the future success of the mission, though, he had to leave his artillery, infantry, and 350 troopers behind. Now, leading just less than 2,000 men, Jones rode downstream, reaching Old Fields about dark. Van Meter wrote that "our Army is around

Reynolds Gap. Courtesy Woodrow Simmons.

us ... it was a great sight to us all ... every house rich & poor cooked & fed them until they left."[21]

The next afternoon, April 25, Jones left the village and marched across Patterson Creek Mountain to Williamsport and Greenland Gap. That evening, in a bloody skirmish at the western end of the gap, Jones lost nine men killed and thirty-four wounded before finally capturing the two infantry companies, Company G, 23rd Illinois and Company A, 14th (West) Virginia, posted at the narrow pass. From available sources, it does not appear that any of the Rangers fought in the four-hour clash. But Captain Martin Wallace, a former opponent of Hanse and Jesse at the Battle of Lexington, Missouri, did his best "to imitate Lexington" and refused to surrender his company until the rebels finally set ablaze the log church the stubborn captain and his men were defending. When Wallace capitulated and led his men outside, the West Virginians came out of some nearby cabins with their hands up.[22]

After taking time to bury the dead, care for his casualities, and send a small detachment back to Moorefield with both prisoners and his own lightly wounded, Jones ordered his troopers back in the saddle, and not long afterward the men were making the winding, four-mile climb up the Allegheny Front. Upon reaching the crest, they rode another six miles to Mount Storm, a village on the Northwestern Turnpike, arriving there about one o'clock on Sunday morning, April 26. At Mount Storm Jones dispatched Captain Edward McDonald with his 11th Virginia Cavalry squadron to disrupt rail traffic and attack the station at Altamont. Now riding westward on the pike, the Confederates continued to Gorman, Maryland. There Jones wrote, "Colonel (A.W.) Harman was sent with the 12th Virginia Cavalry, Brown's Maryland Battalion of cavalry, and (John H.) McNeill's company of Partisan Rangers to burn the bridge at Oakland and march by way of Kingwood to Morgantown." Jones continued following the pike with three regiments, two cavalry battalions, and a packhorse train carrying kegs of gunpowder to blow up Rowlesburg's three bridges.[23]

Just before five that morning, Harman's troopers torched the turnpike bridge over the North Branch of the Potomac and headed north. Riding out in front was guide Charles "Jim" Dailey, a young Ranger and Oakland native. The route to the town would lead Harman's 650 troopers through Ryan's Glade before crossing Backbone Mountain at Kelso's Gap. As the column moved along, squads of outriders roamed the nearby fields and woods, looking for fresh mounts. The famished men were able to get plenty of food from the farmhouses they stopped at but found few horses; the local "mountain grapevine" had preceded them.[24]

Just before eleven o'clock the raiders neared Oakland. Harman then sent McNeill with a detachment to circle the town and charge in from the north. In the meantime, the colonel would be leading the rest of the cavalry forward. A little while later a shot rang out. Instantly one of the rebels galloped ahead and fired a round at a fleeing bluecoat, just clipping the heel of his shoe. Private Cornelius Johnson kept running but stopped suddenly when the trooper shouted, "Drop that gun, and stop you Yankee. . . . Stop or I'll kill you!"[25]

At that time many of the town's three hundred citizens and Captain Joseph M. Godwin's soldiers of Company O, 6th (West) Virginia Infantry were attending church services or just relaxing. About a mile west of Oakland, a handful of Yankees were on duty at Fort Alice, protecting the railroad bridge over the Youghiogheny. No one in town had heard any shots.[26]

An anonymous Ranger described what happened next:

> Our forces charged on Oakland, down the turnpike, and in the rear of the town, the charge down the pike being led by one of the guides, private Daily, a gallant boy attached to Capt. McNeill's company. The charge in rear of the town was led by Capt. McNeill in person. Your readers may well imagine the panic caused by this sudden and violent intrusion into

the quiet village of Oakland by these mountain dare-devils with "horns!" The good Union people thought old Nick was among them sure enough. The Union shirkers ran and hid; the Yankee women scowled and shook their broomsticks and threatened vengeance.[27]

As some of the Southerners roamed throughout the town gathering up Godwin's dumbfounded soldiers, others took over the railroad station and telegraph office before riding to the trestle, capturing the guards, and setting the trestle on fire. During this time, Private Mark Westmoreland, a Ranger hailing from Georgia, captured "a fine set of telegraphic instruments."[28]

Once everything settled down, Harman allowed the men time to eat. Owners of hotels, restaurants, and even private dwellings reluctantly welcomed the rebels, who paid for their meals with Confederate scrip. After that, the raiders started leaving Oakland but not before witnessing a strange sight. Unexpectedly, an unmanned locomotive pulling eight cars rolled slowly though the town and then ran out of steam just as the front wheel of the engine reached the abutment of the burning bridge. It finally stopped, perched precariously above the river.[29]

Upon riding west, the graybacks crossed the turnpike bridge over the river, then set it alight. Proceeding some distance, they ran across Captain Godwin and another officer and took them prisoner, but shortly thereafter Harman paroled both officers and his fifty other captives. Once across the state line, squads fanned out into the countryside and gathered many horses, and outside Cranberry, Virginia, Harman and two hundred of his troopers ran into some militia but quickly brushed them aside. Later, bushwhackers began taking occasional potshots at the riders. In due course the rebels descended Briery Mountain, then crossing and subsequently destroying the suspension bridge across the Cheat at Albrightsville. The next morning, April 27, they passed through Kingwood and made for Morgantown.[30]

About one o'clock in the afternoon, Harman's vanguard arrived outside the Unionist stronghold, one that the Ranger scribe called "the meanest place in Virginia," and Major Ridgely Brown promptly met with town leaders and negotiated Morgantown's surrender. The Confederates then disarmed the local home guards. At five o'clock the rest of Harman's command arrived and learned from their friends the disappointing fact that many citizens had spirited away their horses. The rebels then fanned out through the town, looking for boots, clothes, hats, food, and whiskey. "Private Westmoreland," the Ranger wrote, "then climbed to the top of the steeple on the C.H., tore down the Union flag with the stars and stripes, and nailed fast the Confederate flag, which floated from that place for the first time since the war."[31]

That evening the raiders, driving a large herd of stolen horses, left town and marched south toward Independence. Early the next morning, April 28, Harman reunited with Jones, whose soldiers had failed miserably in their attack on Rowlesburg, and not long afterward McDonald's squadron also showed up. It was then that the men first learned that Sergeant John Dailey, Company D, 11th Virginia Cavalry, had boarded an unmanned train at Altamont Station and accidentally sent it up the track—to end hovering over the river outside of Oakland.[32]

After the Confederates broke camp, Jones headed north to Morgantown, and once again the Rangers, along with the 1st Maryland Cavalry, led the way. Along the road two hunters fired on the vanguard and killed two horses before running off. Westmoreland and others quickly captured the perpetrators, locals Lloyd Beall and Andrew Johnson, and a short time later Captain Frank Bond, 1st Maryland Cavalry, ordered their execution, along with Albert Robey, another mountaineer, who unfortunately had just happened along. The rebels promptly seated the first two atop stumps and shot them as, meanwhile, Robey pleaded his case. When that failed, the man asked for a moment to pray. As he was kneeling, a rebel fired from behind and hit him in the shoulder. He fell face forward and played dead—and then, after the raiders left, he got up, not badly injured, and went to get help.[33]

After Harman rode off, the people in Morgantown had relaxed their guard and were not expecting the graybacks to return. As a Ranger recalled, "The Abolitionists were worse surprised than ever they had been when the Confederates first opened their eyes to the fact that 'the d——d Rebels' were in the neighborhood." Since many of the citizens had already brought their horses out of hiding, the Southerners had easy pickings, and Jones also sent riders out into the surrounding farms to round up more horses. Meanwhile, the rest of the soldiers roamed freely about the town.[34]

While in Morgantown, Lieutenant Welton somehow came across and detained a young female slave who that winter had run off from his Petersburg farm. According to the story, she was General Milroy's "sweetheart." The writer claimed "that the refined and polished gentleman had seduced, not stolen her from Lt. Welton." On the way back "the poor privates in McNeill's company were honored with permission to escort the gallant Gen. Milroy's 'second choice' to her old home."[35]

That evening the Confederates left Morgantown, crossing the suspension bridge over the Monongahela River, and then, after resting for a time, they rode south for Fairmont. The next morning, April 29, Jones's fighters attacked the

Union force guarding the town, captured 260 federals, and later fought off a relief force led by Colonel Mulligan that had traveled hurriedly from Grafton to Fairmont by rail. That evening, in one of the most spectacular incidents of the raid, Captain John Henderson blew up the B&O's six hundred–foot iron bridge over the Monongahela River.[36]

But, as far as the Rangers were concerned, there was controversy. Using the letters O. P. H. as his pseudonym, a soldier correspondent to the *Rockingham Register*, deriding the Rangers' performance in the fighting that day, wrote, "Capt. McNeil's company was also present but was mostly engaged in charging upon stables and pasture-fields for horses."[37]

In a subsequent letter to the paper, however, a Ranger disputed his claim, stating:

> As we neared the town, the command was ordered to charge; they did so, . . . and found, near the village some three or four hundred Yankees and citizens drawn up for battle; sharpshooters were called for, and one hundred and fifty responded out of the whole command. Capt. McNeil, with ten of his men, were among that number, that being all the long-ranged guns in the company, five others went and pledged their pistols to get guns, and went into the fight. Now see what is the proportion: fifteen out of forty-one, rank and file; and one hundred and fifty from the whole Brigade of twenty or three hundred. Now, Messrs. Editors, this thing of those living in glass houses throwing stones, don't pay. I would just here remark that there are some others as well as Capt. McNeil's company who charge upon private property of a different class from horses. Neither is Capt. McNeil's company known by the name of the "Calico" Regiment, and if Mr. "O.P.H." left his calico and goods in the stampede when the Yankees charged upon their rear, he ought not to get mad at Capt. McNeil's men for following after them and picking up a little of what got too heavy about that time and had to throw away.[38]

The next day the rebels continued toward Clarksburg, but Jones, finding the city too heavily defended, then turned east and rode to nearby Bridgeport. There the Southerners destroyed a Northwestern Virginia Railroad bridge, captured a few soldiers, and ran a locomotive into a creek. On May 1 the general and his men arrived in Philippi, after which Jones sent the 6th Virginia Cavalry and the Rangers back to the Shenandoah Valley with the captured cattle, horses, and soldiers, including one of the Snyder clan, the notorious Union guerrilla fighters from Randolph County. In a day or so Jones recalled the 6th Virginia, and Colonel John S. Green turned the livestock and prisoners over to Captain McNeill.[39]

A few weeks later both Jones and Imboden were back at their respective camps, having completed their campaign into the Alleghenies. Although the bridges at Rowlesburg were still standing and few recruits had been added to the ranks, both the B&O and Northwestern Virginia lines had been damaged and, most important of all, thousands of heads of cattle, horses, and mules had been spirited out of the northwest to be used by the Army of Northern Virginia. And on May 9 Jones had also destroyed Burning Springs, an important oil field along the Little Kanawha River.[40]

CHAPTER 6

The Gettysburg Campaign

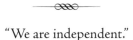

"We are independent."

By the time all of the raiders got back from the raid into northwestern Virginia, plans were well underway for General Lee's second invasion of the North. Due to the mortal wounding of Stonewall Jackson by his own troops at the Battle of Chancellorsville and the large size of the army's First and Second Infantry Corps, Lee had decided to install a smaller, more manageable three-corps system. In the reorganization, Lieutenant General James Longstreet still commanded the First Corps, while Lieutenant General Richard Ewell replaced Jackson at the head of the Second Corps. Lieutenant General A. P. Hill would lead the new Third Corps.

On June 7, as the Army of Northern Virginia got ready to begin its sweep to the Potomac crossings, Lee ordered Imboden to march his brigade north from Churchville into Hardy and Hampshire Counties, collecting livestock and supplies along the way. He was to fight any federal force out of Cumberland or New Creek that came against him and do as much damage to the railroad as possible. Lee also told the brigadier to "cooperate with any troops you may find operating in the Valley."[1]

During the upcoming campaign, Imboden added the Rangers to his command. In the meantime, however, the band, now numbering about sixty-five riders, was roaming through the lower Shenandoah Valley. On the afternoon of Saturday, June 6, McNeill and his men were scouting near Berryville when they came across a small enemy wagon train traveling the pike between there and Winchester. The Rangers attacked immediately, killing two bluecoats, wounding two others, and capturing twenty. The raiders also took twenty-four horses, including four from Major General Milroy's staff wagon, along with harness and other equipment. Instead of torching the wagons, the men used axes to disable them. A dead horse was McNeill's only casualty.[2]

The editor of the *Rockingham Register* opined: "The Yankees had better not drive their teams into Dixie if they don't want McNeill to take them. He's a sort of a High Sheriff in these 'diggins' clothed with the right to 'levy on' whatever property our dear old 'Uncle Sam' may send into the Confederacy. He seems to have a special hankering after Yankee trains and teams."[3]

The Rangers then traveled south to Harrisonburg, turned the prisoners over to the provost marshal, and sold their booty. That Thursday, June 11, the command left town and rode back down the valley to Winchester, arriving outside the city about three o'clock on Saturday afternoon. They quickly discovered that Ewell's troops, the vanguard of Lee's gray tide, had just begun their efforts to force Milroy's defenders out of their fortifications. "Skirmishing," a Ranger wrote, "continued throughout the evening."[4]

It appears that about this time a small Ranger detachment was in Romney. One secondary source places Captain McNeill there on June 15, and two days later 18th Virginia Cavalry trooper Private I. Norval Baker noted in his diary that Jesse McNeill was in Cumberland during the regiment's brief occupation of the town, concocting a tobacco smuggling scheme with a local merchant.[5]

After heavy fighting on Sunday, June 14, Milroy decided to abandon Winchester and retreat to Harpers Ferry. Early the next morning, four miles north of Winchester at Stephenson's Depot, Major General Edward "Allegheny" Johnson's division blocked Milroy's way and decimated his command. Some Yankees, including the hated "Gray Eagle," escaped to Harpers Ferry, while others fled north by way of Bath and Hancock, Maryland, before finally reaching safety in Bloody Run (now Everett), Pennsylvania.[6]

During the day on Sunday, the Rangers had suffered under heavy shelling, but that evening they rode north to Martinsburg on a scout with Major Harry Gilmor's recently enlisted partisans. Upon returning the next morning, the men found that "Milroy and his minions had deserted their boasted fortifications and were skedaddling in every direction. Thinking that some of them might get lost in the mountains and never get home, we concluded that the best plan would be to stop them." The Rangers rounded up 125 to 150 soldiers, 80 to 90 horses with all their saddles and harness, and many "revolvers, carbines, sabres, etc." One of the highlights of the action was when a trio of Rangers captured a band of 21 of the enemy. In its June 30 edition, the *Daily Dispatch* reported the company's military success and noted that "the property taken by them was sold in Winchester and purchased by the C.S. Government for $40,325."[7]

After cashing in their plunder, McNeill's boys were back in the saddle, riding down the valley toward the Potomac. On June 16 the Rangers bypassed Martinsburg and then traveled west on Warm Springs Road to Hedgesville and Johnsontown before striking the B&O depot at Cherry Run. There they ran into some Yankees, and a one-sided fight broke out. When it was over, the Rangers had captured at least twelve Northerners. Once again, McNeill's scribe described the action: "Two of our boys charged 18 Yankees and completely routed them. Here Capt. McNeill was charged upon and surrounded by a squad of Yankees who, after receiving the contents of the captain's double-barreled shotgun and revolver were glad, those that were able to get away in double-quick, apparently well-satisfied with their short, but to them painful interview with the gallant Captain."[8]

Later, according to the soldier-correspondent, the outfit headed downriver to Williamsport. But he left a few things out. On June 17, Elisha Manor, a local miller, noted in his diary "that some Southerners passed through Johnsontown." The next day he recorded "that those Southerners who went through Johnsontown burned Sleepy Creek Bridge, some canal boats and Back Creek Bridge, and took ——— Miller, ——— Paine, and J. Albright prisoners to Hedgesville but there released them." Hancock merchant James Ripley Smith wrote in his diary, "They burnt Sleepy Creek Bridge and boats on the canal." Another Hancock citizen later told a reporter, "The lock gates at Millstone Point were also torn out and the canal boats burned."[9]

After crossing the Potomac at Light's Ford, McNeill spent some time in Williamsport before riding west to Clear Spring. Arriving there on the evening of June 18, the rebels discovered that they were in one of the most pro-Union locales in western Maryland. But what disappointed them most was finding out that many townsmen and nearby farmers had left the vicinity, taking most of their horses to hideaways deep in the nearby mountains. Although Captain William Firey's Company B, 1st Maryland Potomac Home Brigade Cavalry, was patrolling the area and had been skirmishing with other Confederates, their units did not cross paths.[10]

The next day the Rangers continued west in heavy rain. Outriders looking for horses scoured the countryside. By late afternoon they had covered fourteen more miles and were now just east of Hancock, a thriving Potomac River town that owed its prosperity to its location on the National Pike and the Chesapeake and Ohio Canal. Also, just a short ferry ride across the Potomac was Alpine Depot, Virginia, an important stop on the B&O.[11]

James Ripley Smith owned a store along Main Street that faced the canal. For many years the prosperous businessman meticulously recorded important Hancock events. During the war, he was especially observant, noting Union troop movements through the town and the occasional Confederate incursion. In his entry for June 19 Smith wrote, "About 5, 40 Southern cavalry made a

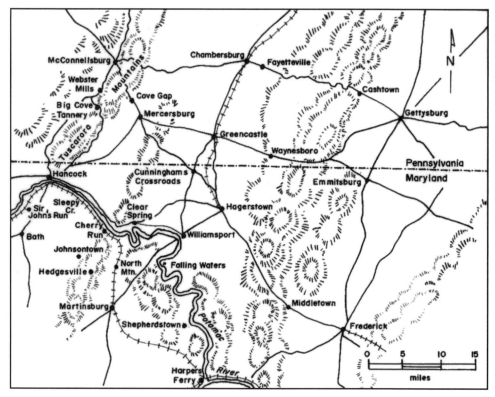

The Gettysburg Campaign (John Heiser).

dash into this place for the first time, and took two Union soldiers with them and paroled several. . . . They conducted themselves very well."[12]

McNeill's charge into Hancock had been so sudden that the eight bluecoats there were unable to defend themselves or escape. In the meantime, as the Rangers galloped up Main Street, many people greeted them with loud cries of "Hurrah for Jeff Davis." And it was then, once things had calmed down, that they found out that Hancock, unlike Clear Spring, was home to a number of Southern sympathizers.[13]

Right away these people started welcoming the rebels into their homes and treating them to supper. One Ranger remembered that "the citizens very cordially invited us to partake of some refreshment with them. Accepting their generous invitation we were soon comfortably seated around tables that were almost groaning under the load of good things that were heaped upon them for us poor rebels."[14]

After supper their hosts asked the men to come back for breakfast. The rebels did not disappoint their new friends and showed up early the next morning for another hearty meal. Before leaving town, Hanse formed his troopers in line along Main Street and delivered a short speech, thanking the Marylanders for their hospitality. When the captain finished, the men gave the people three loud cheers.[15]

After that the rebels burned some canal boats and helped themselves to Smith's stock of boots. Then, passing under the canal via the road culvert, they forded the Potomac and pillaged Alpine Depot. Following the track west, the Rangers soon traveled the five miles to Sir John's Run and in a while rode on another four miles to Great Cacapon.[16]

A B&O employee later recorded the significant damage the raiders inflicted on the line: "McNeill's cavalry destroyed water-station, blacksmith shop, wood-house, sand-house and supervisor's office at Sir John's Run; the water station at Rockwell's and Willett's Run, and Great Cacapon trestling, and a number of sand and tool-houses, hand and truck cars were also destroyed."[17]

Finishing up in Great Cacapon, the Rangers headed south, following a rough road that paralleled the Cacapon River before crossing the stream and going over Little Mountain to Bloomery Gap. Arriving at the gap on Sunday, June 21, they found the Northwestern Brigade camped along Bloomery Run. By this time, Imboden's command had gathered much livestock, occupied Cumberland, and inflicted serious damage on upper-Potomac railroad bridges and portions of the canal.[18]

The day before, a courier had showed up in Imboden's camp with a message from "R.E. Lee" praising the general for his brigade's thorough destruction of the B&O bridges and property from Cumberland east to Little Cacapon. Before ending his note, Lee made the following suggestion: "Should you find an opportunity, you can yourself advance north of the Potomac; and keep on the left of this army in its advance into Pennsylvania." He cautioned the brigadier to "repress all marauding."[19]

On Monday, June 22, Imboden's troops marched north to Bath, completing the twenty-three-mile tramp to the old resort town by that evening. McNeill and Captain Frank Imboden's companies, however, continued another four miles and camped in the fields opposite Hancock, where a few troopers even visited. The next day merchant Smith noted, "Rebs took nearly all the goods in Hancock & let the water out of the Canal at Road culvert." About this time, the soldier who had been chronicling McNeill's exploits for the *Rockingham Register* fell ill and returned home. He closed his letter to the paper, writing, "I left the boys well and in fine spirits."[20]

On Wednesday morning, Imboden moved his command to the fields along the Potomac opposite Hancock. That night, just after midnight, he sent the Rangers and thirteen other mounted companies across the river to the town. Once there, he promptly divided his force into three wings and then proceeded on a raid across the Mason-Dixon Line into nearby southern Fulton County, Pennsylvania. The general led his detachment west to Warfordsburg, while another raided along Timber Ridge. Colonel George Imboden took his troopers, which included McNeill's company, ten miles north to the village of Needmore, where he established a collection camp for cattle and horses. The Rangers and some other troopers, however, continued to Big Cove Tannery and Webster Mills.[21]

At Big Cove Tannery, some of the raiders robbed the S&L Robinson store, taking or destroying over $5,000 worth of goods. McNeill rode on a mile and a half to Webster Mills, the location of William Patterson's store and post office, twenty miles from Hancock. Just past noon an anxious neighbor arrived and warned the family that rebels were on the way. Taking heed, young D. H. Patterson and two of his friends sprinted across the log footbridge over the creek and up the wooded hill to where they had stashed their horses. William followed closely behind, carrying Tip, his small dog, while the womenfolk remained inside the house. After crossing the creek, the trio looked back and spotted Confederate outriders.[22]

A few Rangers chased the boys; others went into the store. According to D. H., the riders first fired a few warning shots and then surrounded them. The boys were terribly frightened, but one, Bob Shirtz, walked up to a trooper, shook his hand, and said, "Why how do you do? I'm glad to see you—how did you leave the folks at home?" The man replied, "Shut your damned Yankee mouth."[23]

The Confederates were sure they had seen four men, but the boys denied anyone else was about. Meanwhile, William hid in the granary with his hand over the dog's mouth. Luckily for him, when the barn door opened, as D. H. wrote, "it covered and concealed the granary door completely." After the Rangers gave up their search, the soldiers took the friends back to the store. Thinking that the teenagers were probably Yankee soldiers out of uniform, they threatened to take them along. Fortunately, Henrietta Patterson then appeared and convinced McNeill to release her brother and the others. Afterward, D. H. continued, "they confiscated and destroyed the entire stock of goods in the store." The family lost an estimated $2,510 that day.[24]

The Rangers then left, but rather than returning to Maryland as Imboden's troopers would, they rode east on Hunter Road toward Tuscarora Mountain before stopping to camp. That evening, however, a few came back to guard the

Patterson Store. Author's collection.

house. D. H. complimented McNeill's men, noting, "At no time during this raid was a disrespectful word spoken to my mother or sister."[25]

On the morning of June 25 the Rangers saddled up and began arguably their most controversial raid of the war. Bypassing McConnellsburg, just six miles north, they rode over the mountain in a pouring rain, reached the Mercersburg Pike, and descended on the small community of Cove Gap, the birthplace of former president James Buchanan. Happily, for many of the always thirsty graybacks, the village had a distillery. During the afternoon, the Southerners raided farms in the neighborhood and reportedly burned a local's barn and robbed his house after he fired a shot at them. That evening McNeill led his men another three miles to the western outskirts of Mercersburg and camped in Ritchey's Woods. When it got dark, the Rangers rode into town, looking for a blacksmith.[26]

In 1863 Mercersburg was a thriving town with a population of twelve hundred, which also included a substantial number of free blacks and some escaped Virginia slaves. With its economy based on the abundant foodstuffs and livestock of the surrounding farms, a number of town businesses and small manufacturers prospered. Mercersburg was also the site of the well-respected Marshall Theological Seminary.[27]

Other Confederates had visited the city before. On October 10, 1862, Jeb Stuart and eighteen hundred picked troopers stopped in Mercersburg for a time before riding on to Chambersburg. During the current campaign, on June 19,

Colonel Milton Ferguson of Brigadier General Albert G. Jenkins's cavalry brigade led some two hundred horsemen through Mercersburg and back on a raid to McConnellsburg. On June 24 Brigadier General George "Maryland" Steuart, also on his way to McConnellsburg, arrived in town at the head of a large contingent of infantry and cavalry. All these previous forays had resulted in the locals losing goods and livestock, but nothing had prepared the people for McNeill's Rangers. As Dr. Philip Schaff, a professor at the seminary, would later write, "Thursday, the 25th—Saturday, the 27th—The town was occupied by an independent band of guerrilla cavalry who steal horse, cattle, sheep, store goods, negroes, and whatever else they can make use of, without ceremony, and in evident violation of Lee's proclamation."[28]

It was still raining hard when the gum-coated rebels arrived at the black-smith shop. The *Mercersburg Journal* reported, "Their first demand was to have their horses shod. No blacksmith being on hand, they threatened to burn the shop. At last their wish was gratified." As the man worked, McNeill and some Rangers rode to the center of town, where the captain promptly addressed a crowd of curious bystanders that had gathered outside the Mansion House, a local inn. According to Dr. Schaff, the captain had a "red and bloated face" and "threatened . . . to lay the town in ashes as soon as the first gun should be fired on one of his men. . . . He gave us fair warning that the least attempt to disturb them would be our ruin." After McNeill finished, the people responded, telling him that they posed no threat to his men. They would rely on the army and militia to do the fighting.[29]

After the Rangers returned to camp, one of the pickets brought in a local boy who wanted to see McNeill. Sixteen-year-old Cephas Richie Hallar, origi-nally hailing from Independence, Missouri, quickly introduced himself and then made a deal with the captain. If McNeill would enlist Hallar, who had five older brothers in Confederate service, the next day he would point out where the town's merchants had hidden their goods. For good measure, Hallar mentioned that there were escaped slaves hiding in and around the town. The grateful captain quickly accepted Hallar's offer.[30]

That Friday morning McNeill sent four Rangers with the boy. After im-pressing a wagon, they rode to the gap and took the rough, steep trail over Cove Mountain to the Little Cove, the narrow valley running south toward the Potomac River.[31]

Of this, local historian James F. L. Harbaugh later wrote:

This young traitor knew where the goods . . . were concealed and lost no time imparting this important information to his new made friends. He first directed them to a place near the mountain where they found

Richie Hallar. Courtesy Ben Ritter.

some of the booty, and then informed them that McKinstry's and Fitzgerald's goods were in the Little Cove. Some of them were at the farm of Mr. John Fitz . . . and others were concealed at a place further down the Cove . . . (they) found the goods and succeeded in getting away with them.[32]

While this was going on, Constable George Wolfe decided to capture the rebels when they came back down the mountain, recover the stolen property, and hang the boy. Wolfe gathered up a handful of nervous volunteers and started out on the pike, but after hearing an alarm bell ringing in town, most of his troop deserted. Meanwhile, Wolfe and merchant William McKinstry kept on going, finally reaching the Fitz place, where they learned bad news. Not only had the rebels taken the store owner's wares, a $3,000 loss, but they had also rounded up seven or eight African Americans.[33]

Returning to Cove Gap, Hallar's outfit halted at Mrs. McFarland's house and took some barrels of whiskey, a prize worth forty dollars a gallon back in Virginia. A little while later they stopped at a farm about a mile outside of Mercersburg and uncovered a stash of valuable hardware hidden by Mr. Shirts, a local store owner. The men, telling Shirts that the merchandise was worth at least $5,000 in Virginia, offered to sell it back to him for $1,200 in U.S. notes, but he declined.[34]

Meanwhile in Mercersburg, Captain McNeill had already sent a detachment with a wagon or two full of plunder back to Virginia. Not long afterward, Hanse, flanked by two heavily armed outriders on each side, rode slowly down Main Street. About that time, Presbyterian Reverend Thomas Creigh looked out his window and saw McNeill stop and make an announcement. He then rushed outside, where a neighbor told him that the rebels "intend to search all houses for contrabands and that wherever they discover either they will set fire to the house."[35]

No locals ventured forward, and when time expired McNeill speedily sent his men to search the town's colored section and the seminary. While in the school, they discovered, the *Journal* reported, "a poor, ragged contraband woman and her three children, besides two muskets and accoutrements." The infuriated captain then turned his men loose. It became, Schaff wrote, "a regular slave-hunt, which presented the worst spectacle I ever saw in this war." The *Journal* continued: "The behavior of this rowdy crew was anything but decent. When remonstrated by citizens they impudently said they were guerrillas, and not subject to Lee's orders about private property, were dealing on their own responsibility, and gave account to no man." Dr. Schaff said that one of the Rangers told him, "We are independent and come and go where and when we please."[36]

Throughout the rest of the morning and rainy afternoon, the partisans systematically looted the town and the outlying farms. Besides the fact that their haul in goods and livestock was enormous, McNeill's only casualty that day was a broken arm one of his roughnecks suffered while breaking into a church. Back in camp that evening, the satisfied raiders no doubt celebrated their success with some of the whiskey Hallar and company had brought in.[37]

On Saturday morning the captain and thirty riders moved slowly through Mercersburg on their way back to Winchester. At the head of the column, Mrs. Hallar and her daughter rode in a carriage, closely followed by two wagonloads of booty. Seated atop the stolen goods were twenty-one African Americans, at least four of whom were town residents. Farther back, drovers pushed a small herd of cattle, some horses, and at least five hundred sheep. Other "land pirates," as the Pennsylvanians called them, galloped up and down the street, keeping close watch on the crowd that now lined Main Street.[38]

As the caravan moved along, the people and rebels bantered with one another. While passing some women, one of Mrs. Hallar's guards asked playfully, "Any more ladies going to Richmond?" When Mrs. R. F. McFarlands's purloined flock of three hundred sheep came by, she shouted to a Ranger, "So the Southern chivalry has come down to sheep-stealing. I want you to know that we regard sheep thieves as the meanest of fellows. I am too proud to ask for them back, but if I were a man, I would shoot you with a pistol." The partisan called her bluff and presented her his sidearm. But she would not take it, telling him to give it to her son. Especially upset at the plight of the blacks, Professor Schaff asked one of the guards, "Do you not feel bad and mean in such an occupation?" The man replied, Schaff said, "that he felt very comfortable." Then they were gone, leaving only a few gun hands behind. The *Journal* noted that "these wholesale robbers kept riding back and forward after the main body had passed; behaving with much boldness and insolence."[39]

McNeill's slow-moving caravan left on Hagerstown Road. Upon reaching Cunningham's Crossroads (now Cearfoss), Maryland, the rebels turned south and headed for Williamsport. Once there, the wagons and cattle forded the river, but it was necessary to use Lemen's Ferry to transport the sheep. The partisans did not arrive in Martinsburg, approximately thirty-five miles from Mercersburg, until June 30.[40]

Colonel Bradley Johnson was also in Martinsburg that Tuesday. The Marylander and some other officers were riding north to link up with the army. The colonel viewed the procession with disgust. In a message to Secretary of War Seddon, Johnson said, "Captain McNeill, guerrilla passed down the Valley road with 740 head of sheep, 160 head of cattle, and 40 horses from Pennsylvania. Private property is respected."[41]

That same day, Major John S. Mosby's partisan rangers also arrived in Martinsburg. Years later, Private James J. Williamson recalled that on June 28 Mosby and about fifty men "left Glasscock's Burnt House and . . . started for the Valley. . . . It was Mosby's intention to join Lee in Pennsylvania." But for some unknown reason the major, once reaching the vicinity of Martinsburg, did not follow the direct route north into Maryland and Pennsylvania but led his men west. On June 30 Elisha Manor recorded "Some forty or fifty cavalry passed through Johnsontown and took H. Johnson's horses."[42]

Early on July 1 the raiders crossed the Potomac, at either the mouth of Cherry Run or upriver from Sleepy Creek, turned north, and between twelve and one o'clock descended on Mercersburg, "where," Williamson wrote, "we expected to find a portion of the army." Upon finding no Confederate force there, Mosby decided to return to Virginia. Soon, according to the *Mercersburg Journal,* Mosby left with most of his men but not before dispatching "a drunken outlaw band left to do mischief." Once again, partisans ransacked stores and captured some local African Americans. Schaff called the incident "the boldest and most impudent highway robbery I ever saw." Williamson failed to mention any loot taken from the stores or from private citizens but did record gathering up "218 head of cattle, 15 horses and 12 negroes." Some evidence exists that McNeill's men may have even guided Mosby to Mercersburg. On July 2 the *Philadelphia Inquirer* reported that "a few that had been at Mercersburg previously returned a day or two since and robbed the people of watches, money, hats boots, shoes, etc." Although Williamson stated that Mosby had fifty Rangers with him, Dr. Creigh places the number at "about 60," while the *Mercersburg Journal* reported "about four score." That evening Clear Spring farmer Otho Nesbitt noted that "the Rebels about 75 or 100 strong went past the stone church this evening with about 500 cattle and about two dozen Negroes and some horses."[43]

Over the next week, little information is available on McNeill's Rangers and their whereabouts. It seems, though, that at least some of the men rejoined

Imboden's command in Pennsylvania and on July 2–3 helped guard Lee's reserve train as it traveled from Chambersburg to Cashtown. On July 4–5 they also participated in guarding Imboden's "Wagon Train of the Wounded," as it rolled slowly from Cashtown to Williamsport. John Fay noted that Rangers "took an active part in guarding Lee's wagon train in Maryland and Pennsylvania, before and after the Battle at Gettysburg."[44]

On the evening of July 6 the partisans were part of a 2,700-man force General Imboden assembled hurriedly not only to defend the crossing at Williamsport, but over 1,200 parked wagons carrying rebel wounded from the three-day fight at Gettysburg, plunder, and supplies. Since four o'clock on the afternoon of July 4, Imboden's brigade had been escorting the wagons from Cashtown, Pennsylvania, back to Virginia. Beset by torrential rains and sporadic attacks by Union cavalry, the first wagons reached Williamsport at two o'clock on Sunday afternoon, July 5. Upon discovering that Light's Ford was flooded and that Union raiders had destroyed the Confederate pontoon bridge five miles downriver at Falling Waters, Imboden started housing his wounded in churches and public buildings and forming a defensive line along a ridge a half mile outside of town.[45]

The following morning McNeill and some of his men were in Clear Spring impressing cattle. Otho Nesbitt was determined not to lose his property to the rebels but failed. As his diary entry for July 6 noted, "The Rebels, Capt. McNeal, Major Vandiver, and others took my bull off worth $50. I followed them on the other side of little Conococheague, but they wouldn't give him up."[46]

Late that afternoon, dismounted troopers from Brigadier General John Buford's 1st Cavalry Division attacked the right and center of the Confederate line. During the battle, later dubbed "the Wagoner's Fight," Imboden skillfully moved his troops and thwarted Buford's attempt to capture Williamsport. At about six o'clock, Brigadier General Judson Kilpatrick's 3rd Cavalry Division threatened to attack and overrun Imboden's left, but reinforcements led by Stuart and Brigadier General Fitz Lee soon arrived and drove the Yankees off. During the engagement, the Rangers fought alongside Smith's 62nd Virginia in attacking Buford's troops on the far right.[47]

In the days immediately following the Battle of Williamsport, General Lee ordered his soldiers into defensive positions where they would have to remain until the waters of the Potomac receded enough to allow the army to cross. As part of this effort, Imboden sent the 18th Virginia and the Rangers a few miles west of Williamsport to guard Clear Spring Road. On July 8, fifteen forage wagons rolled out of the Confederate lines, headed for two gristmills near the canal at Four Locks. Captain Wesley Makely, Company D, 18th Virginia Cavalry, and Jesse McNeill led the troopers guarding the train. Although Hanse told Jesse to stay put, he ignored his father's advice.[48]

Until this time rebel scouts had not sighted any large force of federals west of Williamsport. That morning, however, General Kelley, just completing a forty-mile forced march from Cumberland, led a large contingent of Yankees into Hancock. Kelley immediately sent Captain Andrew J. Greenfield and his sixty troopers of Company B, Ringgold Battalion, to "destroy all ferry boats or means of crossing the Potomac River from Hancock to Williamsport." The Pennsylvanians then followed the towpath fifteen miles downriver to Four Locks before leaving the canal and riding over to Clear Spring. Arriving there about noon, Greenfield then rode west to a lookout high on the southern slope of Fairview Mountain. From that vantage point he could see the Confederate bridgehead at Williamsport.[49]

Soon Greenfield spotted the wagon train: "While viewing the Confederate encampments at Williamsport and Falling Waters through a field-glass from Fairview . . . I discovered a train of the enemy's forage wagons, with cavalry guards, coming out for supplies. I immediately determined to undertake to capture them." Greenfield then told Lieutenant William B. Kelley, the general's son and aide, of his decision. According to Greenfield, Kelley said, "Go ahead, and I will stay here and watch you." Then the captain, accompanied by scout Joseph Kitchen, a Virginia Unionist, ordered his men back in the saddle and started down a heavily foliaged mountain path.[50]

The front of the train had just reached Four Locks Road when one of the outriders spotted the Northerners at least two miles off. Makely promptly ordered the teamsters to turn around and get back to their lines. Once the wagons got rolling, the captain and Jesse followed with the rear guard. Not long afterward, as the hard-charging bluecoats drew near, Makely stopped and formed his troopers in line on a slight rise and awaited the coming onslaught.[51]

The federals were now closing in. "I pursued them rapidly," Greenfield wrote, "and a brilliant chase followed through mud and water. . . . We were cheered on the route by some of the Union ladies of Maryland, who came out of their houses and waved their handkerchiefs." Finally, only a deep, muddy ditch separated the foes. In an instant, most of the hard-charging Ringgolds jumped their mounts over the obstacle, smashed into the outnumbered rebels, and overwhelmed them; other troopers galloped ahead and stopped the wagons. Greenfield's men captured Makely, Lieutenant Jacob Rosenberg, and twenty other graybacks. Jesse McNeill escaped, suffering only a slight cut on his thumb. According to Greenfield, "Captain John McNeill . . . was only a few hundred yards away at the time of our attack, having come out to their relief."[52]

The soldiers quickly unhitched the teams, and once the captives were mounted, Greenfield made for Fairview. Not far behind, a rescue force made up of troopers from the Rangers and the 18th Virginia was fast closing in on the Yankees. But Greenfield had too much of a head start, and the rebels, wary of running into an ambush, slowed down. As the Pennsylvanians galloped by, Nesbitt added, "they went toward the mountain on the old road in a pretty lively gait." Heading back to Hancock via the National Pike, the Pennsylvanians eventually met the rest of the command coming to their aid.[53]

That evening from Hancock, General Kelley dispatched a message to Washington, noting the captain's small triumph and that "several of the enemy were killed and wounded. Captain Greenfield had three men wounded and three horses killed." A week later the *Washington Reporter* in Pennsylvania praised its local hero, writing, "The numerous friends of Capt. Greenfield will be rejoiced to hear of his signal success in an enterprise alike hazardous and responsible, and requiring in its execution, the utmost celerity of movement."[54]

Two days later, fighting again erupted near Fairview between Kelley's cavalry and the rebels. Nesbitt wrote, "In the afternoon, 250 cavalry came and ran the pickets back to the foot of the mountain where they had a little scrimmage. 2 or 3 Union men wounded and 2 or 3 Rebel horses and perhaps 1 or 2 Rebels." Fay noted the fight and added that another dustup the next day resulted in the slight wounding of six Rangers—Thaddeus W. Clary, Sprigg Lynn, John Reed, Wayne Cosner, John L. Harvey, and M. V. Ohaver.[55]

On the rainy night of July 13–14, Lee, using the rebuilt pontoon bridge at Falling Waters and two seldom-used fords at Williamsport, evacuated his troops, and by noon the army was back in Virginia. In the meantime, the Rangers moved on. By July 16 the partisans were resting in camp at Fisher's Hill, just south of Strasburg. A week later the July 24 edition of the *Rockingham Register* contained a notice that would have seemed ironic to the citizens of Mercersburg. Written by Sergeant Abel Seymour, it read, "Stolen from Captain McNeill's camp at Strasburg the 16th, two horses."[56]

CHAPTER 7

Fight in a Graveyard

—⟨∞⟩—

"My God, John,
what are you doing here?"

On Saturday, August 1, the Rangers left Fisher's Hill for Moorefield. Arriving there on Monday, the captain found out that a small squad of Yankees under a Lieutenant Henkel was then in Petersburg and would soon be guarding a small wagon train bound for New Creek. The next morning, the Rangers mounted up and rode west to intercept the wagons.

Not long after reaching Patterson Creek Valley, McNeill discovered that the federals had already passed by and split up. Henkel had taken some prisoners on a shortcut to New Creek through Greenland Gap while the train and its guard continued toward Burlington. McNeill went after the wagons. After passing through Williamsport, he found out that some of the Yankees were just two miles ahead at the Williams farm, feeding their horses. Writing to the *Rockingham Register*, Private Charles E. Watkins described what happened next:

> We then charged up to Mr. W's and captured three Yankees with their wagons. The remainder had gone on.... We then followed the remainder in a drenching rain, to within two miles of Burlington, captured four more of the Yankees, one of whom rode Gen. Kelley's riding horse, a beautiful sorrel. Part of the company returned with the prisoners to Moorefield, and the remainder went . . . with Captain on a scout near New Creek and returned to Moorefield on Thursday evening Aug. 6.[1]

Writing sixty-two years later, J. Forsyth Harrison, a fifteen-year-old cavalryman at the time, said the federals left Petersburg going to New Creek with six recently captured rebels in tow. Harrison recalled that it was about four o'clock and raining hard when they suddenly spotted "a few men wearing blue uniforms out on the road." The boy and his companions went to investigate, and "when we got pretty close to them a volley of guns went off and McNeill's whole company was laying for our command, about 11 men of the Ringgold Volunteer Cavalry." Shortly, Harrison and some of his companions were McNeill's prisoners.[2]

Fortunately, the youngster knew some of his captors, and four of them gave him $125 in Confederate currency before others carted him off on the first leg of his journey to prison. The Southerners also captured three wagons. In his listing of important Ranger actions, John Fay noted that, besides grabbing seven prisoners that day, some Rangers also burned the Greenland Gap blockhouse.[3]

On Thursday, August 6, a fifty-man patrol led by Second Lieutenant Thomas Kerr, Company C, 14th Pennsylvania Cavalry, left General Averell's command at Baker and began riding up the Lost River Valley. The general, then moving on Moorefield via Wardensville Road, had ordered Kerr to sweep the valley for rebels and then cross Branch Mountain to the South Fork. By that time Averell would be in Moorefield. If all went as planned, Kerr would be able to capture some graybacks that his compatriots would flush out of town.[4]

As they moved along, Kerr's scouts, a dozen or so troopers wearing gray uniforms, picked up a few unsuspecting Southerners. That afternoon at Angus Wood's house, 11th Virginia Cavalry lieutenant John Blue and recent recruit Private Ephraim Herriott were getting ready to eat dinner. Just then a local named George Turley arrived and alerted the pair that Yankees were not only now in Moorefield but also nearby. Figuring that Turley was just crying wolf, the hungry men disregarded his warning and sat down to eat. A few moments later, Wood's daughter squalled, "'Yankees!" Blue spun around, glanced out a window, and spied a rider aiming a carbine at him. Then, looking out another window, he saw six more.[5]

The men were soon astride horses, each under the watchful eye of a personal guard. The company, guided by William Branson, a young grayback Kerr shanghaied to lead the way, then continued up the valley. Upon reaching Howards Lick Road, the column turned and headed west. Along the trail the scouts captured a few local men and rebel soldiers who happened along.[6]

Occasionally during the journey, one of the prisoners would suddenly spur his mount into the brush and escape, but otherwise so far things had been uneventful. Toward sundown, however, the Yankees stopped to talk to three small boys. Blue, who had previously noted that his captors were now starting to become nervous, had the following comment: "At length one of the little boys said, who are you fellows, anyhow? Oh, said one of the Yankees, we are

Rebels. No you are not, said the boy, you are Yankees; you better look out, Mr. McNeill's horse company is down at Mr. Randolph's. From that time on, the Yankees were very much demoralized."[7]

The Pennsylvanians now moved along very slowly. According to Blue, after they reached the western foot of Branch Mountain, Kerr ordered his men to shoot the prisoners if bushwhackers fired on the column. Then, just as the lieutenant began to think that his chances of rescue were getting slim, the Rangers struck.[8]

Earlier McNeill's scouts had informed him of Averell's force in Moorefield, and then Captain William Harness arrived in camp with news of federals on Howards Lick Road. In a little while after that, Hanse decided to get out of harm's way and to lead his company farther up the South Fork. Before he could start, though, Ranger Private Jesse Heavener rode in with information garnered from Joseph V. Williams, a rebel who had escaped from Kerr's bluecoats. Heavener told McNeill the Yankees had a number of prisoners, including civilians, with them. Upon learning this, Hanse promptly gathered his riders and set out to waylay the Northerners.[9]

The captain did not travel very far before stopping and setting his trap. He picked a spot where the road passed through heavy timber. It was a narrow, heavily eroded section of the trail that was bordered by banks three or four feet high on each side. McNeill secreted his men along the south side of the road and took his position on the far right of the line. Hanse wanted to make sure where the prisoners were in the column before firing his shotgun, his signal for the rest of the soldiers to open up.

Eventually the enemy came along. By this time, however, it was very dark. As they were passing by, McNeill, trying to distinguish friend from foe, peered out from behind a tree; a Yankee spotted the veteran rebel and shot at him. Blue recalled that "a pistol shot rang out in the stillness of the night, instantly followed by a blinding flash, and rattle of near a hundred carbines and double barrel shot guns not ten feet away."[10]

For a time it was pandemonium. Out in front, Branson fell, seriously wounded; friendly fire grazed Herriott. In the meantime, as the Yankees fought back, the rest of the prisoners dove off their mounts and sought cover. Blue jumped onto the bank, sprinted into the darkness, tripped, and fell over a log. When his head cleared, the lieutenant heard "a great deal of talking going on, well striped with profanity." By now he realized that the Confederates had prevailed. Blue then promptly arose, and after sliding down the bank, came face to face with the barrel of a revolver. By chance John Lynn, his Ranger friend from Cumberland, was pointing it at him.[11]

John Fay recorded that the action had resulted in "wounding 4, taking twenty prisoners, and 30 horses, arms, accoutrements, etc., besides releasing a number of Confederates they had captured." Averell later reported that "a company of the Fourteenth Pennsylvania . . . falling into an ambush after dark, lost its prisoners and thirteen men captured. Four of the Fourteenth were wounded." The general also claimed that "three of the enemy were killed and five wounded," and although no rebels died in the actual fray, Private Edward Beck of Kerr's company later succumbed to his wounds. After the skirmish, the Rangers moved off to the Shenandoah Valley. That Sunday, August 9, as Harrisonburg's happy citizens gathered round their heroes, McNeill turned his prisoners over to the provost marshal. The editor of the *Staunton Spectator* remarked, "Captain McNeill always manages to come off winner in every game he plays with the Yankees."[12]

In mid-August Jemima McNeill, Sarah Emily, and John Jr. were aboard a B&O passenger train, headed east. They had left Missouri some time back and had lived for the past year with relatives in Chillicothe, Ohio. Now they were on their way to Moorefield. When the trio reached Oakland, someone there recognized Jemima and soldiers took the three into custody. When General Kelley got the news, he decided to ship Mrs. McNeill and her children under guard to Camp Chase, Ohio, to be confined there as civilian detainees.[13]

On September 19 Robert Ould, Confederate agent of exchange, wrote his Union counterpart, Brigadier General Solomon A. Meredith, about the McNeills' plight: "They left Chillicothe for the purpose of paying a visit to Hardy County. Will you permit them to accomplish their visit? In fact, will you release them from Camp Chase?" In time the three gained their freedom, but from then on the captain was looking for a way to get even with "Old Ben" for his unnecessary mistreatment of Jemima and the children.[14]

On August 9 Averell, leaving Major Thomas Gibson's battalion behind at Moorefield, marched for Petersburg. After resting there for over a week waiting for various supplies, Averell headed south on a raid, which ended in failure when, on August 26, Colonel George S. Patton defeated him at the Battle of White Sulphur Springs. Although General Imboden's command and the Rangers both attempted to catch the raiders, they failed to do so, and by early September Valley District commander Imboden was back along the South Fork, ready to strike Gibson's Moorefield outpost.[15]

Even though Averell had moved out of the area, General Kelley still had substantial numbers of troops posted in Hardy and Hampshire counties. By August 15 Colonel Campbell's brigade, along with some artillery and five companies of the Ringgold Battalion, were still manning the fort at Mechanicsburg Gap, while Colonel James Mulligan's brigade, along with Company D of the Ringgold Battalion, occupied Petersburg and were hard at work constructing a fort there. That same day, Major Edwin W. Stephens Jr., of the 1st West Virginia Infantry, led six companies totaling 177 men from Petersburg to Moorefield to replace Gibson. He also had on hand a two-gun section of Captain John Rourke's Illinois Battery, consisting of 33 artillerymen, plus Captain Andrew Barr's 48 troopers from Company F, Ringgold Battalion. According to Farrar, "The infantry camped on the hill east of town, where they dug some rifle pits; the cavalry stationed near the cemetery, and the artillery on the high points south of town."[16]

Barr's patrols eventually stirred things up and caused a few isolated skirmishes with the Rangers and troopers from the 7th Virginia Cavalry. On August 27 a Ranger detachment, despite outnumbering Lieutenant B. W. Denny's troopers two to one, lost an encounter along Petersburg Road. The Pennsylvanians captured two partisans and nine horses.[17]

About three o'clock on the morning of September 4, Sergeant B. F. Hassan and six troopers left to scout South Fork Road. Some two hours later the men spied rebel pickets posted near a ford. Hassan quickly sent Corporal Samuel Hallam back to camp with the news. In the meantime, Hassan and the other soldiers pushed the pickets back toward their lines and then retreated. In a little while the bluecoats ran into Jesse McNeill and some Rangers and, after a short skirmish, surrendered.

By now, though, Hallam had made it back to Moorefield and sounded the alarm. Barr promptly ordered a dozen troopers into the saddle and galloped away to help. But when he came across the Confederates, the captain decided to turn his outnumbered command around and get back to camp. Meanwhile, in town, Major Stephens strengthened his defenses.[18]

Finally that day, Imboden's forces marched on Moorefield. The brigadier also sent Captain Abel Scott with two companies to block the Petersburg Gap. In the meantime, as soon as Stephens alerted Mulligan, the colonel promptly got the 23rd Illinois moving. But after marching three miles, Scott's graybacks, positioned in the high rocks above the gap, opened fire on the column. After a brief fight, the colonel turned the relief force around, hurried to Petersburg, and then continued north to Williamsport. On September 5 Stephens evacuated Moorefield and withdrew across Patterson Creek Mountain to Williamsport.[19]

The next day Imboden, still fearing that a force out of Petersburg might attack him, left Moorefield and returned to camp. After leaving behind four companies to keep watch, the general marched his brigade and McNeill's Rangers on to Brock's Gap. Not long afterward, two companies left the South Fork and rejoined the rest of the command, leaving Frank Imboden and Captain McNary Hobson, with about seventy men, to take care of the scouting duties. Captain Imboden took his squadron to a sheltered spot "in the dense woods four miles above Moorefield." In the meantime, Mulligan ordered Stephens back to his station.[20]

On Wednesday, September 9, a slave discovered the rebel camp and reported its location to Mulligan. The colonel and his officers quickly got busy devising a scheme to capture the Virginians. The next day Mulligan contacted Major Stephens and told him the plan. He would be sending an infantry company from Petersburg. "Captain Fitzgerald will start from this point at 9 p.m., intending to arrive at the camp of the enemy at daylight, and, if possible effect a surprise and capture." Mulligan wanted Stephens "to send to-night Captain Barr's company of cavalry and one company of infantry with instructions to move on the reported camp of the enemy to arrive at daylight, and act in concert with the force moving from this point." At three in the morning of September 11, Barr moved out with eighteen troopers, followed by Captain James E. Morrow and thirty-five West Virginians.[21]

The previous evening, however, Captain McNeill returned to the South Fork with plans of his own. On September 9 he had left his camp on Branner's Farm in Rockbridge County with fifty mounted and thirty dismounted troopers. In an emotional speech given to his men before departing, he said the purpose of the raid was for "drawing some blood from the enemy, or getting some drawn from us by them." Upon arrival, McNeill immediately met with both captains to discover what intelligence they possessed of the Moorefield defenses. After getting that information, McNeill decided upon a predawn attack. He gathered his Rangers and Imboden and Hobson troopers and set off. John Fay, who was on his first mission with the company, later wrote, "McNeill moved cautiously out of the woods and down through the bottom fields east of the South Fork until he reached the foot of the ridge about a mile from Moorefield." Then the men dismounted, and after leaving their horses with five Rangers, moved silently in single file up a heavily wooded ridge, not far from the enemy camp on Olivet Cemetery hill.[22]

That night Major Stephens had posted pickets on every road and had at least fifty soldiers deployed as skirmishers. To bypass these guards and get to the rear of the camp, McNeill needed to find the mountain trail that, Fay wrote, "ran along the northern edge of these woods, and coming from the town passed over the top of Cemetery Hill." Now, with their intrepid captain leading the way, the Rangers crawled silently on their hands and knees through briars and heavy brush, expecting every second to hear a rifle shot or an alarm sounded from the Yankee camp. Finally they reached the road and were safely between the pickets and the camp. Only one more guard remained, and the Rangers moved noiselessly past him as he slept. In a few moments McNeill got his troops in line and ready to advance on their sleeping enemies. Then the anxious men marched down the hillside toward their objective, all the while waiting for Hanse to let loose with his double-barreled shotgun and open the ball.[23]

As the rebels closed in, not even a dog barked to give their slumbering masters a warning; Fay was certain they were walking into a trap. But suddenly McNeill's war whoop, followed by the men's wild yells and a pistol shot, broke the silence, and the hillside exploded as the Confederates poured lead into the tents. Although a few Yankees put up a fight, most of them surrendered meekly. Some of the pickets rushed in to rescue their comrades, but the graybacks quickly corralled them. When it was over, Fay estimated that the Northerners had suffered 160 casualties, including fifteen wounded, three mortally.[24]

The attack had its humorous incidents. Stephens was one of the lucky ones that morning, escaping capture, the *Richmond Examiner* reported, "by a precipitate flight through Moorefield in shirttail. Citizens of Moorefield . . . thought at first they had caught a glimpse of a belated ghost returning to his tomb." When Private Westmoreland called on one officer to surrender, the bluecoat unwisely replied, "I am an officer sir and will only surrender to an officer." The Georgian then raised his gun and exclaimed, "It is perfectly immaterial to me, sir, whether you surrender or not! We are on terms of equality here, sir!" The man immediately gave up. Fay even captured his friend, Sergeant George Tippett. Upon recognizing his former "Queen City" companion, Fay said, "Hello George, how are you old boy?" Tippett jumped up shouting, "My God, John, what are you doing here? Why didn't you join the Union army?"[25]

By now, the raiders had rounded up all their prisoners and gathered the spoils. Before they could move out, however, their winded captain needed rest. He lay beneath a tree and, "for a time," Fay recalled, "seemed to be on the verge of a nervous collapse." McNeill soon recovered, though, and got his men moving.[26]

As the column hurried along South Fork Road, McNeill had no idea that Mulligan had previously sent two Union outfits to strike Captain Imboden's camp. Now, two miles above Moorefield, Barr's troopers and Morrow's foot soldiers lay hidden on a heavily wooded hillside west of the road, ready to bushwhack his fighters. When the Southerners came by, the Yankees suddenly opened up. Fortunately, most of the bullets sailed high, but some horses went down. Lieutenant Bernie Dolan quickly signaled his fifteen troopers forward; Frank Imboden grabbed some men and closed in on the enemy's left flank. After a sharp skirmish, the bluecoats disappeared into the mountains. During the confusion, some of the prisoners got away. Captain John W. Daugherty jumped on a horse and escaped; a handful of other soldiers ran off into the brush. Besides losing one man mortally wounded, the rebels also lost twelve horses.[27]

Farther along, Jesse and the vanguard turned onto Howards Lick Road. About this time, scouts spotted Fitzgerald's soldiers and a squad of Swamp Dragons marching on another trail toward them. Jesse hurriedly went back, gathered some riflemen, and set up a defensive line far enough away from the road so the column had room to pass by safely. In the ensuing clash Hanse McNeill was lucky, just missing a serious, possibly fatal wound by inches when a bullet clipped his mustache. When the fighting was over, the Unionists had to be satisfied with wounding a few troopers and killing the horses that were pulling a captured ambulance. For their part, the Virginians were glad that Fitzgerald had not arrived sooner and barricaded the road. If he had, they all agreed that the outcome of the fight would have been much different.[28]

When McNeill reached Brock's Gap, he met with General Imboden and recounted his greatest feat to date. In his subsequent report of the action to General Lee, Imboden tallied up the substantial Union losses, which included 146 prisoners, 10,500 rounds of ammunition, 133 muskets, 29 revolvers, 46 horses, 9 wagons, 2 ambulances, and a plethora of miscellaneous equipment. Besides having "8 to 10 men" captured and the mortally wounded man in Hobson's company, two Rangers had serious wounds. Lieutenant Welton took a bullet in the leg and Private William Maloney suffered a wound in his left arm. Diarist Van Meter noted, "they had quite a fight as they went up the Fork, two of our Men badly wounded (Welton and Malona [*sic*]) was brought to town, several of theirs wounded, two of theirs died since."[29]

Although McNeill's previous feats had attracted the attention of the Southern press and public, nothing he had done so far could match this. Later that month General Lee responded to a letter from J. M. McCue, a member of the Virginia House of Delegates. McCue had written the commander requesting that Lee give the captain permission to increase his partisan command and operate independently from Imboden. Lee, however, disagreed with McCue, writing, "Much incontinence has already been experienced from these organizations, and I am satisfied that they do not accomplish as much as the same number of men in the regular service." Lee did mention that he would prefer McNeill increasing "his command to a battalion or a regiment for regular service."[30]

CHAPTER 8

The Charlestown Raid and a Wagon Train Fight

"Halt there boys. Where are you going?"

On July 21, Robert E. Lee had appointed General Imboden to succeed Grumble Jones as commander of the Valley District. By the time Imboden's new command was organized, it consisted of his own Northwestern Virginia Brigade, McNeill's Rangers, Major Harry Gilmor's independent partisans, Major T. Sturgis Davis's Maryland Cavalry battalion, Major Robert H. White's 41st Virginia Cavalry battalion, and Colonel Gabriel Wharton's infantry brigade. In total, Imboden had approximately three thousand soldiers to defend the area between the Blue Ridge and Allegheny Mountains extending from the Potomac River south to the James River in Botetourt County.[1]

That October, after three months of relatively light military activity, Lee seized upon an opportunity to march north from his line along the Rapidan River and strike the Army of the Potomac. Imboden's part in the plan was to provide a diversion west of the Blue Ridge by marching down the valley and threatening the Union posts at Charlestown and Harpers Ferry. According to one soldier, they were "to destroy the Baltimore and Ohio Railroad either by burning or blowing up bridges or by tearing up the track at some point south of the Potomac." Lee's effort, however, ended in failure, when on October 14 Major General George Meade's soldiers mauled part of Lieutenant General A. P. Hill's Third Corps at the Battle of Bristoe Station. But Imboden, despite having only fifteen hundred cavalry and mounted infantry available for his foray, had great success.[2]

On the evening of October 17 the rebel vanguard reached Berryville and surprised a federal patrol. The bluecoats who escaped the fracas galloped another eleven miles to Charlestown and reported the dustup to Colonel Benjamin Simpson. Although aware of the danger posed by the raiders, Simpson chose to follow Brigadier General Jeremiah Sullivan's order of the previous week to conduct a fighting retreat to Harpers Ferry if attacked. Simpson, whose command consisted of his own 9th Maryland Infantry and some cavalry, completely ignored Major Henry Cole's urgent warning to get out of Charlestown immediately.[3]

In the meantime, Imboden received news from sympathetic locals that led him to believe he could surround and capture the garrison. When the march began about two o'clock the next morning, Gilmor's forty partisans and Colonel George Imboden's 18th Virginia Cavalry led the way. Upon arriving some three miles from Charlestown, these two units took a wide detour around the city, eventually getting into position to block Harpers Ferry Road.[4]

Just before daylight, skirmishing broke out on the southern outskirts of town. The federals gradually fell back to the center of Charlestown, where the Marylanders took refuge in the fortified courthouse, jail, and a few other buildings. Just about this time, Gilmor and George Imboden's men stymied the Union cavalry's breakout attempt. Upon reaching the town, Imboden got Captain McClanahan's guns ready to shell Simpson's defenses. Before opening fire and endangering civilians, though, the general sent McNeill and Captain F. B. Berkeley to offer surrender terms.[5]

Riding in under a white flag, Hanse handed the general's note to Lieutenant Colonel Thomas Cloudsley, and the officer took it back to the courthouse. In response to Imboden's demand to surrender in five minutes, the colonel replied forcefully, "Come and take us if you can." In a little while Imboden sited one of the cannons and fired the first shell into the courthouse, More followed quickly and soon stampeding federals were pouring into the street, and despite Simpson's and his officers' best efforts to form them in column, "the men," the colonel recalled, "broke and ran in every direction." During the commotion, Imboden ordered McNeill to round up all the Yankees still in the town.[6]

When the disorganized infantry came along, Gilmor charged the frantic soldiers, who fired one wild volley and then threw away their rifles. Simpson and some officers, however, galloped off toward the B&O stop at Duffields Station before going on to Harpers Ferry.[7]

The Confederates hurried their prisoners back to town, filled up as many wagons as they could with plunder, and despite the pleas of the grateful townspeople imploring them to stay and fight, started moving out. Over in Harpers Ferry, Sullivan ordered Colonel George Wells to go help Simpson. Soon Wells cobbled together a seven hundred–man force that included his own 34th Massachusetts Infantry, plus Cole's Battalion, the 10th Maryland Infantry, the 17th Indiana Battery, and a company of Connecticut cavalry. Within an hour, Cole's horsemen were fighting Imboden's rear guard on the northern outskirts of Charlestown.[8]

Jefferson County Courthouse. Courtesy of Jefferson County Museum, Charles Town, W.Va.

On the way back to Berryville, Imboden's rear guard held off repeated attacks by Cole's troopers and Wells's foot soldiers. In a subsequent letter to the *Staunton Spectator*, a rebel described one of these fights:

> It was in one of these retrograde movements, that by the rapid withdraw of the artillery, and a misconstruction of orders, the 18th and McNeill's Rangers were thrown into temporary confusion, and were driven back several hundred yards by the enemy thus encouraged; but being sustained by the 62nd regiment in a gallant stand, they reformed and maintained, during the day, the reputation they had gained by their conduct in the first action of the morning.[9]

At dark Wells broke off the pursuit. Imboden, however, kept on going until reaching Front Royal. The day's work had netted the Confederates 434 prisoners, 360 from the 9th Maryland alone, at a cost of about 40 casualties. Wells reported that his force lost 6 killed and 43 wounded, but this total is low since Cole's cavalry lost 9 killed.[10]

It was during this period that Texan Henry M. Trueheart joined the Rangers. Before coming to Virginia in June 1863 and joining Company F, 7th Virginia Cavalry, Trueheart, a native of Galveston, fought in Major General John B. Magruder's January 1, 1863, recapture of the island from federal land and naval forces. On September 21, during a skirmish near Orange Court House, Virginia, Truehart accidently stabbed himself in the knee with his own saber, and it was at some point in his convalescence that he decided to leave his company and ride with McNeill. His occasional letters to his brother and other family members paint a vivid picture of partisan life.[11]

On November 6 Rebecca Van Meter recorded that "some of Capt. McNeill's men were seen today about town." Most locals were glad they were back. For the past few weeks Mulligan, who was intending to winter part of his division in Petersburg, had his quartermasters and teamsters scour the countryside collecting hay, corn, potatoes, and any other supplies they could root out. Over the next few days the women of the Old Fields community baked bread for the Rangers, who were roaming about the nearby mountains. Van Meter noticed that enemy forage trains were now staying away from Old Fields, adding, "It seems they are a terror to the Yankeys."[12]

In either late October or early November, "Missouri John" Cunningham rejoined the company. On July 20 some bluecoats had captured Cunningham at Moorefield. Shipped off by his captors to prison at Camp Chase, Ohio, Missouri John soon found himself quartered with a number of Brigadier General John

Hunt Morgan's men, captured during the daring rebel cavalry commander's June-July 1863 unsuccessful foray through Kentucky, Indiana, and Ohio.

During Missouri John's imprisonment, a Captain Ross, said to be an engineer in General Braxton Bragg's army, supervised the construction of a tunnel "16 feet in length with an entrance of 6 feet at each end." For three weeks the men, using only case knives, painstakingly dug their way to freedom. On September 20 Cunningham, along with nineteen of Morgan's men, broke out. Later, when he reached Harrisonburg, Cunningham narrated the thrilling story of his escape to *Rockingham Register* editor John Wartmann. The Ranger said that the other prisoners chose him to lead the way that night because "he was one of 'McNeill's Roughs' and seemed to be born 'for luck' even though some of it sometimes was 'bad luck.'" Once outside, Cunningham made it to cover; then he looked back and noticed a problem. One prisoner was too large to get through the hole. Missouri John waited around for a time "until he began to conclude that he had better leave if he expected to get off at all."[13]

On Sunday, November 15, eighty wagons loaded with "quartermaster and commissary stores," and accompanied by several sutlers' wagons, left New Creek for Petersburg. Captain Clinton Jeffers, Company B, 14th West Virginia Infantry, was in charge of the mile-long train and commanded an infantry force consisting of Lieutenant George C. Hardman and fifty soldiers from the 14th West Virginia and Lieutenant David Edwards and forty men from the 2nd Maryland Potomac Home Brigade, some of whom were mounted. Upon reaching Burlington, twenty-nine miles from their destination, Jeffers called a halt for the night. There he could rely on Captain A. L. Holtz's company, posted at the crossroads, to help guard the wagons.[14]

Snow was falling lightly the next morning as Jeffers got the men and wagons ready to leave. Hardman with forty mountaineers would lead the way, while the Marylanders covered the rear. Jeffers kept six West Virginians with him in the middle of the caravan and posted another four, as he wrote, "forward between myself and the advance guard as a signal party." At seven o'clock the first wagons rolled out.[15]

For the past week or so, the Rangers "had," according to one of their number, "been lying around Moorefield . . . watching and anxiously expecting a Yankee train to come along." Two troopers of Major White's battalion had spoiled their surprise, though, when they "deserted to the enemy and communicated McNeill's design." The captain then decided, "to look and go elsewhere for a grab." Somehow, McNeill found out about the wagon train and decided to take it. On the evening of the fifteenth, as Private Charles F. Miller remembered, "we started from White Oak flats below Moorefield." The captain's 111-man force included 67 Rangers, plus Lieutenant John B. Moomau and 33 soldiers from the 62nd Infantry and Lieutenant Samuel Fleming leading 8 guerrillas. Approximately 60 of the men were on horseback.[16]

After an all-night march, the Confederates were lying in ambush on the east side of the road between two and three miles south of Burlington, in the same vicinity where the guerrillas Captain Enright and Fleming had recently been attacking squads of Yankee mail carriers. Hanse ordered Jesse McNeill and Moomau to take the dismounted soldiers and attack the front of the train. They quickly positioned their men along a hillside and in an abandoned house. The captain and his horsemen would charge the rear wagons once the fighting up front started. McNeill's guide, "Captain" John T. Peerce, a hard fighting, forty-five-year-old private in Company F, 7th Virginia Cavalry, who lived nearby at his farm, Fairview, joined Hanse.[17]

At approximately nine o'clock the rebels ambushed the front of the slow-moving train as it was passing through some woods. When their first shots killed Lieutenant Hardeman, his fall instantly threw the West Virginians into disorder. Fortunately, Sergeant Silas W. Hare kept his head, got the soldiers in hand, and led them in a fighting retreat far back into heavy brush, west of the pike. The Southerners then came out of hiding and captured the wagons.[18]

When the fight started, the center of the train was passing an abandoned house, not far from Peerce's brick mansion. Jeffers quickly sent his remaining men forward and made ready to ride back and bring up the rear guard. At that instant a band of raiders concealed inside the house suddenly appeared and rushed the wagons. As Jeffers tried to escape, a rebel bullet killed his horse. He then sprinted forward and joined his West Virginians, who, he reported, "had taken up a position behind a fence, from which they kept up a spirited and telling fire upon the rebels." Meanwhile, McNeill's cavalry struck the Marylanders guarding the rear wagons, and despite their stiff resistance, drove them into the nearby woods.[19]

A few days later, a Ranger recorded:

The capture was made by a charge in front and rear at the same moment, Capt. McNeill with our cavalry striking the rear, and Lt. Moomaw with our infantry pressing the front. The Confederates went in with a yell that made the enemy think we had several regiments at hand. The enemy at once ran from the front, but the infantry and cavalry in the rear stood up for a few moments against McNeill, who couldn't get at them well at once on account of a gate that stood in his way. Capt. McNeill, however, soon opened the gate and charged in among them, when they followed the example set at the other end of the train, and abandoned their goods and chattels.[20]

Writing many years later, Private Charles F. Miller recalled that when the Yankees came along, they failed to notice the graybacks standing on the hill. Suddenly Lieutenant Cunningham, a one-armed veteran of the 7th Virginia Cavalry, shouted, "Halt there boys! Where are you going?" Almost instantly, the startled West Virginians opened fire. The rebels, however, replied with a devastating volley and charged, capturing a few bluecoats and chasing the rest off into heavy timber some distance away. Once there, the mountaineers regrouped and began shooting. As some of the men unhitched the teams and gathered the horses, Jesse McNeill and the rest of the soldiers hurried to the rear.[21]

The long-range fire from the woods made getting the horses a dangerous task. Luckily, the Yankee bullets failed to strike any rebels, but at least ten animals went down. The men led the rest out of range as fast as they could. When Miller was finished, he mounted a saddled horse and rode to find Jesse. Upon reaching the lieutenant, Miller said, Jesse "ordered me to cross some open ground and ask Capt. McNeill what move to make. The captain said, 'Get out of here at once,' which we did."[22]

Some of his compatriots later told Miller of the attack on the rear guard. With their way blocked by a fence, Ranger Sergeant Joe Vandiver and Corporal Davey Parsons headed for a gate. Just as they reached it, Vandiver and his horse were both hit. When the horse fell, its body propped the gate open for the charging rebels. What Miller heard about the captain, however, really impressed him: "Captain McNeill rode up to the fence near the gate on his old roan and fired both barrels of his shotgun. Neither he nor his horse was hit. Captain McNeill enjoyed a scrap like this as much as he did a fox chase. I do not think that he thought for a moment of being killed. He relied much on that old shotgun, which he never used until in close range."[23]

With the exception of some wounded horses, McNeill's only casualty was Vandiver, who, although hit badly in the leg, could still ride. Moomau, however, had three men injured seriously. The West Virginians had inflicted mortal wounds on Sergeant William Sites and Private James Keister. Another soldier, Private Thomas Rymer, took a bullet in his right thigh.[24]

Knowing that it would not be long before federal cavalry would be after them, the rebels set fire to some of the wagons and put their thirty-four prisoners, mostly white and black teamsters, on captured horses. With another 211 animals available, the rest of the raiders were mounted, and the command rode east. Moomau left the dying Sites behind.[25]

Hoult and his company soon arrived from Burlington, too late to fight the raiders, but just in time to save many of the wagons. Jeffers later figured his losses among his men at two killed, six wounded and one missing in the 14th West Virginia and six wounded and four missing in the 2nd Maryland. He estimated that the train had lost 150 horses.[26]

That same day Brigadier General Averell's brigade was making its way north from Petersburg to New Creek. Just back off a long raid into southern West Virginia and a significant November 6 victory over Confederate forces defending Droop Mountain, Averell's horsemen were looking forward to meeting the supply train with its much-needed food before traveling on to New Creek and taking a long rest.

At about eleven thirty that morning, they were near the Moorefield-Allegheny Junction when two troopers galloped in and told the general what had happened near Burlington. Hoping to cut off McNeill's escape, the brigadier promptly ordered Lieutenant Colonel Francis W. Thompson to take his 3rd West Virginia Mounted Infantry and Gibson's Battalion and, Thompson wrote, "to go in pursuit . . . , in the direction of Moorefield, to pursue them vigorously and subsist off the country." Averell also sent a galloper back to Petersburg to alert the post commander, Colonel Joseph Thoburn.[27]

After getting one of the two men to guide him, Thompson headed across the mountain for Moorefield but soon found the pike blocked by cut trees. After removing the obstacles, the horsemen continued, arriving in the town at three o'clock that afternoon. Thompson left Gibson there and then marched east toward Wardensville. By dark the West Virginians had reached the intersection of the North River Pike. Proceeding another mile on that road, Thompson called a halt and gave his weary men and horses a chance to rest.[28]

Earlier that afternoon, at about two o'clock, Averell's courier had reached Petersburg and given the general's message to Thoburn. The colonel quickly summoned Captain Greenfield and ordered him, as Farrar wrote, "to take all the available cavalry of our battalion (about 100 men) proceed down the South Branch and co-operate with the force sent by Averill." Two hours later the Pennsylvanians reached Moorefield. There Greenfield met with Gibson, who told the captain that Thompson had ordered him to remain in town and guard the road to New Creek. After a brief rest, Greenfield pressed on and sometime that night arrived in Thompson's camp.[29]

When Thompson refused to push his exhausted men and worn-out horses any farther, the captain then led his squadron to Grassy Lick Road. There a local told him that McNeill had passed by that afternoon "with horses only." He then sent a rider back to Thompson with the suggestion that they combine forces and try to catch up to them. The colonel, however, nixed Greenfield's idea. The raiders had a big head start, and since Thompson's horses were in no shape for the hard riding the pursuit required, "it would be useless to try to overtake them."[30]

Without Thompson's help, Greenfield figured the rebels would greatly outnumber him. Disappointed, he then led his horse soldiers back to Petersburg. But his informant had misled the captain; McNeill was still behind him. Moving slowly through the mountains until dark, the old hero had stopped and rested. Later on he led his men through Reynolds Gap and Old Fields before crossing the South Branch. Colonel Thoburn later reported that a captured teamster, who had escaped the rebels near Brock's Gap, told him "that McNeill did not cross the pike until after midnight, and then passed within 600 yards of Thompson's camp." Diarist Van Meter wrote that "Captain McNeill . . . passed through the old Fields somewhere sunday night, their tracks only were seen." Earlier, in Springfield, Colonel Campbell, had dispatched Lieutenant Colonel John Linton with soldiers from the 54th Pennsylvania Infantry and some other units to be in place near Moorefield should Averell's cavalry compel McNeill to double back. On the morning of November 17, Linton reached Reynolds Gap but discovered that the graybacks had already passed through.[31]

Upon arriving safely in Harrisonburg, Hanse once again turned his prisoners over to the provost marshal and prepared to sell the livestock and any plunder his Rangers and the other soldiers did not need. On Friday, December 4, auctioneer James Steele advertised in the *Rockingham Register* that he would be auctioning off "Yankee harness," taken by McNeill on Monday.[32]

Besides considerable profit from his share of the booty, the wily partisan once again received praise from Imboden and Lee. Jeffers, however, had a different fate. After reading reports of the action, Mulligan had the captain arrested and held for court-martial. Mulligan added that "the loss inflicted was owing to a want of precaution, a want of skill, and a want of fighting." On March 1, 1864, Jeffers was dismissed from the service.[33]

Toward the end of November, Hanse captured Michael Yoakum, a notorious Swamp Dragon, and sent him off to General Imboden, and over the next few months McNeill's action caused a flurry of activity. On December 12 Colonel Thoburn sent a squad from Petersburg to Old Fields and arrested citizens Jesse Fisher and William Van Meter to hold as hostages for Yoakum's release. Prior to this, however, Evan C. Harper, Yoakum's captain, petitioned West Virginia governor Arthur I. Boreman to authorize him to arrest Hardy County secessionists Streight Cunningham, Thomas Seymour, and Felix Welton and keep them until the Confederates decided to exchange Yoakum. Boreman agreed and sent Harper a letter authorizing him to make the arrests. About a month later Harper journeyed to Petersburg to meet with Thoburn, who refused to allow the captain to carry out the governor's order. In a letter to Boreman the colonel noted, "It is not deemed expedient that anymore arrest be made."[34]

General Lee was even willing to assist Yoakum in his plight. Imboden had determined to give the guerrilla a military trial, charging him with "outrages committed upon the persons and properties of some of our citizens of that (Hardy) county." Yoakum, though, demanded that a civil court try his case. Lee agreed, telling Imboden that since Yoakum was not a regular soldier, "I desire that you surrender the accused to the civil authorities."[35]

Jubal Early. Library of Congress.

On December 10 William Boyd, now a colonel currently commanding the 21st Pennsylvania Cavalry, left Charlestown with a force of approximately two thousand cavalry and infantry on a raid up the Shenandoah Valley. Boyd's main purpose was to divert Imboden from sending soldiers westward to stop General Averell's raid on the Virginia and Tennessee Railroad. Imboden, however, chased after Averell with most of his available force, leaving scant numbers to defend the valley. On December 20 Boyd reached Harrisonburg, "where," Captain James Stevenson wrote, "he learned that Gen. Early, with a large force, was advancing down the Valley to meet him, while General Rosser had been dispatched from the Luray Valley to get in his rear." After hearing this, Boyd decided to retreat.[36]

Just north of town that Sunday morning, Private James Shryock had an exciting encounter with some Yankees. According to the *Rockingham Register*, "Prior to this engagement, Shryock had been scouting for twenty-four hours without being out of his saddle; and had been side by side with his commander, Capt. McNeill, when that daring chieftain was pressing the enemy in flight through Harrisonburg." After Shryock shot one trooper, the Unionists chased after him. At the tollgate just south of Harrisonburg, Shryock turned on his pursuers, emptied his revolver, and then rode off. The Winchester native had called out for other rebels to come help him, but they turned tail and galloped away.[37]

On the night of December 30 a squad of Rangers closed out their 1863 activities by raiding the home of James Carskadon, a West Virginia state senator who lived in the Patterson Creek Valley, north of Burlington. Even though the Rangers had surrounded the house, Carskadon and a friend escaped, but the rebels did capture a local schoolteacher. Unable to seize the senator, the partisans contented themselves with rounding up the few horses he had left. Shortly afterward the Rangers went to Locust Grove, the home of Thomas R. Carskadon, the senator's brother. There they took two African Americans and made off with his horses. Before long, though, the freemen escaped. In a letter to the *Wheeling Intelligencer*, Senator Carskadon said, "One of the blacks dodged them before they were fairly underway, and the other escaped after going some distance, by taking to the bushes. They fired at him as he ran but without effect."[38]

CHAPTER 9

Trouble with Rosser

❧

"They won't fight;
can't be made to fight."

With Major General Jubal Early's infantry division, Major General Fitz Lee's cavalry division, and Colonel Thomas "Tom" Rosser's cavalry brigade—Grumble Jones's old command—all now in the Shenandoah Valley, the local scarcity of food and supplies for the troops became crucial. East across the Blue Ridge, the Army of Northern Virginia was also on short rations. On December 22 General Lee ordered Early, now in temporary command of the Valley District, "to collect and bring away anything that can be made useful to the army from those regions that are open to the enemy. . . . I hear that in the lower Valley and, particularly in the country on the South Branch of the Potomac there are a good many cattle, sheep, horses, and hogs."[1]

On December 31, Fitz Lee led all of the cavalry out of Mount Jackson for Moorefield. It was raining, and, as the weather got colder, it started to snow. "The day was terrible in the extreme," Major Harry Gilmor wrote, "a heavy snowstorm prevailing, and extremely cold." In the mountains that day, the artillery and supply wagons could not navigate the steep, icy road that led over the mountains to Hardy County. The disappointed general sent them back and continued. The month of December had been cold, but its weather would seem mild compared to the bitter conditions that the troops of the expedition endured during the first week of the new year. As Private Milton Boyd Steele, of the 1st Virginia Cavalry noted on January 1, "This is the coldest day I ever felt. Water froze so hard in a well 12 feet deep that you could not break it with a bucket."[2]

Upon arriving at Moorefield, Lee found out that Thoburn and his troops still occupied Petersburg. Now reinforced by McNeill's Rangers, Lee sent scouts off to reconnoiter the federal fort. They later returned with the news

77

that the Yankees there "were intrenched with abatis." Without his artillery, the general decided to bypass Petersburg and march instead on New Creek. He left Gilmor's and McNeill's partisans behind to watch the Petersburg Gap and scout the country.[3]

On Sunday, January 3, Lee's column, with Rosser's Brigade leading the way, rode west on the Moorefield and Allegheny Turnpike toward the Patterson Creek Valley. Upon arriving atop Patterson Creek Mountain that evening, the Confederates spotted an enemy wagon train moving slowly north, passing through the Moorefield-Allegheny Junction. In the attack that followed, the 7th Virginia and 11th Virginia regiments captured the 40 wagons and teams, most of the teamsters and guards, about 250 head of cattle, some hides, and artillery ammunition. A reporter noted that "the rebels rushed down from the hillside woods like an avalanche, and the escort fell back to an elevation and contested the possession of the mules . . . but were finally compelled to yield to superior force." The Southerners lost two men killed and two wounded. Before marching to Burlington, Lee sent Major Edward McDonald and some troopers back to the valley with the livestock, prisoners, and spoils.[4]

That night, the raiders burned the blockhouse at Greenland Gap, scattered the Yankees posted at Burlington, and burned the blockhouse there. According to one rebel, "On Sunday night, we made a haul of about 50 Yanks in a church. It was a surprise. The Yankees had not the remotest idea that the Confederates were about until Fitz Lee ordered them to surrender or fight, whatever they preferred." Farther west, some troopers drove in Mulligan's pickets outside New Creek. The Southerners stopped at Ridgeville and prepared to attack the rail center and supply depot the next morning.[5]

Not only was it bitterly cold, but overnight another snowstorm arrived. Despite the harsh conditions, at about four o'clock that morning Fitz Lee ordered his men to move out. Some six miles from his objective, however, he turned back "on account of the suffering of my men and the impassibility of the mountain passes to my smooth-shod horses was unable to proceed farther." Soon the gray riders were on their way back to the Shenandoah Valley.[6]

Meanwhile, after capturing the wagons Fitz Lee had sent Gilmor orders "to go down the Valley towards New Creek, and thence to the wire suspension bridge, to scout towards the Potomac." Taking the Rangers along, except those suffering frostbitten fingers and toes, the major rode north. Sometime on January 4 Gilmor reached Romney and then prepared to attack the Springfield camp of Companies G and F, 54th Pennsylvania Infantry. Before the raiders got there, though, Kelley wired the commanding officer to abandon the outpost and fall back to Green Spring. When the partisans reached the village,

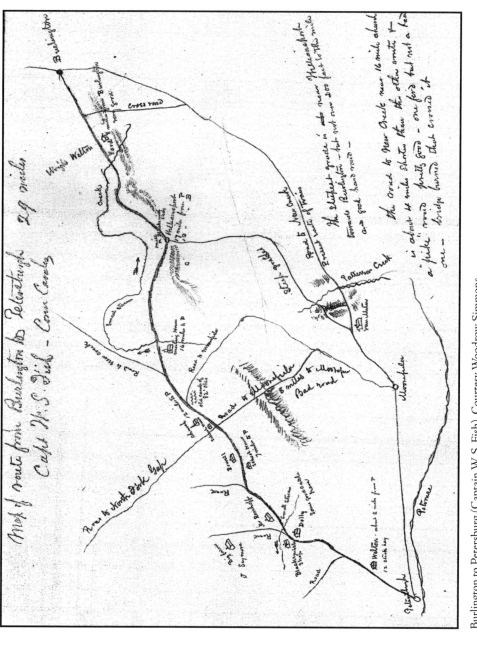

Burlington to Petersburg (Captain W. S. Fish). Courtesy Woodrow Simmons.

they quickly occupied the deserted camp and found many provisions. Gilmor reported, "I captured . . . all the stores and brought off twenty loads of bacon, crackers, sugar, salt, and leather besides burning their winter quarters and a large quantity of stores I could not distribute among the people or give away." Lee later noted that Gilmor "brought off about 3,000 pounds of bacon and some hard bread, nails &c."[7]

After gathering all plunder they could carry, the rebels retreated. Upon reaching the suspension bridge over the South Branch, a local girl warned Gilmor that some Yankees had sabotaged it. After making some hasty repairs so the structure would not collapse with them, the raiders crossed the bridge, continued to Romney, and a day or two later were camped at the village of Lost River. The major recalled that "never have I witnessed as much suffering among the troops as on that trip and glad was I to camp again on Lost River." About a week later Gilmor was back at Mount Jackson; McNeill returned to the South Fork.[8]

On January 11 Rosser penned a blistering attack on the partisan ranger service and sent it up the chain of command to General Lee. He was extremely upset about men deserting his regiments to become partisans. Rosser's letter became the final nail in the coffin for many of these companies, as it would lead on February 17 to the Confederate Congress revoking the Partisan Ranger Act. In the letter, he mentions his close observations of all the area's partisan bands but specifically refers to Major John Mosby's 43rd Battalion. Rosser believed that the irregulars "are a nuisance and evil to the service. . . . a band of thieves, stealing, pillaging, plundering . . . a terror to the citizens. . . . They never fight; can't be made to fight." Although their leaders were brave men, most partisan fighters "have engaged in this business for the sake of gain." Continuing, Rosser emphasized to Lee that the numerous attractions of partisan life kept many men from joining the regular army, that the liberties of these irregulars had caused "great dissatisfaction in the ranks," and that this discontent "encourages desertions."[9]

After commenting at length on problems he was having keeping some of his troopers from deserting and joining Mosby's command, Rosser encouraged Lee to ask General Early about "the evils of these organizations." He also suggested that the commander get Fitz Lee's opinion about the partisans "from his experience with them in the valley the last few weeks."[10]

When Rosser's letter reached Stuart, the major general defended his friend Mosby, noting that "Major Mosby's command is the only efficient band of rangers I know of," but for the most part he agreed with his subordinate, writing that "such organizations, as a rule, are detrimental to the best interests of the army at large."[11]

General Lee concurred with Rosser's assessment of the situation, and upon forwarding the letter to Secretary of War Seddon, he recommended "that the law authorizing these partisan ranger corps be abolished. The evils resulting from their organization, more than counterbalance the good they accomplish."[12]

For the past sixteen months the Rangers had been in numerous skirmishes, but despite losing a man here or there, most notably Second Lieutenant Charles Johnson, wounded and captured at Burlington on December 3, 1863, McNeill had yet to have one of his followers killed in action. Soon Private Robert "California Joe" Rosser—no relation to Tom—would be the first to fall.[13]

Harry Gilmor. Author's collection.

On January 14 California Joe was talking to a few Rangers when, according to a local who occasionally rode with the partisans, "he remarked . . . that he expected to fall, and giving them his brother's address, to write to him in case he should be killed." The next day Rosser was among some Rangers concealed in a wooded ravine near the Petersburg Gap, ready to ambush an oncoming Yankee patrol. That day, Sergeant Armour Thompson was leading a small squad of horsemen from Company B, Ringgold Battalion. Thompson, who Private Samuel C. Farrar described as a "a wiry little Irishman," spotted the Rangers before they could spring their trap and hurriedly ordered a retreat. The sergeant's horse, however, was tired, and Thompson soon fell far behind his fleeing comrades. In the meantime Rosser, mounted on a fast thoroughbred raced far ahead of his compatriots and closed in quickly on his prey.[14]

Knowing that if he kept going his pursuer would soon either capture or kill him, Thompson suddenly spun his horse around and, revolver blazing, charged Rosser. His third shot hit California Joe in his right eye, and he tumbled into the road, dead. As his stunned compatriots reined up, Thompson dismounted, quickly stripped Rosser of his LeMat revolver, shotgun, and sword, and then jumped on the rebel's charger and sped away under a hail of lead. General Kelley later commended the sergeant for his heroic feat "and presented him," Farrar wrote, "with the horse, arms, and equipment."[15]

The Rangers then gathered up their friend's corpse and took it back to Moorefield for burial in Olivet Cemetery. In a subsequent letter to the *Rockingham Register*, the unidentified local wrote, "Thus passed away one of the most gallant, heroic, patriotic men of the land. Long may his memory be cherished by both the officers and the men of the company." That afternoon, Lieutenant Colonel James Quirk led four companies of the 23rd Illinois Infantry from Petersburg to Moorefield and chased the Rangers from the village. Captain McNeill then returned to the Shenandoah Valley for recruiting and relaxation.[16]

Despite the extremely bad weather the troops had endured, Fitz Lee's early January raid had been moderately successful. He had returned to the valley with a few hundred head of cattle, three hundred horses and mules, and some prisoners. But it was far short of what Early needed. Toward the end of the month "Old Jube" was ready to try it again. On January 28 Early led Rosser's brigade, Gilmor's partisans, McNeill's Rangers, and three guns from McClanahan's battery out of Timberville and marched for Moorefield. That same day Brigadier General Edward L. Thomas's infantry brigade and another of

McClanahan's guns left camp near New Market and followed in the cavalry's wake. Imboden's command remained behind at New Market to guard the upper valley.[17]

The general reached Moorefield the next day, and after having Rosser's troops slap together some temporary bridges across the two rivers there, waited for the arrival of the infantry. In the meantime, scouts showed up that evening with news that a wagon train on its way to resupply the Petersburg garrison was now at Burlington. Early and Rosser quickly made plans to attack it.[18]

But overnight Captain Andrew J. Greenfield and twenty men slipped

Thomas Rosser. Author's collection.

through the Confederate picket line south of Moorefield and made a quick reconnaissance of the enemy camp. When Greenfield got back to Petersburg, he brought along one prisoner, who told Colonel Thoburn that "Rosser's brigade and some other detachments was there." Knowing that vital goods and provisions were on the way, Thoburn dispatched a galloper to Burlington to tell Colonel Joseph Snider, 4th West Virginia Cavalry, to hurry the wagons. In the meantime, he also alerted Lieutenant Colonel James Quirk who, with a force of two hundred soldiers from the 23rd Illinois Infantry, was presently atop Patterson Creek Mountain engaged in blockading the Moorefield and Allegheny Turnpike.[19]

The next morning, January 30, the rebel horsemen headed west to intercept the train. In the forenoon, near the top of the pass, they ran into Quirk's ax men busily cutting down trees. Rosser's soldiers chased the federals off, and within an hour they had removed the obstacles from the road. Upon reaching the crest, heavy fighting broke out and lasted until sharpshooters drove the Yankees down the steep slopes into the valley. Quirk then retreated north a mile or so and met the wagons at Medley. Snider, who now had over eight hundred soldiers, promptly halted the train, formed a battle line, and prepared to meet the Confederates.[20]

Rosser soon arrived and saw that the enemy had the numerical advantage. Quickly sending out three to four hundred dismounted troops as skirmishers, Rosser then ordered the rest to "charge him front, flank, and rear." Although the Yankees fought off the first charge, the next, bolstered by the fortunate arrival of one cannon, was successful. As the beaten federals scurried off into the hills, the Confederates snared ninety-five wagons and many horses and mules.[21]

A few of the wagoners and their loads did escape, but nonetheless Rosser's haul was astounding. A trooper noted that "it was a rich prize—nearly 100 wagons well-loaded with corn, oats, bacon, rice, beans, flour, sugar, coffee, molasses, pickled pork, clothing, blankets, and others were loaded with luxuries such as candy, raisons [*sic*], cigars, tobacco, oysters, sardines, cakes, crackers, brandy peaches, cherries, and, in short, everything nice and good."[22]

Since many of the teamsters had hopped on a mule and rode off and a good many other animals were dead or wounded, Rosser was only able to send fifty loaded wagons back to Moorefield. He burned the rest, but not before each soldier gathered as much booty as he could carry. In the action Rosser lost 24 men while inflicting 120 casualties on the enemy, including Major Nathan Goff Jr. Unfortunately pinned to the ground by his wounded horse, Goff, the young son of an influential Clarksburg, West Virginia, Unionist, was Rosser's most important capture.[23]

The next morning, January 31, Rosser marched up the valley for Petersburg. In the meantime Early and the infantry were also advancing on the town. When the Confederates arrived and started shelling the fort, they quickly discovered that no one was there. At noon the day before a rebel deserter had come into the federal lines and told Thoburn that Early intended to attack either the railroad or Petersburg. After receiving this intelligence, the colonel decided to evacuate his defenses and sent a message to Snider to turn the train around. That evening, scouts brought in a prisoner who said that Early would attack the fort at dawn. Thoburn then decided to get moving. As he reported, "At midnight . . . the command moved off quietly. . . . I was compelled to take an unfrequented and difficult mountain road, through Reels gap to the base of the Allegheny Mountains, and from thence to Greenland Gap."[24]

After doing as much damage to the fort as possible and gathering up some small arms ammunition, commissary stores, and forage, Early ordered Rosser back down Patterson Creek Valley to gather cattle and strike the railroad. The commander then accompanied Thomas's brigade back to Moorefield.[25]

Rosser reached Burlington on February 1. Along the way the headstrong young Texan and Captain McNeill had another argument. Rosser told Hanse to take his company and Gilmor's men to the top of the Allegheny Front and get some cattle. At first Hanse argued against heading into the high country but then gave up and moved out. Rosser took Gilmor along with him to scout. In a message to Early, he noted, "It was very difficult to induce McNeill across the mountains, and I think he will do nothing after all."[26]

On February 2 at Burlington, Rosser sent Lieutenant Colonel Thomas Marshall and the 7th Virginia Cavalry to block Mechanicsburg Gap. Early that afternoon the rest of the brigade, except those troopers who were rounding up livestock, descended upon the B&O's Patterson Creek Bridge. After killing two, wounding ten, and capturing forty or so federals guarding the structure and setting it on fire, rebel troopers headed upriver in what proved to be an unsuccessful effort to burn the North Branch Bridge. Rosser men also "destroyed one engine, all the property belonging to the road, the bridge for the pike across the canal, and one canal lock." When he received an urgent message from Marshall that Averell was trying to force his way through the gap, Rosser decided to get back to Moorefield, rather than attack Cumberland. As soon as the raiders left, railroad workers rushed back to Patterson Creek and put out the fire.[27]

The next day Rosser arrived in Old Fields with a large herd of cattle and five hundred sheep and reunited with squads who had camped there on February 2, as Rebecca Van Meter wrote, "with 3 droves of cattle and 3 droves of sheep." No doubt he was surprised to see McNeill with three hundred head of cattle.

In Cumberland that morning Kelley had received news that McNeill was on a cattle raid atop the Allegheny Front and telegraphed Mulligan to try to intercept him. By then, however, Mulligan was on Rosser's trail.[28]

On the morning of February 4 Early ordered the captured livestock and wagons back to the valley. At eight o'clock, however, Mulligan, leading three hundred cavalry and one section of artillery, began forcing a crossing at Goings Ford. Once over the South Branch, six hundred other troops who had marched up Trough Road from Romney joined Mulligan. The federals soon began pressing Rosser's fighters back toward Moorefield. While this was happening, Early recalled Thomas's foot soldiers and ordered Rosser to retire through town and take up a position along the South Fork. Once all his men were in place, the general waited. Despite shelling the rebel positions, the Yankees failed to attack by midday, and the Confederates resumed their retreat, reaching the Shenandoah Valley on February 5.[29]

It was about this time that a young Marylander named James Vallandingham joined McNeill's outfit. In an article for the *Philadelphia Times*, written many years later, he described the captain:

> He was then at the zenith of his fame as a partisan leader, and well deserved his renown, for in nearly fifty skirmishes and raids, he had never been defeated. . . . He was then about 52 years old, six feet in height, and straight as an arrow, very heavily built, in fact, inclined to be fleshy. His beard was gray and flowed over his large chest almost to his waist. His eyes were blue, keen as a falcon. . . . He had on a high, black broad brimmed hat turned up on one side and ornamented with a heavy black plume. Over his shoulder was swung his formidable shotgun loaded always heavily with slugs and buckshot. This was his favorite weapon, and on many occasions, he had used it with fatal effect. By his side, hung a large size revolver. . . . he was certainly a most striking and war-like figure.[30]

On February 17 the Confederate Congress voted to rescind the Partisan Ranger Act and arrange for individual partisans to join regular army units. But the Congress also allowed Secretary of War Seddon to "except from this act some such companies that are serving within the lines of the enemy, and under such conditions as he may prescribe."[31]

It may have been to plead his case with Seddon that Hanse took some time out to visit Richmond. Nevertheless, on the evening of February 22 he was at the American Hotel, attending a serenade to Baltimore's former marshal

George P. Kane. When the celebrated backwoods fighter strode out onto the balcony and stood beside Kane, many in the lively crowd shouted for him to speak. McNeill then, a reporter noted, "indulged in a few remarks, fervent and appropriate to the occasion."[32]

After two arduous expeditions into the mountains, the Rangers took time to rest their bodies and to get their horses back in top shape for the upcoming spring campaign. With plenty of money usually stuffed in their pockets, Harrisonburg's merchants always welcomed the devil-may-care freebooters. With all their extra cash, most Rangers usually had better boots, coats, hats, and uniforms than other graybacks. On February 13 Jesse McNeill got his hair cut at a local barbershop but then walked out and forgot his coat. In an ad offering a hundred dollars for its return, Jesse described the expensive garment: "It is a heavy gray overcoat, with red flannel lining, and a very deep, heavy cape."[33]

Back in Hardy County the federals had not reoccupied their Petersburg fort, but Mulligan did establish an outpost at Greenland Gap. Quirk commanded a force at the narrow canyon that included the 23rd Illinois Infantry, Work and Barr's Ringgold companies, and one section of Carlin's Battery. "Active scouting was required," Farrar commented, "for the country was suffering from marauding bands, who robbed, and occasionally murdered loyal citizens and kept them in a state of terror."[34]

The federals also posted soldiers at Burlington. On the evening of February 28, Lieutenant W. D. Pearne led twenty 15th New York Cavalry troopers on a scout from there toward Petersburg. That night, after covering about seventeen miles, the officer spotted some campfires in the distance. Taking just four men along with him, he discovered a camp of "Ross' brigade and Mc-Niel's rangers—and they had two parties, one of fifty, and one of twenty five men, scouring the country." Before leaving, the intrepid Pearne somehow slipped into the camp and quietly made off with two rebels.[35]

On March 1 Captain George Work received orders to take all available troopers and ride from Greenland to Petersburg. Once there his men would guard some supply wagons that a force going to break up the rebel saltpeter works near Franklin would leave at the fort. Departing camp in the midst of a heavy snowstorm, Work and his thirty-three troopers did not reach Petersburg until eight o'clock that night. There he met Lieutenant Colonel Augustus I. Root, who on the evening of February 29 had led the 15th New York Cavalry and a detachment of Ringgold troopers, over four hundred men, from Burlington.[36]

Because of the terrible weather, Root postponed marching to Franklin until the evening of March 2. He arrived there the next afternoon and took a squadron to the saltpeter works, which the men destroyed. Also on March 2,

Work had led a patrol to Moorefield, discovering, before returning to camp, that Confederate cavalry had been there. Just about dark Lieutenant Benjamin W. Denny and thirty-seven more horsemen arrived at the fort to reinforce Work. The next morning, the captain, concerned that a large rebel force might be lurking nearby, sent Denny with twenty-six men to reconnoiter to Moorefield. This time, though, Jesse McNeill would be waiting for them.[37]

Everything was fine until the patrol got to within three miles of the town There, Jesse lured the lieutenant into his trap. First he had a handful of Rangers charge the Pennsylvanians and then suddenly retreat. Denny took the bait and chased them, his men shooting a few of the partisans and some of their horses. By now the Yankees were within fifty yards of their prey. An anonymous bluecoat recalled, "But we were not the boys to be scared by the hideous yells of traitors and the whizzing of bullets." Suddenly, however, a Ranger band stormed out from their hiding place and quickly closed in on the federal rear. Up front the rebels turned and charged. "We could do nothing but retreat," the trooper wrote, "and our only way was up a precipice, and across a deep ravine in the woods." Denny and a handful of men on fast horses reached the South Branch, plunging their steeds into the river and swimming them across. Some soldiers jumped off their mounts and disappeared into the brush. Later on the partisans, after fruitlessly tracking these Yankees in the snow, gave up the chase. In all, Jesse's squad had succeeded in capturing seven of the enemy and rounding up thirteen horses. Of the troopers taken, six later died in prison.[38]

Although the brief combat had resulted in a victory for the young officer and his men, the cost had been high. A Yankee bullet mortally wounded twenty-one-year-old Private Charles W. Miles and another struck Corporal David Hopkins, one of the original Rangers. Although Hopkins recovered and later made it back to the company, Miles only lasted another month, dying on April 3. After the fight, Jesse took his prisoners on to Harrisonburg, where one scribe exclaimed that, "in his chivalrous dash and courageous bearing seems to be a 'chip off the old block.'" Noting the absence of their captain, he went on to write, "Capt. McNeill has not been paying his attention to the Yankees so frequently of late; but he has promised himself increased activity and diligence, and as the Spring opens, he expects to attend to them as usual."[39]

The ambush made Work jumpy. Now concerned that the rebels would slip in and overrun his small force, the captain sent a messenger to Greenland Gap for reinforcements and, in the meantime, moved his men five miles north of Petersburg. When Root arrived at the fort on March 5, he found it empty and continued to Burlington. By then Work and his troopers had returned to the gap.[40]

Later that month Private Samuel C. Hopkins came home to Harrisonburg to die. The son of Colonel John C. Hopkins, the Yankees had captured the eighteen-year-old near Moorefield on September 10, 1863. Imprisoned for six months, upon exchange Hopkins was a patient at Chimborazo Hospital in Richmond for a short time. When he arrived in Harrisonburg, an onlooker later commented, "He returns with a shattered constitution. He is such a complete wreck of himself, that his intimate friends scarcely knew him when he got off of the stage." According to company records, the young Ranger passed away on March 31.[41]

About the end of March, rebel deserters informed Union officers that McNeill and five hundred men were on their way to the South Branch Valley. Soon federal cavalry was roaming the countryside trying to find the raiders. In an April 14 letter to his sister, Cally, Private Henry M. Trueheart described the adventurous life the men were leading. The illustrious McNeill fascinated the wandering Texan, who had joined the Rangers the previous fall. And he thoroughly enjoyed all the extras, including romance, that the partisan service provided a young soldier. He told his sister that recently two regiments of federal cavalry were constantly pursuing them. To keep the bluecoats guessing, the wily McNeill had his men camp "in the hollow and gorges of mountains" during the day. While the men bided time, the captain relied on his pickets posted atop "a commanding hill . . . with spyglass in hand," to warn him if the enemy got too close. Late each afternoon detachments would ride to the nearest farms and get bundles of corn and hay for the horses. Just before dark, McNeill would lead the company to another out-of-the-way spot and remain there for the night unless "the Yanks were near and known to be watching us." If that were the case, the men would get fires going and then disappear. Before ending his note, Trueheart also described a typical Ranger ambush. "At other times our comd. is concealed along the road where the enemy is expected, and when the opportune moment arrives, a wild yell and a charge—the charge preceded by a *discharge* is the only warning the poor Yanks have."[42]

During this time, the only recorded action the Rangers fought in was a mid-April fight along the South Fork near Peru by a portion of the command against Captain John Bond's Hardy County Scouts. On April 29, 1864, Bond sent a letter to Governor Arthur I. Boreman describing the skirmish his company had had with the Rangers:

> Some ten days ago 18 of my men met this Rebel McNeal in a gap of the South Fork mountain with 43 men fired on them repulsed them wounded 5 of them (2 severely) killing one of his horses wounding one and capturing 3 with several stacks of corn which they had stolen from

some of the Union men in the mountain. . . . We drove them from the Mountain got everything out had 2 men slightly wounded We are now invaded on the S and SE by Rebel McNeal on S & SW by 62nd Va. Reg Smith's command we are in great need of assistance but will do the best we can and wont complain we are in much need of our Money Rations and some clothing. . . . I would further state that there are many citizens in our district who would assist us on many occasions but for want of ammunition they are not able to get powder for their rifles I hope that you will provide a way for them to get it.[43]

CHAPTER 10

Bloomington and Piedmont

———— ✺ ————

"My God! It's ——————
hard to be gobbled up in this way."

During the first two weeks of April, the federals continued beating the bushes in Hampshire and Hardy Counties, looking for the elusive captain. Although some of his soldiers were still out in the mountains, McNeill was resting near Harrisonburg, suffering with recurring fevers. Trueheart recorded that he and his fellow compatriots were "lying inactive, recruiting our horses . . . till he recovers." All of McNeill's men knew that Secretary Seddon would soon make his decision on their partisan status, but most were confident that he would exempt their company from Congress's February repeal of the Partisan Ranger Act.[1]

Besides being sick, Hanse needed to stay close to town for another reason. Recently General Imboden had preferred charges against the veteran warrior for failing to have his accounts in order for some unspecified transaction and for "knowingly receiving and entertaining a deserter from other than his own company and refusing to deliver him up." Trueheart, though, thought that the charges had something to do with McNeill's "snapping a shotgun at a man and then breaking it over his head for disobedience . . . while close to the enemy."[2]

On April 12 a military tribunal in Harrisonburg found the captain innocent of the first charge. In the second court-martial, held on April 15, the verdict was the same. Coincidentally, about the same time Harry Gilmor went on trial for allowing his men to rob passengers during the February 12, 1864, holdup of the B&O Express West at Brown's Shop (now Bardane), West Virginia. The court, made up of officers from the 7th Virginia Cavalry, Gilmor's former regiment, found him innocent. Not long afterward, the major formed the 2nd Maryland Cavalry Battalion, mostly made up of men from his former partisan command.[3]

But as far as each officer's command was concerned, the secretary of war had already made his decision. On April 21 Seddon issued a statement that read, "Mosby's and McNeill's commands I prefer to have retained as partisan rangers." Five days later the assistant adjutant general, Major Samuel W. Morton, ordered Gilmor and his men to be mustered into a new Maryland cavalry battalion. Virginians riding with the colorful officer had the option of staying with him or transferring into an Old Dominion unit.[4]

By the last week of April Franz Sigel, now a major general and the newly appointed commander of the Department of West Virginia, was at Martinsburg assembling a force to march up the Shenandoah Valley. Sigel's advance was part of Commanding General Ulysses S. Grant's multipronged strategy to bring the Confederacy to its knees. With Grant accompanying Major General George Meade's Army of the Potomac, Meade's overall aim would be to destroy the Army of Northern Virginia. In the meantime, additional Union forces would advance simultaneously on other important objectives. Trying to force General Lee to deplete his army by sending troops to defend the capital, Major General Benjamin Butler would advance up the peninsula toward Richmond. Farther south, Major General William Tecumseh Sherman would be invading northern Georgia attempting to destroy General Joseph E. Johnston's Army of Tennessee and capture the vital rail center of Atlanta. In southwestern Virginia, portions of Sigel's command, led by Averell and Brigadier General George Crook would lead separate columns against the Virginia and Tennessee Railroad.[5]

As Sigel got his army ready for the upcoming campaign, he transferred the 54th Pennsylvania Infantry and the Ringgold Battalion, now part of the recently formed 22nd Pennsylvania Cavalry, east. By May 1 their replacements, hundred-day National Guard troops from Ohio, were still not in place along the railroad.[6]

Now, with Sigel pulling troops away from the line, McNeill realized he had an opportunity to make a powerful attack on the B&O similar to the one he had envisioned leading against Rowlesburg the year before. But in that instance, changes ordered by General Lee to Imboden and McNeill's original plan made the captain play second fiddle to Grumble Jones. Now, though, Sigel's actions gave McNeill another chance to test his theory that a small, fast-moving force could sneak through Union lines and inflict a painful blow to "Lincoln's life-line." Not only could he put the railroad out of commission for a time, but a successful attack against the line might force Sigel to send some of his troops back from the valley to guard the line.[7]

McNeill's aim was the destruction of the B&O shops and roundhouse at Piedmont, West Virginia. On Tuesday evening, May 3, he left Moorefield with about sixty partisans. When the Rangers stopped for a time at Old Fields, his trusted compatriot Captain John Peerce joined the riders. Taking the road over the mountains to Williamsport, the men stayed in the saddle most of the night, stopping just before dawn somewhere between Patterson Creek and Mill Run. They hid there, out of sight, the rest of the day.

Once it was dark the Rangers broke camp, crossed Knobly Mountain at Dolls Gap, and taking a seldom-used path, they started the long, steep ascent up the Allegheny Front. Finally on top of the mountain, they crossed the Northwestern Turnpike and, as Peerce wrote, "We followed the Elk Garden Road a short distance to the intersection of a road leading to Piedmont and Bloomington."[8]

Just after dawn on Thursday, May 5, the Rangers descended upon Bloomington, Maryland. As they surrounded the station, one trooper shinnied up a telegraph pole and cut the line. Upon questioning a startled B&O employee, McNeill found out that a few eastbound freights and one passenger train were on their way down the track. The captain halted his men and waited to capture the prize. Soon a steam whistle signaled a freight coming through the Savage River gorge. As it approached the village, a half-dozen Rangers rode out and flagged the engineer down.[9]

Loaded with military supplies, there was plenty of plunder in the cars, but it would have to wait. After moving the train down the track, McNeill told "the engineer to detach the engine," Peerce recalled, "and sent Lieutenant Dolan and one or two others on it with a flag of truce to demand the surrender of the guard at Piedmont, two miles distant." Hanse then left Peerce there in charge of ten Rangers, and with the rest of the men he followed the engine to Piedmont. Along the way, a local who knew McNeill spotted the raiders and rode off to New Creek to alert the federals. Upon reaching Camp Jessie, he warned Colonel Nathan Wilkerson that the partisans were nearby, but according to a later rumor the officer ignored him.[10]

That morning only a skeleton force consisting of a sergeant and ten soldiers from the 6th West Virginia Infantry guarded the vital rail yard. Although the week before, B&O president John Garrett had sent an urgent message via the master of the road, W. P. Smith, to Sigel emphasizing the importance of Piedmont, Smith had mistakenly forwarded Garrett's concerns to Cumberland, rather than the commander's Winchester headquarters. When the rebels arrived at seven o'clock, the telegraph operator saw them, and just before one of the raiders severed the wire, hurriedly sent a hasty communication down the line. The surprised bluecoats took refuge inside a nearby brick house and prepared to resist, but after Dolan told them that New Creek had already fallen, they surrendered. Shortly afterward McNeill sent two scouts eastward to picket New Creek Road.[11]

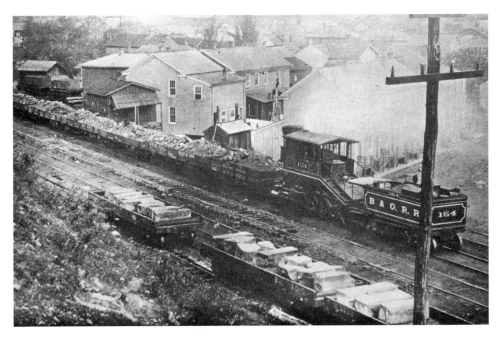

Piedmont. Courtesy of the B&O Railroad Museum.

With the Yankee garrison only five miles away, McNeill put his men to work and got busy paroling the prisoners. Within a short time, according to a B&O report, "a detachment . . . set fire to and burned the machine and paint shops, sand and oil houses, and partly destroyed one of the extensive and costly engine houses." In his report to Seddon, McNeill said, "We burned some seven buildings filled with the finest machinery, engines and railroad cars; burned nine railroad engines . . . and sent six engines with full heads of steam towards New Creek." Not far from town, the runaway locomotives crashed just below the "Rat Tail," a "narrow area strung along the inside of the B&O as it curves eastward out of Piedmont." A few partisans tried to burn the Georges Creek Railroad Bridge, but some determined local women stormed the structure and kept putting out the flames. A handful of rebels also ransacked the telegraph office, while others went into a nearby army stable and grabbed between thirty and forty horses belonging to Henry Gassaway Davis, a local Unionist who purchased mounts for the army. The raiders, however, did not destroy or take any private property or rough up any citizens.[12]

Not long after the operator's wire reached New Creek, Lieutenant Charles Bagely, Battery L, 1st Illinois Light Artillery, got his men ready to move out. Backed up by Second Lieutenant John Brown and seventy-five soldiers from the 23rd Illinois, Bagely marched for Piedmont, taking along one cannon. At

Rangers wreck the B&O at Piedmont, West Virginia, by Garnet Jex. Courtesy Sharpsburg Historical Society.

the railroad station an engineer had a locomotive and five cars ready to speed the soldiers up the line. But Bagely, probably fearing an ambush or a head-on collision should the Confederates decide to send a locomotive barreling down the single track, refused it.[13]

Just after the relief force left, bystanders saw a citizen galloping out of New Creek, then racing past the bluecoats. In a letter to the *Baltimore American*, a man who identified himself only as "A Delayed Passenger," wrote:

> I am informed by those who were on the adjacent heights at Piedmont that they saw a horseman come up the New Creek road at full speed, and when he approached McNeill's outer picket, he reined up for few moments. They then moved on to the second picket, stationed nearer the town, and the three passed into the town, ... and in a very few minutes after he was seen to leave in full gallop, the way he came, and McNeill's forces were immediately put in motion to leave, which he did, and when the troops from New Creek arrived, McNeill and his party were some three miles off and they well mounted, and the pursuing party afoot, and fatigued at that.[14]

The Rangers followed the track back to Bloomington. The federals, however, crossed the Potomac to Westernport. After marching another two miles, the tired Yankees arrived atop the heights overlooking the track. In total it had taken them between ninety minutes and two hours to get there. Just below, they could see three trains ablaze and a few rebels still trying vainly to damage the B&O's stone arch bridge. As Brown deployed his riflemen, Bagely's gunners made ready to fire.[15]

About a half hour after McNeill rode off from Bloomington, his soldiers left behind in the village could clearly see a column of smoke rising from Piedmont. By now Peerce's detachment had stopped another freight train, and the captain had graciously told the appreciative townsfolk "to help themselves." After sending B&O conductor Mose Everett and a guard up the track to flag down the next train, a sympathetic local told Peerce that a man had fled up the mountain to Frankville, to wire a message to Oakland to stop an oncoming passenger train. He also said that the next train would be full of soldiers, but Peerce thought his informant was mistaken.[16]

Just to make sure, the captain dismounted his troopers and sent them up the line to keep watch. In the meantime Peerce rode up onto the station's platform so he could get a good look at the riders once the train stopped. Just as the locomotive came into view, Peerce heard one of his men shout, "loaded with soldiers." He promptly ordered his men to mount up and join him. By now the captain could see at least two cars full of armed troops.[17]

The night before, the Mail Train East had pulled out of Wheeling bound for Baltimore's Camden Station. According to company records, it "consisted of the engine and tender, with one baggage, one mail and four passenger cars." A total of 104 Union officers and soldiers sat in the first three cars. In the rear coach, mostly filled with women, the 25 passengers included Mrs. Susan Wallace, wife of Major General Lew Wallace. Two other notables on board that morning were W. R. Porter, the B&O superintendent of construction, and Kentucky congressman William H. Wadsworth. In the mail car an Adams Express messenger guarded a safe loaded with cash, including a substantial sum on its way to Nodlinger and Company in Baltimore.[18]

As the train slowed down to stop at the station, Peerce had to decide whether to ride off or try to capture the soldiers. If he stayed there with his small band and the Yankees chose to fight, the captain was at a great disadvantage. On the other hand, if he retreated into West Virginia, the soldiers on the train and any pursuing force from New Creek would have McNeill's detachment trapped between them.[19]

"I resolved, in my mind," Peerce wrote, "that if the train could be reached before they could be informed of our numbers, we could capture them and relieve McNeill." When the locomotive stopped and conductor Samuel Gill got off, Peerce asked to see the captain. Along the track, his men ranged themselves on each side of the train, brandishing revolvers. Gill quickly pointed out a man standing on the landing of the rear car. Riding across the platform, Peerce leveled his revolver at the officer and demanded that he surrender his troops. The astonished captain replied, "My God! It's ——— hard to be gobbled up in this way, but I have no alternative. I have no ammunition." In the meantime, on the other side of the train Private Charlie Watkins, a Ranger from Baltimore, was riding alongside the cars, keeping up the ruse by shouting out, at the top of his lungs, for companies F and G to come forward.[20]

As soon as the soldiers disembarked, Peerce sent a rider to find McNeill and tell him "that I had one hundred prisoners and no one to guard them." The captain then rode back to the last car containing a number of frightened ladies and "informed them that we were Southern soldiers and that no lady need feel the slightest alarm in the hands of Southern gentlemen." Peerce also told the civilians to go to the baggage car and get their luggage.[21]

A few guards walked the passengers and prisoners across the railroad bridge into West Virginia. Meanwhile, other Rangers searched the train and discovered eighteen loaded revolvers. Although the rebels later claimed that they molested no passengers, at least one man reported losing a gold watch.[22]

Years later, W. R. Porter told a somewhat different story about the Confederates' taking of the train. Porter claimed that Ranger Private Benjamin Worting, whom the superintendent described as a "rough, double-fisted man," came aboard and demanded the surrender of the train. According to Porter's tale, when the captain asked him to whom he was surrendering, Worting replied that it was to "General McNeal." The partisan went on to say that they were three thousand strong and had captured Cumberland and New Creek and burned Piedmont. Since the officer could clearly see a pillar of smoke rising from the direction of Piedmont, he decided to surrender. Porter said that as each soldier disembarked, "his gun was taken from him, the muzzle struck over the edge of the platform and the gun thrown aside."[23]

Thirteen-year-old newsboy Charles Hambright worked the evening run between Cumberland and Grafton, and then back. He was on his way home that morning when, at 6:30, the Rangers interrupted his journey. Years later Hambright recalled that the partisans lined both sides of the train, each one holding two revolvers. After being ordered off the train, the passengers were, Hambright said, "marched down the track, across the bridge over the Potomac River, up along the slope of Hampshire Hill."[24]

By the time Peerce had everyone across the river, McNeill's detachment had arrived and was busy ransacking the freights. After parking the mail train

Bloomington Bridge from Hampshire Hill; single track prior to the 1900s. Author's collection.

atop the bridge, all three trains were set on fire. With the federals out of New Creek still on the march, the raiders took their time and made a good job of the destruction. In total they destroyed that train, plus two engines and eighteen freight cars. From his post nearby in West Virginia, Peerce was happily watching the Rangers go about their work while sharing a bottle of whiskey with some of his captives. As the vandalism continued, Private John Lynn stopped and handed Hambright some letters addressed to Lizzie Blocher, the boy's aunt, who ran the Potomac House in Cumberland.[25]

As the civilians and most of the paroled Yankees started walking down the line toward Piedmont, McNeill ordered his men back in the saddle, and they started up Hampshire Hill. Peerce, still along the track, suddenly heard a loud explosion, and on looking up he spotted a Yankee cannon just across the way. The Illinois riflemen also opened fire on the rebels. The walkers stopped in their tracks and watched the exciting spectacle.[26]

Many of the Rangers were leading captured horses up the steep grade. Henry Trueheart, though, had decided to ride one of them and lead his mare along. Suddenly, a shell burst right behind him, killing Watkins's horse. He stopped to help the man out and loaned him the mare. Trueheart recalled that as Watkins was changing his saddle, "the shells bursting all around us made it a slow business and very uncomfortable, and as soon as he was mounted, my mare flew up the mountainside, leaving me and my windblown horse in the rear of the command." Despite the Yankees' heavy fire, it was not very accurate, and all of the Rangers escaped unhurt. There is some evidence, though, that a shell burst either killed or wounded a local man who had joined the Rangers in their flight.[27]

Unfortunately, a few innocent civilians also became casualties. Irish immigrants Edward and Mary Walsh and their children lived in a log cabin on the side of Hampshire Hill. That day Mrs. Walsh's sister, a Catholic Sister of Charity, was there visiting. Hambright remembered that "we were standing on the railroad tracks while the shooting was going on. . . . One of the bullets from the cannon went through the Walsh house . . . and killed a little girl four years old and cut a boy's arm off at the shoulder." Years later, the obituary of John Thomas Walsh published in the *Piedmont Herald* told what happened. "He was asleep in his crib when a 'pumpkin ball' from a large caliber rifle went through the Walsh house. . . . His sister, Mary, a girl not yet ten, crouched over the crib to protect the baby as bullets tore through the frame dwelling. The 'pumpkin ball' struck her inflicting fatal wounds and mutilated the baby's arm." A shell fragment injured the nun's foot.[28]

Once atop the hill, the Rangers met Joseph Dixon, a hearty ninety-year-old fellow, who volunteered to be their guide. Curious about the huge column of smoke he could see rising from Piedmont, Dixon had ridden out on the heights to get a better look. He ended up piloting them for about ten miles. Finally stopping to hide in the forest the rest of the day, that night the raiders crossed the Northwest Turnpike at "Stony river bridge," west of Mount Storm, then turned east, and after riding some distance they made their way down off the Allegheny Front and on to Petersburg. According to Colonel Wilkinson, who had organized a pursuit of the raiders, "they left the roads and paths and passed along the mountains, through the woods, moving for Reels Gap, ten miles south of Petersburg and escaped."[29]

By the time they reached the town, Trueheart recalled, "the men and horses were badly used up, many of the men bleeding at the nose from fatigue and loss of sleep, and I saw horses, for the first time, drop on their knees, go fast asleep." The next day the Rangers rode over to Moorefield and, while resting, amused themselves reading personal letters taken from the train.[30]

Almost immediately, B&O repair crews got to work, and by that afternoon they had cleared the track east of Piedmont. But the heat from the fires at both places, especially Bloomington, prevented any further work until things cooled off. By noon the next day, however, the track was once again open, and trains resumed running. The westbound express, whose passengers included Major General Robert Schenck's daughters, then went to Piedmont and Bloomington, picked up any stranded passengers still there, backed up to New Creek, and dropped them off.[31]

Oddly enough, the Rangers' raid on Piedmont would give their nemesis Ben Kelley's military career a boost. After Sigel replaced him as department commander in February, the tough old warrior had remained in Cumberland, hoping for another assignment. On May 6, without notifying Sigel, Secretary of War Edwin Stanton had ordered Kelley to take charge of the defense of the railroad between Wheeling and Monocacy Junction, Maryland. In the meantime, Kelley's railroad troops would soon be receiving reinforcements, as considerable numbers of Ohio National Guard and West Virginia soldiers were now eastward bound to help protect the line. Two days after passing through Piedmont on May 14 and seeing the destruction there, Private Clinton Nichols, 152nd Ohio National Guard, noted in a letter home to the *Springfield Daily News* that "the sight of these ruins aided us to appreciate that we were in an enemy's country."[32]

As Kelley began reorganizing the defense of the road, on May 7, stung by the Piedmont debacle and Stanton's actions, Sigel sent a message to General Grant. "In regard to the affair at Piedmont," he wrote, "I beg leave to state that I could not obey the orders given to me and still guard the railroad from Parkersburg to Monocacy against the enemy raids. . . . However, I take full responsibility for the affair." Before closing, the general added, "Last night 500 cavalry were sent to Moorefield and Petersburg to cut off the raiders." Sigel was sure that this force commanded by Colonel Jacob Higgins would either capture or scatter the Rangers and protect his army's right flank from Confederate attacks as it marched up the valley. To guard his left flank from being harassed by other guerrillas and partisans, Sigel sent Colonel William Boyd at the head of a large detachment east across the Blue Ridge after Mosby's Rangers. On May 12 Boyd and his men turned west, passed through Manassas Gap, and continued to Front Royal.[33]

Higgins left Winchester at three o'clock on the morning of May 7. The expedition included 225 troopers of his 22nd Pennsylvania Cavalry and Lieutenant Colonel Root leading 220 horsemen from the 15th New York Cavalry. Leaving about half of the 22nd behind to guard Sigel's wagons, Higgins took with him veteran companies from the old Ringgold Battalion. That spring the regiment had been formed with the addition of five new companies. Since that time, most of the Ringgold troopers had resented the fact that Higgins was in command of the regiment rather than the experienced guerrilla fighter Andrew J. Greenfield, now a lieutenant colonel.[34]

From the start, the troopers were in bad humor. The evening before Higgins had ordered the men "to saddle up and be ready to leave at a moment's notice." The soldiers, now anxious to go, became angry as hour after hour slipped by. Then, when they finally started moving out, many grumbled about the colonel's decision to take along twelve wagons. The old hands knew the wagons would only slow the column down and might cost them any chance they had of cornering McNeill.[35]

The command camped at Wardensville that night. The next day, May 8, the bluecoats were about seven miles from Moorefield when the wagoners stopped to water their teams. Shortly, some bushwhackers shadowing the column opened fire from the mountainside, killing Corporal William White and wounding a few horses. The Pennsylvanians returned fire and later learned from some of the locals that they had hit a guerrilla or two. In a letter to the Pennsylvania paper *Washington Reporter,* a trooper described the incident. "While resting on the shady banks of a stream," he wrote, "a party of guerrillas fired on us from the high rocks above, killing Corporal White. . . . The event so sudden, was painfully sad."[36]

It was about four o'clock in the afternoon when the Yankees finally arrived in Moorefield. Far out in front, Sergeant Hopkins Moffitt shot at a gray horseman and then chased after him. The man, Ranger Private Samuel Daugherty, jumped off his mount and then, according to John Elwood, "he ran into a mill and jumped into a barrel of flour." Hopkins quickly collared him, but in the meantime, about a mile south of Moorefield, an alert Captain McNeill was getting his men ready to gallop away with their captured horses and other spoils.[37]

The captain ordered Lieutenant Dolan to stay behind with a dozen Rangers and hold Toll Gate Hill, an eminence commanding the Petersburg Pike, for as long he could. Meanwhile, Colonel Higgins, much to the disgust of Farrar, was taking the time to deploy the whole command. "We formed immediately east of the town," Farrar wrote, "and with the precision of a dress parade advanced towards the enemy, who immediately formed on a point to receive us. . . . If Greenfield would have been in command, the only word would have been, 'Come on, boys!' and we would have followed with a yell."[38]

Once clear of the village, the now major Henry Myers waved his sword and shouted for the men to come on; Captain Hart's company surged forward. As the bluecoats came charging up the hill, the rear guard waited until the last instance before firing and then scampered off. Although there was plenty of flying lead, no bullets struck any soldiers on either side, but the Northerners did capture John Fay. In a letter to his wife, Private Aungier Dobbs noted, "We charged on him ... after firing one round at us he fled and we caught but one of his men." Afterward the soldiers found out that some of the mail the Rangers had taken off the train was letters from their wives and girlfriends back in the Keystone State.[39]

Higgins and his men camped on a hill just outside of town that night. The next morning, May 9, Myers took a squadron and conducted a long reconnaissance, first riding to Petersburg and then to Greenland Gap, before returning that evening, a circuit of forty-eight miles. Outside Moorefield that day patrols had roamed the nearby hills and mountains looking for the Rangers, but their searches proved fruitless. Higgins had planned to stay in Moorefield overnight, but a report that Imboden was heading that way with 4,500 soldiers caused him to move up his departure. At ten o'clock that night the Northerners mounted up and began riding back to Winchester. Myers's tired men and horses formed the vanguard, while Major George T. Work's squadron protected the wagons. But Imboden was not coming to Moorefield. Instead he was pushing his troops toward Lost River Gap, hoping to intercept the Yankees before they reached Wardensville.[40]

On May 8 a Captain Bartlett of the Confederate Signal detachment located atop a lookout at the northern end of Massanutten Mountain reported to Imboden that two large cavalry commands had left Winchester. Bartlett noted that one was heading west over North Mountain toward Moorefield Road and the other eastward. The brigadier immediately recognized an opportunity: "These facts convinced me that Sigel, before venturing to advance, meant to ascertain whether he had enemies in dangerous force within striking distance on either flank; an investigation which would consume several days. As there were no troops except my little band ... it was manifestly important to attack these detachments as far from Strasburg as possible and delay their return as long as possible."[41]

Imboden did not waste any time cobbling together a force to go after Higgins. On May 9 he telegraphed Major General John C. Breckinridge at his headquarters in Staunton about McNeill's success at Piedmont and that "thirteen hundred cavalry have gone out from Winchester to intercept McNeill." He added, "I proceed with two regiments cavalry and one section of artillery to the relief of McNeill." Imboden would leave Colonel George H. Smith at Woodstock with the 62nd Virginia Mounted Infantry, four of Captain Mc-Clanahan's guns, and a hundred or so miscellaneous troopers. In a subsequent wire, Imboden told Breckinridge he would "return to the Valley in four or five days." To deceive Union spies, Imboden floated a rumor that he was moving his cavalry nearer North Mountain to get better grazing. Then, sometime late in the afternoon, he rode out taking the 18th and 23rd Virginia regiments and two cannons with him. After crossing North Mountain at Devil's Hole, Imboden marched his men through the night and arrived at Lost River Gap the next morning. There Imboden, with the help of some Rangers he had encountered on the trail, set up an ambush.[42]

That morning, at around six o'clock, the blue vanguard was entering the fog-shrouded pass when it ran into Imboden's pickets. Upon hearing some gunshots, Higgins dashed forward and ordered Myers to clear the gap. The major immediately sent Captain Hart's company forward and followed close behind with the rest of the squadron. Higgins formed the rest of the command on the right of the road in support.[43]

Hart quickly drove back a thin line of rebels, but he suddenly ran into trouble a half mile beyond. There Imboden's whole force, drawn up in the river bottom, was waiting for him. Private Dobbs noted that "we did not know their number but we made a charge and was met by 3 or 4 times out number. [W]e received and returned several rounds at them . . . we was compelled to retreat and they pursued." Another trooper wrote, "Our little column was hurled back with an impulse commensurate of its former momentum. We had caught hold of the beast, and it was now a question, 'How to let it go!'" Hart lost two troopers captured but was able to fall back and rejoin Myers before the rebels overran his outmatched force. The major reported the situation to Higgins, who promptly ordered a retreat. "Here," Elwood remembered, "began a ride for life, forty miles from our lines, without any chow to feed our faithful animals that had gone all night without anything to eat."[44]

Higgins, Myers, and a small squad of troopers then started for Romney. Other bluecoats quickly followed, but trying to save the wagons, Major Work and Lieutenant Colonel Root took their time forming a rear guard. "The train," Farrar wrote, "which had been turned back, was ordered to move up lively, while the rear-guard fell back slowly to enable the train to get out of the way." At first the Confederates did not pursue, but eventually Work sent Captain James Chessrown to check on the wagons. In the meantime the rear guard formed on a hill just outside of Baker, and when Imboden's horsemen finally came along, met them with a volley, killing Private Andrew Baker of the 23rd Virginia Cavalry.[45]

After riding on a few miles, a surprised Chessrown found the wagons, their teams unhitched, parked in a grove along Grassy Lick Road. About midday the wagoners, mistakenly thinking that they were now out of danger, had stopped to feed and water the famished, thirsty animals. While they were there, most of the troops responsible for guarding the wagons moved on. Upon hearing sharp gunfire to their rear, a handful of terrified African American teamsters started running away. Wagon master Sergeant H. B. Hedge ordered them to halt. "I demonstrated with my revolver," he recalled, "telling them it was sure death if they did not go back to work; they soon found their places and we moved on."[46]

Not long afterward Imboden's fighters pushed back the outnumbered rear guard and chased after the wagons. To lighten their loads and gain some speed, the helpers cast heavy boxes of supplies off into the brush. Finally, with the Confederates fast closing in, the teamsters stopped, unhitched and jumped on their horses, and scampered off. The remaining guards, however, killed some of the other animals to prevent them falling into rebel hands. The Northerners lost all of their wagons and the one ambulance.[47]

The race to reach Romney continued. As many of their exhausted horses played out, troopers got off and ran into the woods. Some escaped; the rebels collared others. Upon finally reaching the turnpike just east of town, the Northerners continued through Romney, heading north for Green Spring. By this time, most of Imboden's men had given up the chase.[48]

About an hour after the last Yankees had passed through Romney, Dolan arrived in town leading a Ranger detachment. Hoping to rescue his friend Fay, Trueheart wrote, he picked "ten of the best mounted men," and "pursued them nine miles to Springfield at half-speed." Upon reaching the suspension bridge over the South Branch, Dolan spotted a number of federals and their prisoners ascending the hill across the stream. Sergeant John Corbitt was bringing up the rear, leading his horse with Fay aboard. Upon turning and seeing the partisans galloping across the bridge, and with bullets now kicking the dust up around him, Corbitt sprinted into the woods. Soon Dolan had rescued Fay, Daugherty, and a few other rebels. According to Trueheart, they killed one soldier and captured "eight Yanks and ten or twelve horses." On their return to town, some ladies treated them to supper.[49]

Lieutenant Joseph S. Isenberg, adjutant of the 22nd, led the first troops into the B&O station at Green Spring and promptly telegraphed a message to Sigel about Imboden's attack. Later, when Higgins and other soldiers arrived, the colonel ordered his men to cross the river to Old Town. The next morning Major Myers arrived at Kelley's Cumberland headquarters and filled him in on the inglorious retreat. He also told the general that besides losing their wagons, he estimated at least "50 in killed wounded and missing." Kelley wired Higgins to bring his command to Cumberland.[50]

By May 11 Imboden was back at his station at Mount Jackson. He reported to Breckinridge that "I thrashed parts of three regiments in Hardy yesterday, ran them twenty-four miles, killed 5, wounded a number, captured only thirteen, as they fled to the mountains; captured their train—12 new wagons and one ambulance, 20-odd horses."[51]

After having effectively eliminated close to five hundred troopers from Sigel's cavalry force, Imboden turned his attention to slowing the general's advance up the valley and finding and destroying Colonel Boyd's three-hundred-man scouting party, now supposed to be in the Luray Valley. On May 13 Imboden's cavalry surprised and routed Boyd's column as it descended Massanutten Mountain, near New Market. Two days later Breckinridge repulsed Sigel at the Battle of New Market, thereby ending the Union threat for the present to the Confederates guarding the upper valley.[52]

CHAPTER II

The Timber Ridge Fight

———— ✺✺ ————

"The brave fear no danger
when duty calls."

On the evening of May 22, Kelley wired Higgins at Green Spring and ordered him to send Captain Hart out with a squadron to scout along Trough Road to Moorefield. Since Hart was familiar with the area, Kelley issued no specific instructions but emphasized that he wanted "McNeill killed, captured, or driven out of this valley."[1]

Hart left the next day, but when he reached Moorefield, a usually trustworthy source told him that McNeill and his men were over in the Shenandoah Valley. Returning to Green Spring, Hart reported this information to Higgins, who in turn relayed the news to Kelley. The general, however, suspected the partisans were still around and ordered his soldiers guarding the line to remain vigilant.[2]

The information that Hart received was partly true. On either May 21 or 22 Captain McNeill had taken fifty-four Rangers to the Shenandoah Valley, leaving sixty-five men behind with Jesse. In the following weeks Sigel's army, now commanded by Major General David Hunter, once again advanced up the valley, attracting the immediate attention of the captain and the rest of the Confederates in the area. Meanwhile, over on the South Fork Jesse kept his men busy looking for opportunities to ambush enemy patrols.[3]

On May 29, from New Creek, Colonel Wilkerson notified Kelley that a large rebel force under Imboden and McNeill was encamped at Petersburg. That evening Kelley wired Higgins, wanting to know who had told Hart that McNeill was in the valley. Two days later the general ordered Hart back to Moorefield. In his message to Higgins, Old Ben wrote, "Let him take a wagon and ten days rations of hard bread, sugar, coffee and salt, and depend on the country for forage and cattle." On June 1 Hart, Second Lieutenant James Gibson, and ninety troopers left camp. By evening they had reached Reynolds Gap, where they stopped for the night.[4]

It was raining the next morning when the patrol started out. Arriving in Moorefield, Hart was unable to find out any information from the people there on McNeill's whereabouts. Nevertheless, Hart suspected that the Rangers might attack Colonel Robert Stevenson's 154th Ohio National Guard stationed at Greenland Gap and decided to go there. Along the way, the troopers noticed horsemen off in the distance tailing them.[5]

Upon reaching Greenland and finding everything quiet, Hart had his men draw five days' rations, and to make better time he left his wagon there. By the evening of June 3 the Pennsylvanians were back at Old Fields, camped in a wooded grove. Sometime that day, Sergeant John Elwood recalled, the captain discovered that the Rangers and Major William Harness "were following him with full purpose of capturing his entire command; when the opportunity came." Harness, who in October 1863 had resigned from the 11th Virginia Cavalry rather than face a court-martial, was now leading his own independent company of cavalry.[6]

Thinking that he might be able to draw the rebels out into the open and smash them, Hart led his men back across Patterson Creek Mountain. The Southerners, however, kept their distance, hanging near the base of the mountain. After stopping to rest at Williamsport, the troop then rode south toward Petersburg, Hart learning from a citizen along the trail that no Confederates were then in the town. That night the men camped along the banks of Lunice Creek under the watchful eyes of Ranger scouts. The next morning, June 6, Hart backtracked to the Moorefield and Allegheny Turnpike and once again headed for Moorefield.[7]

While Hart and his troopers had been away, one of the captain's friends back at Green Spring grew apprehensive about the men's safety. When Major George Work awoke on the morning of June 4, he was very disturbed by a strange dream he had had. In it he saw Hart's patrol in peril, surrounded by the enemy. Although Work put his troubling vision off at first, he finally approached Higgins about taking some men to search for Hart. Meanwhile, in Cumberland, Kelley had earlier received intelligence that Hart's patrol might be in danger, so even before Work asked about leading a relief force, the general had telegraphed Higgins about sending Hart reinforcements. Later Work called on Captain James Y. Chessrown, Lieutenant Felix Boyle, and some thirty troopers to accompany him on the expedition. The Pennsylvanians took along a mountain howitzer and ten days' rations.[8]

After getting a late start and only reaching Springfield by dark, Work stopped for the night. The next morning he set out for Greenland Gap. Arriving there later that afternoon, Work found out that the patrol had been in the area the day before. The major, figuring that Hart would be scouting to either Moorefield or Petersburg, rested his men and horses at the gap that night before riding over to the Moorefield-Allegheny Junction. There Work discovered that Hart was now traveling to Moorefield. Work followed along, and upon reaching the top of the mountain, he discovered where the company had stopped for a time. The major, estimating that he was only about a half-hour behind Hart, hurried the men forward.[9]

In the meantime Jesse and Harness were busy setting up their trap The partisans hid themselves on the eastern slope of Timber Ridge, just about three miles west of Moorefield—"at a bend in the road," Farrar wrote, "where the bank on the upper side is high and covered with a thick undergrowth." Another soldier said, "An eight foot perpendicular bank, and the thick under-brush that lined its margin, was all that concealed the wily guerrilla chieftain and his murderous clan."[10]

Sergeant Hopkins Moffitt led the way down the ridge. Although he was an old hand at backwoods fighting, this time Moffitt failed to spot the enemy. As the bluecoats moved along slowly, McNeill let about twenty soldiers ride by before signaling his men to fire. "The sharp ringing of two hundred Rebel carbines," one participant remembered, "accompanied by the whizzing sound of swift passing leaden messengers, first told our boys of the presence of the enemy." A number of troopers pitched out of their saddles; terrified horses bolted forward. The rebels had cut the company in two.[11]

A squad of mounted graybacks chased the front of the company down the hill. But as they closed in, Lieutenant Gibson and Moffitt suddenly rallied a handful of men and charged the rebels, who turned and scattered. Just about this time Work's contingent was passing through nearby Walnut Bottom when the shooting started. Spurring their mounts, they quickly reached the crest of the ridge. Once the gunners got their cannon in place and started shelling the Confederates in the woods, they retreated to a new position. Chessrown then led some dismounted troopers into the brush, and finally spotting the rebels, shouted to alert the gunners to where they were. In an instant the howitzer commenced its deadly work, and the Southerners took to the hills.[12]

When the fight was over, Hart, whose horse had suffered three wounds, gathered up his men and counted his losses. The rebels had killed Corporal James C. Smith and Privates A. Smith Morton and Joseph Wright and had mortally wounded Private James E. Smith. They had also wounded eight other troopers, killed three horses, and wounded a number of others. That afternoon, after leaving the dying Private Smith behind with a local family, Work took charge and started the command back to Green Spring. The soldiers arrived there the next morning. Now safe, Hart's troopers praised Work and his men for coming to their rescue. One of the grateful men said, "The brave fear no danger when duty calls."[13]

Although the Rangers had had victory within their grasp, the sudden arrival of Work's squad had foiled the ambush. While not shot up as bad as their opponent, Jesse's detachment had suffered some losses, including Private Richard Clary, killed, and Sergeant Jim Dailey and Private Erasmus Tucker, wounded. The Rangers later buried Clary, one of a trio of Ranger brothers from Cumberland, in Olivet Cemetery.[14]

After he learned of the incident, Kelley wired Sigel, now charged with guarding the supply depot in Martinsburg that he would be putting Mulligan, who had just returned with the 23rd Illinois to New Creek, in charge of the soldiers guarding the track between Sleepy Creek and Piedmont. For now, "Old Ben" would "take immediate steps to drive McNeill and Harness out of the South Branch Valley." On June 13 Work and about 150 troopers left camp for Moorefield. Meanwhile, Mulligan ordered Stevenson to march 300 soldiers from Greenland Gap to the town. Both columns were operating under Kelley's orders that "the country around Moorefield and Petersburg will be thoroughly scouted, and the force of McNeill and Harness either killed captured or driven out of the country." By the time the Yankees reached Moorefield, though, their crafty foes had once again vanished.[15]

Over in the valley, Imboden's outnumbered fighters, only about 1,000 men, had been busy nipping at the heels of Hunter's 8,500-man army as, after crossing Cedar Creek north of Strasburg on May 26, it slowly made its way toward the Confederate rail center and supply depot at Staunton. With General Breckinridge and most of the defenders of the Shenandoah now fighting Grant's legions east of Richmond, Imboden was just trying to slow down Hunter's progress long enough to allow time for reinforcements to arrive on the scene.[16]

Captain McNeill's detachment started harassing Hunter's column when it reached the vicinity of Mount Jackson. Besides scouting, the Rangers picked off Union foragers out scouring the countryside for food and plunder. While Hunter was camped at New Market, Hanse led his men on a complete circuit of the enemy's position, gaining an accurate count of the numbers Imboden faced. During this mission, Trueheart wrote, "We wounded & killed several, capturing a few prisoners and some horses."[17]

Hunter reached Harrisonburg on June 3. While McNeill kept watch, Imboden established a strong defensive position astride the Valley Pike at Mount Crawford. Years later, in 1900, an anonymous rebel veteran recounted meeting McNeill at this time. The man, a telegrapher, had been watching the Yankees around New Market, tapping the line in various places and sending up-to-date information on the Yankee advance to Confederate authorities in Staunton, the authorities then forwarding it to Richmond. As the Northerners marched toward Harrisonburg, he and his assistants fell back.[18]

Just after midnight on June 4, the man ran into some Rangers at a blacksmith shop west of Harrisonburg, near the village of New Erection. He described the scene:

> McNeill's company of Rangers lay that night asleep and snug in a small strip of timber, which then stood in the fields east of New Erection church. Before sunrise next morning (Saturday) Hunter was stirring. Lloyd C, a young Marylander, the picket on the hilltop east of us, rode rapidly into the little hidden bivouac, and shook the old war horse, Captain John H. McNeill, wrapped in his buffalo, fast asleep in the leaves in a fence corner.
>
> In an instant, he mounted and led his men to the crest of the wooden ridge, near and a little south of the Eversole place. From this point, the hill being cleared to its crest on its east side, the enemy was plainly seen with his glass.[19]

A few moments later Hanse became concerned because he could not see any federals marching south on the Valley Pike. When one of his men suggested looking east toward Port Republic Road, he immediately spied the Yankees. McNeill, realizing that by using this route Hunter would eventually turn south, bypass the defenses at Mount Crawford, and then descend on Staunton, needed to warn Imboden immediately. Hoping to prevent the federals from capturing his messengers, the captain then sent the first of three couriers in a roundabout way via Bridgewater to inform the general of this new development.[20]

That same morning Southern troops, led by Grumble Jones and Brigadier General John C. Vaughn, arrived at Mount Crawford. Grumble, due to seniority, took command of the rebel contingent, which Imboden estimated numbered "all sorts of troops, veterans and militia, something less than 4,500 men." Vaughn, however, figured that the force consisted of some 5,600 soldiers. Only fourteen cannon backed up the butternut cavalry and infantry.[21]

McNeill and his boys were soon in the saddle and skirmishing with some of Hunter's outriders on the right rear of the Union advance. This fighting continued for about three hours but did not amount to much. Trueheart remembered only "wounding one and capturing one." Upon disengaging, McNeill rode over to Mount Crawford and found Jones in command. Despite his earlier warnings, though, the troops had not yet marched men east to contest the Yankee advance.[22]

Jones finally got moving, and "On the 5th," Imboden wrote, "our forces were concentrated about half a mile north-east of the village of Piedmont. . . . After repelling two attacks, our left wing was doubled up by a flank attack, Jones was killed, and we were disastrously beaten. Our loss was not less than 1500 men." The Rangers watched the four-hour fight from a safe distance. Not long before the battle ended, Jones called upon McNeill and ordered him, Trueheart said, "to go to the rear and attack their trains—that all was well in front & he could manage them there." But before the Rangers got a chance to leave, the Yankees suddenly broke through the Confederate lines, killing the general and overrunning the defender's position. The partisans spent the rest of the day helping some of the wounded to escape. That night they kept a sharp lookout for Union patrols.[23]

Reaching Staunton on June 6, Hunter's soldiers quickly confiscated or destroyed anything of military value. On June 8 Crook's and Averell's troops arrived in town and linked up with the command. Two days later Hunter started marching south for Lexington. For a time following the Battle of Piedmont, McNeill kept watch on Hunter, but on June 8 he turned his attention to a well-guarded train of 217 wagons rumbling toward Staunton. McNeill sent word of the train's approach to Vaughn and expected him to send his horsemen to help destroy Hunter's supplies. But after shadowing the wagons for some eighteen miles and receiving no reinforcements, McNeill decided not to risk heavy casualties attacking with his small band. On June 11 Hunter captured Lexington, burning the Virginia Military Institute and Governor John Letcher's house. Not long afterward the general turned his army east, crossed the Blue Ridge Mountains, and marched on Lynchburg. Meanwhile, Hanse led his detachment back to the South Fork.[24]

CHAPTER 12

Johnson's Run and Springfield

❧

" . . . killed all we could lay our hands on
—three."

On June 4 Captain John S. Bond wrote West Virginia Governor Arthur I. Boreman from New Creek: "Dear Sir: My ammunition is nearly exhausted. Will you please have a supply sent me to this station immediately to the care of Thos. P. Adams Esq."[1]

In mid-June a wagon train defended by approximately a hundred soldiers from a few West Virginia Home Guard companies wound its way north from Petersburg bound for the supply depot at New Creek. Rather than risk a Ranger ambush along the Patterson Creek route, Captains John Boggs and John Bond followed the rougher, but safer, road that passed through Greenland Gap. Upon reaching New Creek, the soldiers intended to load their wagons with ammunition, military supplies, and other necessary items courtesy of the state and federal governments. Also accompanying the train were a few citizens, including some women looking to buy things in New Creek that were in short supply back home.[2]

As has been noted in a previous chapter, at the beginning of the war many men in Hardy and Pendleton Counties remained loyal to the Union and supported the newly formed Reorganized Government of Virginia, located in Wheeling. According to the late Harrison M. Calhoun, an author, educator, and lawyer in Franklin, West Virginia, who in his lifetime did considerable research on guerrilla warfare in that remote area, "Three guerrilla companies of Union sentiment were organized on the lower South Branch in the Mill Run District." Captains Michael Mallow and Isaac Alt led Hardy County companies while Captain Bond led a mixed band from Hardy and Pendleton. These companies sometimes coordinated their efforts with Captain John Snyder's company, composed mostly of men from Randolph County and a few others from Pendleton County. Calhoun noted that "these companies were originally called State Troops and Home Guards but later called Swamp Dragons and still later Swamps." Throughout the conflict, a number of Confederate deserters drifted back home and joined Swamp Dragon companies, especially Snyder's outfit.[3]

Although scores of mountaineers enlisted in regular Confederate units, some Southern sympathizers who stayed behind also formed guerrilla bands. The "Dixie Boys," one of the first, consisted of secessionists from Pendleton, Randolph, and Tucker Counties and included Captain Ezekiel Harper, a noted guide and scout. Later, the Pendleton contingent left the group and formed another company also called "Dixie Boys." The Pendleton Reserves, consisting of the oddly dubbed "Pizarinktums" and a seldom-used group of old-timers called the "Groundhog Battery" also supported the Confederate cause.[4]

As the war progressed, guerrilla fighters on both sides went after each other vigorously. They became adept at arson, horse stealing, robbery, and murder. Roadside ambushes and nighttime raids were their forte, but when accompanying regular troops on expeditions through the Alleghenies, they more than proved their worth as guides and scouts.[5]

In July 1863 the legislature of the new state of West Virginia passed "An Act for the defense of the State." This new law led to the formation of West Virginia Home Guard companies whose soldiers would be armed, paid, and supplied by the state. In Pendleton County Captain Evan Harper soon organized the Pendleton County Scouts, and not long afterward he took ten of his men to New Creek for arms and supplies. When they stopped at a house near Greenland Gap for breakfast, three of the men decided to ride on and eat somewhere else. Later, when Harper and the others heard a distant shot, they made haste to help their companions. But the men were too late; a party of McNeill's Rangers had captured the trio. All three ended up in Richmond's Castle Thunder prison.[6]

On April 18, 1864, the Dixie Boys raided the farm of old Jesse Harper and shot down his sons Evan and Perry and his son-in-law Eli Harman. On April 28 the soldiers of Evan's company met and unanimously elected John S. Boggs, a veteran guerrilla fighter and former member of the West Virginia House of Delegates, to replace their fallen leader. When Boggs visited Wheeling on May 7, he reported that "since the cold-blooded murder of Captain Harper and his brother. . . . there is no such feeling as humanity longer existing in the minds of the people[.] Several rebels supposed to have been engaged in the murder of the Harpers have been captured and killed."[7]

On June 18 Boggs's and Bond's companies were on their way back home from New Creek. Loaded down with supplies, the wagons had already passed through Petersburg and forded the South Branch. Earlier McNeill had been getting his men ready to ride to Pennsylvania when news came into camp about the wagon train. Subsequently Dolan led about sixty fighters to a spot just south of the river and set up a two-pronged ambush. He placed twenty-five dismounted men in cover near an icehouse on the east side of Franklin Road, just beyond Johnson Run. Farther back, hidden in the trees along a farm lane, the lieutenant's mounted party lay in wait.[8]

About a hundred yards after the mountaineers' vanguard crossed the run, some of the men spotted rebels in the brush, but the graybacks promptly opened fire and scattered the surprised Unionists. Instantly the mounted detachment charged the rear wagons. Most of the Swamps jumped off their horses, scurried up the steep bank of a nearby hill, took cover behind some trees, and returned fire, while a few stayed and defended the wagons. After some fierce skirmishing, Boggs led his men in a furious counterattack and recaptured all of the wagons, except one or two that the rebels burned. The Rangers made off with nineteen horses.[9]

The battle had been costly to both sides. The Swamps had lost Henry Harman, Godfrey Kesner, John Ours Sr., and Arnold Kimble, killed, and a few wounded. According to Calhoun, "Nimrod Borrer and Ezra Borrer were taken prisoner and neither ever returned." Local author E. L. Judy added that the same fate befell Isaac Murphy.[10]

McNeill, though, might have suffered a bigger loss. In Boggs's counterattack, Dolan went down with a mortal wound and fell into the hands of the enraged West Virginians. A few of them wanted to finish him off, but others, knowing he would soon die, stopped them. The only other partisan wounded was Private Frank Davis, who took a bullet in the thigh. Oddly, another Ranger, nineteen-year-old William Coakley, collapsed from sunstroke during the fight and soon developed a fatal case of pneumonia. When the combat was over, Boggs sent a messenger to New Creek with an account of the ambush. Kelley later wired Sigel about the skirmish, telling him that Major Work, now scouting around Moorefield, was going after the rebels.[11]

The next day a determined band of Rangers set out to recover Dolan's body. Upon arriving in Petersburg, locals tipped them off that some of the Home Guard, figuring that the partisans would be back, had returned to the skirmish site and were waiting on top of the same hill. Not wanting to stumble into an ambush, the partisans backtracked through Petersburg Gap and then took a long roundabout course from Durgon around Gap Mountain, and after warily crossing Franklin Road, came in silently behind their prey.[12]

From their perch atop the hill, Lieutenant Adam Yoakum and his men had watched the Rangers ride into town and then leave. Hoping they would return, the Home Guards lay hidden in the woods and were completely unaware of the approaching Confederates until the Southerners opened fire. John Yoakum and William Shreve fell to the ground dead, and Clark Shreve was wounded. The Rangers suffered no losses and soon recovered Dolan's corpse. "On the 19th went after his body," Trueheart penned, "and finding that the Swamps were waiting for us, killed all we could lay our hands on—three."[13]

The Rangers returned to Moorefield and laid their young hero to rest in Olivet Cemetery. On June 27 the *Wheeling Daily Intelligencer* reported his death; in its next edition, the editor added more detail:

> We learned yesterday that the person killed is Barney Dolan, who was formerly a clerk in the store of the Messrs. Handlan, at Ritchietown. He left this town with the Shriver Greys. His parents resided, and we believe, still reside, at Benwood. Of the one hundred deluded young men who left this city to join their fortunes with the rebellion, not more than ten are now with the army.[14]

On Wednesday night, June 22, McNeill and sixty-five partisans left Moorefield and rode north. General Kelley, however, did not find this out until Saturday. At once he suspected that the Rangers intended to cross the Alleghany Front to raid a horse farm, located between Oakland and Red House, that the army used to rehabilitate broken-down mounts. He promptly telegraphed the commanding officer at Oakland to be on the alert "and inform Captain Godwin, at Fort Pendleton." Kelley also wired Altamont and ordered Captain Joseph A. Faris, 6th West Virginia Infantry, to take "fifty men with five days rations, and go over by the Red House and scout the country in toward the Horseshoe." Kelley's hunch, however, was wrong.[15]

Just after midnight on June 24, Lieutenant William D. Nichols, Company D, 153rd Ohio National Guard, received orders to march his company from Green Spring to Romney and there meet Lieutenant Colonel Francis W. Thompson's 6th West Virginia Cavalry. About three hours later Nichols had his men on the road. Marching along in the early morning hours, he became very apprehensive. "There are no U.S. forces in this country and it is infested with guerrillas. . . . There are two hundred of them under a Captain McNeill who always stay in the area and bushwhack, steal horses, and gather up small parties of Federal soldiers." Nevertheless, by noon the Buckeyes had safely reached their destination and took up quarters in the Hampshire County Court House. The next evening, around 5:00, Thompson's horse soldiers reached Romney. Shortly afterward the West Virginians and their Ohio compatriots left for Springfield, arriving there about four hours later. With his mission accomplished, Nichols led his company back to Green Spring.[16]

That same day, Saturday, June 25, McNeill found out that Union cavalry was traveling west on the turnpike. Hoping to get some horses, the Rangers mounted up and eventually reached the road some two miles east of Romney. After setting up their ambush, they learned that the federals had already passed by. Trueheart recalled that he "saw two young ladies running up the road in a broiling July sun to tell us that five hundred Yankee cavalry were in Romney." Shortly, though, his scouts told McNeill that the enemy had already passed through town and was on the road to Green Spring.[17]

Moving on, Hanse sent some men ahead and followed at a distance with the rest. Either later that night or early the next morning, his outriders reported that the enemy cavalry had stopped in Springfield. They noted that troopers were guarding the Wire Bridge, and the foot soldiers had gone on to Green Spring. Now that he knew the situation, McNeill decided to strike the Yankees by using a backwoods trail and cross the South Branch a "mile or two" below the bridge.[18]

The next morning Thompson's troopers were scattered about, seemingly unconcerned and not anticipating any trouble. On the banks of the South Branch east of the village, Captain Gailema Law, commanding Company K, was in charge of a squad guarding the ford at Millisons Mill. Except for those men on duty, most of the mountaineers were unarmed, either having left their weapons back at camp or propped up against nearby trees. To pass the time, many soldiers had stripped off their clothes and jumped into the stream for a refreshing bath. Others were sleeping under the trees, while a few guarded the unsaddled horses grazing in a field of clover.[19]

At around ten o'clock Hanse spotted the unsuspecting Yankees, formed his men in line, and then signaled a charge. As the rebels surged forward, they shot down the few bluecoats who resisted, but most of the rest threw up their hands and surrendered. Trueheart figured that the company "took 58 prisoners-104 horses, saddles, bridles, etc.—killed three & wounded two that we know of."[20]

Moving quickly, the Rangers were able to get their prisoners, horses, and booty back across the river and well on the way to the Lost River Valley before Thompson could come to his men's rescue. After telegraphing Kelley a short message, Thompson gathered up a squadron and took off in pursuit. At eleven o'clock, Kelley wired Sigel with the news and told him that the raiders were probably "McNeill's and Harness' cavalry."[21]

As soon as Nichols found out about the raid, he immediately ordered all of the soldiers into the Green Spring blockhouse. Until the scare was over,

they remained behind its stout walls. In a letter written later that day, he noted that "some of Thompson's wounded are coming in, and many escaped troopers without arms or horses, some bareheaded, all tired and hungry. They lost a captain, two lieutenants, and fifty-five men captured, six wounded, and one killed. They also lost 100 men and 100 rifles. It was McNeill's men who surprised them."[22]

The next day Kelley contacted Sigel again and said, "I will send an officer to investigate and report in regard to the capture at Springfield yesterday. I fear it will turn out to be a disgraceful affair. . . . It was, as I expected, McNeill and Harness' men, under command of McNeill himself, who had just returned from the Shenandoah Valley."[23]

When word of McNeill's triumph got back to Richmond, the old fighter was once again the man of the hour. The *Daily Dispatch* soon received a letter from a Harrisonburg citizen reporting the details of the one-sided skirmish. The paper noted that some of McNeill's prisoners had commented unhappily that "their term of service had just expired and that they were on their way home to return no more when McNeill pounced on them and concluded to detain them a little while longer in Dixie."[24]

The scribe continued:

Capt. McNeill does as efficient service as any other officer in the Southern command. With his company of partisan rangers of not more than 80 or 90 men, within the past year he has captured some 600 to 800 (perhaps 1000) prisoners, killed and disabled more Yankees than his entire command, and in arms and ammunition, stores, and horses, his captures have been very large. He has also destroyed immensely in property and stores of the enemy. Many persons in this section of the country . . . entertain the opinion that the efficiency of this valuable force would be greatly added by increasing it to a battalion of five hundred men at least, and the promotion of the gallant commander to . . . Lieut. Colonel. It must be borne in mind that this last affair of the Captain's is only one of many equally daring and successful in character, performed through a series of many months. Singular to add, the Captain has rarely lost a man, killed wounded or captured.[25]

Opposite: Green Spring Blockhouse. Courtesy *Civil War Times*.

CHAPTER 13

To the Gates of Washington

"You could not see more than a horses length
& that indistinctly."

Once back in Harrisonburg, McNeill discovered that Jubal Early, now a lieutenant general recently promoted to the command of the Second Corps, had beaten back Major General David Hunter's attempt to take Lynchburg. "Black Dave" and his army had then retreated over the Blue Ridge, across the valley, and disappeared into the mountains of West Virginia. Now Early's soldiers, along with Breckinridge's troops, were in Staunton, preparing to advance down the valley toward the Potomac crossings at Shepherdstown and Williamsport.[1]

At this time Hanse gave part of the herd of horses captured at Springfield to some Missourians, soldiers who were members of Captain Charles Woodson's Company A, 1st Missouri Cavalry, a unique band made up of men the Yankees had previously captured in Missouri. In a letter home, Henry Trueheart noted that "a company of Missourians who distinguished themselves very highly in the Newmarket fight . . . has been told by the Genl that they might attach themselves to any comd they pleased, joined us with 35 men who we mounted—thus furnishing us with a most valuable reinforcement."[2]

Earlier in the war, Woodson had served with the Missouri State Guard and later Colonel Joseph C. Porter's 1st Northeast Missouri Cavalry, a guerrilla band. In September 1862 the federals captured Woodson, and he eventually wound up in the Alton, Illinois, prison. On June 13, 1863, his jailers paroled Woodson and twelve hundred other captured Missourians and sent them cross-country to City Point, Virginia, for exchange. Toward the end of June 1863, Woodson and compatriot Edward H. Scott met with Secretary of War Seddon and received his permission to form a cavalry company made up of other exiles. Within a few weeks, Woodson and Scott recruited about seventy men, and the 1st Missouri Cavalry Company A was born.

But the new captain had a serious problem: none of the men had horses. That September the Missourians joined Colonel George Hugh Smith's 62nd Virginia, a regiment that Smith was presently converting to mounted infantry. On October 18 at Charlestown, Woodson's troops fought on foot in Imboden's victory over Colonel Benjamin Simpson's 9th Maryland Infantry. In the following months, though, the men saw little action. On January 1, 1864, the company took over provost duty in Harrisonburg, where it remained until spring.[3]

It seems that their stay in town was very enjoyable. In early February Woodson wrote a letter to the *Rockingham Register* thanking two local sisters for knitting socks for his men. In a postscript, editor John Wartmann commented that "Capt. Woodson is a gallant Missourian . . . as are also a large majority of noble fellows under his command. They are justly entitled to this mark of grateful recognition and sympathetic regard."[4]

That spring the patriotic soldiers of Woodson's company, tired of their soft duty and itching to get into action, reenlisted for "forty years or the war." Wartmann, impressed by the resolve of these exiles to fight on, remarked, "There is not, we venture to say, in the Confederate service, better soldiers than these Missouri boys. They have seen hardships enough, since they entered the service, to chill the ardor of any man not thoroughly imbued with the spirit of patriotism. . . . They are . . . not only good soldiers, but intelligent, sober, high-minded gentlemen."[5]

Before long the company rejoined the 62nd. At the May 15 Battle of New Market, the sixty-two Missourians, led into the fight by Lieutenant Scott, took a terrific pounding. Advancing with the regiment on the left center of General Breckinridge's line, the company lost, according to the *Staunton Vindicator*, at least thirty-eight killed and wounded. Another source, however, figured the casualties at sixty, while Scott counted fifty-six.[6]

Soon Robert E. Lee summoned Breckinridge east to help defend Richmond. The 62nd Virginia, including Woodson and seventeen of his men still able to fight, were among the twenty-five hundred soldiers the former U.S. vice president took with him. On June 3 the company fought in the bloody Battle of Cold Harbor. Four days later Lee again had Breckinridge's troops moving westward in response to Hunter's success at Piedmont. Finally, on June 18, Breckinridge and Early, whose Second Corps had arrived in Lynchburg just the day before, turned back Hunter's advance on the city, compelling the Yankees to retreat.

Now with Hunter out of the area, Early marched down the Shenandoah Valley to Staunton, reaching that city on June 26. Once again he commanded all Confederate forces in the valley. At Staunton the general reorganized and rested his troops before marching north on June 28 to invade Maryland.[7]

As the cavalry brigades of Brigadier Generals John McCausland, Bradley Johnson, and W. L. "Mudwall" Jackson fanned out and headed for the Potomac crossings, Early ordered Imboden's forces, including the Rangers, Woodson's company, and Harness's guerrillas, to strike the B&O in Hampshire County. While Imboden's brigade marched for the Lost River Valley, McNeill led the others to Moorefield, arriving there about eleven o'clock on Sunday morning, July 3. Just as in the Gettysburg Campaign, Imboden's troops would form the western flank of the invasion force. If the gray riders were successful in seriously damaging the line, they would prevent Hunter's army, by now camped at Parkersburg, West Virginia, from moving east by rail and attacking Early.[8]

That same day, "Old Ben" Kelley received a message from Greenland Gap. Colonel Stevenson said that Moorefield resident Jacob Powell had arrived at the pass the night before and reported that Early and Imboden were camped along Lost River and that he expected them to reach Moorefield the next evening. But a scouting party sent out by Stevenson that later viewed the Moorefield Valley from the crest of Patterson Creek Mountain, as well as another dispatched by Lieutenant Colonel Thompson from Old Town to Romney, failed to discover any rebels. In the meantime reports reaching Cumberland from Harpers Ferry, Martinsburg, Cherry Run, and other points along the B&O line had more or less convinced Kelley that the main Confederate thrust was far to the east of Cumberland. Imboden, however, was moving his way. Also on July 3, his men surprised a patrol made up of seventy-two 153rd Ohio National Guard soldiers at North River Mills. The Virginians killed one man and captured thirty-six others; the rest escaped to Paw Paw.[9]

Early on the morning of July 4, Imboden, commanding the 18th, 23rd, and 62nd regiments plus McClanahan's battery, attacked Captain James McKinney's Company B, 153rd Ohio, posted in a two-story blockhouse at South Branch Bridge and a 6th West Virginia Infantry contingent manning a "Monitor" armored railroad car. The five-hour contest was spirited, but, besides McClanahan's gunners putting the two-cannon ironclad out of commission and the rebels burning the east side of the bridge and tearing up some track, the damage did not amount to much. By the time Lieutenant Nichols and some men finally made it down from Old Town, the fighting was over. He wrote, "We . . . found the blockhouse still standing and the men in it. The gunboat car had been burned. . . . The bridge was burning on one end." After the rebels moved off eastward to French's Depot and Bloomery that afternoon, local farmer Lou McAleer reported to Kelley that "they captured only one man from this post and did little damage to the railroad. . . . Imboden's forces cannot exceed 500 men. They are mounted on indifferent horses. They took all my horses and grain; burned several canal boats."[10]

Prewar Patterson Creek Bridge. Courtesy of the B&O Railroad Museum.

About the time the fighting at the bridge started, Captain McNeill and his hundred-man detachment had descended on the Carskadon farms in the lower Patterson Creek Valley and were eating breakfast, courtesy of the Unionists. Later that morning Kelley received an urgent message from Lieutenant Colonel John F. Hoy, 6th West Virginia Infantry, commanding officer at New Creek, informing him that one of the Carskadons had just arrived with the news that at ten o'clock the raiders had left for Springfield. Shortly afterward Kelley wired Hoy and reported that "Patterson Creek has just been occupied by the enemy. I had withdrawn the company to North Branch Bridge. I presume it is McNeill's company."[11]

When the Rangers arrived at the bridge that afternoon, they discovered that the troops guarding the structure, a company from the 153rd Ohio, had already evacuated the place and retreated up the track to defend the North Branch Bridge. With these soldiers and others from the 152nd Ohio, Kelley had between two and three hundred troops at that spot, backed up by another "Monitor" and two ironclad rifle cars. Still, even with these numbers, the general suspected he did not have a sufficient force to protect it. Kelley even considered Cumberland to be in danger. Earlier the general had called on Major John B. Lewis, at nearby Clarysville General Hospital, to arm all his patients that were well enough to fight and send them to Cumberland.[12]

"On the 4th of July," Trueheart noted, "we reached the RR at Patterson Ck Station—six miles from Cumberland—burning an important bridge, RR depot—large brick tank & machinery for filling it etc. Just as we had completed it, we were attacked by 250 mt. inftry." In the meantime, at North Branch, Captain Henry Pease, 23rd Illinois, reported that advanced pickets were now engaging the enemy and requested Kelley to send some cavalry. Before long the general ordered Thompson, who had earlier left his post at Old Town to help the soldiers at the South Branch Bridge, to proceed to Patterson Creek. Not long afterward the colonel and his 150 mountaineers were riding up the C&O Canal towpath.[13]

Sometime after six o'clock that evening, Thompson was opposite the mouth of Patterson Creek. When he saw that the rebels were still about and up to their destruction, Thompson dismounted his troopers and led most of them across Frankfort Ford. The bluecoats caught the Rangers by surprise and quickly drove them off toward Frankfort. Before long, Thompson had the men's horses brought over, and the chase began.[14]

Five miles up the road, the West Virginians caught up with the Rangers. This time, however, the rebels were ready for them. "They followed us," Trueheart wrote, "when we formed and charged them killing three & capturing three Yanks and one horse. . . . Our loss one man slightly wd & two horses killed." Lieutenant Scott remembered that "Capt. McNeil was just behind some Federals, his long beard streaming in the air, and his shot gun . . . aimed for deadly fire, and woe to the one who came within its range." Nichols, whose foot soldiers had followed the cavalry to the bridge, pegged Thompson's losses as three mortally wounded and a few captured. After their thrashing, the mountaineers fell back to the bridge and Thompson sent a courier to North Branch with an appeal for forage. Pease telegraphed the request and news of the skirmish to Kelley. The disappointed commander replied, "I regret Colonel Thomson turned back, he should have followed McNeill and revenged the capture of his men at Springfield."[15]

The next day Kelley personally inspected the damaged bridge and reported to both Hunter in Parkersburg and Sigel, who, on Early's advance, had evacuated Harpers Ferry and crossed the river to the defenses atop Maryland Heights. He informed them that repairs to the trestle works there would take about two days. "Old Ben" speculated that a locomotive with three ironclad cars operating east of the South Branch, along with reinforcements that he was sending to Great Cacapon and Sir John's Run, could keep those posts from falling into Imboden's hands.[16]

On July 5 the Rangers and Woodson's company rode to catch up with Imboden's main force, but since their progress was slowed by a herd of fifty cattle, they did not fight on July 6 in the brigade's unsuccessful attempt on the railroad bridge at Great Cacapon or its repulse by troops posted at Sir John's Run. That evening the partisans caught up to the brigade either at, or near, Alpine Depot.[17]

Just about this time, the general fell ill with typhoid fever and turned command of the brigade over to Colonel Smith, then traveling to Winchester for medical treatment. Over the next two days Smith pushed the men to catch up with Early's invasion force, now marching on Frederick, Maryland. On the evening of July 8, Smith's forward units reunited with Early near that city. Later the general gave McNeill command of the rear guard.[18]

The next day, just south of Frederick, the advancing rebels found General Lew Wallace and 6,000 federals defending a line on the far side of the Monocacy River. After a hard-fought contest, the defeated Wallace withdrew toward Baltimore, leaving Early with an open road to Washington, D.C. On Sunday, July 10, Early marched most of the army toward the federal capital, leaving behind Major General Stephen D. Ramseur's division at Monocacy Junction to destroy the railroad bridge and other B&O property. Meanwhile, McNeill, with about 150 riders, patrolled to the north and west of Frederick. About ten o'clock that morning, scouts spotted Yankee horsemen approaching the city from the west. McNeill quickly formed his troopers on Market Street, between Patrick and South Streets, and got ready to waylay them.[19]

As the three hundred bluecoats were coming into Frederick, Captain Morgan McDonald, commanding Company M, 12th Pennsylvania Cavalry, noticed that some of the rebels seemed to be in a hurry to leave. Determined to sweep the Southerners out of the town, he signaled his men forward. McDonald and the vanguard rushed down Patrick Street, while another band of troopers galloped down South Street. Both detachments had no idea that the partisans were waiting for them. McDonald soon struck the right of McNeill's line.[20]

Years later, Private Scott M. Jones, of Company M, described the scene:

> Mac and his boys made a bold dash down the street to the center of town, thinking to assist in and expedite any further arrangements . . . the Rebels needed to leave the town. . . . Near the intersection of the two streets at this point, on the one running north and south, but far enough inward to be unperceived by the chargers until too late, 200 Confederate cavalry, formed in ambuscade, welcomed the boys with blunt and unkindly greetings. . . . Although causing a momentary check to the advance of the little loyal band in blue, it was quickly responded to by lively manipulation of carbine and revolver.[21]

As the enemy riders neared them, the Confederates unleashed a terrific volley. Knocked down by a blast from Hanse's double barrel, McDonald's horse lay dead in the street, its rider terribly wounded. Then saber-wielding fighters on each side went after one another viciously, their terrified mounts stirring up such a cloud of dust in the melee, that, Trueheart wrote, "you could not see more than a horses length, & that indistinctly."[22]

When the partisans gave ground, McDonald summoned up enough strength to get to his feet and order another charge. As a few soldiers helped the captain over to the nearby home of dry goods merchant Fred Markell, his troopers, Jones recalled, pitched into "the solid phalanx of horsemen" again, driving them back upon a line of Confederate infantry, which fired on the pursuers and ended the contest.[23]

Keeping their distance, the federals trailed the rebels a few miles before breaking off and returning to Frederick. Although his doctors and others thought McDonald mortally wounded, he eventually recovered. The regiment lost three men, Sergeant Augustus Singer and Privates Francis (Frank) Gallagher and John Griffith, killed in the fight. On the Confederate side, Trueheart said, "Our loss was one wounded & five missing—two of them known to be killed."[24]

On July 11 Early reached the capital's undermanned outer defenses. That afternoon skirmishing began near Fort Stevens and continued throughout the next day before Union reinforcements finally turned the tide. That night the Confederates withdrew toward Poolesville and the Potomac River. Also on July 11, the Rangers linked up with McCausland's cavalry and held a position on Early's right flank in front of Fort Reno, about four miles west of Fort Stevens, until the army retreated. Trueheart, for one, was perplexed that Early did not enter Washington. "It could have been done easily the first day and from a small sacrifice from the best lights before me." When McNeill pulled out, leaving Private James Saunders, stricken with typhoid fever, behind, the Yankees captured Saunders, along with a number of wounded rebels, at Silver Spring.[25]

But not all of the Rangers were with the company that July, during their brief sojourn in the Free State. Though seventeen-year-old Jefferson W. Duffey had only been in McNeill's company for a few months, many years later he penned a newspaper article describing a thrilling escapade that he had while riding with a small partisan detachment trying to catch up with Early's command. Upon arriving in Martinsburg, locals told the men that they were far behind the main body of troops. After talking their situation over, the soldiers decided that it would be too dangerous for their small unit to ride into Maryland.

After stopping on North Queen Street to feed their horses some oats, the men went to the Everett House, a hotel owned by George Ramer, Duffey's uncle, to plot their next move. Just as the youngster started to dismount, he heard "a pistol shot soon followed by a volley." Looking up the street, Duffey spied a squad of federal cavalry bearing down on them. Vaulting into their saddles, the graybacks sped off, with the teen bringing up the rear. Just one block away the Southerners turned right at the town square, heading for Valley Pike. When Duffey rounded the sharp turn, though, his mount slipped and fell. Pinned for an instant, he somehow got his horse back up. Noticing that one of his spurs was in the street, Duffey had just started to reach down for it when he heard a youngster shout, "Mister, you had better hurry, they are right on you."[26]

Duffey kicked his steed in the ribs and sped away. The Ranger knew his thoroughbred was fast enough to outrun his pursuers, but, as the bullets whizzed by, he feared getting hit in the back. After going five blocks, Duffey turned left onto the pike. There, to his surprise, he saw his compatriots lined up, waiting to pounce on the Yankees. In an instant, the enemy horsemen turned the corner, and the Southerners opened fire, checking their advance. Now the pursuers quickly became the pursued as the partisans chased them back up the street. After a few blocks, however, the rebels broke off the chase when they spotted more Federals waiting around the square. Duffey remarked, "We called it a drawn game and left Martinsburg."[27]

CHAPTER 14

Helping McCausland

⬡

"What could have induced such a foolish act
is a mystery to me."

On Early's return to Virginia, the Rangers and the Missourians took the lead, scouting far to the front. Once across the Potomac, the federals shadowed the Confederates and fought a few engagements with them. On July 22 General Averell reported that upon reaching Middletown, he had sent a detachment off to the west looking for the Rangers. His riders failed to catch them, however, because by July 19 the partisans were in Moorefield. For the next few days they rested their weary bodies and rundown horses. Although the men had quite a few adventures during the campaign, many regretted that the company captured only a handful of horses in Maryland.[1]

Over in Cumberland, Kelley had been anxious to locate the partisans. On July 6 he notified Colonel Stevenson that he expected McNeill to attack the railroad "at some point west." Kelley advised him "to keep the country well scouted, and keep yourself fully advised of his movements." The general also ordered out a patrol to scout a circuit from New Creek "via Knobley Road to Sheets' Mill, thence to Burlington and return via Ridgeville."[2]

On July 10 Stevenson reported erroneously that McNeill, leading two companies, was in Petersburg. Despite the fact that scouts out of New Creek had failed to locate any rebels, Stevenson's message convinced Kelley that McNeill was preparing to strike the railroad "west of New Creek." Nothing happened, but wild rumors about the Rangers' whereabouts kept reaching headquarters. Four days later Kelley wired Hunter, whose forces, after being transported by rail across West Virginia, were now camped in the river bottoms at Sir John's Run, that, "McNeill was at Romney, this a.m." He also alerted the other post commanders stationed along the track from Great Cacapon to North Branch Bridge.[3]

Since his nemesis was presently with Early, however, Kelley's search proved fruitless. On July 19 the general once again ordered Stevenson to "keep your scouts constantly active and well out in your front, be thoroughly and correctly advised of McNeill's movements." After cautioning the Ohioan that some of the Confederates now back from Maryland might be coming into the South Branch Valley, Kelley closed his message with a question: "What is your latest information of McNeill?"[4]

By the last week of the month Kelley knew that the partisans were definitely in the area. On July 26 local Unionist Abe Hinkle provided the commander with the intelligence that he expected McNeill to go after a herd of 250 cattle then grazing in the lush meadows atop the Allegheny Front. Two days later Hinkle, who would act as guide, arrived at New Creek with orders for Stevenson to send one company of the 11th West Virginia Infantry into the mountains to thwart the rebels' designs. In the meantime, however, McNeill, following Early's orders, intended to strike the railroad somewhere between Green Spring and the North Branch Bridge. First, however, the captain planned to give his men a payday.[5]

On the night of July 29–30 McNeill and a hundred partisans rode down Wagner's Hollow to the Wolford farm, crossed the track about two miles west of Green Spring, and then forded the river. Later some of Captain Archibald McNair's pickets at Green Spring heard cavalry riding over the upper canal bridge into Old Town. Shortly McNair had his men ready for action. From their position near the railroad the bluecoats could hear men talking in the distance, but they finally concluded they were probably just some 6th West Virginia Cavalry troopers returning from a patrol.[6]

In the meantime, once across the canal, a handful of Rangers fanned out and sealed off all of the exits from the village. The rest of the outfit then broke into the town's few stores and robbed them. After gathering up their plunder, along with one unfortunate soldier and two horses, the raiders crossed back into West Virginia. There they cut the telegraph lines and knocked down three poles, but they did not have enough time to damage the railroad. Upon reaching Wolford's, the rear guard gathered a dozen cattle and twenty sheep.[7]

Once again the Buckeyes heard riders crossing the upper canal bridge. This time, however, Lieutenant Nichols suspected something was wrong. Taking two men with him, he hurried over to Old Town. When they got there, the last of the partisans had just left. The trio rushed back to camp, where Nichols gathered up nine more soldiers, and hoping to catch a straggler or two, started after the graybacks. Upon approaching the Taylor farm, about a mile from camp, the group spied a lone rebel riding up the lane to the house and then watched him dismount. When they rushed out of the woods, hoping to surround the dwelling and capture the man, he spotted them, mounted up, and took off. Nichols wrote, "George Sargent fired at him first. Bill Hillis next, then John

Stall, then all the rest, and if he didn't lay flat on his horse and go it! Hillis' ball struck him along the side of his head and wounded him severely. He hurried the rear guard up and that was the last our folks could see of them."[8]

Three or four hours later the partisans reached Springfield. Suddenly, though, Thompson's 6th West Virginia came charging into the village from the west. The Rangers, swiftly jettisoning their purloined livestock and any other plunder that would slow them down, galloped off. The bluecoats kept on their trail through Romney and followed them another six miles out of town, before stopping their pursuit.[9]

Although Kelley had his mind firmly fixed on stopping McNeill's depredations, some events then transpiring in the Shenandoah and Cumberland Valleys would soon get his full attention. On July 24 at Kernstown, just south of Winchester, Early's forces routed General Crook's Army of West Virginia, inflicting approximately twelve hundred casualties on the federals and killing Colonel Mulligan. Two days later Crook was north of the Potomac. In the meantime, Early's men once again inflicted significant destruction on the B&O line.

On July 28 McCausland and Johnson's brigades, numbering approximately fourteen hundred men each, rendezvoused at Hammond's Mill, near Hedgesville. Previously that day, Early had instructed McCausland to take both brigades to Chambersburg, "capture the city and deliver to the proper authorities a proclamation which General Early had issued, calling for them to furnish me $100,000 in gold or $500,000 in greenbacks." If the citizens did not pay the ransom, he was to burn the city. The commander's harsh order was in retaliation to Hunter's cavalry's burning of a number of private residences in the lower Shenandoah Valley earlier that month.[10]

At dawn on July 29 McCausland's horsemen began crossing the Potomac at McCoy's Ford, and after some skirmishing with Union forces later that day east of Clear Spring and south of Mercersburg, they reached the latter around five in the afternoon. The Confederates moved on through the night, and despite encountering some resistance from a small band of federal troops, arrived on the western outskirts of Chambersburg about dawn. After firing some shells over the town, the rebels started entering the city at five-thirty. Following breakfast at a local hotel, the general got to his task.[11]

McCausland had planned on meeting with city leaders and presenting Early's demand. The brigadier and his staff, however, were unable to find any of the officials. After reading a proclamation to the folks gathered in the Diamond, the center of town, McCausland gave them time to gather the funds. But many of the people thought the Confederates were bluffing, and they did not intend to hand over any hard-earned money to McCausland and his band of

ragamuffins. Even if they had wanted
to, though, bank officials, previously
alerted that raiders were about, had
already spirited most of the needed
funds northward. After waiting two
hours for the people to deliver the
ransom, the general gave the order
to burn Chambersburg. His soldiers
went about their work quickly, and
over the next few hours started fires
that destroyed 559 businesses, private
dwellings, and other buildings.[12]

About midday the Southerners
left town, riding west on the Bed-
ford-Chambersburg Turnpike. After
traveling some twenty-five miles,
the gray horsemen reached McConnellsburg that evening. As his men
robbed citizens along the streets and
ransacked the stores, McCausland

John McCausland. Author's collection.

requisitioned two thousand meals from the frightened locals. That evening
his brigade camped on the eastern edge of McConnellsburg, while Johnson's
men rested in the fields along Great Cove Road, just south of the village. The
next morning, July 31, the two brigades headed south for Hancock.[13]

By this time Averell's troopers were following them. Early on the morning of July 30, couriers had informed the brigadier of the rebels' advance on
Chambersburg. Instead of riding directly into the town and chasing them
off, he decided to gamble that after leaving Chambersburg the Confederates
would strike east. He first led his men from Greencastle to New Franklin and
then to Greenwood, located on the Cashtown Turnpike, about ten miles east
of Chambersburg. While waiting to intercept his prey, Averell was greatly surprised when he viewed a tremendous column of smoke rising in the distance.

That afternoon, once the general became convinced that the raiders were
not coming his way, he led his men into Chambersburg, where they witnessed
a scene of utter desolation. Passing on through, that evening Averell's horsemen
stopped at the eastern base of Tuscarora Mountain. The next morning his
advance easily routed some Confederates posted at the crest of the mountain
before descending into McConnellsburg. After pausing to get something to
eat, the troopers swung back into the saddle and rode south.[14]

Shortly before noon that Sunday, the Southerners appeared in Hancock. Quickly attracting some attention from the guns of a "Monitor" car parked at Alpine Depot a few well-aimed shells from the rebel artillery struck the locomotive's firebox and smokestack. Captain Peter H. Petrie, 2nd Maryland Potomac Home Brigade Infantry, immediately ordered the engineer to back up the track and out of range. Later on, about a hundred soldiers guarding the depot broke off long-range skirmishing with rebel marksmen across the Potomac and then jogged about a mile and boarded the train. Now Petrie moved on to Sir John's Run. Once there, the officer telegraphed Kelley the news from Hancock and then ordered the engineer to continue to Great Cacapon.[15]

Throughout the afternoon, rebel soldiers robbed Hancock's stores, torched a few canal boats, and accosted some locals, including a Catholic priest who was relieved of his gold watch by one raider. Later McCausland decided to levy on the citizens a tribute of $30,000 and five thousand meals. He emphasized to them that failure to comply would result in his troops burning the town. When Johnson, who was still disturbed over the burning of Chambersburg, heard this, he confronted the general and issued a strong protest. Johnson explained that not only was Hancock in Maryland, with many Southern sympathizers among its inhabitants, but it was impossible for the people to meet his monetary demands. McCausland, though, refused to rescind his order, and for a time it appeared as if the two headstrong officers and some of their loyal troops might settle the matter with their revolvers.

While all of this was going on, Averell was closing in on Hancock. At about six o'clock that evening, Yankee skirmishers and the rebel rear guard started exchanging rifle fire in the pine hills and fields along Baptist Church Road, just north of the town. Meanwhile, McCausland hurriedly ordered his troops back into the saddle, leaving Major Harry Gilmor's 2nd Maryland Cavalry Battalion behind to slow the Yankees down. The raiders rode west on the mountainous National Pike toward Cumberland, the tired men and horses plodding on throughout the night before finally stopping at the hamlet of Bevansville about three o'clock on the morning of August 1. Since leaving McConnellsburg, the rebels had ridden over forty miles. Back in Hancock, Averell had broken off pursuit the previous evening, his men and horses almost completely exhausted.[16]

Over in Cumberland, an anxious Kelley, now sure that McCausland intended attacking the Queen City, had been gathering his troops and even local volunteers, and he positioned many of them across a ridge, about two miles east of town, that commanded the pike. Near Old Town, Colonel Israel Stough had 450 soldiers from his 153rd Ohio National Guard, plus a few other miscellaneous

W. W. Averell. Library of Congress.

troops, ready to stop any rebel force from crossing the river. Later Petrie's train arrived at Green Spring to reinforce the Buckeyes.[17]

Sometime between three thirty and four in the afternoon along the pike, fighting broke out between the rebel vanguard and the well-dug-in Yankees. During the engagement, now called the Battle of Folck's Mill, McCausland quickly realized that it was going to be impossible to force his way into Cumberland. The brigadier, fearing that Averell might arrive suddenly and capture his artillery and baggage train, ordered Gilmor to find a route to the nearest river crossing. The major soon found an unwilling local, who, at the point of a gun, reluctantly led the scout some distance back down the pike to Old Soldiers Road, a rugged track that led south toward the ford at Old Town. Gilmor then notified McCausland about his discovery. After breaking off the four-hour skirmish at dusk, the general waited another three hours before retreating.[18]

That night, slowly making his way along the rough mountain trail, Gilmor led his 2nd Maryland battalion, followed by the rest of the column, to Williams Road and, turning east, continued to its junction with Mill Run Road. The guide indicated this track intersected the Braddock Road, some distance west of the village. It was hard going. During their night march, according to the recollection of Private Clifton M. Nichols, 152nd Ohio National Guard, "The Rebels ... left a large quantity of artillery ammunition in the mountains—also several caissons."[19]

Nearing Braddock Road, Gilmor ran into a Yankee ambush. Luckily for him, however, their bullets sailed high, and the major and his companions were uninjured. After establishing a skirmish line, he sent out scouts to reconnoiter Old Town. The major also dispatched a rider back through the column to tell Johnson to hurry. At dawn on August 2, his scouts returned with the bad news that there were, as Gilmor remembered, "eight hundred infantry and an iron-clad battery at the ford, to dispute our crossing." Gilmor, desiring to capture the upper canal bridge at the western end of town, started his men forward in a dense early morning fog. The advance, commanded by Lieutenant William Kemp, quickly stumbled into another Yankee trap, losing one man killed and two wounded. Not long afterward General Johnson, the major, and his battalion attempted to reach the bridge before some bluecoats, whom they spotted working hard taking up its flooring, could finish the job. But Stough's main force posted atop Alum Ridge, a hill between the canal and the river, fired on the Marylanders and forced them to take cover.[20]

Stymied there, Gilmor and his men soon worked their way to the east end of town and the lower canal bridge. In the meantime, other rebels finally captured the upper bridge and quickly cobbled together enough flooring to get across.

Eventually they forced the Ohioans off Alum Ridge and across the ford to Green Spring. Once there, Petrie's guns and marksmen posted in the blockhouse backed them up. Subsequently they repulsed—bloodily—numerous grayback attempts at crossing the North Branch.[21]

Finally, however, Gilmor convinced Lieutenant John R. McNulty to take a section of the 2nd Maryland Artillery, cross the upper bridge, and get in a good position to shell the train. Despite a harrowing charge, in which two of his horses were killed and had to be dragged along in their traces, McNulty reached the top of the ridge about ten o'clock that morning and swiftly put the ironclad's locomotive out of commission with a shot through its boiler. Unfortunately for the Confederates, he was not able to bring his guns to bear on the blockhouse. Inside the fortification, its stout wooden walls impervious to bullets, the Ohio riflemen commanded the river crossing.[22]

By this time most of the defenders had boarded another train and sped off to Cumberland. During all of the confusion, one of Stough's officers had mistakenly thought that everyone was aboard and ordered the engineer to depart, leaving the colonel and eighty-three men stranded.[23]

To keep from losing any more troopers and to prevent a pursuing federal force from trapping them, about midday Johnson sent a messenger under a white flag to the blockhouse. He met with the colonel and presented McCausland's demand for an immediate surrender. Stough soon sent back a list of four conditions, which included a demand that McCausland parole all of his soldiers. Upon reading Stough's requests, both generals agreed. After a short meeting with Johnson, the colonel ordered his troops to lay down their arms and evacuate the blockhouse. The Confederates then proceeded to destroy the fortification, along with the "Monitor" car, the nearby engine house, and water station. Their effort to burn the nearby South Branch Bridge was partially successful.[24]

At about four o'clock that afternoon, the raiders rode south to Springfield, and once there Johnson's troops camped along the South Branch, just east of the village, while most of McCausland's Virginians gathered atop a hill to the west. In the meantime, Harry Gilmor's battalion scoured the local farms upriver for fresh mounts. It was during this time that Captain McNeill met McCausland and reported the destruction that day of the Wire Bridge. His men had cut one of the structure's suspension cables, throwing its deck into the water.[25]

Not many days before, Early had ordered McNeill to destroy the bridge, which, to this point of the war, had been useful to both sides. In his entry for August 2, 1864, local farmer George W. Washington recorded:

I heard a lot of Rebels had gone down this morning on their way to Cumberland. I met Michael Blue, who informed me that the rebels had thrown down the wire bridge. What could have induced such a foolish act is a mystery to me. When I got there, sure enough, I found it in the river. They must have known it would be a great public loss. I wish from the bottom of my heart, the originator of the thing had been caught under it and sent to the bottom of the river.[26]

That evening Hanse rode out of Springfield with a hundred men to strike the railroad. About six miles west of Cumberland they crossed the North Branch at Brady's Mills, and according to a B&O report they "cut telegraph wires on the 2nd, also destroyed 22 feet span over Warrior's Run and two culverts on the 184th mile from Baltimore." The Rangers also captured two Union soldiers at Brady's Mill, Sergeant Michael Dunn and William H. Helm, of Company I, 6th West Virginia Infantry.[27]

After fording the river back into West Virginia, on August 3 the partisans began sweeping Patterson Creek Valley looking for cattle and horses. Captain Dennis B. Jeffers, 6th West Virginia Cavalry, notified Kelley from Frankfort that the raiders had taken all of "Seymour's cattle. They are scouring through the country in the direction of Burlington and gathering all stock, cattle, and horses; all they can find." Later that day Kelley received a report from New Creek that "McNeill had captured Maryland cavalry at Sheet's Mill."[28]

After completing the raid, most of the Rangers began driving the livestock to Moorefield. The captain and a few others, however, rode to Romney, where McNeill met McCausland, whose troops earlier that day had entered the town. Hanse reported damaging the track west of Cumberland and added that only three hundred soldiers protected the important Union supply depot at New Creek.[29]

Acting on McNeill's information, McCausland decided to attack the rail town. The commander, now needing to move as fast as possible, had already sent many of his dismounted and wounded men, wagons, and broken-down horses on their way back to the Shenandoah Valley. McCausland, accompanied by McNeill and some Rangers, subsequently led his brigade to Junction, camping along Mill Creek, and the next morning, August 4, he was ready to move on the federal stronghold. A little while later Johnson's horsemen arrived on the west side of Mechanicsburg Gap.[30]

That afternoon the Confederates attacked New Creek, seizing the unmanned Fort Piano, perched on the steep heights above the town but failing to oust the garrison from Fort Fuller. Stevenson's troops then held the rebels at bay until reinforcements from Cumberland, slowed down by having to change to another train at Warrior's Run Bridge, arrived at four o'clock and, in fierce fighting, pushed the Southerners back. Later on a disgruntled McCausland broke off the engagement and retreated to Burlington.[31]

On August 5 the raiders marched for Old Fields. Upon reaching his destination, McCausland posted Johnson's brigade in and around the village, while his men camped just across the South Branch. During this time Hanse tried to advise the general "where and how to post the pickets," but the twenty-seven-year-old commander ignored the suggestions. The miffed captain then washed his hands of the matter and led the company to Peru.[32]

In the meantime Averell, his command now reinforced by troopers from the 1st New York Cavalry and the 22nd Pennsylvania Cavalry, was on his way to chastise the Confederates, and on the morning of August 4 he crossed the Potomac at Hancock. After stops in Sir John's Run and Bath, he continued to Bloomery, reaching the gap at midnight. On August 5 the federals marched to Slanesville, then over South Branch Mountain, before finally reaching Springfield about five o'clock in the afternoon. The trip was demanding on man and beast. Two days of hard marching had already cost Averell a hundred horses and riders. Now his column numbered only sixteen hundred men.[33]

After being resupplied with food and forage—and, most of all, getting some rest—the bluecoats were back in the saddle the next morning. They rode into Romney at approximately eleven o'clock. There Averell soon learned that McCausland was near Moorefield, and before long the general, figuring that the rebels would probably return to the Shenandoah Valley via Wardensville, ordered Major Work to take a battalion and block Lost River Gap. In a little while Work and his men left town on Grassy Lick Road, and that afternoon Averell and the rest of his command moved out for Moorefield.[34]

Ranger Private William H. Maloney was also in Romney that day. When the federals came into the town, the teenager quickly rode west, but then he stopped and hid in the woods near the ruins of the turnpike's covered bridge. From a distance he watched the bluecoats ford the river and estimated their numbers as being between seventeen hundred and two thousand men. After the federals had moved on, Maloney hurried down Trough Road, using the shorter but more rugged route to Moorefield. Along the way he picked up his friend Isaac Parsons. At first the pair made good time, but then a hard rain slowed them down. Just after midnight on August 7, they finally reached town. Upon discovering McCausland's headquarters were at Samuel A. McMechen's house along Main Street, Maloney hurried there and reported his news to the general. When the private suggested ambushing the Yankees in Reynolds Gap, the general replied."When I need your advice, I may send for you." Afterward McMechen permitted the Ranger to stay there for the night.[35]

McCausland soon dispatched a courier to Johnson's headquarters at Daniel McNeill's mansion, Willow Wall, in Old Fields to inform Johnson of this new development. Shortly the brigadier sent out patrols to look for the enemy, but his men, hampered by dense fog, came back empty-handed. A few hours later, though, just beyond Reynolds Gap, gray-clad Yankee horsemen surprised and captured his pickets. Later Averell's horsemen swept through Johnson's camp, crossed the river, and after a sharp engagement routed McCausland's men. When the fighting was over, rebel casualties numbered 464, including 417 captured. Averell lost just 47 men.[36]

In Moorefield that morning, a blissfully unaware Maloney had already been out to the barn, fed and saddled his horse, and was just about to eat breakfast when a servant yelled,"Run, Mr. Maloney! De town am full ob Yankees!" Maloney sprinted outside, mounted his steed, and luckily escaped with the mob of graybacks fleeing the town. Ignoring the calls of furious locals shouting for them to stay and fight, they soon disappeared.[37]

Once safely out of the village, Maloney watched from a distant hilltop as the conquering federals entered Moorefield along Main Street. But the proud victors did not stay in town long. After Averell crossed back over the South Branch and retired through Reynolds Gap, Maloney and some compatriots went out to the battlefield, where they tried to help some of the wounded and later got around to the tough job of burying the dead.[38]

In a few days Early ordered McNeill to send his men out to gather cattle for his army. During the coming weeks, portions of the company and Woodson's riders traveled into the Alleghenies, and keeping a sharp lookout for federal patrols and local bushwhackers, gathered up what livestock they could and drove it over the mountains to help feed Early's always hungry, always malnourished fighters. Although the Rangers were not now actively involved in Early and Sheridan's bloody struggle for control of the Shenandoah Valley, that would soon change.[39]

CHAPTER 15

Meems Bottom

"I can do no more for
my country."

The military and political concerns raised by Early's attack on the capital and McCausland's burning of Chambersburg led U. S. Grant on July 31, 1864, to order Army of Potomac cavalry commander Major General Philip Sheridan to the Shenandoah Valley. In Grant's original plan, Major General Daniel Hunter was to remain in command of the Department of West Virginia. If he decided to accompany his forces in the field, Sheridan would lead the Sixth Corps, but if Hunter chose to remain at headquarters, Sheridan would command all troops on the march.[1]

On August 6 Sheridan met Grant at Monocacy Junction. There Grant informed his lieutenant of Hunter's sudden resignation and that the thirty-three-year-old West Point graduate was now in command of the Middle Military District.[2]

At their conference, Grant ordered Sheridan to first concentrate his forces around Harpers Ferry and then follow Early and attack him "wherever found." He cautioned "Little Phil" not to extend his army too deep into the Shenandoah Valley and authorized him to take from the valley farmers all the livestock and provisions he needed and then destroy the rest.[3]

After settling in at Harpers Ferry, Sheridan estimated that "the force I could take in the field at this time numbered about 26,000 men." It included the Army of the Shenandoah, made up of Major General Horatio Wright's three-division Sixth Corps and Brigadier General William Dwight's division from the Nineteenth Corps, along with George Crook's two-division Army of West Virginia. Sheridan gave Major General Alfred Torbert, just arrived from outside Petersburg, Virginia, with his cavalry division, command of the army's entire mounted arm, including Averell's horsemen, not yet back from Moorefield.[4]

As the combative general got his troops ready to go after Early, over in Cumberland, Kelley's main concern was locating the Rangers. In an August 15 message to his adjutant, Captain P. G. Bier, the recently promoted brevet major general remarked that since the hundred-day enlistments of his Ohio National Guard troops would soon expire, he feared not having enough soldiers available to protect the rail line or public property. He also noted, "We have 1500 sick in the hospital, liable to capture by McNeill."[5]

Two days later Kelley ordered Stevenson to send "one company of the Eleventh Virginia and a detachment of cavalry—say twenty men" to investigate a report that McNeill and some of his men were at Mechanicsburg Gap. The patrol left New Creek and traveled by Knobly Road to the pass, and then on to Romney, but found the Rangers long gone. On August 22 mountain guide Abe Hinkle and Stevenson both wired Kelley of a large rebel force in Moorefield, leading the general to suppose that McNeill intended to raid toward Oakland. Kelley ordered the colonel to send a force to Greenland Gap "to learn, if possible, the movements of McNeill." He then wired Captain Joseph Faris at Oakland and told him to be on the lookout for McNeill.[6]

Six days later Kelley telegraphed Faris to say that some dismounted Rangers had been spotted east of Fort Pendleton and ordered the captain to "send a scout of twenty men . . . to assist Captain Godwin in driving them out." The general also told Colonel Hoy to dispatch a twenty-man patrol from New Creek "to the Junction on Allegheny Mountains to ascertain if any of McNeill's men are in the neighborhood. Get Hinkle to go with them."[7]

While Kelley was watching what was going on in the high country, things were starting to heat up closer to home. That same day Captain Charles J. Harrison, Company I, 153rd Ohio National Guard, wired Kelley from South Branch Bridge that he had a "report that McNeill was coming down the South Branch, for purpose, as is supposed, of getting on the railroad at some point." In the meantime Harrison sent a scout to Romney to watch for the Rangers and posted some soldiers along a ridge near Springfield to waylay the partisans if they came that way.[8]

The next afternoon the captain reported that a Mr. Caldwell said that the Rangers were at Romney the night before and that at least one partisan had flanked Union pickets and scouted the camp at Green Spring. On August 30 he added that some Confederates had been in Springfield shoeing their horses. A "colored man" had also told him that Imboden's command was somewhere between Romney and the Wire Bridge. Just before ten o'clock that night, another message from Hinkle reached headquarters. "McNeill left Moorefield yesterday morning," he wrote, "with about 300 men, started in the direction of Romney, and from all I can learn he is making a raid on the railroad east of Cumberland."[9]

Nevertheless, Kelley still expected McNeill to launch his company on a livestock raid into the Alleghenies and cautioned Hoy to "keep your scouts active and on the alert I think McNeill intends striking west instead of east of this point." On the thirty-first, though, he was finally sure of McNeill's location, noting in a message to Averell that McNeill and 250 men were between Romney and the Wire Bridge. For a time, however, there was no other mention of the partisans' activities.[10]

Meanwhile, over in the Shenandoah Valley, Early and Sheridan kept their armies active until September 19, when, in a bitterly contested daylong fight, Sheridan's forces drove Old Jube's tenacious though outnumbered fighters out of Winchester. Three days later, at Strasburg, the Northerners smashed rebel defenses on Fisher's Hill and forced the badly beaten army to retreat farther up the valley.[11]

During September, reports of McNeill's whereabouts were rare. On the seventh, Trueheart wrote to his brother Charles that he was just coming off a long cattle raid into the Alleghenies and was now leading "twenty men guarding a wagon train through a country infested with Swamps." Four days later Home Guard captain John Boggs reported to West Virginia governor Arthur I. Boreman that the Rangers were also buying cattle and hogs from so-called sworn men, who would drive livestock to Franklin or Petersburg and sell them for hard coin at auction. That same day, September 11, Confederate riflemen seriously wounded Captain John Bond in a skirmish along South Mill Creek, near Petersburg. But it was not until the twenty-ninth that a patrol led by Captain George M. Ellicott, Brigadier General Alfred Duffié's chief of scouts, ran into some of the Rangers at Washington's Ford. He attacked them and later reported killing one, wounding one, and taking two prisoners. That night McNeill struck Ellicott's camp near the Widow Reese's residence. The Unionists, though, were able to hold their ground and suffered no casualties.[12]

Back along the South Fork, McNeill knew of Early's plight and decided to help. In his story about the Rangers, Missourian W. D. Vandiver related that in late September McNeill and his men had just returned from another raid into the Alleghenies. "The cattle were left grazing on the sides of the mountains," he wrote, "and McNeill with sixty of his men was undertaking a desperate raid into the Shenandoah Valley, fully believing that Sheridan would be driven back, and he would intercept his retreat."[13]

Private Duffey noted that McNeill understood that Sheridan's army, now camped in and around Harrisonburg, had one serious disadvantage: the commander's Winchester supply base was sixty-seven miles away. "Captain McNeill concluded," Duffey wrote, "to make a reconnaissance of the immediate territory with a view of intercepting one of Sheridan's supply trains." On September 30

McNeill divided his command, leaving Lieutenant Welton and half the men at the Cove, a remote campsite in the rugged mountains of eastern Hardy. Hanse then led fifty or more troopers to the valley. Private James Vallandingham added that McNeill left men behind because "his forced marches had so broken down many of the horses." But before riding off the captain stated "that those who chose to do so could make up small squads and harass small bodies of the enemy between their main body and their base of supplies at Winchester."[14]

Upon reaching the Orkney Springs vicinity that evening, the captain sent Privates John and Joseph Triplett off to reconnoiter Mount Jackson, their hometown, and see what they could find out. Before the brothers returned, though, Hanse got word of a supply train nearing Edinburg, some seven miles north of Mount Jackson. Quickly calling on his troopers to mount up, he started leading them down Back Road, a byway just west of the Valley Pike. Soon the raiders were in position to strike, but after a careful reconnaissance of the heavily guarded wagons, McNeill called off the attack.[15]

That night the hungry graybacks camped in the hills with nothing to eat. The next day, Sunday, October 2, the partisans retraced their tracks up Back Road. Along the trail, McNeill received information that a hundred Union cavalrymen were guarding the turnpike bridge over the North Fork of the Shenandoah River at Meems Bottom, just south of Mount Jackson. Right away, Hanse started planning a dawn attack on the camp. Not only could he burn the bridge, but also, if successful, the men could get some food and capture some badly needed horses. In the meantime, the men began hearing the sound of heavy cannonading southward.[16]

Thinking that he might cause Sheridan problems if Early's fighters somehow forced the Yankees to retreat, McNeill swiftly sent four troopers to torch an unguarded bridge at Edinburg. Although the people were happy to see the quartet ride into town, they became frightened when the troopers told them their mission. The women, fearing Yankees would burn the town if the men destroyed the structure, steadfastly refused to give the rebels any matches or firebrands. The four, however, readily sympathized with the locals' plight and decided to set fire to a nearby pile of wet straw. The rising column of smoke fooled McNeill and the others into thinking they had burned the bridge.[17]

When the cannonading finally subsided, McNeill decided to return to his original plan of attacking the bridge. That night Captain Hugh Ramsey Koontz, Company K, 7th Virginia Cavalry, guided the now thirty or so partisans on a roundabout eight-mile trek that ended just four hundred yards east of the camp. McNeill, seated aboard his "swift, tough little roan," then sent three men ahead to get a closer look. When the trio returned, Hanse spread his horsemen out

Meems Bottom. Author's collection.

in a long line. Although he had planned a dawn attack, McNeill knew it would be too dangerous to tarry any longer. At four in the morning of October 3, the intrepid captain signaled his troopers forward.[18]

"The advance was made in order and quiet," Duffey remembered," even the tramp of the horses was muffled by the sod of the meadow." Suddenly, about two hundred yards from the camp, an alert sentry called out and promptly fired. McNeill shouted "Charge!" and his howling Phantoms of the South Fork surged into the camp.[19]

Captain James Jackson was commanding the cavalry guarding the bridge that morning. His sixty-man detachment consisted of troopers from Companies E, F, and G, 14th Pennsylvania Cavalry. Jackson also had a small squad on picket duty at the north end of Mount Jackson, and about a mile to the south, other soldiers were on lookout atop Rude's Hill. Apprehensive of a night attack, Jackson had earlier ordered his men to keep their horses saddled and bridled.[20]

The Pennsylvanians had been in the forefront of the August 7 attack on Bradley Johnson's camp at Old Fields. Now, half awake, they were in the same position that their foes had been in that morning. The charging partisans wounded six men, including two stragglers from the supply train, and captured most of the rest. Lieutenant Albert Hague and nine enlisted men, however, made it over the bridge and safely reached the picket post north of town. Lieutenant John H. Neismith and three soldiers galloped away to the south. The fight had lasted just five minutes.[21]

The Rangers only suffered one casualty, but it was a most important one. While the men were busy corralling the prisoners, gathering horses, and torching the bridge, no one noticed that McNeill was down. At last Corporal Davy Parsons discovered Hanse on the ground, shot in the back, "lying on his left side," Duffey recalled, "with his head raised on his elbow." As the men gathered around their stricken leader, the captain summoned enough strength to make clear the escape route he wanted them to take. Then McNeill gave his Rangers an order: "Move at once and leave me to my fate." But his devoted followers ignored him, and five of the band gently hoisted the captain onto his mount and then moved slowly up the pike toward Rude's Hill.[22]

Shortly, however, all realized that the captain was hurt too badly to continue, and they would have to leave him behind. After traveling less than a mile, the Rangers and their forty-four prisoners stopped at Locust Grove, the home of the Reverend Addison and Elizabeth Weller. The men helped Hanse off his horse and laid him carefully on the ground. Elizabeth remembered that as his followers gathered close to bid farewell, McNeill roused himself to speak. "Jesse, my son, take charge of the prisoners and you and my men do the best you can and move on." To the rest, he added, "Goodbye my boys, leave me to my fate. I can do no more for my country." As the graybacks mounted up and began to ride away, Private Nelson Kiracofe got off his horse and returned to offer a petition to the Lord for his mortally wounded chieftain. After he finished, Kiracofe, who had followed the old man for about a year, rejoined the column. Mrs. Weller added that "the captain's eyes followed them as long as they were in sight."[23]

As the Rangers and their captives headed west, some unidentified Yankees rode after them. Trailing at a distance, the bluecoats fired a number of stray rounds, making sure they did not hit their friends. Seeing that they could do no good, however, the troopers soon gave up the chase. Upon reaching North Mountain, Jesse sent Parsons to Hardy County to get Jemima McNeill. In the meantime, others paroled most of the prisoners but kept their horses. "Sworn on the virgin rocks and released," Duffey wrote, "they scampered down the mountainside like children let out of school." On October 7 General Sheridan, mistakenly identifying them as troopers from the 8th Ohio Cavalry, reported to U. S. Grant that "I learned that fifty-six of them have reached Winchester."[24]

Back at Locust Grove, McNeill had asked Elizabeth to help relieve his severe pain. According to her account, the bullet had lodged at the base of his spine, paralyzing him. Trying to ease his misery, Elizabeth first got him a cup of coffee and then gave him some morphine a Union doctor had left with her.

Weller House, 2016. Courtesy Nancy Grandstaff Shrum.

When McNeill drifted off to sleep, the Wellers and some of their servants rolled him onto a blanket and carried the captain into the house. After some difficulty, they got McNeill upstairs to the couple's bedroom.[25]

When Hanse awoke, Elizabeth told him that some Union soldiers had been there and left. Not long afterward, McNeill agreed to her request to cut his hair and shave his beard. She reasoned that his new appearance could fool any Northerners who might stop by. If it did not, they would haul him off and most likely burn the house. Elizabeth wrote, "His appearance was completely changed, and I told him that if anyone came in he must be rational but let me do the talking." Later that afternoon some soldiers stopped by and dropped off a wounded Massachusetts officer named Welch. No doubt that when these men got to camp they reported that McNeill was at Locust Grove. The rumor spread fast, and that evening at his headquarters in Weston, West Virginia, General Kelley received a wire from his son, William, in Cumberland: "Harness in command of McNeill's and his own company; McNeill wounded."[26]

As a hard rain fell, McNeill passed a restless night. The next morning, October 4, some Yankee doctors who had stopped by to treat Welch, walked upstairs to see the patient. Heeding Mrs. Weller's advice, Hanse lay still and did not speak. A few hours later, though, a squad of troopers arrived at the house and asked if McNeill was there. Mrs. Weller replied that there was only "Lieut. Welch and a man Hanson, by name, of the Southern army." She took them into his room, but they did not recognize him. When the soldiers were leaving, one said that "they would return and bring someone who would know whether it was Capt. McNeill or not." Vallandingham remembered hearing that Brigadier General George A. Custer had sent the soldiers after hearing a report that McNeill was there and "determined if possible to get hold of him."[27]

That evening Jemima, Jesse, and a few of the men finally arrived. Mrs. McNeill promptly took over as her husband's nurse. Sometime before they showed up, Dr. Leonidas Triplett, father of the two Rangers from Mount Jackson, came by and examined the captain. "The ball," Duffey wrote, "had entered near the spinal column on the left side, between the lower rib and thigh." The surgeon concluded that one of McNeill's own men had mistakenly shot the captain. He then sent John Triplett to find a chicken. When he returned, the famished captain eventually got some soothing hot broth and an egg.[28]

Once they thought about it, some Rangers concluded that McNeill's wounding had not been accidental but the result of a run-in with a wandering rebel who had recently attached himself to the band. Reflecting on it years later, though, Duffey related, "A mature judgment, however, has discredited that suspicion." Welton, who had not been at the skirmish, agreed. "It can never be definitely known whether he received this wound from friend or foe." As he wrote, "He may have been shot accidently in the dark, and in a hand-to-hand fight it is hard to tell friend from enemy."[29]

Vallandingham described George Valentine, the suspected assassin, as "a good soldier and had become somewhat popular in a short time, for he could tell a good joke with much humor and sung in a charming style songs of the sea and of love and war."[30]

But even after twenty years, Vallandingham firmly believed that Valentine was the guilty party:

A few nights before the fifty-seven were chosen . . . near Orkney Mountain, some chickens were stolen. . . . Complaint was made to the captain and upon investigation; he concluded that George Valentine . . . was the guilty party. He put Valentine under arrest and used most violent and abusive language towards him. Valentine swore he would have revenge for this. Yet so magnanimous was McNeill (who never harbored revengeful feelings) that he forgot and overlooked the matter and took Valentine with him on the desperate attempt to destroy the bridge over the Shenandoah at Mount Jackson.

When the men formed in line to charge, Valentine was in the center. As soon as the charge began, after hanging back a minute, he rode rapidly in the rear of the line towards the right where Captain McNeill was. Just as the order to cease firing was given, Captain McNeill was mortally wounded by a shot fired from his right rear. No man of McNeill's command has ever seen Valentine since that day.[31]

According to Mrs. Weller, "It was three days before the Yankees returned bringing with them Simon Miller, a Ranger deserter." According to company records, Miller, before disappearing on April 13, 1864, had been with the Rangers for about thirteen months. Well known for his bravery and devotion to the cause, the Rockingham County native ran off just after recovering from a serious wound. The troopers brought Miller into the house. As he entered, the man immediately recognized Elizabeth, a former friend. As Miller passed by, she touched his arm discreetly. Once in the bedroom, he looked straight into the eyes of his old commander. To her relief, Elizabeth then heard him say, "No gentlemen, you are mistaken in the man."[32]

Now Sheridan's army began moving down the valley. By this time his troops had burned two thousand barns and seventy mills. They had also taken tons of foodstuffs and slaughtered livestock for their own use. On October 7, from Woodstock, Sheridan wrote Grant: "In moving back to this point the whole country from the Blue Ridge to the North Mountains has been made untenable for the Rebel army."[33]

A day or so before, Sheridan had stopped at Locust Grove. Accompanied by his surgeon, Major William McKinley, and some other officers, the general entered the house and went up to McNeill's room. At first, according to Duffey, "Little Phil" quizzed McNeill about the attack on the bridge. Suddenly he asked the stricken warrior, "Are you not McNeill yourself?" McNeill replied, "I am." At this time, the doctor walked over to the bed, put out his hand, and expressed his sadness. "Captain McNeill," he said, "I know you, and am sorry to find you in this condition. I was once a prisoner in your hands, and your treatment was so magnanimous, I now hold myself ready to render you any service in my power." His promise to help Hanse proved true. Before departing the next morning, the doctor left him some food, painkillers, and "liquid spirits."[34]

Sheridan was certain that McNeill was going to die. In the same October 7 message, he told Grant that "McNeill was mortally wounded and fell into our hands. This is fortunate, as he was the most daring and dangerous of the bushwhackers in this section of the country."[35]

By this time, however, McNeill was probably resting in Hill's Hotel in

Harrisonburg. In her version of the captain's escape, Elizabeth Weller wrote, "That very night we procured a carriage and moved him beyond the lines of Harrisonburg." Duffey later recalled that sometime after Sheridan left the premises, the general sent back a squad with an ambulance to pick up McNeill. "The Weller family," Duffey wrote, "had conjectured the ominous silence of General Sheridan, and, but a few hours before, with the assistance of others, had placed McNeill in a Confederate ambulance en route to Harrisonburg."[36]

CHAPTER 16

Kelley's Tigers

"I saw from the looks of some of the men . . .
that a terrible retribution would occur."

McNeill's men were now scattered throughout the Shenandoah Valley. Before their leader's regrettable wounding, some had been riding with Captain John Q. Winfield. The captain, previously commander of Company B, 7th Virginia Cavalry, now led a contingent of the Valley Home Guards. As Sheridan's army fell back, Winfield's riders stayed on its flanks and captured a few soldiers. According to Trueheart, about this time a rumor began circulating among the partisans that "Sheridan has ordered all of Mosby and McNeill's men falling into his hands to be shot."[1]

At least a few of the Rangers found their way across the Blue Ridge and became the main actors in an incident that won them additional respect from the Ringgold Cavalry. On October 13 troopers from the 2nd West Virginia Cavalry of Colonel William Powell's brigade were on patrol when they found the body of a Union soldier. These men soon discovered that two locals named Chancellor and Myers had killed him. Despite the fact that the dead man was a deserter, the Yankees wanted revenge.[2]

Later, stopping at a blacksmith shop at Gaines Crossroads, the West Virginians captured two of Mosby's men. When Colonel Powell heard this, he ordered the troopers to execute one of the prisoners in retaliation for the murder of the soldier. The next morning, at the Marlow farm along Chester Gap Road, an officer had Private Albert G. Willis and an unidentified partisan pick straws, to determine their fate. When the latter selected the short straw, the man began sobbing uncontrollably. He kept shouting out about what would become of his poor family and fearing death because he was not a Christian. Willis, a one-time Baptist divinity student, promptly stepped forward and volunteered to take his place. After the especially brutal hanging, the soldiers left Willis in the poplar tree with a placard around his neck that read, "A.C. Willis, member of Co. C Mosby's command, hanged by the neck in retaliation of the murder of a U.S. soldier by Messrs. Chancellor and Myers."[3]

On October 10, near Upperville, some of Mosby's Rangers had captured Private Francis M. White, of Company A, 22nd Pennsylvania Cavalry. Earlier he had been one of the squad Sergeant Hopkins Moffitt had led into the hills to destroy a still house. After completing the job and returning to camp, White, realizing he had lost his saber, promptly turned around and rode back to get it. He never returned.[4]

Not long after Willis's execution, Mosby, now in possession of White, decided to even the score. As his men were preparing to hang White, a few of McNeill's Rangers showed up and asked what was going on. They questioned the captive and found out that he belonged to "old Ringgold." The men interceded immediately, relating how these Pennsylvanians had helped many people in Hardy County and asked Mosby to halt the execution. When he refused, Elwood wrote, "They drew their revolvers, surrounded the prisoner, and declared that they would die to a man before they would see a man belonging to the Ringgold cavalry executed that way."[5]

According to the story, Mosby relented and called off the hanging. Company records show that White was among the thousands of bluecoats confined in the Confederate prison at Andersonville, Georgia. At the close of the war, White, broken in health, returned home to Beallsville, Pennsylvania. He died there on July 5, 1865.[6]

On October 12 Major Peter J. Potts led a patrol from the 6th West Virginia Cavalry out of New Creek. Upon reaching Greenland Gap, Potts joined forces with the newly formed Kelley's Tigers, an "independent company of scouts and rangers." Led by nineteen-year-old Captain Tappen Wright Kelley, an accomplished scout and another of the general's sons, Company M, 2nd Maryland Cavalry Independent, the official name of Kelley's Tigers, had surprised their comrades in New Creek a few weeks before by returning from their first mission with a small herd of cattle and twelve prisoners in tow. On October 13 the Northerners reached Petersburg, where some Swamp Dragons came on board. Upon questioning a number of loyal citizens, Potts found out that an enemy force numbering between three and four hundred men was camped in Moorefield. Commanded by Woodson, it consisted of his company along with "Harness', McNeill's and part of Scott's command." On the fifteenth, when Potts got back to New Creek and reported in, Lieutenant Colonel Rufus E. Fleming telegraphed the news to Cumberland.[7]

That same day Captain Kelley became involved in a brutal incident that illustrated how vicious the war in the mountains had become. According to the author of an October 21 letter to the *Rockingham Register*, civilians Seymour Baldwin and Isaac Pratt had heard that their stolen horses were at Kelley's camp at Schell's Gap. The middle-aged men left their farms near Rig, traveled over to the Knobly Mountain pass, and met with the young officer. After finding out what the two wanted, an irritated Kelley told them they had thirty minutes "to take themselves off home," or he would have them shot.[8]

The men were soon on the way back to their farms. A short time later, though, some of Kelley's troopers caught up with the pair and told them that the captain wanted both back in camp. When Baldwin and Pratt returned, Kelley said they would "have to go to New Creek for their horses." The grateful men promptly set out for the rail town and were soon on Walker's Ridge when some soldiers or Swamps waylaid them—and on Sunday, October 16, locals found their bullet-ridden corpses. The incensed *Register* letter writer demanded, "Should Capt. Kelley ever fall into our hands, his life should pay the forfeit of the deed and his vile carcass thrown out for the buzzards." In a postscript, the man noted that since the murders, the Swamp Dragons had called a Mr. Judy out of his house and shot him. "He is not dead, but improving," he added.[9]

According to Vallandingham, two days after the news of the outrage reached camp, Sergeant Joe Vandiver gathered a squad of about thirty troopers and set out, bent on revenge. He wrote, "I saw from the looks of some of the men who were enlisted from that neighborhood that a terrible retribution would occur." After telling the soldiers to leave their sabers behind, Vandiver ordered them to follow him. Soon they were in the highlands beyond Petersburg, heading for a known Swamp Dragon lair. The Rangers moved stealthily through the night, and just before dawn they arrived near the isolated homestead.[10]

After dismounting and talking to Vandiver, Sergeant Isaac Judy took seven troopers, and hoping to surround the cabin, crept silently through a cornfield. In a little while Vandiver led the rest of the troop forward. By the time he got the men into the barnyard, though, the other detachment had already opened fire on the house. Shortly three men burst out of the dwelling and ran to the stable to get their horses, but Judy's soldiers captured them. "Sergeant J was heard in exultant tones," Vallandingham wrote. "By the Lord Harry, Joe, I've got em."[11]

As four Rangers brought "three of the most miserable looking mortals ever seen from the stable," Vallandingham said that about that time, a trio of women ran out of the house to plead for their men. The oldest cried out, "Oh Lord, spare them, spare them! Don't kill or nor yet take them away. They didn't do it." Vandiver immediately said, "They didn't do what, Madam?" The frightened woman replied, "I mean they didn't tell on them." Her husband shouted,

"Mammy, oh Mammy! You have made it worse. Why didn't you say they were not with Mr. Kelly when the men were killed?"[12]

Vandiver allowed the prisoners a few moments to say their farewells. He then mounted the Swamps on their horses and put them in the middle of the column. When they arrived in Petersburg, Sergeant Joe bought his boys a jug or two of applejack. He then went over to the mountaineers, Vallandingham recalled. "'Take some,' Vandiver said, 'you may need all your nerve for a long trip.' The poor creatures took it freely, but their confidence was not restored. They continually turned their eyes from side to side unwilling to meet the gaze of anyone."[13]

In a little while Vandiver and some of the others were starting to get drunk. While joking with his compatriots, he told two soldiers to unbind the prisoners' feet. The sergeant then ordered Vallandingham and a handful of younger men to ride to Petersburg Gap and guard the South Branch ford, about three miles away. They were to wait there until the rest of the troop arrived.[14]

The youngsters rode off and presently reached their station. Just a few moments later, they heard a sudden flurry of shots from the direction of Petersburg. One of the boys raced back to see what was going on. He returned quickly and advised his friends to "ask no questions." Finally Vandiver and his men showed up, bringing with them three saddled horses. In a few moments the sergeant told the youngsters that they were now the rear guard. Before moving out for Moorefield, he remarked, "They tried to get away, and we had to shoot them."[15]

In the meantime, Confederate fortunes in the Shenandoah Valley had taken a turn for the worse. On October 19, at Middletown, Sheridan's forces had decimated Early's Valley Army. In the morning phase of the battle, the Confederates had surprised the federals and driven them from their camps. Later, however, the combative general arrived suddenly just north of the town and reinvigorated his fighters. Subsequently, Sheridan led his men in a counterattack that overwhelmed the rebels and swept them from the field. Although still defending the upper valley, Early's force was now just a shell of what it once had been.[16]

On October 25 Unionist Lou McAleer reported to army headquarters in Cumberland that "a force is congregating around Slane's Cross-Roads [Slanesville] for the purpose of capturing the garrison at Green Spring." That same day Lieutenant Charles Lyon and Brevet Lieutenant Lorenzo Hatch of the 15th New York Cavalry were gathering a squad of sixty-seven men from their West Virginia hilltop camp, just across the river from Cumberland. Hatch, a native of Syracuse, was a hard-fighting combat veteran now back with his outfit after recuperating from a serious wound he had suffered some months earlier, on July 19, in fighting at Berry's Ford along the Shenandoah River. The New Yorkers were to relieve the company guarding the post at Green Spring.[17]

On the evening of October 31, Jesse McNeill and Captain Woodson led their men toward Green Spring. Later, sometime after three the next morning, the rebels approached the federal camp. Fortunately for them, the blockhouse destroyed by McCausland and Johnson's forces on August 2 was still in ruins, and the New Yorkers, sleeping in their tents, had little protection. Within the next hour a few Confederates silently captured the camp pickets, and when they returned the raiders advanced, leaving a quarter of the men behind to hold the horses.[18]

As the graybacks rushed forward, they ran headlong into an unexpected obstacle. About a hundred yards or so from their camp, the federals had placed trip wires to thwart any surprise attack. Although many of the Missourians and Rangers stumbled and crashed to the earth, the Yankees were sleeping so soundly they did not hear the commotion. Once back on their feet, the raiders formed a line and fired a tremendous volley into the tents. The surprise was complete.[19]

Regimental historian Private Chauncey Norton later wrote that "the men rallied as quickly as possible in the darkness and confusion and made a vigorous resistance, but the death of Lieut. Hatch deprived them of their leader and becoming disheartened were easily taken prisoners." Including Hatch and the seriously wounded Lyon, the bluecoat losses were high. Norton counted "sixty-four killed, wounded, and missing only four managed to escape." An official regimental record listed four killed, nineteen wounded, and twenty-three missing. The rebels later boasted of "capturing twenty-three Yankees and a negro, killing three or four, and wounding several more of the enemy, and capturing forty-four very fine horses and some equipments." The partisans also filled their pockets with their captive's recently received pay. On the Southern side, Woodson lost William H. Zumwalt killed and Jeremiah Knight wounded. Private Marcellus Alexander was the only Ranger wounded.[20]

The Confederates also came close to grabbing another prize. As they were plundering the camp, the graybacks heard the sound of a train coming up the track. It proved to be the Express West on its nightly run to Wheeling. Some distance from the station, the train came under fire. The engineer quickly stopped the express, and some troops jumped off and started shooting. Choosing not to fight it out, the Southerners gathered up the captives and spoils and rode away. As soon as news of the attack reached Cumberland, Kelley ordered his cavalry after the rebels, but they returned empty-handed.[21]

Three days later "Old Ben" received information that four hundred guerrillas had rendezvoused at Moorefield, intending to strike his weakened lines and

George Latham. Library of Congress,

disrupt the upcoming November 8 national and state elections. Hoping to grab the initiative, the general proposed to "capture or drive the enemy's out of these valleys, and thereby prevent a large amount of forage and subsistence from going to Early's army." Kelley then briefed Major General George Crook's assistant adjutant general, Major Robert P. Kennedy, on the plan. Besides sending a force from New Creek to attack the rebels and another from Cumberland into the Lost River Valley, Kelley had Townsend wire Brigadier General William H. Seward at Martinsburg to ask him to dispatch some cavalry to Moorefield via Wardensville Road. Townsend also telegraphed Crook at Strasburg and asked him to send "a small cavalry force . . . into the Lost River Valley."[22]

At nine thirty in the morning of November 6, Colonel George R. Latham, now commanding the post at New Creek, led 225 troops from his own 5th West Virginia Cavalry and the 6th West Virginia Cavalry, along with a gun from Battery L, 1st Illinois Light Artillery, toward Greenland Gap. A lawyer hailing from Grafton, Latham was a staunch Unionist possessing an excellent war record. At this time he was also a candidate for Congress. Two days later voters elected the thirty-two-year-old colonel to represent West Virginia's Second Congressional District in the United States House of Representatives.[23]

The column reached the gap at five o'clock in the late afternoon of November 6 and stopped to eat supper and feed their horses, and four and a half hours later the troops were back in the saddle. Just before dawn the mountaineers surrounded Moorefield and quickly rooted out a few rebels who boarded in town. Latham, however, still had not discovered the partisan camp, which was located some distance south of Moorefield.[24]

When it was light, Confederates riding into town for breakfast spotted the West Virginians, and skirmishing began. Only facing about a hundred fighters, Latham pressed his numerical advantage, and the grayjackets beat a hasty retreat up the South Fork, eventually crossing Shenandoah Mountain and escaping to Mount Jackson. Latham wrote, "We captured eight of them, wounding one, all of whom we brought in." Upon questioning the prisoners, he found out that "the rebel force at Moorefield was preparing for a raid upon our lines when we reached this place."[25]

After leaving Moorefield, the bluecoats spent the rest of the day in Old Fields, rounding up livestock. Many of the animals belonged to herds gathered by the partisans and intended for Early's army. All total, besides a few horses, Latham counted "46 cattle (beef) and 460 head of sheep." Rebecca Van Meter recalled that "they took three hundred sheep from Mr. D. McNeill & 2 Yoke of Oxen, took 180 of Cousin Jac's fine ewes."[26]

The soldiers also grabbed Rebecca's two oxen. When she found out that her animals were gone, Van Meter followed the raiders until she came upon Latham, asleep in an ambulance. The woman woke him up and demanded that he return her animals. Latham told her "Col. Fleming had authority over the cattle." Farther along, she caught up with Fleming and convinced him to give them back. After that, and later that afternoon, the federals moved off through Reynolds Gap. Their progress slowed down by the sheep, they did not make it back to New Creek until the next evening.[27]

In the meantime, over in Harrisonburg Captain McNeill was still barely clinging to life. Finally, on November 10, surrounded by Jemima, Sarah Emily, Jesse, young John Jr. and a few other relatives, the bold partisan chieftain joined the "Great Majority." A day or two later he was laid to rest with Masonic and military honors, and on the eleventh McNeill's Masonic brothers of Rockingham Union Lodge No. 27, AFAM, issued a memorial proclamation noting that "we unhesitatingly declare that the country has lost one of its truest friends and best soldiers, the Confederate Army one of its bravest and most efficient officers, and afflicted family, a most devoted, kind and affectionate husband and father." While in succeeding years, his fame would never reach the heights of such renowned American irregular fighters as French and Indian War hero Major Robert Rogers, Revolutionary War legend Francis "The Swamp Fox" Marion, or his contemporary John Mosby, McNeill's accomplishments in two years of constant partisan warfare certainly rank him alongside them.[28]

CHAPTER 17

Old Maid's Lane

—— ∞∞∞ ——

"It was awful, I don't know what saved
our people from being killed."

Although Hanse had passed on command of the company to Jesse, a number of the men doubted his ability to guide the outfit. None of the men questioned his bravery, but some would have rather had the steadier Welton in charge. According to Duffey, who admired Jesse, "the young leader was known to be quick-tempered and impetuous, bordering on rashness." The Rangers also knew that he liked the bottle. But Trueheart said that about this time the lieutenant alleviated their fears on this count by vowing "never to touch another drop of whiskey."[1]

Toward the end of the month Kelley got word that McNeill and Woodson's companies were back around Moorefield. Once again, he decided to strike them. This time "Old Ben" would not count on Crook or Seward to close the trap but would give the job to his own cavalry and the Swamp Dragons. Kelley instructed Latham to send one force into Moorefield from the north and another from the east via Wardensville Road. In the meantime the Pendleton County Home Guards would move into the South Fork Valley to stymie any Confederates attempting to flee through there to the Shenandoah Valley.[2]

Latham chose a mixed force of horsemen from the 5th and 6th West Virginia to carry out the proposed November 28 attack. He ordered the Swamps to block the intersection of South Fork Road and Howards Lick Road by 4:00 A.M. The colonel was also counting on help from another quarter. Upon hearing of Kelley's threat "that if they continue to harbor and feed McNeill's men . . . the whole valley will be laid waste like the Shenandoah Valley," a group of South Branch Valley men met with Latham in New Creek. They promised him that they would "take measures to rid the country of McNeill's men and to cooperate with us for that purpose."[3]

At nine o'clock on the night of November 26, Major Peter J. Potts left Burlington with 155 men. Potts stopped for the night at Romney, where a day or two before some of his troops, a civilian reported, had robbed "the people of money, watches, & @c." The next morning he traveled up Grassy Lick Road to the intersection of Wardensville Road at Baker. By nightfall the major was camped "within a few miles of Moorefield." About the time Potts left Romney that Sunday, Lieutenant Colonel Fleming rode out of Burlington at the head of 120 troopers and an artillery crew and one 12 pounder from Battery L, 1st Illinois Light Artillery. In his report written early the next morning, Fleming lamented the force at his disposal: "Two of the companies were armed with Enfield rifles and had never been in action. The other company was armed partly with revolvers and partly with Enfield rifles." Later that afternoon, about two miles from Old Fields, some scouts, who had already skirmished briefly with a few enemy troopers picketing Goings Ford, rode in. They told Fleming that Brigadier General Tom Rosser was either now in Moorefield or would be the next morning. Almost instantly, Fleming decided to forget Latham's orders about attacking the partisans and marched through Old Fields to the South Branch. Once there he promptly sent Lieutenant Richard Blue's company across the river to discover Rosser's whereabouts. To back them up, Fleming posted his cannon and the other two companies atop the forty-foot-high bluff that commanded the ford.[4]

On November 26 Rosser and about six hundred troopers rode out of Timberville for the South Branch Valley to gather much-needed supplies. While there, Rosser also intended to attack and take New Creek. Some time prior to this, he had sent scouts John T. Peerce and James L. Williams to spy on the post and map its defenses. The men completed the mission successfully, and their subsequent report convinced the general that even though its fortifications were strong, there was a good chance he could catch the federals napping and capture the place. According to Captain William N. McDonald, "He had with him his own and Payne's brigade and a few of the choice spirits of the cavalry and artillery left behind, among who were Capt. James Thomson, Maj. Robert Mason, Lt. Charles Menegrode, and Maj. James Breathed."[5]

While crossing the mountain from Mathias to Moorefield that night, Rosser sent a courier to find McNeill. The general, fearing that once he neared town roving federals or Unionist spies might discover his force and spoil the surprise he had in store for New Creek, wanted Jesse to picket the roads around Moorefield. The courier finally caught up, in Petersburg, with the lieutenant, "who," a soldier wrote, "was searching for any straggling Yankees that might come that

Rufus Fleming. Author's collection,

way." After reading Rosser's orders, McNeill quickly dispatched squads of men northward to Goings Ford and other locations. Trueheart recalled that "a dispatch reached us that caused a great stir in camp & in less than two minutes, we were on our way to Moorefield." In the meantime, Rosser halted along the South Fork, four miles from town.[6]

About two hours after McNeill's troopers arrived at the ford, some of Fleming's scouts, clothed in gray, appeared on the far bank. The strange horsemen called out that they were McNeill's men and invited the pickets to come over. The wary rebels, however, kept to their side. Shooting soon erupted, and the Rangers galloped away to warn their comrades. The federals dashed back to inform Colonel Fleming.[7]

Meanwhile, Rosser and his staff had reached Moorefield and found McNeill. After telling the general about the latest development, Jesse took the Rangers and Woodson's company and rode out to see what was going on. About this time, they were joined by fifteen men from Company F, 7th Virginia Cavalry. As the hundred Confederates moved toward the river, McNeill kept his men out of sight, hidden behind a low ridge until he reached a patch of woods just behind Caledonia, James Heiskell's house.[8]

Just then four of Blue's men were approaching the front of the dwelling, followed, at a distance, by the lieutenant and the rest of his troopers. "Doubtless we would have captured them," Duffey later speculated, "but at that juncture some wild man from our company gave a yell . . . and before we could get through the barnyard gates they were in full retreat." As Company F private L. H. Davis remembered, "We moved at a rapid gate down through the field . . . Our enemies now retreated faster than they had come." Another soldier recalled that "at this point, McNeill and his men broke from the woods with a yell, and gave the Yankees close pursuit to the river."[9]

Opposite: Sketch of action of Rosser's Cavalry near Moorefield, Va., November 27, 1864 (Jedidiah Hotchkiss). *Atlas to Accompany the Official Records of the Union and Confederate Armies*. Washington, D.C.: U.S. Government Printing Office, 1891–1895.

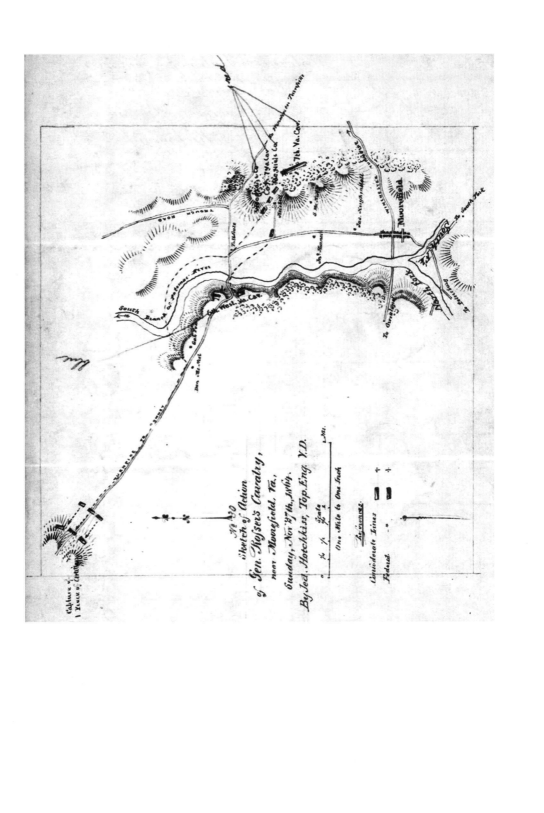

Nº NO
Sketch of Action
of Gen. Rosser's Cavalry,
near Moorefield, Va.,
Sunday, Nov. 27th, 1864.
By Jed. Hotchkiss, Top.Eng. V.D.

Scale
One Mile to One Inch

Confederate Lines
Federal.

Slowed down by a stout fence across their path, the Southerners could not catch the West Virginians before they splashed across the ford. Once their comrades were safe, the rest of Fleming's soldiers opened fire on the oncoming rebels, putting them in a tight spot. "Just as we reached the river," Trueheart wrote, "their whole force . . . rose & attempted to protect the crossing of the river, pouring in a terrible fire of grape from a 12 lb. gun & making the air musical with the hiss & whiz of smaller missiles." Years later Davis recalled that "I have very distinct impressions, to this day of the impression produced on my ears by those flying missiles of death."[10]

So far, though, casualties had been few. Fortunately for the rebels, the bullets and grapeshot were passing just over their heads. But to stay there meant certain death. At last McNeill called out, "Men follow me," and led his wild riders in a breakneck race downriver to Fox's Ford. In the meantime, as his artillerymen tried vainly to hit their fast disappearing mark, Fleming ordered his troops back in the saddle and retreated down the pike, hoping to reach rugged Reynolds Gap and take cover among the rocks.[11]

As soon as Fleming reached the vicinity of Willow Wall, however, he spotted the Confederates congregated at the lower crossing. The colonel promptly ordered his gunners to unlimber and open up, but shortly the graybacks were across the river. As Jesse led a band of horsemen through the fields to get ahead of the mountaineers, another detachment closed in on the rear guard. "I intended to make a stand in the gap," Fleming wrote, "but was so hotly pursued that I could not rally any portion of my men until it was too late."[12]

By this time McNeill and his riders were pushing their steeds as fast as they could go, hoping to head off the Yankees at the intersection of the pike with Old Maid's Lane, the narrow farm road to Van Meter's Traveler's Rest. According to Duffey, "Captain McNeill was in the lead. The short mane of his mettled bay flying erect in the air and closely followed by others, at whom the fleeing Federals, who packed the road, were discharging their revolvers with a rattling fire like pop crackers exploding by packs."[13]

From her house, Rebecca Van Meter heard cannon fire and "a most awful scream, it was the Rebels rushing down through the fields to head them, the Yankeys staying down the Pike as hard as their wagons and horses could go." As the now frantic bluecoats raced for the protection of the gap, they shot wildly at the Southerners, thundering through the nearby meadow. Once the soldiers fired their Enfield rifles, though, it was almost impossible riding at a fast clip for them to reload. Finally, some of the rebels reached the end of the lane and blocked the pike. In an instant, a vicious hand-to-hand fight broke out with

Fleming's trapped rear guard. But Southern revolvers and sabers soon won the day. As some graybacks corralled the battered and bloodied Northerners, others kept up the chase.[14]

At the entrance to the gap, a few Rangers stopped their pursuit and claimed the wrecked 12 pounder. During the chase, a wheel fell off and the gun ran into a ditch, breaking an axle. It was the first, and only, cannon the Rangers captured during the war. Other Confederates pursued the West Virginians through the defile and toward Purgitsville, but their prey finally got away.[15]

In addition to losing their gun, the federals also lost an ambulance and a wagon. According to the *Rockingham Register*, their casualties numbered five or six killed, a few wounded, and forty men captured, along with fifty to sixty horses. Once out of danger, Fleming dispatched a messenger to Latham. When Fleming finally reached headquarters sometime after midnight, he reported, "I cannot at the present ascertain the entire loss, but twenty men will cover it, 6 or 8 of whom were wounded and killed." Fleming also noted that a detachment of his scouts on the west side of the river had spotted "a column of 500 men which never moved out of Moorefield."[16]

Despite the fact that the rebels had been under some cannon and heavy small arms fire, only Sergeant Charles Hopkins and Private John Hoard, of the Rangers, and 7th Virginia trooper Private Jacob Gassman suffered wounds, a fact so amazing that few could believe it. Duffey noted, "Another feature is the extraordinary amount of ammunition used up and the inconsiderable casualties reported."[17]

By eight o'clock that night, the victors were back in Moorefield, watching Rosser's men leaving for New Creek. Earlier, the general had personally congratulated Jesse on his outstanding feat. When he moved out, Rosser left the Rangers and Missourians behind to watch the roads.[18]

About four o'clock the next morning, Major Potts and his soldiers broke camp and headed for their scheduled rendezvous with Fleming's column at Moorefield. Along the South Fork the Home Guards from Hardy and Pendleton Counties were already in place to waylay the Confederates, should the federals push them upriver. Just east of Moorefield, Potts's men silently captured a rebel picket post. After that the Yankee vanguard charged into the village and immediately encountered Sergeant John Fay leading a swarm of angry partisans, who met and chased them off. According to Potts, his own men corralled some enemy troopers while losing one man captured and having two soldiers slightly wounded. Down along the South Fork the Missourians skirmished with the Swamp Dragons, who, now realizing that Kelley's plan had failed, scampered off to their isolated mountain sanctuaries.[19]

Rather than returning to New Creek through Reynolds Gap, Potts retreated across Patterson Creek Mountain to Williamsport. Upon reaching the hamlet, the major, now knowing that Rosser's force was in the area, chose to take a backwoods trail that led across Knobly Mountain at Harrison's Gap. From there the Yankees, wanting to reach Piedmont, took a path toward Elk Garden Road. Soon, however, Potts spotted a Confederate camp blocking his way. The major then took another obscure track into the mountains before stopping to camp overnight in the highlands just west of Bloomington. Departing early the next morning, he reached the Frankville B&O station at four o'clock. Six hours later Potts and his men, along with the rebels taken in Moorefield and some of Rosser's stragglers captured along the way, arrived safely in New Creek. They found the place still in an uproar over Rosser's lightning raid the previous day.[20]

Private Davis said that just before leaving Moorefield, their officers told the men that their objective was New Creek. That night the column took the Moorefield and Allegheny Turnpike to Patterson Creek Valley, and just before dawn it reached Joseph Arnold's farm, some five miles south of Burlington. There they stopped to feed and water their horses, get something to eat, and sleep. The men, no doubt, kept a watchful eye on the old Dunkard preacher so he would not steal away and spread the alarm.[21]

While there, Rosser summoned his leading officers for a council of war. Although all believed that no Yankees had spotted them, some were anxious that, by now, Fleming's bluecoats had reached New Creek and sounded the alarm. These men urged Rosser to call off the attack. About this time, however, John Peerce spoke up. The crafty old scout was sure the West Virginians had spread the alarm, "but that information, in his opinion," according to Captain William McDonald, "would only make the Federals more careless, for they would think that Rosser would not dare approach the fort." When Brigadier General William H. F. Payne, who had earlier been discussing with Captain Thaddeus Fitzhugh the latter's idea on how to capture the fort, concurred with Peerce's logic, Rosser decided to press forward. Not long afterward the raiders broke camp and traveled cross-country to reach the turnpike.[22]

Private Davis remembered that "our route now led us over Mike's Run, then across the hills by way of Davis Mill, thence by the Henry Harrison farm, where we intersected the northwestern turnpike about a mile from the New Creek ford."[23]

With Payne up front, the 6th Virginia Cavalry led the way, followed by the 5th and 8th. Just after cresting Knobly Mountain, the column turned onto the road leading to New Creek Turnpike. Shortly afterward Rosser sent Major Edward McDonald's 11th Virginia down a backwoods trail that ran alongside

Limestone Run. This rough track, skirting the front side of Abram's Ridge, ended about one-half mile east of the depot. Upon reaching the B&O, McDonald's
troopers were to cut the telegraph wires, damage any bridges and track, and then
join the assault on the garrison. Next Rosser met with Fitzhugh, Company F,
5th Virginia, and ordered him to pick thirty reliable men who were wearing
blue overcoats and riding U.S. horses. Fitzhugh wrote that "Rosser ... ordered
me to keep two or three hundred yards in advance of his command, and when
coming in sight of the federal pickets not to fire on them."[24]

As some Southerners had feared, Latham and his troops were expecting
them. Kelley had already warned his subordinate that he anticipated the
Confederates making the attempt. Just after Fleming's galloper finally reached
headquarters, at nine o'clock that night, "I extended and strengthened my
pickets," Latham wrote, "and had the post put in proper state for defense." Although he had approximately 700 men, Latham's force was much weaker than
it seemed. Of the total number of defenders, 200 were artillerymen, and out
of the rest only 160 were armed. Four miles west of New Creek, Captain John
Fisher, commanding Company A, 6th West Virginia Infantry, was guarding
Piedmont's vital B&O workshops with only 35 soldiers. Another 20 of his men
were just up the track at Bloomington. On the morning of the 28th Latham
ordered "pickets and patrols eight miles out." At Fort Fuller, called Fort Kelley
by the rebels, a party of 20 scouts was just ready to depart for Burlington when,
at eleven thirty, disaster struck.[25]

About four miles from the town, Fitzhugh encountered an old woman on horseback. She told the Virginian that the first picket post was "three-fourths of a mile
down the pike" and that there were six soldiers there. As they passed farmhouses
along the way, people, thinking that they were Union soldiers, came outside to wave
at them. These loyalists were amazed, though, when, in just a little while, outriders
from the main column surrounded their dwellings and forced them indoors.[26]

Fitzhugh's blue-clad troopers had no trouble taking the oblivious pickets,
who, anxious for Potts's arrival, had no idea the rebels were about. "On our
approach," Fitzhugh wrote, "they all lined up to learn the news of the fight and
desired to know the fate of some of their men in the engagement." When the
Virginians drew their pistols and Fitzhugh ordered them to surrender, they
were dumbfounded. The captain and his men continued down the road and
easily captured the next two posts. Soon the Southerners were within a half
mile of Fort Fuller.[27]

Led by Payne and Rosser, the 6th Virginia Cavalry now came up and began
moving slowly toward the citadel. Inside the stronghold the men of Battery H,

1st West Virginia Light Artillery, were not alert to the oncoming danger. In fact, at that time many of the mountaineers were away from their post and in town. The others, supposing Fitzhugh's riders were their own soldiers returning to camp, had gathered in front of the fort to greet them. The captain, however, swiftly detoured to the left, galloped across a meadow to the fort, jumped the parapet, and captured the flag. When the 6th Virginia had closed to within thirty yards, "they set up a horrible yell," a witness reported, "and charged down with great fury upon the fort." Instantly, many soldiers and citizens suddenly realized what was going on and were now sprinting toward the North Branch to escape capture by swimming into Maryland. Although many officers tried to stop the stampede, all order had been lost. When a few armed soldiers reached the far bank, though, they took cover and started shooting at the Southerners. Meanwhile, riders from the 5th Virginia were bearing down on the guns of the Illinois Battery positioned atop Church Hill. Abandoned by his men, one brave officer was just about to fire a parting shot when Major James Breathed cut him down with a blow from his saber.[28]

The *Wheeling Daily Intelligencer* reported what occurred during the next five hours:

> The Rebels, about 1,000 in number, now had everything their own way. They burned the commissary stores and government and other private property, and captured about two hundred and fifty citizens and soldiers, including the greater portion of Holmes' battery, some who have since made their escape. They also captured about two hundred and fifty cattle, eight hundred horses, three thousand pair of pantaloons, as many shirts and some other government clothing and property.[29]

When McDonald arrived, Rosser ordered him to take his regiment and destroy the B&O shops and facilities at Piedmont, the same property that Hanse McNeill had seriously damaged on May 5. After that the major was to proceed to Elk Garden, gather up all of the cattle that he could, and then march to Petersburg. McDonald soon got on his way, but Captain Fisher was waiting for him. Already aware of the attack on New Creek, Fisher had recalled his twenty soldiers from Bloomington and then marched the whole company about a mile from town, posting them in a strong hillside position commanding the road from New Creek. When the Virginians came into sight, a spirited fight broke out. Soon, though, the outnumbered mountaineers fell back to town, ran across the bridge into Maryland, and took cover.[30]

Arriving in Piedmont at five o'clock that afternoon, McDonald ordered some men to the rail yard and sent a detachment to roust out the snipers on the Maryland hillside. His men made two attempts to cross the North Branch, but both times heavy fire from Fisher's riflemen drove them back. While the fighting raged, other soldiers burned, as a B&O official reported: "Round Front House, Machine shop, with stationary machinery; Carpenter Shop, with a large quantity of valuable lumber; four cars and two tender cars that were under repair and could not be moved." McDonald later said he would have burned some other shops, but he feared setting the town ablaze. Still under sporadic fire, the Virginians moved out into the gathering darkness. According to Captain Fisher, "They left one man killed and one mortally wounded."[31]

About that same time, five o'clock, Rosser's troops left New Creek, accompanied by approximately 450 federal prisoners, a large number of civilian captives, the three guns of the Illinois battery, about 250 horses, and lots of plunder. Back in town at least one man—Samuel Cox, one of assistant quartermaster Captain George W. Harrison's civilian employees—was dead. The Confederates had also spiked Fort Fuller's siege guns and burned a number of government buildings. General Kelley later estimated that the rebels had either ruined or taken an estimated $90,000 in federal goods. Local businesses suffered severe losses, and on December 6 the *Wheeling Daily Intelligencer* reported that "T. B. Davis & Company . . . store was plundered and afterwards burned by the chivalry."[32]

Darkness soon enveloped the column as the raiders herded their captives south. Soon, as rebel vigilance waned, along the trail many Unionists, including Abe Hinkle and John Carskadon, escaped into the brush. Well-known Greenland Gap Unionist Abijah Dolly sprinted off, and upon reaching his farm, he drove his stock beyond the reach of the oncoming Confederates. Hinkle later told a reporter:

Nearly all the Rebels had supplied themselves abundantly with commissary whisky. They nearly all got stone blind drunk. And they had as much as they could do to look after the mule's load of booty which each of them carried. They had also lost a great deal of rest previous to the attack on New Creek, and for these reasons the men were not very watchful.[33]

After stopping in Petersburg on the morning of November 30 to rest and reorganize, Rosser moved on to the Shenandoah Valley with not only his remaining prisoners, captured horses, mules, and supplies but also over four hundred head of cattle and some sheep gathered up along the way. The partisans remained behind and took to the mountains to track down the Yankees who had slipped away. On December 3 Potts returned to New Creek from trailing the rebels and reported that the only Confederates left in the area between Petersburg and Moorefield were "McNeill's and Woodson's commands . . . about 150 men."[34]

On December 1 Kelley had Latham arrested and sent "to Grafton to await trial by general court-martial." In the meantime, Sheridan first dismissed Latham from the service but then reconsidered his decision and ordered him to be court-martialed. During the trial, which began on December 17 in Cumberland, the tribunal rejected Latham's main argument in his defense, first made in a statement to General Kelley that "I feel most deeply the disaster, and especially the stigma of a surprise, but without standing picket myself, I cannot see that I could have been more vigilant." On January 11, 1865, the officers found him guilty of "neglect of duty, disobedience of orders, and conduct to the prejudice of good order and military discipline." The court punished the disgraced colonel by stripping him of his rank and dismissing him from the service. Despite the fact that Latham had been one of the president's most ardent West Virginia supporters, Lincoln approved the verdict. On March 4, though, Latham took his seat in Congress, and two weeks later the War Department reversed his dismissal and gave him an honorable discharge.[35]

Back in Cumberland, Kelley did not escape his commander's wrath. Sheridan, who labeled the brigadier's three-pronged attack on Moorefield as a "Don Quixotic expedition," criticized his subordinate's decision to send the troops to capture the partisans. "The expedition sent out by General Kelley to Moorefield," he wrote, "was sent without my knowledge, and on the bragging system, which always embraced too many combinations, and turns out to be bad strategy for guerrillas in a mountainous country."[36]

Once the Richmond papers with stories describing Rosser's expedition reached Moorefield, many of the Rangers and Missourians questioned why they did not receive any special recognition for their important role in the general's successful campaign. In his brief November 30 report to Early, Rosser did not mention the partisans' role in the attack and rout of Fleming's command but made it appear that his troopers alone had done the job. "After capturing the artillery and wagons at Moorefield," he wrote, "on the 27th I moved on to New Creek."[37]

On December 16, however, the editor of the *Richmond Whig* published a long letter penned by H, an unidentified writer from Hardy County, who thoroughly described the Old Fields action. In the opening paragraph H noted that "we think it justice that Lieutenant McNeill and his brave and heroic little band should receive the praise they so richly won by the part they played in this expedition."[38]

The controversy over Rosser's slight carried over into the next century, with other writers echoing H's call to give the partisans more recognition. In a 1914 article, written long after both McNeill and Rosser had died, the former private, now reverend, L. H. Davis remembered, "I also feel confident that the responsibility of planning and executing of this movement rested solely with Capt. McNeill." A year later John Fay remarked, "It added no feather to the General's cap when he failed to give the credit so justly due to McNeill and his men for their gallant feat at Moorefield."[39]

Although the dying Hanse had given Jesse command of the company, Jesse's leadership during the November 27 fight at Moorefield had now earned him the position. From then on he would be the unquestioned chief of the partisan band. In 1918 Jefferson W. Duffey reflected on the skirmish and concluded, "That young man, Capt. Jesse Cunningham McNeill, met a crisis in the career of the company. He displayed qualities of leadership of exceptional ability and effectiveness."[40]

CHAPTER 18

Punishing the Swamp Dragons

—⟨∞⟩—

" . . . he's a damned old Yankee,
and I hope you have killed him."

The New Creek fiasco caused Department of West Virginia commander George Crook, now a major general, to call on local Unionists to help stamp out the partisan threat. On December 9 his assistant adjutant general, Major Robert P. Kennedy, issued the following circular:

As the borders of this department are infested with small disreputable bands of men, who in civil times, would be called horse thieves and murderers, but who dignify themselves with the title of guerrillas, claiming to belong to the so-called Confederate States . . . it becomes necessary that some measures be taken by citizens living within this department, and whose property is threatened, for their own protection.

Citizens are called upon to organize for the destruction of all bands of these villains . . . and all possible assistance for their destruction will be given them.

Such men, banded together for purposes of plunder and dishonorable personal advantages, are unworthy of, and should receive, no quarter, and when taken, any disposition that may be deemed necessary by the captors themselves towards their persons will be fully upheld and justified. It is impossible to hunt down and destroy these parties by large military organizations, while citizen residents-able to know of their whereabouts-may speedily organize for their destruction.

Citizens living within this department must protect themselves in the same manner as in civil times, when over-run by these plundering,

166

marauding and thieving bands, and rise up with a determination to rid themselves of them at once, and for all, resting upon the assurance that all assistance possible will be given them by the department commander.[1]

Snow was falling when Lieutenant Gus Boggs and a squad of Rangers showed up in Old Fields on Sunday, December 11, to round up livestock that the partisans had previously gathered and drive the animals to the Shenandoah Valley. And they had to move fast. According to Rebecca Van Meter, the Rangers "had captured the orders that the Yankeys to take all stock, burn all barns, & grain and take McNeills and Woodsons Companies."[2]

For some time the two companies had been supplying most of the meat for Early's thinned ranks. Ranging far into the mountains of western Maryland, small bands of men worked hard stealing and then driving herds of cattle through enemy territory. Those not involved in this activity scouted the country, "constantly watching & dogging the every movement of the enemy both by ordinary road and R.R." Trueheart wrote, "And at the same have probably killed wounded & captured as many Yanks during that time as any other two companies in the service."[3]

Meanwhile, over in the valley rations were growing short. That same day Colonel Elijah White led his 35th Battalion of Virginia Cavalry, the hard-fighting "Comanches" of the Laurel Brigade, from his camp eight miles south of New

George Crook. Author's collection.

Market toward the Alleghenies. The battalion, made up of Marylanders and Virginians, had been on Rosser's New Creek raid, and at first the men balked at the idea of heading back into the rugged terrain. Finally, though, White ordered his officers, as Captain Frank Myers related, "to take all the men in camp, who had horses fit to travel." In total, however, they probably only gathered about a hundred.[4]

After arriving in Petersburg, the 35th joined forces with McNeill, Woodson, and Company F, 7th Virginia Cavalry. On December 19, his ranks now swelled to about three hundred troopers, White left Petersburg to sweep the valley between

Elijah White and friends; White is front row center. Author's collection.

there and Franklin. Not only looking for food and plunder, the raiders were also determined to chastise the Swamp Dragons, whom they considered no better than the one-time "Highland outlaws of Scotland." Along the way, several Home Guard units began harassing the rebels. Occasionally a shot would be fired by a bushwhacker from a distant hillside but would fall short of the Confederates. About midday some Swamps drew closer, but Private John Mobberly led a charge on them, killing one and chasing off the others. Young Mobberly, one of White's best scouts, usually roamed the Short Hill section of Loudoun County, Virginia, with his own small, brutal guerrilla band. Due to his vicious ways, many Yankee soldiers and Unionists in that locale considered him one of the most notorious murderers in the Confederate service. Years later, Private Magnus Thompson, who knew Mobberly quite well, remembered, " . . . everyone agreed he personally slew more Yankees than any man in Lee's army."[5]

Upon reaching John Bond's place, the rebels ransacked the captain's house and outbuildings, taking almost everything of value the man owned. As this was going on, White suddenly spied riders off in the distance and sent Mobberly's squad to scatter them. In short order the men did their job, and the Swamps vanished into the hills.[6]

That night the Southerners camped along Brushy Run, just north of Franklin. The next morning, White determined to lead his men west into the "Smoke Hole," a remote valley that was in the heart of Swamp Dragon country. Even though some of the Rangers undoubtedly remained with White as guides, the rest of the company returned to Moorefield. Woodson's men and Company F continued to Monterey and then rode over to the Shenandoah Valley.[7]

Captain Isaac Alt was out patrolling the countryside when he spied the Confederates as they were ascending Cave Mountain. Alt, sure they were McNeill's outfit, hurried back home to spread the alarm. When the graybacks reached the crest, White sent riders down the road to search a few houses, while he took six others and scouted southward a few miles. Upon stopping at a roadside cabin, the colonel questioned a handful of mountain women and found out "that their husbands, brothers, sweethearts and all, were out with the Dragons." Suddenly hearing shots off in the distance, White ended his conversation and signaled his men to follow. They made it back just in time to help extricate their hard-pressed compatriots from an ambush.[8]

Next the colonel once again divided his men. One wing descended Cave Mountain to the South Branch and began sweeping down the narrow valley. The other half of the command also marched north, H. M. Calhoun wrote, "by way of the present John Kimble place through the Shreve settlement and thence down through the ridges, towards the Grant [postwar] County line." As the two columns moved along, some troopers ransacked houses just abandoned by the fearful mountain folk, while outriders gathered cattle and horses. Presently a few Swamps started taking potshots at the detachment riding along the river.[9]

In a little while the Comanches reunited, and now, accompanied by a yearling colt and a curious deerhound, the men rode along slowly, nervously scanning the rugged, heavily wooded heights for hidden riflemen. Soon Alt's sharpshooters, posted atop a nearby ridge, opened fire. As the fighting intensified, White led a small mounted detachment through a hollow, then up a steep slope to flank the bushwhackers. Clark Shreve, one of Alt's soldiers posted high atop another ridge, hollered across to his friends, alerting them to the danger.[10]

All but four of the Swamps heeded Shreve's warning and ran away. But Isaac Kimble, his uncle John Kimble, Jacob McDonald, and Benjamin Shreve Jr. remained in place and kept shooting. John was a hard-nosed old-timer who earlier that day, had ignored his family's pleas to stay put, picked up his ancient flintlock, and marched off with the younger men, determined to fight.[11]

White and his handful of tough, veteran fighters now closed in on their quarry. When the four mountaineers saw them coming, three ran off into the woods, but John, partially hidden in the brush, kept his position, and drew a bead on the colonel. Private Nicholas Dorsey, though, spotted Kimble and shouted out a warning to White. Captain Myers described what happened next. "White . . . instantly fired on him with his pistol, wounding him in the hip, and at the same moment, Alonzo Sellman shot him in the side, and the old man rolled over with the load still in his rifle." Other Comanches killed Isaac Kimble and slightly wounded Shreve Jr.[12]

John was barely breathing, but some troopers still picked him up, along with his flintlock, and "placed him behind John Walker." As the rebels moved off, they left Isaac's corpse in the woods. The old man did not last long; he died on the way down the mountain. Later White halted at a nearby cabin and placed the body on the ground. The rebels moved on quickly, but the deerhound stayed there, licking the dead man's face. Myers related that farther down the trail "a woman, mounted man-fashion, on a horse, met the command, proclaiming she was a rebel." After spying John's flintlock, she exclaimed, "Its daddy's gun; I know it, he's a damned old Yankee, and I hope you have killed him."[13]

That night the Comanches camped around the house of Solomon Shirk. When they arrived, either White or another officer cautioned Shirk "to keep away from the men as some of them have been wounded and they were in bad humor." At daybreak the ones who had slept outside awoke beneath a cover of deep snow, with more coming down, but after breakfast they were back in the saddle and on their way to Petersburg. Pressing on through the storm, the Southerners arrived in town that evening and then rested there for a few days before heading back to the Shenandoah Valley.[14]

Although White's battalion had carried out the raid, the West Virginians believed that it had been the work of the Rangers. The deaths of Isaac and John Kimble and the wholesale looting of the mountaineers' houses and livestock only intensified their blood feud with the partisans.[15]

Sometime during the Christmas season, Jesse fell from his horse and severely sprained an ankle, putting him out of action for the next six or seven weeks. After turning over command to Lieutenant Welton, his men took him to the home of Felix Welton, located along the way to Petersburg, about four miles south of Moorefield. As McNeill remembered, "I was confined there for two or three weeks, during which I suffered much." Others later moved him to the home of R. B. Sherrard, where he continued to recuperate.[16]

On New Year's Eve Crook issued orders reorganizing the Department of West Virginia. Brigadier General Isaac Duval would command the First Division, while Kelley's troops, "including the post at Wheeling, will form the Second infantry division." At Harpers FerryBrigadier General John D. Stevenson's soldiers guarding the B&O line through the eastern panhandle of the new state "will constitute the Third infantry division." Colonel John S. Oley's troops in the Kanawha Valley "will form the First separate brigade." Crook placed Captain H. A. DuPont, 5th U.S. Artillery, in charge of the division's long arm.[17]

The beginning of 1865 brought extremely harsh weather to the mountains, and for a short time, things were quiet. Some of the partisans took advantage of this respite by journeying to Harrisonburg, exhuming Captain McNeill's corpse, and bringing it back to Moorefield for reburial in Olivet Cemetery. By the second week of the month, though, fighting between the partisans and Swamps flared up. On January 10 the *Rockingham Register* reported that Welton, leading a squad of "25 or 30," ambushed a detachment of Hardy County Independent Scouts along the North Fork River in Pendleton County. They killed "a man named Yoakum and one named Branneman, both notorious amongst the 'Dragons' for their thieving operations." Upon getting back to camp, the lieutenant sent two captured Swamps along with two Union deserters picked up in Petersburg back to Harrisonburg.[18]

On January 15, however, Captain James Rohrbaugh of the Hardy County Scouts described the raid in a letter to West Virginia adjutant general F. P. Pierpoint. Bad weather and poor roads, though, prevented him from sending it until two weeks later. According to the captain, whose story was completely different from the *Register*'s account, the partisans had first captured Private Henry Goldizen at his house before nabbing Private Bethnel Watts along the river. Both men belonged to Captain John Yoakum's company. The Rangers, whom Rohrbaugh estimated to number about fifty, then moved on to the Yoakum farmstead, where they killed nineteen-year-old Private Michael Yoakum, who, according to company records, was "at his home, while sick."[19]

The next stop for the raiders was the Rohrbaugh home place. The Southerners robbed the captain's brother and sister and then commenced plundering the house. Rohrbaugh wrote, "They destroyed all our flour and other provisions we had on hand, took some cooking utensils, all my brother's Samuel's clothing, a new bolting cloth, . . . a side of sole leather, a side of harness leather, . . . and all my brother's papers."[20]

While this was going on, some of the Rangers spotted Private Aaron Stonestreet, Rohrbaugh's nephew, running into the woods and gave chase. They failed to catch the fleet youngster, but while out in the brush the men fortunately stumbled across a six hundred–round cache of rifle ammunition.

Not long before, Rohrbaugh had borrowed the bullets from Captain Boggs and hid them in what he thought was a safe place.[21]

The Rangers then moved on to the home of Private Isaac Hartman. When he tried to escape, the rebels chased after him, Rohrbaugh adding that "after pursuing him some distance into the woods, killed him, apparently after he had surrendered, for he was shot in the face, on the left side of the nose." Before leaving, the partisans took Hartman's "revolver, all his money, and all of his and Geo. Day's clothing."[22]

In closing, the captain reported that the surprise had been complete because "the rebel's came across the mountain opposite Yoakums, at a place where no hostile approach could be expected." Rohrbaugh assumed that they had been "piloted by someone well acquainted with the topography of the country." In a postscript, Rohrbaugh asked Pierpoint to send rations for Hartman's wife and two small children: "They are entirely destitute, and the deceased was a good man and soldier."[23]

On January 11 some of Woodson's men, led by Private J. Kelly, skirmished briefly with twenty or so Home Guards, who were raiding somewhere along the South Fork. After the Missourians chased them away, the Swamps descended on Solomon Dasher's farmstead at Peru and started robbing the place. The rebels, however, soon arrived and drove them off. The *Rockingham Register* commented that "it will be seen that some of McNeill's and some of Woodson's men are still deposed to 'peg away' whenever a chance offers at these pests."[24]

That same day Major Elias Troxel, commanding two hundred troopers from the 22nd Pennsylvania Cavalry left New Creek for Petersburg, hoping to get there quickly and attack the partisans before they had a chance to take flight. When the federals arrived, though, the river, its banks full from the rains of the last two days, was too high to ford. Just across the raging waters, about a hundred rebels watched them.[25]

Troxel then turned his men around and headed for the North Fork. On the evening of January 13, the Pennsylvanians arrived at the mouth of Seneca Creek. There Troxel received a message from Captain John Boggs that four companies of Confederates, along with two pieces of artillery, were camped in Franklin. In a little while Boggs and forty men arrived at Troxel's camp. At once the major determined to advance on the town and capture the rebels.[26]

After a physically demanding, all-night march on a rocky trail that took the Yankees across North Fork Mountain, the bluecoats arrived outside Franklin at five o'clock in the morning. Troxel had hoped to catch the butternuts napping but found out they were gone. Locals told the major that someone had warned the Southerners of his approach. After resting a few hours, he led his men back to their previous camp. Along the way guerrillas hidden in the rocks and trees high on the precipitous ridges took potshots at his soldiers, but they hit no one. Upon leaving Seneca Creek, Troxel moved on to Petersburg. There he reported that "I drove McNeill's command, they scattering to the mountains and, eluding pursuit, fired at me from the mountainsides." Following this skirmish, the Pennsylvanians returned to New Creek.[27]

CHAPTER 19

Capture of a Cavalier

———⊶∞⊷———

"I tried to be cheerful, but
it was hard to bear."

Sometime after the first of the year, General Early ordered Harry Gilmor to transfer his battalion from the Shenandoah Valley to Hardy County. Once there, he was to take command of McNeill's and Woodson's companies and conduct raids against the railroad. When Colonel Gilmor—promoted that previous September—arrived in Moorefield, sometime after the middle of the month, he had about a hundred of his own men, and he estimated that there were another two hundred rebels in the area.[1]

Once Gilmor informed the Rangers and Missourians that he was now in charge, the officers and men of both outfits promptly refused to acknowledge his authority. Their resistance, combined with the deep snow and frigid temperatures, led Gilmor to postpone any raiding. In the meantime, while waiting for the weather to moderate, his Marylanders either camped outside or boarded with the locals and worked hard to keep their horses well fed and in shape.[2]

When word got back to Early that Gilmor was having trouble with the independents, he decided to play another card. On January 31 the general wrote Robert E. Lee asking the commander to request that the War Department "revoke the exemption granted McNeill's company from the operation of the act abolishing partisan rangers." Despite the Rangers' previous valuable service to his army, he added, "The fact is that all those independent organizations, not excepting Mosby's, are injurious to us, and the occasional dashes they make do not compensate for the disorganization and dissatisfaction produced among other troops." Lee concurred with his lieutenant's opinion and forwarded the message to the War Department. It would be up to newly appointed Secretary of War John Breckinridge to make the final decision.[3]

To the subsequent delight of the partisans and their allies, though, Breckinridge never took any action on the matter. On February 5 Union forces captured

Henry Young. Author's collection.

Gilmor and removed him from the scene, and in the meantime the secretary received a February 2 letter from Captain Woodson, pleading his case to keep his company intact. Woodson, then hospitalized in Harrisonburg, feared that this conflict with Early and Gilmor might lead to Breckinridge ordering his Missourians back to Smith's 62nd Virginia Mounted Infantry. In the missive, he pointed out to his former commander the company's distinguished service under Breckinridge at New Market and elsewhere. Woodson also noted how disruptive Early's appointment of Gilmor to command had been.[4]

Sometime in mid-January Sheridan had received intelligence indicating that Gilmor was at Harrisonburg. Soon a pair of his so-called Sheridan Scouts, a band of gray-clad veteran troopers, who specialized in penetrating the rebel lines, left Winchester to track down the elusive Baltimorean. In a few days they returned and reported that Gilmor was then on his way to Moorefield. The general, who considered him "the last link between Maryland and the Confederacy," determined to remove this thorn in his side. Sheridan then ordered his chief of scouts, Major Henry Young, to send two other spies into Hardy County and find out where Gilmor was staying. According to Sergeant Joseph E. McCabe, Young's second in command, the major also sent a "widow, one of the Unionists Young used for information, to find out what Gilmor and McNeil were doing."[5]

On Tuesday, January 31, Private Archie Rowand and an unidentified partner left Winchester for Moorefield. With the area now swarming with Confederate horse soldiers home on leave or looking for remounts, the disguised pair had no trouble reaching the town and mingling with the rebels. In addition Rowand, who had spent part of his childhood in Greenville, South Carolina, spoke with a Deep South accent "that seemed to identify him with the gray." Two days later they were back at headquarters, disclosing to the commander "the whereabouts of Harry Gilmor and command." About the same time the widow showed up and made a report of "how their troops lay and where their headquarters were."[6]

Edward W. Whitaker. Library of Congress.

Now Sheridan ordered Lieutenant Colonel Edward W. Whitaker, of the 1st Connecticut Cavalry, to lead a force to Moorefield and grab Gilmor. Soon Whitaker had put together a three hundred–man contingent, some from his own regiment, plus troopers from the cavalry units 1st New Hampshire, 2nd Ohio, 8th New York, and 22nd New York. At six o'clock on the morning of February 4, with Major Young and his scouts in the vanguard, Whitaker left Winchester and rode south for Wardensville and Lost River Gap. The skies were clear, but it was bitterly cold.[7]

Upon arriving in Wardensville, Whitaker ordered a halt and rested his men before pressing on. Up the trail, the scouts suddenly ran into some rebel pickets but easily brushed them aside. Whitaker had been counting on using the bright moonlight to assist his raiders in an early morning attack on the enemy camp. As he neared his objective, though, the skies became cloudy and the wind started to pick up, foreshadowing a snow squall moving in rapidly from the west. At about twelve-thirty in the morning on Sunday, February 5, he halted his men some four miles from the town and began preparing to strike the enemy at dawn. Before long, though, some of Young's scouts returned from reconnoitering Moorefield and reported to the major that they could not find "Gilmor or his camp." The fearless Rhode Islander informed Whitaker of this development and then headed for the South Fork with his twenty men, to search some suspected partisan hideouts a few miles upstream.[8]

It was snowing heavily when Whitaker reached the town. Before following after Young, the colonel left his 2nd Ohio contingent to picket the village and roust out any Confederate bedded down there. Meanwhile, moving up the east side of the river, Whitaker soon spotted enemy riders on the far side of the stream, shadowing the column.[9]

Farther along, Young had already divided his men and pointed them in the direction of two large houses, on opposite sides of the South Fork. Rowand, guide Nick Carlisle, and a handful of others rode to Mill Island, home of the Williams family. In a few minutes they surrounded the place and captured one of General Tom Rosser's horsemen. At the same time Young, McCabe, Sergeant George D. Mullihan, and the rest of Young's band forded the narrow stream and descended silently on Moray Randolph's house, better known as The Willows, and toward a bloodless rendezvous with their prey. The Rangers, following their practice of not camping more than one night at the same place, were bedded down about a mile away.[10]

On the second floor of the dwelling, Gilmor and his cousin Hoffman Gilmor were still soundly asleep in their comfortable bed. No doubt, Gilmor felt he was safe: reliable compatriots were guarding all of the roads coming into

Moorefield, and if they failed to sound the alarm and strangers approached the house, the loud barking of his trusty bloodhound would surely warn him. What he did not know at the time, though, was that the blinding snow and freezing temperatures had driven some of the pickets from their stations, and his dog was either fast asleep, bedded down where it was warm, or off on an early morning jaunt.[11]

As the scouts approached the dwelling, Young noticed a number of horses in the stable. When the officer dismounted and walked over to investigate, he came across a young servant girl tending to her early morning chores. The major immediately asked her about the animals and found out that "they belonged to Major Gilmor." Young rushed over to the back door of the home and came face to face with Moray Randolph's wife, who told him straightaway that only her family was inside. While his men secured the grounds, Young and Mullihan brushed the defiant lady aside and commenced searching the place. After running up the steps and opening a door, they spied two men, in bed. "We got up Thair," Sergeant Joseph McCabe wrote, "into his Room Befor he knew it." Awakened suddenly by the noise, Gilmor started to get up but realized he was cornered; it was too late to fight.[12]

A reporter later interviewed the participants: "Major Young in an instant was at his bedside, seized Gilmor's pistols, which were on a chair, and then asked Gilmor who he was. He replied 'Major Gilmor,' and then added to his confronter, 'Who the devil are you!' The major replied, 'Major Young of General Sheridan's scouts.'"[13]

Young kept the pair covered with his revolver, while Mullihan went to the stable and saddled two horses; McCabe grabbed Harry's fleet black mare. After the Marylanders got dressed, Young led them downstairs and out into the yard. Just before the soldiers put their prize "on a sorry old horse," his devoted dog finally showed up. To keep the animal from being "confiscated" by the Yanks, Gilmor kicked him in the ribs, and with a yelp he scurried off.[14]

Now ready to go, Young took his prisoners across the shallow ford and reunited with Whitaker. For a time the colonel had been watching numerous graybacks "collecting on the bluff over the house and river and on my right flank and rear." Just when Young and Mullihan brought Gilmor to the front of the column, skirmishing broke out. Hoping to be rescued, the intrepid cavalier shouted "Give them the devil, boys." Immediately, Whitaker gave the order to move out. In the rear, Lieutenant Brown and thirty-eight men from the 1st Connecticut opened up on the rebels, but fifteen marksmen armed with rapid-firing Spencer rifles soon convinced the pesky graybacks to back off.[15]

When the bluecoats rode back through Moorefield, many young women rushed out of their houses to bid their handsome hero good-bye. As the ever-romantic cavalier remembered, "I tried to be cheerful, but it was hard to bear." Rather than return to Winchester via Wardensville, Whitaker followed Young's advice and took Trough Road to Romney. Far in front of the column, Young's scouts, whom one rebel described "as desperate a set of guerrillas as ever graced a saddle," kept on the lookout for unsuspecting butternuts they could first deceive and capture.[16]

The men had good hunting that day, rounding up twelve Confederates and killing one, the 18th Virginia Cavalry's legendary Captain George Stump. Six Rangers—Privates Manny Bruce, W. W. Harness, John Lynn, James McNeill, John Rafter, and R. Payton Tabb—were among those whom Young's gray-clad impostors tricked into surrendering and then hustled off to the rear for Fleming's troopers to watch.[17]

William Maloney, however, had better luck. According to his story, the young Ranger was at David T. Parson's house, about eight miles from Romney, when he peered outside and spied some riders coming down the road. At first he thought they were friends, but Maloney soon knew he was in a tight spot when a few of them entered the dwelling and started strong-arming the people "and demanding money and jewelry." Quickly darting into another room, he hid his coat, plopped onto a couch, and since it was Sunday started reading a prayer book. In an instant, two scouts burst through the door and spotted him. Accused of being a rebel, Maloney at last convinced them that he was just an innocent farmhand. About the time they started to rob him, Young arrived and called them off.[18]

The day before, Captain Stump, accompanied by Rangers Lynn and Bruce and 11th Virginia troopers John Casler and Joshua M. Lovett, had been on the trail returning home. Known by the nickname "Battery" Stump for his penchant for always being heavily armed, the stocky 6-foot, 240-pound grayback was still on the mend from a serious head wound. That evening Stump stopped at his sister's house to stay the night. Casler, who had nursed the captain for a time during his convalescence, decided to bunk there too; the others rode on. The next morning Stump left to see his parents, who were staying at Hickory Grove, his brother William's house, not far from Romney. There are various tales as to what happened next. Some said it was murder, while others claimed the captain only got what was coming to him.[19]

According to George Mullihan, it was just about noon when he spotted a house in the distance and told Young he was going over to get something to eat. While there, a servant girl told him that it was Captain Stump's house. Mullihan later wrote, "Knowing that Captain Stump was one of McNeill's scouts, with the reputation of hanging and cutting the throats of Union prisoners, I made further inquiry about him." After finding out the man was at church,

George Stump. Courtesy Ben Ritter.

the sergeant and some companions went there but discovered that the services were over and he was already gone. At first fooled by the men's gray uniforms, some parishioners volunteered where they could find Stump. Taking Carlisle with him and leaving the others to guard the churchgoers, Mullihan hurried down the road. Upon reaching the two-story brick mansion, they had started to search the basement when the captain dashed from the house to make his getaway. Upon hearing the commotion, the pair ran out into the yard and saw Stump mounting his horse. Mullihan shouted for him to surrender; then both men fired. Hit in the leg, the captain fell to the ground. As he started to rise, Stump reached for one of his guns, but by that time Mullihan had run up, put a pistol in his face, and forced the captain to his knees. When Mullihan and Carlisle questioned him, Stump denied strongly being the notorious rebel, insisting he was William.[20]

After disarming the painfully wounded man and helping Stump aboard his horse, the scouts took him to Young, and shortly after that he finally admitted to the major his identity. Mullihan related that Young said, "I suppose you know that we will have to kill you. But we will not serve you as you served our men, cut your throat or hang you. We will give you a chance for your life. We will give you ten rods start on your own horse, with your spurs on. If you get away, all right. But remember, my men are dead shots."[21]

In a few moments, a grinning Stump spurred his horse and took off at a gallop. When he had traveled the agreed distance, the Yanks opened fire, and their nemesis pitched into the road, dead. Although Gilmor made no mention of this incident in his memoirs, Mullihan quoted him as remarking, "Everything considered, I can't blame you."[22]

A *New York Herald* correspondent posted in Winchester later talked with some of the men and got the full scoop of Gilmor's capture and Stump's death. During the next week, other Northern, and even some Southern, papers published all or portions of the *Herald* article. The February 11 *Boston Evening Transcript* reported that "Stump . . . made a desperate resistance to his capture, and was only induced to surrender when perforated with bullets from the pistols of our men, from the effects of which he died." The piece went on to note the "three revolving pistols of a very novel and peculiar English manufacture" that Stump was carrying in his waist belt.[23]

But there was another side to the story. Over a month later the *Rockingham Register* published a letter to the editor filled with lurid details describing Stump's murder. The author, identified only by the letter M, related that he had learned the facts of Stump's death "from a person who was captured by the same party, who was an eyewitness to the tragedy, and who subsequently made his escape." According to the eyewitness, the Yankees first put Stump on his horse without giving him treatment for his "dangerous and disabling wound through the hip." As they went down the road, Stump passed out from the pain and tumbled off his mount.[24]

M continued:

> Then it was that the "perforating" commenced. He was deliberately shot through the head and then beaten over the head with a fence stake as long as he exhibited any sign of life. . . . It was nothing more than a most foul and fiendish murder. The wretch who fired the ball through his head, afterwards boasted of his act to his superior, Young, and received his commendation.[25]

Another Southern account claimed that as the scouts began to move out, Stump became too sick to ride. When one of them told Young, the major supposedly said, "Make him sicker." The men then shot the captain multiple times, stripped him, and left him lying in the road.[26]

Earlier that day Young's men had also collared John Casler. As he was riding along under guard, Casler grew apprehensive about Stump's fate but at length concluded that his friend probably had escaped. Finally, just past the Stump place, "I saw him lying dead in the road, with nothing on but his pants and shirt, and his face all black." On the way to Winchester, Casler questioned a pair of scouts about the incident and got two different versions. In the first, Stump, after being wounded, "said he could whip all of them if they would give him a chance, and that when they got out in the road, they gave him a chance, and commenced firing on him till they killed him." Casler, however, believed the other Yankee, who told him that Young "said that he was an old guerrilla chief, and told them to kill him, which they did."[27]

Despite the falling temperatures, Whitaker did not halt at Romney but kept pressing on, not stopping to rest and feed the horses until about nine o'clock that night. During this break, Private Manny Bruce sprinted off and vanished into the dark woods. He was the only prisoner Fleming's men lost on the way back to Winchester.[28]

According to Whitaker, they arrived at Capon Bridge "after midnight." Once there, he put most of the rebels in one house and bunked with Young, some of the scouts, and Gilmor and his cousin in another. The command left Capon Bridge about daylight and arrived in Winchester just before noon. "I reached Winchester with prisoners," the colonel wrote, "having ridden near 140 miles in a little over forty-eight hours, over a mountainous country, across swollen streams filled with floating ice, and within enemy lines, fully accomplishing the object of the mission without the loss of a man."[29]

Except for Gilmor, whom Young personally escorted to Boston's Fort Warren prison, Sheridan sent the rest of the captives to Fort McHenry. Casler recalled that at "Little Phil's" meeting with the men, he declared, "we were guerrillas of notorious character, and should be kept in close confinement at Fort McHenry, Baltimore, Md., during the war, and not be exchanged." The next day guards marched them five miles through a driving snowstorm to Stephenson's Depot and put the prisoner in an unheated Winchester & Potomac cattle car for the twenty-six-mile trip to Harpers Ferry. Once there they stood outside in the cold for four hours before boarding a B&O passenger train for the final leg of their trip.[30]

CHAPTER 20

The Kidnapping of the Generals

——— ⚬⚬⚬ ———

"You know me General, I suppose."

None of the Rangers shed any tears over Gilmor's capture, but they had to be embarrassed that the Yankees had slipped into their territory and ridden away with some of their own comrades. When Jesse got the news of their misfortune, he was determined to go ahead with a plan that he hoped could get the men released from prison. By now, with the devoted care of Sarah Sherrard, his nurse and future wife, Jesse was well on the mend. During his recuperation, he worked on a scheme that Sergeant John Fay had first proposed to the late captain. Enraged by General Kelley's August 1863 arrest and short imprisonment of his wife, daughter, and young son, Hanse had been determined to repay "Old Ben," but he never got the chance. Now the young company commander was considering taking a small force into Cumberland and grabbing the general. When, in late January, Cumberland native John Lynn requested a furlough to return home, Jesse granted him leave and "instructed him to find out all he could bearing upon the enterprise under contemplation and report to me on his return."[1]

Subsequently captured by Sheridan's Scouts, Lynn never returned from his reconnaissance, but meanwhile, according to Jefferson Duffey, Fay, another Queen City native, had made two trips to the town and secured knowledge of picket posts and the hotel where Kelley was staying. It was about this time that the idea originated to seize General Crook as well.[2]

After meeting with Fay and some others, Jesse decided to press ahead with the plan. If they could capture the generals and get them to Richmond, he hoped to trade the pair for the five Rangers confined in Fort McHenry. McNeill ordered Fay and Private Richie Hallar to "proceed to Cumberland, secure all the information they could, and report to me at the Hampshire County Poorhouse on the night of February 19." Hallar, the teenaged Missouri refugee who had joined the Rangers in Mercersburg, Pennsylvania, during the Gettysburg Campaign, was now one of the outfit's best scouts. Fay, who picked the youngster to go with him, described Hallar as "well tested of courage and prudence."[3]

A few nights later Fay and Hallar forded the river five miles above Cumberland, hid their horses, and then walked a short way to the house of railroad worker George Stanton, an Irishman whom Fay knew well. Fay gave his trusted friend specific instructions for an important spying mission. On the evening of Monday, February 20, Stanton was to go into town, taking a young neighbor along to help. One of the men was to make sure that each officer "had turned in for the night." The other man was to meet the raiders "at a designated time and place."[4]

The scouts were soon back on their horses and splashing across the ford. They stayed in the saddle for the next twenty miles, until reaching Vause Herriot's house at dawn. A trusted ally, the bachelor lived on an isolated farm about five miles north of Romney. When the cold, famished men arrived, Herriott quickly fixed them breakfast. After finishing his meal, Fay penned a message to McNeill and handed it to Hallar. Not long afterward the youngster headed south, disappearing quickly into a sudden snow squall.[5]

Fay's message read: "Dear Jesse: I have been across the Potomac and find all O.K. Meet me here on Monday evening. Haller will give you all other particulars. The attempt, if carried out, will certainly prove successful. J.B.F."[6]

Jesse had been quite busy while his spies were away. First he met with Welton and Boggs. After filling them in on the plan, Jesse ordered the pair to make "the needed preparations for the trip by having the horses shod, getting together rations, etc." On the night of February 18, his leg in splints and still having to rely on crutches, McNeill left the Sherrard farm, accompanied by Rangers "Missouri John" Cunningham and Joe Vandiver, along with Private Joseph Kuykendahl of Company F, 7th Virginia Cavalry. They finally stopped to bed down at Jacob Smith's house, located east of the South Branch, four miles below Moorefield.[7]

The next morning Jesse traded his crutches for a cane before going downriver to meet with his men. On reaching their camp, McNeill stayed out in the frigid, snowy weather while selecting riders with the best and strongest horses. When Jesse finished, he had chosen Welton, Cunningham, Vandiver, and forty-three other Rangers. The lieutenant also included Kuykendahl and eight top scouts from the 7th, along with six troopers from Company D, 11th Virginia Cavalry. McNeill left Gus Boggs in charge of the rest of the Rangers, ordering him to guard the roads, protect the rear, and "report anything that might threaten the success of our undertaking."[8]

After that the rebels continued down Trough Road to the Hampshire County Poorhouse and waited. At this time, according to one account, Jesse sent a courier back to Boggs to get twenty Union overcoats. That night a tired Hallar arrived with Fay's message, and sometime after ten o'clock on the morning of February 20, McNeill and the men rode north, traveling slowly so as not to tire their horses. Upon reaching the turnpike and passing through Mechanicsburg Gap, Jesse signaled them to move faster, and they finally reached Herriot's house just after dark. While the men fed their mounts and got something to eat, McNeill met with Fay. Before long Jesse called his followers together and told them the goal of the upcoming mission. The young lieutenant went on to say he would only take volunteers. If anyone wanted to turn back, "he could do so without censure." To Jesse's delight, not one balked. "It was gratifying to find all willing to go," he wrote, "and each man conducted himself as if success depended on his actions alone." Nonetheless, he was still nervous about the undertaking, knowing it was up to him to get his men back alive: "I recalled a lecture which my father gave me on his deathbed about my rashness and foolhardiness . . . and telling me to look well for a getting out of a place before going in."[9]

Now it was time to depart. With Fay leading the way, the column moved out, heading for the trail across Knobly Mountain. About three hours later, in what might have been the physically toughest part of the mission for man and beast, the riders began crossing the steep, snow-covered heights. After navigating the icy bridle path up and through the narrow gap, on the western slope they encountered great snowdrifts covering the open fields, "which," Fay recalled, "forced us to dismount and lead our struggling horses." After descending the mountain, the chilled riders stopped at Ren Seymour's farm to get some whiskey. Welton and a few others got off their horses, walked over to the house, and woke him up.[10]

Seymour was glad to fill some canteens for the rebels, but he warned them to go easy on the stuff. Then Ren took Joe Vandiver aside and said, "Van, for God's sake, your sake, your mother's sake, turn back! There are over 8,000 troops in and about Cumberland; you have only a handful; you will never return alive." Edwin Harness, one of Jesse's friends, just happened to be staying with Seymour that night. Harness, from Ohio, was on his way to visit relatives in Moorefield. When the Rangers got ready to leave, Harness bade them good-bye and said that he never expected to see them again. A confident few called back that they would "meet him in Moorefield."[11]

Vandiver recalled crossing the North Branch "in the running ice and slush . . . and the water was high enough to wet every man." Now in Maryland, the graybacks rode silently through the river bottoms until reaching Sam Brady's

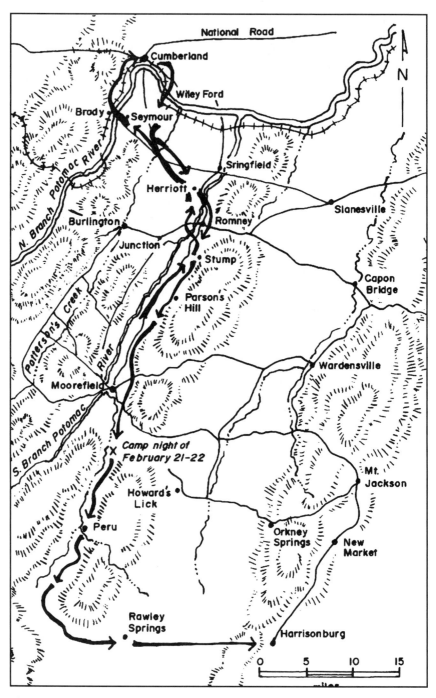

The Kidnapping of the Generals (John Heiser).

house, on the eastern edge of Cresaptown. McNeill left most of the troop in a nearby field, then took Fay, Vandiver, Jim Dailey, Kuykendahl, and some others over to the dwelling. There Stanton and fellow spy John Brady were waiting. Once inside, the Irishman gave the rebels the latest news from Cumberland and added that a cavalry patrol headed for New Creek had passed by two hours before. John Brady told McNeill that he "had left Cumberland about eleven o'clock that night and that everything was quiet when he left."[12]

From Brady's, Fay had planned to lead the raiders north for a while before changing course and riding into town on the National Road, a highway not guarded by the federals. But it was now after two in the morning, and he knew it was far too late to make this roundabout ten-mile trek. If they were to complete the mission successfully, their only alternative was to take New Creek Road and risk a confrontation with Yankee pickets stationed along the way. At this time, Fay remembered, McNeill suddenly considered calling off the endeavor "but to prevent the trip from being an entire failure, he suggested that we should surprise and capture the pickets at the railroad station nearby, at Brady's Mill." Those gathered around him, however, rejected his proposal; Jesse then determined to ride on. At that time, according to Private Sprigg Lynn, both he and Fay understood that they would lead the parties into the hotels to capture the generals, "as," Lynn later wrote, "a compensation for services rendered as scouts."[13]

When the meeting ended, they rejoined the other men and began the five-mile ride into Cumberland. The daring Southerners were now heading into a city garrisoned by 3,500 to 4,000 federal soldiers. That night, though, most of these troops were sleeping at Camp Hasting, located west of town. In total there were five infantry regiments, one battery, and one company of cavalry protecting the "Queen City of the Alleghenies."[14]

McNeill and Vandiver led the way, followed closely by Fay, Kuykendahl, and eight others. Farther back, Welton came with the rest. Fay recalled:

> A layer of thin, crusty snow was on the ground, and although it was an hour and a half before dawn, we could see very well for a short distance. The New Creek road skirts the base of Will's Mountain, running almost parallel with the railroad and river and all three come close together at the mouth of a deep ravine, about two miles from Cumberland. Here the road deflects to the left and winds up through the ravine and over the hill to the city. A cavalry picket was stationed at the mouth of the ravine and as we neared this point, a solitary vedette was observed standing on the roadside.[15]

Seymour House. Courtesy Mark Jones.

They were almost to the B&O water station when a voice cried out, "Halt! Who comes there?" "Friends and scouts from New Creek," was the immediate reply. The soldier, one of a trio of bluecoats guarding the road, may have thought the riders were Major Young's men or Kelley's Tigers. He called for one man to dismount, come forward, and give the countersign. Instantly Jesse kicked his horse in the ribs and dashed ahead. When the surprised guard shouted for him to halt, McNeill shot at the Yankee but missed. In the meantime, Fay and the vanguard rushed forward and seized the man, who was a German immigrant, and his two companions. Fortunately for the Southerners, the soldiers farther down the road at the reserve picket post did not hear the gunshot.[16]

The raiders soon discovered that their captives belonged to the 3rd Ohio Independent Cavalry Company. If they were to pass the next set of pickets successfully, McNeill needed to get one of them to tell him the countersign. At first the soldiers refused, the German even standing his ground when Jesse put the barrel of his cocked revolver between the man's eyes. Finally, though, after one of the graybacks put a halter strap around the stubborn hero's neck and prepared to lynch him, the frightened horse soldier suddenly blurted out, in his thick German accent, "Bool's Gap [Bull's Gap]." Many years later, General Crook commented, "By threats they made the ignorant Dutchman ... give them the countersign." Fay and Kuykendahl now took the lead; Welton, whose men were to follow and guard the prisoners, ordered the pair guarding the German to shoot him if, at the reserve picket post, "Bull's Gap" proved to be wrong.[17]

A mile farther along, at the intersection of the "old Frostburg pike," the advance came to the reserve post, manned by five soldiers of the 1st West Virginia Veteran Infantry. Seated inside a shed, the men were playing cards, a roaring log fire nearby providing them some heat and plenty of light. As one got up slowly and asked for the countersign, the raiders moved forward swiftly and grabbed the surprised mountaineers. After disarming the bluecoats and destroying their rifles and ammunition, the rebels released them on a parole of honor after they agreed to remain there until their captors returned. Now McNeill divided his men and gave them their final orders. Due to his injury, Jesse could not dismount and conduct the actual capture of the generals, so after privately meeting with Vandiver and Kuykendahl, he picked Vandiver to lead a squad into the Revere House to get Crook, while at the same time Kuykendahl would take another band to the nearby Barnum House and seize Kelley. He subsequently ordered Fay and Hallar to ransack the B&O telegraph office and cut the wires, while John Arnold and George Cunningham were getting horses from the military stable. When Lynn told Fay that Jesse had changed their roles, the disgusted scout, still fuming over Jesse shooting at the German, replied, "I can stand it if he can."[18]

By three o'clock that morning, the column was entering the city. Traveling down Greene Street, the rebels passed by a brick house where some Yankees were quartered. As one blue-clad rebel told the unsuspecting guards, they were "Scouts from New Creek." Others were singing or whistling Yankee tunes. Continuing, they soon passed over the iron bridge spanning Wills Creek and descended onto Baltimore Street. Upon approaching the Saint Nicholas Hotel, Sprigg Lynn spotted a soldier outside that establishment and another at the Barnum, just across Saint George Street. He quickly dismounted, and followed by Rangers George Carrell, Charles Nichols, and 11th Virginia trooper John Dailey, walked over to the Saint Nicholas and silently captured the unsuspecting sergeant. Both men then crossed the street to the Barnum House, and as the riders were passing by, Lynn quickly got the drop on the other soldier. In a few moments the vanguard halted outside the Revere House, and the rear of the column pulled up at the Barnum. As McNeill and the rest of the men waited, the soldiers in each detachment dismounted and departed on their missions. In the meantime a few others went forward and captured the B&O's night watchman. Then the waiting began. Years later Jesse stated, "As I sat up on my horse surveying my surroundings . . . I must confess that doubt was uppermost in my conflicting emotions."[19]

Outside the Barnum, Lynn turned one prisoner over to his friends. By that time Kuykendahl, John Dailey, and William Maloney had arrived and followed Lynn as the scout took the sergeant along with him to find Kelley's room. Going up the steps to the second floor, the men first entered the room of Captain Thayer Melvin, Kelley's assistant adjutant general. A week later an anonymous Ranger described the scene: "They . . . found him in bed with his wife, who happened to be a blushing bride and as quickly but as gently as possible, succeeded in making the blissful bridegroom into a miserable poor devil of a prisoner." If this incident actually happened, the woman was certainly not Melvin's wife; the twenty-nine-year-old was a bachelor.[20]

In a few moments Kuykendall entered the adjoining room and awakened the slumbering old hero. That evening both Kelley and Crook had stayed out late, attending a society dance at Belvedere Hall. The young rebel and Kelley had met before. On January 14, 1862, federals had captured the scout near Springfield and brought him to the general's Cumberland headquarters. Before the Yankees exchanged Kuykendahl that fall, he had served prison stints at Camp Chase and Johnson's Island, Ohio.[21]

On February 28 the *Richmond Whig* published the details of Kelley and Kuykendall's second meeting:

> "You know me, General, I suppose," says Joseph W. Kuykendahl, who had charge of this party. "I do," said the general. "You are ———," giving his name. "General, you had me once, it is my honor to have you now. You are a prisoner." "But," says the general, "whom am I surrendering to?" "To me, sir," was the emphatic response, "No place or time for ceremony, so you will dress quickly."[22]

In a less dramatic recounting of the episode, Fay said that when Kelley asked whom he was surrendering to, the scout replied, "To Captain McNeill, by order of General Rosser." Once Kuykendall got both officers out of the hotel and into the street, Kelley climbed aboard John Cunningham's mount, while Melvin got on another man's horse. By now, though, some of the Rangers were becoming jumpy, Vandiver had still not returned, and just down the street a stock train had pulled into the rail yard. Off in the distance they could see its crew, illuminated by their lanterns, walking around, checking the cars. McNeill immediately sent Cunningham "to tell Vandiver to come with or without Crook, we must be getting out."[23]

While the others were grabbing Kelley, Vandiver's squad had arrived outside the Revere House. The sergeant told the lone guard that he had dispatches

"A Surprise for General Kelley," by Garnet Jex. Courtesy Sharpsburg Historical Society.

for Crook, and then, before the man could respond, collared him. Vandiver then whispered in his ear, "Speak above your breath, and you are a dead man." Then, since Private Jacob Gassman of Company F, 7th Virginia Cavalry, and Jim Dailey were well acquainted with the building, Vandiver chose them to lead the way. The hotel was owned by Gassman's uncle, and he had previously worked there as a clerk. And for some time John Dailey, Jim's father, had been the establishment's proprietor.[24]

The pair now knocked on the door. As soon as night porter Bill Cooper unlocked it, the rebels came in quietly. The young African American promptly recognized Gassman and Dailey but not the others. When asked where Crook was, Cooper said he was not there. But when someone put a gun to his head and whispered, "We want the truth," Cooper replied. "Yes sah, but don't tell 'im I told you." While Gassman headed up the steps to room 46, Dailey and Vandiver went into the office to get a lantern. The pair, however, were not alone; Captain Charles D. Bowen, 2nd Connecticut Infantry, was sleeping soundly in the room, but the rebels did not spot him. Meanwhile, Trueheart remained outside, guarding the entrance.[25]

Suddenly awakened by Gassman's rapping on the door, the usually wary thirty-seven-year-old Crook had no reason to suspect anything was amiss. In fact, in those wee hours of the morning, the general's thoughts might have been far from military affairs. According to Dailey family lore, that evening the general had asked the lovely Mary Dailey, Jim's sister, for her hand in marriage. When Crook asked, "Who's there?" Gassman answered, "A friend." By the time Crook told Gassman to come in, Vandiver, Dailey, and Private Sam Tucker were with him. Vandiver boldly approached the general, who remained in bed, and spoke[26]:

> "General Crook, you are my prisoner." "What authority do you have for this?" inquired Crook. "The authority of General Rosser, of Fitzhugh Lee's division of cavalry, said Vandiver in response." Crook then rose up in bed and said, "Is General Rosser here?" "Yes," replied Vandiver, "I am General Rosser; I have 2,500 men with me, and we have surprised and captured the town."[27]

Crook said later that in the darkness he thought that the stocky, powerfully built rebel was Rosser. Vandiver gave the general two minutes to get dressed. While Crook got up and started to put on his clothes, Dailey and Gassman searched for plunder. Jim picked up the general's field glasses; Jacob grabbed a cap and a pair of corduroy pants. Someone appropriated one of Crook's coats and his sword; headquarters flags were gathered. As they hustled the general out of the room, Gassman spotted some letters lying on a table and picked them up. Later he discovered many of the letters were not important military papers but Mary's romantic missives to Crook. Pockets now full of booty, the Confederates closed the door and began walking softly down the steps; about the only thing they left behind was half a fruitcake.[28]

Before they went outside, one of the men whispered in Crook's ear to keep quiet, and the general obeyed dutifully. A soldier recalled that "he passed out with his escort, as mute as a mummy." Just about the time Crook mounted up, Fay arrived with the news that his squad had wrecked the telegraph office and cut the lines. As the Rangers began to leave, an excited young bellhop named John Chambers came outside carrying a lantern and shouted out, "How many Johnnies have you caught?" Suddenly, John Cunningham took the boy's hat, John Taylor checked his pockets for money, and William Maloney pulled his coat over his head.[29]

The command now reversed direction and headed back up Baltimore Street. Welton's squad, with both generals' headquarters flags proudly displayed, led the way; McNeill brought up the rear. The prisoners were riding double, each seated behind a rebel. Just before reaching the Chain Bridge over Wills Creek, John Arnold and George Cunningham showed up with at least eight horses from Kelley's military stable; a Shetland pony tagged along. Arnold was riding Philippi, Kelley's prized thoroughbred, a cherished gift from his many Wheeling friends. The graybacks now stopped and put each prisoner on a horse, although Crook's mount did not have a saddle. All of this took some time, and now they had been in town twenty to twenty-five minutes.[30]

McNeill was anxious to leave and called upon Fay to lead the way. Joined by Vandiver and Kuykendall, the scout led the troop down Water Street for a short distance before nearing the C&O Canal. Moving steadily, they encountered a dozen soldiers at Guard Lock No. 8, promptly surrounded and disarmed them, then "speedily decamped down the towpath." Some two miles farther along, pickets posted at a bridge that carried a road over the canal to a nearby river crossing halted the rebels. When Corporal Isaac Judy forgot the countersign, one of the Yankees said, "Sergeant, shall I fire?" Vandiver immediately shouted, "If you do, I'll place you under arrest. This is General Crook's bodyguard and we have no time to waste. The Rebels are coming, and we are going out to meet them." Upon hearing this and seeing the flags, the soldiers allowed the raiders to move on. The band then passed under the bridge, rode over to the riverbank, and crossed Wiley Ford into West Virginia. As they moved on, one bluecoat shouted, "Give them the d—l boys, when you catch them." To which a partisan replied, "All right, we'll do it." During this time, Trueheart recalled, "the generals . . . were as quiet as lambs." Once across the North Branch, a Ranger guarding one of the Ohio troopers took his horse and turned him loose.[31]

McNeill planned to reach Romney as fast as he could and then take Trough Road to Moorefield before moving on up the South Fork. The raiders still had to cover close to fifty miles before they would be safe. Once Cumberland's garrison was aroused, all knew that pursuers would soon be coming after them. Likewise, when the federal commanders at New Creek and Winchester heard of the incidents, cavalry would depart those places and try to cut the rebels off before they could get across the mountains above Moorefield and into the Shenandoah Valley.[32]

As they were riding along Old Furnace Road, about five miles from Cumberland, "we heard," as one of them remembered, "the firing of the signal gun . . . boom after boom, rang out." The raiders promptly picked up the pace. Crook, riding bareback, complained to Maloney that he needed a saddle. Although at first the Ranger was puzzled as to where he could get one, Maloney finally rode ahead to a nearby farm. There, after getting Jacob Kyles out of bed and convincing him that he needed a saddle, the man told him to look in the flour barrel. Maloney's effort to get the saddle was greatly appreciated by Crook, who, earlier, had thanked Trueheart for stopping along the road and pulling down the legs of his long underwear, which had bunched up around his knees. An appreciative Crook told the Texan, "Young man, if I can ever be of service to you, call on me."[33]

Three days later a *Fairmont National* scribe, who was certainly no admirer of General Kelley, satirically described the Ranger's early morning escape. The West Virginian wrote:

On they went, as fast as fresh horses could carry them; in the midst of the gallant sixty rode the Major-Generals, with thoughts no longer intent on the "gay and festive" scenes of the ball-room or in cultivating the little arts of coquetry which call around admiring bevies of women whose influence is so potent in subduing the stern qualities of mind so essential in a good military chieftain. But we imagine that our kind hearted Gen. Kelley at last began to realize that he had been betrayed into the hands of the enemy by home Rebels whom he always treated with so much leniency, not to say distinguished consideration.[34]

After crossing Patterson Creek, McNeill turned to General Kelley and said, "What do you think about this?" "Old Ben," who so far on the trip had been deep in his thoughts and silent, replied, "It is a disgrace, that two major generals should be captured by a beardless, broken-legged boy, with a handful of men."[35]

CHAPTER 21

The Getaway

"You boys have beaten me badly."

Inside the Revere House, Major William McKinley, "hearing a slight movement in the general's room and thinking he might be unwell," got out of bed and went across the hall to check on him. Upon finding the room empty, McKinley opened the window, "heard the clattering of hoofs and saw the party disappearing down the street." When the half-awake officer finally realized what had happened, he woke up Crook's other aides. They hurriedly dressed and then rushed up to the Barnum and found out that Kelley and Melvin were also missing. In the meantime, Bill Cooper and others were spreading the alarm. Soon a group of officers that included Brigadier General Rutherford B. Hayes, Brigadier General Joseph "The Fighting Parson" Lightburn, Lieutenant Colonel Andrew J. Greenfield, Major Robert P. Kennedy, Captain James Hart, and McKinley gathered at the Revere House to discuss the situation and organize the pursuit. Within an hour and twenty minutes, Hart and fellow Pennsylvanian Lieutenant William E. Griffith had gathered enough horses to mount a detachment of approximately fifty 23rd Ohio infantrymen and started out to rescue the generals.[1]

Before leaving the telegraph office, Fay's detachment had bound operator A. T. Brenaman, "hand and foot," walked out of the wrecked building, and locked the door. After struggling with the ropes, Brenaman finally broke free and unlocked the office. By then help had arrived, and the men went to work repairing the wires. Although the rebels were sure they had put the telegraph completely out of commission, by six o'clock in the morning the resourceful operator was busy tapping out Major Kennedy's alert to New Creek, sending it out on the wire via Pittsburgh and Wheeling. A short time later, Captain James L. Botsford, one of Crook's aides who had crossed the river and trailed the raiders for a time, returned to headquarters and reported, "They are going direct to Romney, via Springfield, they are riding very fast."[2]

Soon after word of the incident reached New Creek, Major Elias Troxel got about 150 men ready to leave for Moorefield and try to intercept the Rangers before they could vanish into the mountains. Kelley's Tigers pulled out first, and at about seven-thirty the Pennsylvanians followed. In the meantime, Major Work led some troopers to Romney. Later on Lightburn and Greenfield arrived in New Creek by special train. Greenfield hurriedly gathered a squad of horsemen and galloped off to join in the chase.[3]

Immediately after sending the wire to New Creek, Kennedy sent another to Sheridan at Winchester. After providing "Little Phil" with a sketch of what had happened, he wrote, "Cannot parties be sent out from the Valley to intercept them?" In a little while, Sheridan ordered Colonel Whitaker and his men into the saddle.[4]

Back in Cumberland, the excited citizens were now up and out in the streets, speculating on what rebel outfit had pulled off the amazing feat. Some said the kidnappers were Rosser's men, others guessed McNeill's Rangers or the remnants of Gilmor's outfit. Many suspected that local secessionists helped with the planning; a wild rumor implicating Sheridan's Scouts began circulating through the mob. A few Unionists accused Nellie Tidball, a beautiful young Winchester, Virginia, belle, of being involved in the kidnappings, but she quickly proved her innocence.[5]

As an unidentified member of the West Virginia Legislature reported,

> It was, however, the common talk among a certain class of people in Cumberland, that the men who took away the generals, were our own soldiers, and it is said that a distinguished officer connected with General Sheridan's scouts was seen walking around among the rebs, speaking to them in a tone of authority. This conjecture found credence only among the citizens, the military authorities being firmly convinced that it was a bona-fide capture.[6]

Riding fresh horses, Hart's squad made good time, stopping only whenever they saw one of Crook's letters lying in the road. Pressing forward, the Yankees crossed Patterson Creek and followed the rebels' trail a mile upstream to the Johnson place. When Hart halted there to give the horses a breather, McNeill's rear guard spotted them and then rode on.[7]

With Crook's and Kelley's headquarters flags held high, the Rangers entered Romney sometime after nine o'clock on the morning of February 21.

Stump House. Author's collection.

Upon reaching the courthouse, the rebels turned west onto the turnpike and followed it through town to Trough Road. When McNeill's column passed William Stump's house, 11th Virginia Cavalry troopers Sergeant J. L. Sherrard and Private John Poland decided to stop at Hickory Grove, get some corn for their horses, and then ride off to visit their families. According to John Casler, Manny Bruce and a few comrades also dropped in to get something to eat and talk to some girls.[8]

As Sherrard kept watch, Poland went to the barn. A few moments later the sergeant spotted some black objects off in the distance, milling around the burned ruins of the turnpike's covered bridge. At first he thought they were cows but suddenly realized bluecoats were on the way. Sherrard shouted a warning and told everyone to hurry. Soon they were on their horses, racing up the road with the Yanks not far behind.[9]

When Poland's charger started to play out, he forgot about catching up with McNeill, and hoping to escape into the woods, left the road, and started riding up a hill. Sherrard followed close behind, but the others rode on. The climb, though, was too much for the private's faltering steed, and Sherrard had to stop and pick up his friend. Now, with their pursuers closing in fast and shooting at them, the sergeant remembered that he had a B&O time schedule in his pocket. Fearing a hangman's noose if the federals found it on him, Sherrard took the small book out of his pocket, bent low, and pitched it under his horse's hooves. About that time Poland screamed when a bullet clipped his leg; Sherrard pulled on his reins and stopped.[10]

While a few bluecoats gathered around the pair, Hart led the rest forward. About four miles farther on, McNeill stopped and ordered Welton to take charge of the rear guard. Jesse, certain that their pursuers would continue the chase, told Welton to keep the Yankees from rushing in and freeing the prisoners. His fearless subordinate replied, "I will do it, or they will ride over my dead body."[11]

As McNeill and the rest galloped away, Welton dismounted the rear guard and formed a skirmish line along Parsons' Hill. There a steep ridge protected the rebel right flank, and a high cliff descending to the fields along the South Branch secured the left. In the meantime, as Hart neared the hill he saw a chance to capture the handful of fleeing graybacks they had been chasing and waved his men forward. Suddenly, though, he and Griffith realized that the Buckeyes had not followed. As Farrar wrote, "A sharp hand-to-hand skirmish occurred in which Griffith was captured, after he had exhausted his ammunition." Then 11th Virginia private Robert Moorehead, who along with his comrade, Private John W. Urton, had grabbed the lieutenant and taken his revolver. Afterward, Welton held his position for about an hour and before riding on, paroled the lieutenant "with the understanding that he was to be exchanged for Sergeant Joe Sheared."[12]

After tending to Poland's flesh wound, the bluecoats rode back to Romney and left him there. Upon reaching Cumberland that evening, Hart took Sherrard to the provost marshal's office, where he endured intense questioning by a number of officers before winding up in the guardhouse and spending "the night among a lot of bounty jumpers, deserters, and a very hard crowd." The authorities in Cumberland refused to acknowledge Griffith's parole, so on Wednesday morning Sherrard was aboard a B&O train on his way to Wheeling's Antheneum Prison. A day or two later his jailers transferred him to Camp Chase, Ohio.[13]

Somewhere along the way, McNeill dispatched a rider to Moorefield to alert Boggs and Woodson that he would soon be there. Around midday the raiders rode by David Van Meter's farm, just across the river from Old Fields. Upon

Old Trough (River) Road–Parsons Hill. Author's collection.

reaching Zedrick's Hill, they found John Peerce and Woodson's Missourians, ready to lend a hand. While taking a short break, the men suddenly spotted federal cavalry racing through Old Fields toward the river. Jesse swiftly sent a galloper to Moorefield with orders for "Boggs . . . to form his men below town and bluff them as long as possible, and if compelled to retreat to then fall back through town and then up the South Branch, while we would take to the ridges and flank the town, to the left, and come out two miles above on the South Fork."[14]

For a time, Tappen Wright Kelley's hard-charging Tigers and the graybacks, separated by the South Branch, were almost parallel to one another. By now the young captain was close enough to recognize his father and desperately wanted to free him. As the federals neared the lower ford, however, the partisans left the road and disappeared into the woods, causing a disappointed Crook to mutter, "So near and yet so far." Captain Kelley then waited another hour for Troxel, who was still on his way from Purgitsville, to come up. Sometime after two in the afternoon, the Yankees, now reunited, crossed the river, and soon engaged Boggs's squad. After easily brushing the rebels aside and finally reaching

Moorefield, the major continued to Moray Randolph's place. Once there he realized that it was useless to continue the chase. By this time the major knew that McNeill was far south of town and figured that reinforcements sent by Rosser had already joined them. In a little while, Troxel turned his men around and led them back to Old Fields, with three prisoners and five captured horses in tow. There Greenfield was on the scene and took command. That night, the federals camped on the grounds of Willow Wall.[15]

Whitaker's 340-man column, its progress hindered by deep snowdrifts across portions of Wardensville Road, did not reach Moorefield until one thirty in the afternoon of February 22. After discovering that the graybacks had long ago made their escape, the colonel sent an aide to communicate with the federals at Old Fields. While tracking the raiders by torchlight, Whitaker's scouts discovered that after crossing Wardensville Road, McNeill had taken "a wooded path on my right down a steep declivity into woods on my left." Uninterested in continuing a hopeless chase and concerned over approaching bad weather, Whitaker decided to return to Winchester via Romney. Later, along Trough Road, the colonel's courier arrived with Greenfield's reply, saying that he would cooperate with Whitaker if he wanted to continue the pursuit. By this time, however, Whitaker was well on his way back to Winchester and, he reported, "I had moved out to far too return a reply."[16]

After flanking the town, McNeill followed an obscure trail for a while until coming out on South Fork Road. Not stopping to rest, he pressed on until he reached the intersection of Howards Lick Road. Once there McNeill stopped and gave his boys and their horses a breather. He wrote, "Here we rested for the first time since leaving Vance [Vause] Herriot's the night before, having ridden seventy-five miles without food or rest." While they were there, Boggs rode in with news about his skirmish with Troxel. Pleased with the report, McNeill then ordered the officer to have some of his men picket South Fork Road.[17]

It was about this time that "Old Ben" made a request. Incensed that John Arnold was riding Philippi, a horse that was not only expensive but one that the general held in great sentimental value, he asked McNeill to take the animal for his own and keep it. When the war was over, the general promised to buy Philippi back. McNeill refused.[18]

After an hour's rest, Welton took the lead as the Rangers rode deeper into the mountain fastness. Just before dark they reached a safe haven about eight miles from Moorefield and stopped to camp. While some of the men were starting fires to get warm and prepare a welcomed repast of "stale bread and fat bacon," others went into the nearby corncribs and fields to gather grain and hay. McNeill, though, went to the home of George Harness. After his men helped Jesse off his mount and took him inside, the lieutenant, Kuykendahl, Raison C. Davis, Harness, and Vandiver ate supper and then bunked there for the night.[19]

McNeill got little rest. Physically exhausted from the long ride and suffering severe leg pain, he was awake most of the night. Just after three on the morning of February 22, Boggs rode in with news of another Yankee force arriving in Moorefield. McNeill then alerted Welton, who was going to take the generals to Richmond, to saddle his horses and get ready to leave. An hour or so later, though, Boggs returned and reported that the federals had retreated.[20]

That morning Jesse handed Welton a report to deliver to General Early in Staunton. It read:

> I have the honor to report that on the morning of the 21st, I entered Cumberland with about sixty men, fifty from my own company and ten from Co. D. 11th Va. Cavalry, and succeeded in capturing Major Generals Crook and Kelley, Capt. Melvin, Kelley's Adjt. Gen., two privates, and four stands of colors. All of whom I succeeded in bringing off safely. The enemy made desperate attempts to recapture them but failed. I was followed as far as Moorefield by about two hundred and fifty cavalry. I reached this place about dark last evening. Scouts report this morning that the enemy who have followed me have gone back.[21]

Welton took a small squad of soldiers with him to guard the prisoners. The group included Davis, Vandiver, Private Peter Deevemon, and, most likely, John Peerce. Before they left, Crook thanked the Rangers for their kind treatment. Traveling on fresh horses, the riders continued up the South Fork Valley. After thirty miles of hard riding, they reached the intersection of the road to Harrisonburg. Riding on over Shenandoah Mountain and through Dry River Gap, Welton finally halted at Rawley Springs.[22]

Back in Cumberland that evening, the uproar caused by the thrilling escapade was finally settling down. In fact, many soldiers and citizens were enjoying themselves celebrating George Washington's birthday at a Belvedere Hall charity event. Among the scheduled performers was vocalist Mary Clare Bruce, the lovely young daughter of Colonel Robert Bruce, commander of the 2nd Maryland Potomac Home Brigade infantry. Everyone in the audience knew that Miss Bruce and twice-widowed "Old Ben" were romantically involved. Moreover, just two nights before, the twenty-two-year-old beauty had attended the dance there with him. One of her selections, "Of't He Kissed Me, When He Left Me," caused a terrific commotion. As she was singing the words "He kissed me when he left," many heard a drunken bluecoat bellow, "I'll be damned if he did. McNeill didn't give him time." Others, however, reported hearing "That's a d———d lie; he hadn't even time to put his boots on." As the audience exploded in laughter, a flustered Mary Clare ran off the stage, crying.[23]

Early on the morning of February 23, Welton got everyone up and in the saddle for the twelve-mile ride into Harrisonburg. Once in town the men stopped at Hill's Hotel for breakfast. As they were dismounting, Crook spoke to the small crowd that had gathered. "Gentlemen," he said, "this is the most brilliant exploit of the war." Later, as they were leaving the establishment, an Irishman walked up to Kelley and handed him a box of cigars. The general, though, refused the gift, telling the man he "did not smoke," and Crook did likewise. Melvin, however, gladly took the box, in which he later discovered a $100 Confederate bill.[24]

After spending some time in Harrisonburg, Welton, Davis, and the prisoners boarded a stagecoach for Staunton, twenty-five miles away. Arriving there on Friday, February 24, Welton took them to General Early's headquarters.[25]

A *Richmond Enquirer* reporter described the scene: "Upon being presented to Gen. Early . . . , the prisoners were received with the homely but not unacceptable greeting, 'Take seats, gentlemen, I presume you are tired after your ride,' and, added the hero of brilliant victories and stunning defeats, . . . 'I expect some enterprising Yankee will be stealing off with me in the same way one of these days.'"[26]

That evening at supper, Early was most interested in questioning Crook about his part in the Battle of Cedar Creek. Later, he reminded Kelley of his July 21, 1863, attempt to strike the general's camp at Hedgesville. "I intended to have had the pleasure of myself capturing you and your supply train at Hedgesville," Early said, "but you mysteriously gave me the slip. And you didn't leave a cracker behind. My army went without breakfast that morning sir. . . . we had depended on your supplies." Kelley replied, "There might have been enough supplies to go around when you had finished that part of the morning's work—but fortunately you did not get started in time." After their fine meal, the general made sure that his prisoners had good quarters.[27]

On Saturday morning, February 25, Welton and Davis put the prisoners on board a Virginia Central passenger train and escorted them to Richmond. During the ride, they had a chance encounter with the now colonel John Mosby, presently almost fully recovered from a near-fatal wound suffered on December 21, 1864. After finding out what McNeill's band had accomplished, Mosby, who earlier in the war had entered Union lines at Fairfax Court House, Virginia, and spirited Brigadier General Edwin H. Stoughton from his bed, reportedly said, "You boys have beaten me badly. The only way that I can beat this, is to go to Washington and bring out Lincoln."[28]

Arriving in the capital that afternoon, Welton took his prisoners to the provost marshal, who later sent them to Libby Prison. While in Richmond the lieutenant met with government officials and related McNeill's desire for the War Department to hold the generals hostage for his recently captured men, now confined in Fort McHenry as "guerrillas not to be exchanged during the war." When he got back to Moorefield, Welton had a message from the authorities for McNeill, telling him, "This, they could not do, but they would see that my men received such treatment as was accorded prisoners of war." Before leaving town the next day, Davis and Welton bought the generals and Melvin a $65 pint of whiskey and dropped it off to them.[29]

After the prisoners settled into their new abode, some Wheeling expatriates came by to visit Kelley, their former townsman. They offered to help him in any way that they could. He later reported that his onetime friends were "all quite despondent in their talk, although no open confessions of their opinions were made." Melvin also got some company when a few of his old West Virginia friends stopped by to see him. They talked very little about the war, however, being more concerned with assisting him in his needs.[30]

The officers' stay in prison, though, was short. On March 10 Confederate officials paroled them. A day after their release they arrived in City Point, Virginia, where Crook met with General Grant. During their conference, Grant asked Crook to stay there and take command of one of his cavalry divisions, but the Ohioan replied that he would first like the general to restore him to his old command. Grant approved the request and then gave all three men leaves of absence, pending exchange. On March 13 the mail steamer *Dictator* left City Point with over four hundred federal officers and men as passengers. The flag of truce boat arrived at Fortress Monroe the next afternoon. Crook, Kelley, and Melvin then boarded the steamer *Adelaide* and set sail for Baltimore.[31]

Reaching Baltimore on March 16, the generals, according to a reporter, passed the time giving "amusing accounts of their adventures." They assured him that "their captors treated them as kindly as could be expected." Kelley soon left by rail for Cumberland, Crook a few days later. Melvin did not stop off in Cumberland but returned to his home in Hancock County, West Virginia. During the time when the generals had been captured, Grant had assigned Major General Winfield S. Hancock, now in charge of the Middle Military District and headquartered in Winchester, to the command of the Department of West Virginia. Grant picked Brigadier General Samuel S. "Bricktop" Carroll to replace Kelley.[32]

By the time Crook got back to the Queen City, he had been exchanged for Confederate major general Isaac Trimble. On March 20, acting under Grant's orders, Crook reassumed command of the department. Grant, however, had forgotten to inform Hancock, who, the next day, ordered Crook to relinquish the post and report to Frederick, Maryland, "in arrest." In the meantime, Grant tried to clean up the mess by ordering Crook back to City Point. It fell to President Lincoln, though, to soothe Hancock's ruffled feathers. He settled everything by sending the general copies of Grant's orders to Crook.[33]

The general had been right in thinking that his return to command the Department of West Virginia, even for a short time, would help to restore his military reputation. After chastising the *New York Tribune* for attacking Crook, a West Virginia scribe commented: "We are pleased to see that the War Department and the General-in-Chief have not lost confidence in General Crook, and, further, that by restoring him to command, no blame in their opinion attaches to him in the affair resulting in the capture of himself and General Kelley."[34]

But that was not what Captain Melvin thought. Late in life he still believed that the captures might have been the outcome of Crook's romance of Mary Dailey. He wrote, "The fact is on one or more occasion during the Civil War, northern soldiers who had become interested in southern women were either captured or narrowly escaped capture."[35]

For his success in the planning and capture of the generals, the Confederate War Department promoted Jesse to Captain of Partisan Rangers, C.S.A., and on March 24 the *Rockingham Register* noted that "he is a modest and clever boy and will wear his honors as becomes a brave soldier."[36]

CHAPTER 22

The Baker Place Fight and a Train Robbery

⸺᥆᥆᥆⸺

"We are rebels, and we'll have every d———d
one of you!"

On February 27, 1865, Sheridan left Winchester with ten thousand troopers
and some horse artillery bound for Lynchburg. As the bluecoats proceeded up
the valley, Early's woefully thinned ranks evacuated Staunton and tramped ten
miles east to Waynesboro. The only opposition Sheridan encountered along
his march was from Rosser's troopers, who were defending a bridge across the
swollen North River at Mount Crawford. Although the stout three hundred
held out for a time, federal cavalry crossed when the waters fell and easily
brushed aside the gray Spartans.[1]

On the afternoon of March 2, Brigadier General George A. Custer's division
attacked the Confederate defenses at Waynesboro and quickly overwhelmed
the Southerners. Although Early escaped capture, thirteen hundred of his
men were not so fortunate. Before moving on the next day, Sheridan ordered
Colonel John L. Thompson, 1st New Hampshire Cavalry, to usher the prisoners
to Winchester.[2]

Thompson's escort numbered about twelve hundred men, divided evenly
among various mounted squads and a collection of dismounted troopers and
those with run-down horses. It was a while before the Yankees got going, but
after destroying some captured military property and organizing the march,
they moved out. The column traveled slowly, making it only halfway to Staunton
by evening. The next morning, March 4, Thompson ordered Major Edward
Schwartz, 4th New York Cavalry, to ride into town and tell the citizens to get
some food ready for the prisoners. From there Schwartz was to head down the
Valley Pike and post guards to protect two important bridges along the way
to Harrisonburg.[3]

When the procession arrived in Staunton, the town folk had very little food
on hand, so Thompson had his soldiers take "flour and bacon" from the local

John L. Thompson. Courtesy Collections of the State of New Hampshire.

insane asylum. Officers also sent squads to burn some Confederate supplies found in the town. During this halt, a local informed Thompson that Rosser was presently gathering as many men as he could to attempt a rescue of the prisoners, a tip that proved to be true. As the Yankees marched down the pike, Rosser's handful of horsemen skirmished with Lieutenant Colonel Theodore Boice's rear guard and kept foragers from roaming the countryside.[4]

As Rosser kept shadowing the Unionists, other Confederate soldiers and militiamen rode in to help. Near Harrisonburg, some of McNeill's Rangers and another hundred of his own troopers joined in. By this time Rosser's band had grown from fifty to three hundred. Hoping to slow Thompson down until more reinforcements joined him, the general sent a detachment ahead to cross the North Fork of the Shenandoah River to get possession of the fords at Meems Bottom. On the night of March 5–6, Rosser attacked the Union camp, just north of Harrisonburg. and before retreating he was able to liberate a few prisoners. The next morning Thompson marched on, reaching the river at noon. There, to his disappointment, he found the normally shallow stream running high and about two hundred butternuts on the Mount Jackson side ready to contest any crossing. Meanwhile, Thompson had soldiers cut some trees in the hope that his men could build a walkway across the ruined turnpike bridge. A mile south, Boice's 5th New York Cavalry took positions atop Rude's Hill.[5]

After the troops failed in their attempt to rebuild the bridge, the Yankees settled uneasily into camp. That evening they spotted more rebels moving off their flanks. When it got dark, Rosser sent men through the lines, Captain William McDonald wrote, "to mingle with the prisoners and persuade them to revolt and cooperate with Rosser when he should make his attempt at rescue." A number of the prisoners, however, were reluctant conscripts unwilling to risk their lives.[6]

Just after daylight on March 7, Thompson ordered Major Charles Brown to take his own 22nd New York Cavalry and the 1st Rhode Island Cavalry across the upper ford and disperse the rebels. Within ten minutes after crossing, Brown's troopers had captured a few Southerners and chased the rest off. Now the dismounted soldiers and prisoners, hoping to keep the rushing waters from sweeping anyone away, started fording the stream in large groups. Presently Rosser attacked the rear guard, but his hoped-for uprising of the prisoners never materialized, and after some fierce skirmishing Boice's troopers finally repulsed the grayjackets.[7]

By this time, however, many of the prisoners were across the river. Rosser, realizing that his opportunity was slipping away, gathered his men and tried again. Just as before, however, the rear guard held their ground; then they successfully counterattacked and ruined the general's designs. In the fighting that morning the Southerners suffered between forty and sixty casualties, mostly prisoners. Thompson reported one officer and five men wounded. This figure, though, is low; 5th New York Cavalry records list two men killed or mortally wounded, one wounded and three missing, just in that regiment.[8]

Once the Northerners had moved on, the Confederates swarmed into the bottoms, garnering only one useless cannon and a few ambulances the blue-coats had discarded. The general had some of his men trail the column as far as Woodstock, but no farther. Having received intelligence that Mosby was on his way to join Rosser and both would attack that night, Thompson stopped upon reaching the abandoned federal earthworks at Cedar Creek. Resuming the march early the next morning, March 8, the column reached Winchester about midday. Two days later Major General Alfred Torbert was to notify General Hancock of Thompson's outstanding performance in foiling rebel rescue attempts and "in bringing safely to Winchester more prisoners than he started with."[9]

Although Rosser had sent a rider after Woodson, the Missourians did not arrive in time to help. About a week later, though, Major Kennedy telegraphed Hancock's Winchester headquarters with some recent news about the company. Some of the major's "reliable sources" had reported that Woodson, with a hundred men, would soon "raid down Back Creek Valley." Although Kennedy suspected they were after livestock and plunder, he was also concerned for the safety of local Unionists, including noted West Virginia politician Bethuel Kitchen. He suggested that "a party from Winchester could cut off these men if they get into Back Creek Valley, or could disperse them." Later that month Kennedy's fears of increased guerrilla activity along Back Creek proved true, when around midnight on March 27 a dozen unidentified Confederates attacked the home of steam sawmill operator and sometime Union guide Jake Files, hacking through the front door with an ax. Despite suffering two wounds, Files fought them off, shooting their leader dead as he barged into the house.[10]

Early on the morning of March 18, a Swamp Dragon band descended on the neighborhood of Petersburg. According to a local, "After plundering several houses, insulting and threatening to shoot defenseless women, they carried off ten horses, stealing saddles and bridles to rig them up.... They then started to make for the mountains from whence they had come." Joe Vandiver, however, was about, and as soon as he discovered what had happened, he started gathering a squad to go after them. By eleven o'clock he had eight men—two or three Rangers and the rest furloughed troopers from the 18th Virginia Cavalry. Having a good idea the route the enemy would take home, Vandiver soon had his men traveling on a shortcut, hoping to get ahead of the Home Guards and lay a trap.[11]

Twenty-four hours later Vandiver had his gunmen waiting in the brush beside an isolated trail atop the Allegheny Front. When the Swamps finally came along on a nearby path, though, they sensed danger, stopped, and began moving off in a different direction. But before they got very far, the rebels attacked, killing William Davis, John Harness, and John Wratchford and chasing off the rest. After rounding up all of the stolen horses, the rebels returned to Petersburg.[12]

On March 22 the editor of the *Wheeling Intelligencer* made a prediction about those bands of diehards still resisting state authorities: "The thieving gangs of Guerrillas which infest the border and mountain counties of the interior, have already commenced their usual spring depredations, but without their usual success. Their efforts thus far have been promptly met, and they are being rapidly brought to grief. Like all that clings to the waning fortunes of the Confederacy, they are doomed to an early overthrow, and if they persist, to final destruction."[13]

That same day a squad consisting of a lieutenant, sergeant, and ten soldiers of Company H, 14th West Virginia Infantry left their camp at the mouth of Patterson Creek to patrol as far as the Levi Baker farm, located ten miles away in the foothills of Knobly Mountain. For the past month Captain Henry M. Ice's men had been building a blockhouse to protect the railroad bridge crossing the creek.[14]

Sergeant Jesse Sturm had asked Second Lieutenant George W. Joliffe if he could lead a reconnaissance to the Baker place and, from there, descend upon suspected Ranger hideouts. The idea for the patrol had originated from a suggestion by one of Levi's daughters, who had for some time been visiting the Blackburn girls, the daughters of a local Unionist. Sturm's small squad guarded the Blackburn property, and, while there, the sergeant became smitten with Miss Baker. Before she left to return home, the mountain beauty suggested to him, Sturm later wrote, that he bring some men to her house "in about two weeks and she would show me where I could capture some of McNeal's men who were home on furlough."[15]

Sturm, who was far more interested in courting the girl than in tangling with rebels, did not wait two weeks to get started. The next day, March 21, Sturm told Joliffe what he wanted to do. At first the lieutenant put him off, but later he reconsidered, and on the afternoon of March 22 Joliffe approved Sturm's request. The sergeant quickly collected ten trusted comrades, and all well armed with the new Henry repeating rifle, they got ready to go. When Second Lieutenant Isaac Martin, Sturm's cousin, heard about the adventure, the officer asked his relative if he could accompany them. After Sturm told Martin that the real purpose of the mission was romance, he "readily agreed with my plan of action."[16]

After a few minor adventures along the way searching roadside houses for arms, the soldiers arrived at their destination at sundown. Happily, the men found a collection of attractive young lasses in the cabin, just finishing up their quilting bee. The girls soon fixed the soldiers some supper, and afterward Martin and Sturm decided that it would be a good idea to put off catching rebels until the next day. Just then, however, a boy showed up to take his two sisters home. When the wary sergeant suddenly became suspicious and ordered them to stay, a heated argument started. When the irate girls shouted that Jesse McNeill would come to their rescue, Sturm pointed to the new rifles and replied that his men were not afraid. One of the pair, though, got the last word in, saying, "Oh, I just wish that McNeal would come," and at the same time clapping her hands close to the sergeant's face.[17]

The young maid's wish soon came true, but not to her satisfaction. Some time before, as Sturm later discovered, one of McNeill's Cumberland spies had sent Jesse word that an eastbound passenger train carrying important Union officers recently posted in Nashville was to be coming down the line that night. After hearing this, McNeill decided to stop the train at Brady's Mill and capture the men. So it was that, that evening, when Sturm and the others heard horses coming down the road, it turned out to be Jesse and about sixty horsemen, well on their way to the Potomac crossing. A few soldiers and some of the girls immediately went out on the porch and watched as the riders came closer; inside, other Yankees picked up their rifles. When a nearby Unionist picket shouted, "Who comes there?" a rebel shouted, "Friends." By this time, though, the graybacks were up to the fence that bordered the house; the sentinel fired.[18]

As the rest of the soldiers rushed out of the cabin, one of Jesse's men cried out, "We are rebels, and we'll have every d———d one of you!" In an instant the fight was on. For a time, there was great confusion, with the girls screaming and clinging to the nearest soldier as the combatants blasted away at one another. Finally, though, the mountaineers' Henry rifles turned the tide. The Confederates charged the house three times, but the Yankees' rapid fire drove them back. Now the partisans, their force cut in two and suffering some casualties, retreated.[19]

When the shooting stopped, Sturm went to find his girlfriend and discovered that she was "lying on the hearth near the fire wounded." He soon determined the she had suffered a wound "between the hip and the knee," but it appeared to him that the ball, lodged deeply in her flesh, had not done any serious damage. Sturm told her mother to keep "cold cloths" on it, and he would return to camp and get a surgeon. Despite all the flying lead, there were no other wounded, and while at first Sturm thought that two of his men were dead, they soon showed up, no worse for wear. Once everything settled down, the soldiers got on the trail back to camp.[20]

Arriving there the next morning, they first ate breakfast before rounding up a surgeon to examine the girl's leg. As they finally marched out, it was Joliffe who now commanded the party. Upon reaching the cabin, the doctor extracted the ball and sewed up the wound. Then the patrol followed the route of last night's unwanted guests, Sturm writing that "we could tell by the dead horses and blood in the road, that our bullets had been telling." In addition, locals along the way related that the partisans had not fared so well. The people figured that at least two of the enemy were mortally wounded, with another three wounded. The rebels had also lost two horses killed and seven wounded. But upon finally discovering that the Rangers were resting in a village, just five miles away, Joliffe decided to leave them alone and return to camp.[21]

Along the way back the boys happened upon a still, filled their canteens with whiskey, and soon started toasting their success. Later, when news of the mountaineers' stinging defeat of McNeill started circulating up and down the B&O line, "we were for a time," Sturm wrote, "the heroes of the hour." He recalled that the department commander in Baltimore issued a special congratulatory order commending the men for their "bravery and intrepidity."[22]

Although the fighting had ended for Sturm and his friends, on March 23 Vandiver and five companions went to the house of a Mrs. Hull at Ridgeville, looking for Jack and Fred High. For the past year and a half the notorious 7th Virginia Cavalry deserters had been guiding Union forces. When the Rangers got there, they charged the house, and braving heavy fire, burst inside and captured the brothers. But the renegades never made it back to the Harrisonburg jail. About five miles from Ridgeville, as the *Rockingham Register* reported, "they attempted to make their escape through the woods, but both were killed."[23]

It was also about this time that thirty Tucker County Home Guards made a successful foray against secessionist homesteads in Pendleton County. Concentrating their efforts in the upper reaches of the South Fork, the raiders stole forty horses and stripped many families of any good clothing and valuables that they had. Except for a few resolute women, they met very little resistance. When one of these spitfires tried to stop the plunderers, a Swamp hit her in the head with a saber; another whipped an enraged woman with an iron ramrod. The robbers were out of the valley and back into the high Alleghenies before the Rangers, or any other of the local rebel outfits, found out what had happened.[24]

The Sturm squad had accidentally stymied Jesse's first plan to hold up a train, but he still intended to try. So, on the afternoon of March 30, McNeill led a band of between thirty and forty men toward Dan's Run, an isolated trackside hamlet located some three miles east of the Patterson Creek Bridge. His force included a collection of his own men and troopers from Company F, 7th Virginia Cavalry. That evening the raiders arrived there and captured a few B&O trackmen; then, according to a later report, "they forced them to take up a few rails and turn the track, so as to throw the engine off, headed into an embankment."[25]

Earlier, the Mail Train West had left Baltimore's Camden Station on its regular run to Wheeling. Passengers aboard the eight cars included some soldiers, assorted businessmen and travelers, and Walter Quincy, the line's assistant master of the road. The slow train, which made many scheduled stops along the way, normally took a little over ten hours to reach Cumberland, so it was just after six thirty in the evening, as the train was approaching Dan's Run, that the engineer heard a flurry of pistol shots. Fortunately, he stopped the locomotive just in time to prevent a horrendous crash, but nevertheless the locomotive, tender, and two cars ran off the track. The clerk instantly jumped out of the mail car and sprinted up the line to get help, and seconds later "the ruffians entered the cars," a reporter later noted, "with pistols and bowie knifes in hand."[26]

William Wilkerson, a passenger who was riding with two African American men to Cincinnati, watched as the rebels stormed aboard his car. A day or so later he recalled one shouting in a loud voice, "All officers on board of this train must at once surrender." As two captains and a pair of lieutenants raised their hands and walked forward, the leader told some terrified ladies that "no indignity or injury should be offered them, but that they wanted all the money and other valuables on board the train." The officer then ordered the passengers outside. As they exited their coach, the partisans stopped and searched every one of the men, relieving them of their money and jewelry, besides taking some coats and hats and even a few pairs of boots.[27]

Next the graybacks began pillaging the baggage and mail cars. Gathering more booty, they forced Wilkinson's two black friends to help carry some of it. When the Confederates were finished, a few scattered letters throughout the mail car and then set them on fire. Wilkinson claimed that he attempted to extinguish the blaze but stopped his effort when a rebel shot at him. Just then, he recalled an officer shouting, "Fall in Company F." The soldiers then mounted swiftly and with some cheering and others shouting, "Good-bye Yanks," spurred their horses and disappeared down the line into the approaching darkness. Going along with them were the four captured officers and the two African Americans. By chance they had just missed bagging a bigger prize. Vice President Andrew Johnson had been scheduled to leave Washington and catch the westbound train at Relay House, "but," according to the *Hartford Daily Courant*, "he delayed his departure in the hope of seeing the President."[28]

As soon as the rebels were gone, Quincy, the railroaders, and some of the passengers put out the fire in the mail car, and later the passengers and others totaled up their losses. Wilkinson reported that "the quantity taken was upwards of $20,000 in money besides a number of gold and silver watches, rings and clothing." One rider alone lost $5,000. Wilkinson lost $140 but was able to save his expensive watch by hiding it "between his drawers and person." Quincy lost his wallet and watch.[29]

An hour later troops from Green Spring and Patterson Creek arrived at the scene. They found the locomotive, baggage, and one passenger car damaged beyond repair and the chilled riders very anxious to get on their way. Over in Cumberland, Brigadier General Carroll wired New Creek, and at about ten o'clock that night Lieutenant Colonel Greenfield, Captain C. J. McNulty, and two hundred troopers from the 22nd Pennsylvania Cavalry set off after the bandits. But as a disappointed Samuel Farrar recalled, "The pursuit proved fruitless, as the job had been done by experts in that line, who, being well mounted got away with their plunder, before their pursuers were under way." Likewise, another mounted column out of Green Spring failed to catch sight of the rebels.[30]

Carroll had sent some troops from Cumberland to Dan's Run to assist with the track cleanup, but due to a minor accident they did not arrive there until eleven fifteen at night. Sometime after midnight the displaced passengers boarded another train sent down for them and resumed their trip, and a few hours later the soldiers had cleared the track and through rail traffic resumed.[31]

In his report of the incident, Carroll lamented the fact that it was next to impossible to prevent train robberies from "happening until the country in front of the railroad is entirely cleared of these guerrilla bands." Not long afterward, General Hancock suggested to B&O officials that he put armed soldiers on all passenger trains. The company however, insisted that the government buy a ticket for each guard, and immediately after seeing this reply, Hancock dropped his plan. In the meantime, Greenfield beefed up defenses along the river by stationing one company of the 22nd Pennsylvania Cavalry at Green Spring and another at Black Oak Bottom, a crossing about five miles downriver from New Creek.[32]

As one of his last acts while commanding the post at Cumberland, on April 3 Carroll issued General Orders No. 18. Made up of three parts, his first directive stated that the next time guerrillas attacked the railroad, "the property of all disloyal citizens within an area of five miles . . . south of the places of such raids and attacks shall be immediately burned." To compensate loyal citizens for any future financial losses that they would suffer at the hands of the guerrillas, Carroll also decreed that "a levy for twice the amount in value will be at once be made on the property of known disloyal citizens in the vicinity of such outrages for the purpose of restitution to the Union citizen." Lastly, the general commanded that whenever the Southerners murdered a loyal citizen or soldier, "a rebel sympathizer nearest the place of murder will be immediately hung, in retaliation."[33]

CHAPTER 23

End of the Line

∞∞∞

" . . . until we can learn the fate of the
Confecy more fully."

The news of the sudden retreat of the Army of Northern Virginia from its Petersburg and Richmond defenses and Lee's subsequent April 9, 1865, surrender of his battered legions to Grant at Appomattox Court House caught the Confederate forces in the mountains by surprise. By mid-April many rebels had now decided it was time to give up the fight and started coming into Cumberland and New Creek to surrender. In the Shenandoah Valley many of the Missourians started showing up at various federal posts to get their paroles, including Captain Woodson, who got his in Winchester on April 17. But with some Southern forces still under arms, Jesse and the majority of the Rangers were determined to stay in the field until they received orders from some Confederate leader as to what they should do. In fact, Henry Trueheart noted that in an April 22 meeting with federal officers at Petersburg, West Virginia, all but one of the diehards turned down the offer to surrender under the terms granted to General Lee. The Yankees had better luck with Captain Abel Scott's Company E, 18th Virginia Cavalry, when at least a dozen of his troopers laid down their arms.[1]

On April 24 McNeill and thirty Rangers showed up at the outer picket post, south of New Creek. In his subsequent conference with Brigadier General Rutherford B. Hayes, Jesse requested a temporary truce in Hardy County until he could contact his superiors. Hayes gave McNeill permission to camp outside the lines while he telegraphed Major General William H. Emory, now commanding in Cumberland, for his instructions. That evening Emory wired the brigadier "that the armistice asked for is improper and cannot be granted."[2]

The next morning Lieutenant Colonel Greenfield left New Creek with two hundred troopers, hoping to round up McNeill and his remaining followers.

McNeill and companions: John Fay (*front row center*), Jesse McNeill (*right front*), Jim Dailey (*top left*). Courtesy Shaun Dorsey.

Under orders from Emory not "to capture or disturb those who have already been paroled by General Grant or Hancock," Greenfield later descended upon Moorefield, and after surrounding the place, watched as his troops rounded up thirty graybacks. The Rangers, however, were not there.[3]

Although many of the partisans were still on the loose, more rebels were starting to turn themselves in. Samuel Farrar saw a group of fifty who surrendered at New Creek:

> They had no arms; their horses were private property; their saddles were United States or Confederate States, but they were allowed to keep them; in fact, they surrendered nothing but their allegiance to the defunct Confederacy. They were rather good-looking men, and had plenty of money which they spent freely. They purchased quite a lot of clothing, shoes, etc., and scattered to their homes.[4]

For the next few weeks the remaining Rangers continued hiding "in the mountains and woods," Henry Trueheart wrote, "until we can learn the fate of the Confecy more fully." But, hearing nothing, Jesse finally decided to accept defeat, and on May 5, accompanied by Boggs, Dailey, Fay, Trueheart, and others, rode to New Creek to get his parole and negotiate the formal surrender of the company. Five days later the Cumberland provost marshal, Lieutenant Colonel George W. Taggart, and a handful of soldiers crossed the South Branch in a skiff to meet with McNeill and most of his remaining men on the grounds of Sycamore Dale, just west of Romney. Under a previous agreement the partisans, as part of the Army of Northern Virginia, would receive the same terms as Grant gave to Lee. Although those rebels who had lived in what was now West Virginia were free to go home, the ones from Maryland, Kentucky, or Missouri could only return to their native state "by complying with the Amnesty Proclamation of the President and obtaining special permission from the War Department." For a time the ceremony went smoothly, as each Southerner rode forward, tossed his weapons down, took the loyalty oath, and signed his parole. Taggart and the others noticed that the guns were worthless junk, but anxious to get the ceremony finished, they ignored the obvious.[5]

The Rangers could keep their horses, but according to local lore a serious problem arose when the colonel told the men to turn over their saddles and blankets. McNeill considered these previously captured articles as spoils of war and balked at obeying this order. As a result, the two began arguing, and Jesse quickly threatened to call off the ceremony unless they could keep their gear. Finally, Taggart, aware the Rangers were still heavily armed and that the rest of his company was on the other side of the river, relented.[6]

Sycamore Dale. Courtesy Donna Shrum.

Upon their return to Moorefield, Jesse formally disbanded his troops, and in the following weeks most of the Rangers who were not present in Romney came into a federal post and surrendered on their own. A few never did.[7]

Over in Wheeling, there had been great rejoicing after Governor Boreman received General Emory's May 8 telegraph, stating that McNeill and many of the Rangers had already surrendered and others would soon be coming in. The Swamp Dragons and other local Unionists, however, were furious with the federals for the wholesale paroling of men whom they considered bushwhackers and murderers, not soldiers. That same day John Michael of Greenland Gap wrote to the West Virginia adjutant general, Francis Pierpoint, his views on the matter: "I am fearful we will have a great (d)eal of trouble yet in our county. The Authorityes at New Creek is Peroling all the Rebel Bushwhacker and horsthieves and Letting them Run with thare arms and Horses and we can never organise our county under these circumstances for you cannot truest one in five hundred."[8]

It seems, however, that once the Confederates surrendered, things gradually settled down. On June 11 Emory ordered Greenfield to take his regiment to Moorefield "to assist in the enforcement of the laws and preservation of good order in the community." With companies C through G already mustered out, the 22nd now consisted of only seven companies, numbering about six hundred troopers. Over the next month the locals set about reorganizing the Hardy

County government and court. "It soon became evident," Farrar noted, "that there was no necessity for a military force to maintain order and uphold the authority of the court."[9]

Private Aungier Dobbs noted to his wife the easy duty he now had: "There is no gurrilling in this Country and some of the rebs and us have some interesting talks about our Skirmishes we had They are very friendly and commutative and seem desirous to have permanent peace Capt. McNeal is a fine looking young man and a dashing fellow and he is still single."[10]

About the only important event that happened during the regiment's stay in Moorefield was the unexpected death of Sergeant John T. Corbitt, an original member of Company A and an accomplished scout, who became ill and died in the hospital there on July 22. On July 25 the 22nd regiment rode out of Moorefield for the last time, bound for their new post at Clarksburg, West Virginia. The men continued their duties in the Mountain State throughout the summer and early fall. On October 31, in Cumberland, the Pennsylvanians received their discharges from the service.[11]

Thirty-six years later, however, the Rangers invited some of these same bluecoats back to Moorefield to attend a joint reunion. On August 21, 1901, Greenfield, Captain Hart, Lieutenant Felix H. Crago, twenty-six other former officers and soldiers, and thirty-six of their hosts participated in the various festivities. At the courthouse that morning, speakers from both groups gave talks "which," Duffey wrote, "expressed the sentiment of good will and united friendship."[12]

That afternoon a brass band led the way as Greenfield and McNeill started their comrades marching to Olivet Cemetery, and as the old enemies, locked arm in arm, passed by in double file, thunderous cheers erupted from the spectators. Finally the procession and hundreds of town folk reached the top of the hill and gathered around the Monument to the Confederate Dead. After his introduction, Greenfield, standing near the grave of Hanse McNeill, gave a moving address.[13]

Before leaving for home that evening, the colonel invited his former foes to attend the next Ringgold Cavalry reunion. McNeill accepted for the group, and at the end of August 1902, a delegation of Rangers, including Mrs. Sarah McNeill and Mrs. Gertrude Corbitt Parker, journeyed to California, Pennsylvania, for the affair. To their amazement, the Pennsylvanians had prepared a royal welcome for the Southerners. Thunderous cannon fire greeted the train as it slowed to stop at the station, where scores of cheering Union veterans stood ready to welcome the group. After it disembarked, Greenfield received their old adversaries with a few kind words. McNeill, almost overcome with emotion, spoke next. "We were enemies once," he said, "but, thank God, we are friends now."[14]

During his stay in town, McNeill had another surprise. While visiting at the home of John Elwood, Jesse got the opportunity to get together with Captain James Hart. The two, who had chased and fought each other throughout the war, spent much time talking over their long-ago adventures. As Elwood remembered, "The meeting of these two men was one that not one who was present will ever forget."[15]

On August 31, 1910, McNeill's Rangers held their last reunion in Moorefield. Their ranks now thinned by disease and time, only eighteen aging veterans attended. That morning the celebrated raiders assembled at the courthouse. Jesse McNeill presided at the meeting as former Rangers—Judge Raison C. Davis, John Fay, Judge J. E. Pennybacker, and Reverend John E. Triplett—addressed the gathering. Later, Isaac Welton chaired another session at Innskeep Hall. After the recounting of many exciting war stories for the audience, the men marched to Olivet Cemetery and decorated the graves of their former comrades.[16]

Epilogue

After the War

NOTABLE RANGERS

Jesse McNeill: Jesse, soon after the war, married his sweetheart, Sarah Sherrard, a union that over the following years produced nine children. For a time the McNeills farmed in Hardy County but eventually moved to Daviess County, Missouri. Along the way there, the family ran into bad luck when the Mississippi River ferry they were passengers on capsized. Except for an heirloom chest, they lost all of their belongings. Later, seeking better opportunities, the McNeills picked up stakes and moved to Mahomet, Illinois. Captain Jesse McNeill died on March 4, 1912. He was seventy years old. No doubt that when the word of the captain's passing reached Moorefield, more than a few remembered a humorous comment he had made about his onetime enemies. While riding from Moorefield to Keyser (formerly New Creek) to see a dentist, Jesse stopped along the road to talk to some friends. He told them that "a single tooth . . . was giving him more annoyance than all the Union troops in that section forty years before."[1]

Jefferson W. Duffey: The Rangers' most prolific author, Duffey studied for the ministry after the war and subsequently served as pastor for a number of Methodist Episcopal churches. He died November 9, 1929, and today rests in the Confederate Section of Arlington National Cemetery. Duffey Memorial Methodist Church in Moorefield was named in his honor.[2]

John Fay: The intrepid scout eventually became the editor of the *Oakland Democrat*, a position he held for fourteen years, after which he Fay moved to Washington, D.C., and worked for the U.S. Government. A first-rate wordsmith, Fay authored a number of postwar McNeill Ranger articles. On January 16, 1925, he died at Dunn Loring, his home in Fairfax County, Virginia. Duffey wrote of his compatriot, "He made no parade, however, of his friendship, as he did not of literary attainments or moral excellence, and yet his attachments were as hooks of steel, his store of information gleaned from many fields of literature was large and interesting while in matters moral he was above reproach."[3]

Sprigg Lynn: A significant actor in the capture of the generals, Lynn returned to Cumberland, subsequently worked as a coal company clerk, and later engaged in iron ore speculation. Always ready for a scrap, in 1898 the middle-aged Lynn enlisted in a Texas volunteer force and headed out to fight the Spanish in Cuba. On April 9, 1898, the *Baltimore Sun* reported that "a message has been received in Romney, W.Va.[,] that Sprigg Lynn had been killed in Cuba."[4]

William Maloney: The daring young man who warned McCausland of Averell's impending attack on the general's forces camped at Old Fields, and who later participated in the Cumberland raid, served as a Hampshire County magistrate for thirty years. He died in the Queen City in October 1927.[5]

Henry Trueheart: Before leaving Hardy County for Galveston, the hard-fighting Texan married Petersburg belle Annie Van Meter Cunningham. Over the years Trueheart became a successful businessman and financier, and on August 18, 1914, he died at the Grandview Sanitarium in Wernersville, Pennsylvania. He was eighty-two.[6]

Joseph Vandiver: Although he had received a parole at the end of the war, Vandiver claimed that the federals later "offered a reward for my body, dead or alive." After hiding out in the West for eight years, Vandiver returned to Virginia, settled at Millwood, and worked as a horse doctor. From time to time he gave interviews on his role in the kidnapping of the generals. Wounded five times during the war, Vandiver died on August 25, 1892.[7]

Isaac Welton: After the war, the former lieutenant returned to the family farm near Petersburg, West Virginia, and raised livestock. A fixture at Ranger reunions, Welton died February 9, 1923.[8]

Notable Federals

George Crook: In the years following the war, Crook, leading campaigns against various Apache, Cheyenne, and Sioux tribes, became one of the army's most accomplished Indian fighters. Unlike his superior, General Philip Sheridan, however, Crook preferred pacification of the natives rather than extermination. On the morning of March 21, 1890, Major General Crook, commander of the Military Division of the Missouri, died of a heart attack at the Grand Pacific Hotel in Chicago. First interred in the Dailey family plot in the Odd Fellows Cemetery in Oakland, Maryland, the following November, Crook's remains were removed to Arlington National Cemetery. On September 24, 1895, his wife, the former Mary Dailey, whom he had married on August 21, 1865, died suddenly at Crook's Crest, her Oakland, Maryland, home. Today she rests beside her husband.[9]

Andrew J. Greenfield: In 1866, according to research compiled by West Virginia Civil War author Rick Wolfe, Colonel Greenfield moved near Oil City, Pennsylvania, and entered the oil business. The following year he married Louise Castle, and then, moving into town in 1871, he subsequently joined the Oil City and Titusville Oil Exchange and eventually became president of the company. Greenfield later served one term as mayor. In 1883 President Grover Cleveland appointed him postmaster of Oil City. In later life the old veteran moved to Chicago, dying there on January 13, 1931.[10]

James P. Hart: Brevet Major Hart finished the war serving on the staff of Major General Emory, after which he returned to Washington County, Pennsylvania, and went into business. Financial success followed quickly, and he amassed a sizable fortune. During the 1870s, however, his concerns suffered severe losses. In 1878 Hart moved his family to Washington, D.C., and got a government job. Hart died at his home on January 12, 1908, and a few days later he was buried in Arlington National Cemetery. His old companion Sergeant John Elwood later said of him, "He did more hard riding, covering more miles, than any other officer, who ever served in the hills of West Virginia."[11]

Benjamin F. Kelley: Once back from Libby Prison, Kelley never returned to active duty. Sometime later he wed young Mary Clare Bruce, and over the following years Kelley held several U.S. government positions, including superintendent of Hot Springs, Arkansas. The general and Mrs. Kelley made their home at Swan Meadows farm, just south of Oakland, where he died on July 16, 1891. At the time of his death, Kelley, aged eighty-four, was the oldest living former Union Civil War general. Kelley's gravesite at Arlington National Cemetery is not far from George Crook's plot. At the time of his death an army officer remarked, "Kelley made less history for the amount of fighting he did than any other general officer in the service."[12]

Others

Harry Gilmor: After his July 25, 1865, release from Fort Warren Prison, Gilmor worked on a memoir about his war adventures. Published by Harper Brothers in 1866, *Four Years in the Saddle* still gives its readers a fascinating inside look at partisan life. Returning to Baltimore in 1867 with Metoria Strong, his young Louisiana bride, he went into business. In 1873 the governor appointed Gilmor a major in the Maryland National Guard, and the next year, he became one of two of Baltimore's police commissioners. In the latter capacity, Gilmor helped to put down rioting during the July 1877 B&O strike in Baltimore. He died on March 4, 1883.[13]

John Peerce: In 1867, despite the protests of many of his neighbors and Governor Arthur I. Boreman, President Johnson granted Peerce a pardon. Prior to this, the former scout had returned to his large farm south of Burlington and restarted his cattle operation. The well-educated and multitalented Peerce was also an accomplished local architect and builder. Later on he became involved in politics, serving as a Democratic delegate to West Virginia's 1872 Constitutional Convention. He also served a term in the state legislature. Peerce died August 9, 1896, and was buried in the family cemetery.[14]

Rebecca Van Meter: The Old Field diarist who chronicled many exciting happenings just outside the front door of Traveler's Rest spent her last years there. She died on January 15, 1882, aged eighty-two.[15]

Charles Woodson: After getting his parole, the captain returned to Missouri.

He married in 1867 and settled in Salisbury. According to author Thomas F. Curran, "Woodson became a successful contractor and bridge builder and dabbled in local politics." Possibly fearing retribution for his partisan activities, Woodson did not publicize his role in the war, and when questioned about it, usually told a false story. On July 10, 1909, the old rebel died.[16]

Appendix
Duffey's Tribute

———∞∞∞———

In 1918 the Reverend J. W. Duffey penned a fitting tribute to his former comrades in the pages of *Confederate Veteran* magazine. On May 1, 1864, as a seventeen-year-old youngster, he had enlisted in the company and in the war's last year participated in many exciting Ranger escapades. Looking back to those former glory days, he wrote:

No small body of men in the Confederate ranks rendered more effective service than McNeill's Rangers. Authorities on the war and official documents establish that much; but the records do not show . . . how much it cost these men to accomplish what they did. The field of their operations was an outpost nearly a hundred miles from any Confederate troops who could give support in a crisis, environed also by strong detachments of the enemy, and that section infested by lurking informants who would have counted it a prize to betray them. They had no tents or shelter of any kind and rarely camped two nights in the same place. The deep ravines of the ridges and gorges of the mountains were the places of bivouac, not to be entered, however, until after dark; and whatever the chill or storm of the night might be, but little fire, and sometimes none at all, was allowed. The men literally slept on their arms, for no retreat was considered entirely safe.

Every man furnished his own outfit, which was scant at best for man and horse, and he was appraised a "lucky dog" who could afford a change of underwear. Their best accouterments were spoils from the enemy. Many men wore blue trousers, not from choice, but by necessity, and would have donned the blue coat but for the liability of being shot for a Yankee. As for rations, each one, like the little domestic fowl, had to scratch for himself. . . . The best chance for a square meal was to make a daybreak call on the enemy. Old Rangers still recall how good was the taste of Yankee hard-tack, corned beef, pickled pork, and coffee with the luxury of sugar in it.

No man complained of hardships, no one thought it a hardship. That small but heroic band was in it, not for comfort or spoils, but for a constitutional right, and for that right, they were willing to dare and die. Their record is as honorable as it is unique. They were never caught napping, never idled away time in camp, never lost an issue with the enemy, never failed to capture the prize for which they started, and never consented to capitulate until thirty days after General Lee surrendered at Appomattox.[1]

Notes

ABBREVIATIONS

NA	National Archives
OR	U.S. War Department. *The War of the Rebellion: A Compilation of the Official Records of the Union and Confederate Armies.* 128 vols. Washington, D.C.: Government Printing Office, 1880–1891
ORS	U.S. War Department. *Supplement to the Official Records of the Union and Confederate Armies.* Wilmington, N.C.: Broadfoot, 1994.
TFP	Trueheart Family Papers, Rosenberg Library, Galveston, Tex.
WVA	West Virginia Archives, Charleston
WVAGP	West Virginia Adjutant General Papers

PROLOGUE

1. "An Attractive Branch of the Service," *Richmond Daily Dispatch*, April 24, 1862.

2. John Fay, "M'Neill's Rangers," *Baltimore Sun*, Aug. 7, 1906; OR, ser. 1, 33: 1252–53.

3. "Military Notices," *Richmond Daily Dispatch*, May 7, 1862.

4. "Southern Chivalry: Bushwhackers," *Hartford Daily Courant*, May 5, 1862; "Hanging the Guerrillas," *Macon Telegraph*, June 2, 1862.

5. "Partisan Rangers," *Richmond Daily Dispatch*, June 5, 1862.

6. OR, ser. 1, 51: pt. 2, 578–79.

7. *Richmond Whig*, July 25, 1862.

1. THE MISSOURI STATE GUARD

1. Pugh, *Capon Valley*, 60, 63.

2. Ibid., 58; W. D. Vandiver, "Two Forgotten Heroes," 405.

3. Van Meter, *Old Fields*, 6, 60. A "garden of Eden" since Indian times, the farming community of Old Fields is located across the South Branch River about four miles north of Moorefield. Traveler's Rest is at the northern end of the village.

Notes

4. Vandiver, "Two Forgotten Heroes," 405; Compiled Service Records of Confederate Soldiers Who Served in Organizations from the State of Missouri, NA.

5. Piston and Hatcher, *Wilson's Creek*, 45, 47; OR, ser. 1, 3: 385.

6. Ibid., 34; Piston and Hatcher, *Wilson's Creek*, 103–4.

7. OR, ser. 1, 3: 94.

8. Piston and Hatcher, *Wilson's Creek*, 114–15, 134–35; OR, ser. 1,3: 622–23. According to Piston and Hatcher, Cowskin Prairie was "an open area formerly used as a place for slaughtering cattle."

9. Piston and Hatcher, *Wilson's Creek*, 264–66, 335–38.

10. Ibid., 314–15; "Mulligan Surrender," *Rockford Republican*," Sept. 26, 1861; "Highly Important from Missouri," *New York Herald-Tribune*, Sept. 23, 1861.

11. OR, ser. 1, 3: 187; OR, ser. 1, III: 443–47.

12. Pugh, *Capon Valley*, 61; Compiled Service Records of Confederate Soldiers Who Served in Organizations from the State of Missouri, NA; Vandiver, "Two Forgotten Heroes," 405; OR, ser. 1, 53: 437. Pugh wrote that George McNeill was shot on September 17.

13. OR, ser. 1, 53: 437, Mulligan, "Siege of Lexington," 313; *Daily Illinois Journal*, Sept. 26, 1861. According to Jim Creed, longtime student of the 23rd Illinois Infantry, "Gen. Price, commander of the Missouri State Guard (not yet part of the Confederate States) paroled the officers and men of the Irish Brigade in the two days following the surrender. When they got back to federal control, Fremont and Halleck determined that the paroles were legally invalid, because only a belligerent country could issue a parole . . . For the same reason, Mulligan refused his parole and remained the only POW from Lexington to remain in captivity." Creed to author, Feb. 13, 2013. Also, Creed writes: "After some weeks an exchange was arranged, Confederate Gen. Daniel Frost (captured earlier in St. Louis by Lyons) went south and Mulligan went north." Creed to author, Mar. 13, 2017.

14. Vandiver, "Two Forgotten Heroes," 405–6.

15. Ibid., 404.

16. Ibid., 406.

17. Ibid.

18. Ibid., 407; Compiled Service Records of Confederate Soldiers Who Served in Organizations from the State of Missouri, NA; The Civil War in Missouri website, "Military Prisons," 1–3 (civilwarmo.org/educators/resources/info-sheets/military-prisons).

19. Vandiver, "Two Forgotten Heroes," 407; "Widow of Noted Confederate Figure Central Figure at Birthday Party," *Winchester Evening Star*, Sept. 1933; Compiled Service Records of Confederate Soldiers Who Served in Organizations from the State of Missouri, NA. Vandiver believed that Jesse escaped from the slave market.

20. *Columbia Missouri Statesman*, June 27, 1862; Rudi Keller, "150 Years Ago: News of Mass Escape Includes Prisoners from Central Missouri," *Columbia Daily Tribune*, June 27, 2012.

21. Delauter, *McNeill's Rangers*, 18.

2. 1st Virginia Partisan Rangers

1. Delauter, *McNeill's Rangers*, 117, 118, 120, 122, 125; Kaler, *Story of American Heroism*, 545. In his fall of 1862 correspondence with 1st Virginia Partisan Ranger quartermaster Capt. Thomas Shumate, McNeill signs as "Capt. John H. McNeill comm. Hardy Rangers."

2. "Western Virginia," *Wheeling Daily Intelligencer*, Sept. 15, 1862; Newcomer, *Cole's Cavalry*, 15.

3. "Notorious Guerrilla Killed," *Point Pleasant Daily Register*, Nov. 6, 1862; Van Meter, *Old Fields*, 199; "One of Pierpont's Senators in Limbo," *Rockingham Register*, Sept. 19, 1862; Duffey, *M'Neill's Last Charge*, 11. Delauter does list a John W. High but adds "No official record." See Delauter, *McNeill's Rangers*, 120.

4. Delauter, *McNeill's Rangers*, 22; OR, ser. 1, 19: 630–31. A tributary of the South Branch of the Potomac, the South Fork begins in the mountains of Highland County, Virginia, and flows north some sixty-eight miles to Moorefield.

5. "Capture of Yankees in Hardy," *Richmond Daily Dispatch*, Sept. 27, 1862. Bond later escaped from the guardhouse at Staunton. After finally being recaptured, a magistrate later released Bond on bail. He promptly skipped town, returned to the mountains, and by December 1862 he was hard at work forming another Swamp Dragon company. See "The Swamp Dragons," *Rockingham Register*, Jan. 8, 1864. Capt. Lewis Dyche commanded Company F, 2nd Regiment, Potomac Home Brigade Infantry. See Scott, *Civil War Era in Cumberland*, 95.

6. OR, ser. 1, 19: 631.

7. Ibid., 630. Trough, or River, Road starts near Romney and roughly parallels the east bank of the South Branch River to Moorefield. The road gets its name from a steep-sided canyon along its route.

8. Toomey, *War Came By Train*, 78; Scott, *Civil War Era in Cumberland*, 73, 75, 80.

9. OR, ser. 1, 19: pt. 2, 370; Beach, *First New York (Lincoln) Cavalry*, 17. Although Beach states that McReynolds located his headquarters at Old Town, Maryland, telegraph messages from his headquarters, however, show that the colonel camped directly across the Potomac at Green Spring. From there, he could send messages from the B&O station.

10. Bates, *History of the Pennsylvania Volunteers*, vol. 3, 136.

11. Delauter, *62nd Virginia Infantry*, 3; French, "Rebel Land Pirates: Plunder and Retreat," *Washington Times*, Mar. 25, 2006.

12. Delauter, *McNeill's Rangers*, 23; "The Battle of Blue's Gap-Routing of the Rebels by Gen. Kelley's Troops," *New York Herald*, Jan. 14, 1862; "The Enemy in Hampshire: Murder and Outrageous Vandalism," *Richmond Whig*, Jan. 17, 1862.

13. Stevenson, *Boots and Saddles*, 125.

14. Ibid.

15. Ibid., 125–26; *Rockingham Register*, Oct. 10, 1862.

16. Stevenson, *Boots and Saddles,* 126–27.

17. Beach, *First New York (Lincoln) Cavalry,* 179.

18. Ibid.; Stevenson, *Boots and Saddles,* 127.

19. Stevenson, *Boots and Saddles,* 127; applejack is a brandy made from apples.

20. Beach, *First New York (Lincoln) Cavalry,* 179–80.

21. Delauter, *62nd Virginia Infantry,* 3; French, "Rebel Land Pirates," *Washington Times,* Mar. 25, 2006.

22. ORS 59: 751; Bates, *History of the Pennsylvania Volunteers,* vol. 3, 138; "The War in Western Virginia," *Wheeling Daily Intelligencer,* Oct. 6, 1862; OR, ser. 1, 19: pt. 2, 25.

23. OR, ser. 1, 19: pt. 2, 22–24.

24. Ibid., 24.

25. Ibid., 23–25.

26. Ibid., 24; "Capture of Rebel Supplies, Munitions of War and Prisoners," *Daily Times Delta,* Oct. 23, 1862; "Imboden's Guerrillas, Capture of Prisoners and Papers," *Public Ledger,* Oct. 24, 1862.

27. Tucker, *Brigadier General John D. Imboden,* 101; OR, ser. 1, 19: pt. 2, 17.

28. OR, ser 1, 19: pt. 2, 154–55; Van Meter, *Old Fields,* 199.

29. OR, ser. 1, 19: pt. 3, 630; Roy, *Captain Snyder and His Twelve,* 60.

30. Maxwell, *History of Tucker County,* 241, 340.

31. Ranger, "Letter to the Editor," *Staunton Spectator,* Nov. 20, 1862.

32. OR, ser. 1, 19: pt. 2, 156. Early in the war, Milroy's soldiers, impressed by his chiseled facial features and wild shock of gray hair, had dubbed him "Gray Eagle."

33. OR, ser. 1, 19: pt. 2, 157. Prior to June 20, 1863, the date West Virginia became a state, loyal regiments raised in northwestern Virginia were designated as Virginia units. To avoid confusion with Virginia Confederate regiments, I have used the designation "(West) Virginia" up until that date to indicate the Northern, or loyal, troops. According to West Virginia historian Rick Wolfe, "That started after June 20, 1863, but many units continued the Virginia designation even on documents. In 1864 the state started having flags made for each unit with West Virginia's name and state seal." Wolfe to author, Mar. 14, 2017.

34. Ibid.; Ranger, "Letter to the Editor," *Staunton Spectator,* Nov. 20, 1862.

35. *Staunton Spectator,* Nov. 20, 1862; OR, ser. 1, 19: pt. 2, 157–58.

3. Early Exploits

1. Tucker, *Brigadier General John Imboden,* 107.

2. OR, ser. 2, 5: 810.

3. "An Unheard of Monster," *Richmond Daily Dispatch,* Dec. 15, 1862.

4. "Gen. Milroy's Defense of the Folly in Western Virginia," *Wheeling Intelligencer,* Feb. 25, 1863.

5. OR, ser. 1, 21: 35–36; Farrar, *Twenty-Second Pennsylvania Cavalry,* 80–81; "Western Virginia," *Boston Traveler,* Jan. 8, 1863. The Ringgold Cavalry Battalion consisted of seven

Pennsylvania companies. The Ringgold Company, commanded by Captain John Keys, and the Washington Cavalry, commanded by Captain Andrew J. Greenfield, entered the service "in the summer of 1861." Later known as the Pennsylvania Squadron, Keys and Greenfield's men patrolled the mountains of northwestern Virginia and along the upper Potomac. In the autumn of 1862, the Keystone, Beallsville, Monongahela, Patton, and Lafayette Companies joined these two outfits, forming the Ringgold Battalion, or Ringgold Cavalry. Farrar writes, "As these companies were generally stationed at one point, or post, the senior captain commanded the battalion." See Farrar, *Twenty-Second Pennsylvania Cavalry*, 171–72.

6. Farrar, *Twenty-Second Pennsylvania Cavalry*, 80–81; OR, ser. 1, 21: 35–36, 829; Van Meter, *Old Fields*, 202; "Two Companies of Stuart's Cavalry Routed," *Baltimore Sun*, Dec. 8, 1862; McDonald, "A Rough Sketch," 61–62. McDonald wrote his Civil War memoirs for his family. The author is grateful to Louise McDonald for providing him with a photocopy.

7. OR, ser. 1, 21: 825, 855, 877, 940, 976.

8. OR, ser. 3, 3: 123–24; Van Meter, *Old Fields*, 203.

9. Van Meter, *Old Fields*, 203. As noted in the text, Junction is the location of the intersection of the Northwestern Turnpike with the Moorefield and North Branch Turnpike, approximately seven miles west of Romney. It is not to be confused with Moorefield Junction, which is located south of Medley. There, the Moorefield-Allegheny Turnpike meets the Patterson Creek Valley Turnpike.

10. OR, ser. 3, 3: 124.

11. "The Abolitionists in Hardy," *Rockingham Register*, Jan. 2, 1863 (emphasis in the original); "The Enemy's Doings in Hardy County, Va.," *Richmond Whig*, Jan. 6, 1863.

12. Delauter, *18th Virginia Cavalry*, 2; OR, ser. 1, 21: 1076.

13. Imboden, "War Diary," WVA, 1; Van Meter, *Old Fields*, 205–6. Both Colonel George Imboden and Captain Frank Imboden were younger brothers of John D. Imboden.

14. Imboden, "War Diary," WVA, 1.

15. "Capture of Yankees in Hardy County," *Richmond Daily Dispatch*, Jan. 8, 1863.

16. Van Meter, *Old Fields*, 205–6.

17. Van Meter, *Genealogies and Sketches*, 174.

18. Van Meter, *Old Fields*, 207–9.

19. OR, ser. 1, 21: 747; Neese, *Three Years*, 143–44.

20. OR, ser. 1, 21: 746; OR, ser. 1, 25: pt. 2, 92; Keyes, *Military History of the 123d Regiment*, 34; ORS 55: 349.

21. OR, ser. 1, 21: 747–48; Neese, *Three Years*, 144–48; "The Dash into Moorefield," *Richmond Daily Dispatch*, Jan. 10, 1863.

22. OR, ser. 1, 21: 748.

23. Ibid.; Van Meter, *Old Fields*, 212.

24. "Capture of Prisoners and Horses," *Richmond Examiner*, Jan 14, 1863.

25. Van Meter, *Old Fields*, 212–13; Farrar, *Twenty-Second Pennsylvania Cavalry*, 89.

26. Farrar, *Twenty-Second Pennsylvania Cavalry*, 89; Van Meter, *Old Fields*, 213; Keyes, *Military History of the 123d Regiment*, 36.

27. Keyes, *Military History of the 123d Regiment*, 37–38; Van Meter, *Old Fields*, 214; ORS 9: 566, 588.

4. Capture of a Hay Train

1. OR, ser. 1, 21: 1086, 1102.

2. Delauter, *18th Virginia Cavalry*, 2; Delauter, *McNeill's Rangers*, 30–32; John Fay, "M'Neill's Rangers," *Baltimore Sun*, Aug. 7, 1906.

3. Fay, "M'Neill's Rangers."

4. Tucker, *Brigadier General John D. Imboden*, 110; OR, ser. 1, 25: pt. 2, 657; Delauter, *McNeill's Rangers*, 32.

5. "The Capture of That Forage Train near Romney," *Wheeling Intelligencer*, Mar. 2, 1863; ORS 55: 375; Elwood, *Elwood's Stories*, 134; Farrar, *Twenty-Second Pennsylvania Cavalry*, 94; "Caught Again—Another Successful Dash at a Yankee Train," *Daily Constitutionalist*, Feb. 26, 1863. The Moorefield and North Branch Turnpike ran from Green Spring south to Romney. There it met the Northwestern Turnpike. It started again at Junction and continued to Moorefield. Daniel R. McNeill, of Old Fields, was the president of the turnpike company.

6. "Caught Again—Another Successful Dash"; OR, ser. 1, 25: pt. 2, 642–43; Farrar, *Twenty-Second Pennsylvania Cavalry*, 94.

7. "Capture of a Forage Train Near Romney, by the Rebels—A Disgraceful Affair," *Philadelphia Inquirer*, Feb. 26, 1863 (reprint of a *Pittsburg Chronicle* article).

8. Ibid.; "Capture of That Forage Train"; Farrar, *Twenty-Second Pennsylvania Cavalry*, 94.

9. "Capture of a Forage Train Near Romney"; Van Meter, *Old Fields*, 217; Keyes, *Military History of the 123d Regiment*, 38–39.

10. Ibid.; Farrar, *Twenty-Second Pennsylvania Cavalry*, 94; "Army Correspondence," *Washington Reporter*, Mar. 11, 1863.

11. "Another Train Captured," *Wheeling Intelligencer*, Feb. 20, 1863.

12. "Capture of That Forage Train." Devil's Hole Mountain (elevation 2,833 feet) is located in southeastern Hardy County on the Virginia–West Virginia border.

13. "A Brilliant and Paying Dash," *Staunton Spectator*, Mar. 3, 1863. According to Elwood, who years later interviewed Jesse McNeill about the incident, the younger McNeill led the charge. McNeill also said that Sergeant Hopkins "was the bravest man who ever faced him during the whole Civil War." See Elwood, *Elwood's Stories*, 134–36, 283.

14. "Capture of That Forage Train"; OR, ser. 1, 25: pt. 2, 643; ORS 55: 375–76.

15. *Rockingham Register*, Mar. 6, 1863. Romney attorney Royce Saville commented on McNeill's alleged practice of leaving signed paroles with locals to hand out to Union soldiers willing to take them. Interview with Royce Saville, June 14, 2014.

16. OR, ser. 1, 25: pt. 2, 656.

5. The Jones-Imboden Raid

1. Roberts, *West End-Cumberland*, 107, 122, 127.

2. OR, ser. 1, 25: pt. 2, 652.

3. Ibid.

4. Ibid.

5. Ibid., 653.

6. Ibid., 661.

7. Ibid., 660.

8. Ibid., 661, 668, 674–75.

9. Ibid., 710–11.

10. "Another Installment," *Rockingham Register*, April 10, 1863; Van Meter, *Old Fields*, 220; Elwood, *Elwood's Stories*, 137; OR, ser. 1, 25: pt. 1, p, 81.

11. OR, ser. 1, 25: pt. 1, 81–82; Van Meter, *Old Fields*, 220.

12. OR, ser. 1, 25: pt. 1, 82; Elwood, *Elwood's Stories*, 137, 141.

13. Farrar, *Twenty-Second Pennsylvania Cavalry*, 98.

14. Elwood, *Elwood's Stories*, 137.

15. Farrar, *Twenty-Second Pennsylvania Cavalry*, 98.

16. Ibid., 98–99.

17. OR, ser. 1, 25: pt. 1, 82; Fay, "M'Neill's Rangers," *Baltimore Sun*, Aug. 7, 1906.

18. Van Meter, *Old Fields*, 220; OR, ser. 1, 25: pt. 1, 82.

19. OR, ser. 1, 25: pt. 1, 82, 98–99.

20. Ibid., 91, 98–100.

21. Ibid, 113, 123–24, 127, 129, 132, 134–35; A Rough, "Messrs. Editors," *Rockingham Register*, June 12, 1863; Van Meter, *Old Fields*, 221.

22. OR, ser. 1, 25: pt. 1, 109–10, 114, 121, 124–25.

23. Ibid., 117, 125. Captured at Moorefield on Dec. 3, 1862, McDonald "escaped at Greenville, Miss., while on his way to Vicksburg, Miss. to be exchanged." He returned to his company by Jan. 1, 1863. See Armstrong, *11th Virginia Cavalry*, 163.

24. OR, ser. 1, 25, pt. 1, 117, 125; Grant, "Episodes of Cavalry Raid of 1863," 26–27; Hoye, "War in This Section," 20.

25. Ashby and Ashby, "Jones Raid," 84–85.

26. Summers, *A Borderland Confederate*, 59.

27. "The Northwestern Virginia Raid," *Macon Telegraph*, May 23, 1863.

28. Ibid.; Hoye, "War in This Section," 21.

29. Grant, "Episodes of Cavalry Raid of 1863," 26–27.

30. OR, ser. 1, 25: pt. 1, 126, 134; Wiley, *History of Preston County*, 170.

31. Cale, *Gray Days in Morgantown*, 27–30; "Northwestern Virginia Raid."

32. Oates, *Hanging Rock Rebel*, 178; OR, ser. 1, 25: pt. 1, 132, 134.

33. OR, ser. 1, 25: 126; "Northwestern Virginia Raid"; "Gen. Jones' Thirty Day Scout," *Rockingham Register*, June 5, 1863; Cale, *Gray Days in Morgantown*, 31–33. In the author's

opinion, Cale's study, the product of many years of painstaking research, is the definitive work on the raid on Morgantown.

34. Cale, *Gray Days in Morgantown*, 36–38; OR, ser. 1, 25: pt. 1, 118; "Northwestern Virginia Raid."

35. "Northwestern Virginia Raid." Considering the Rangers' intense hatred of Milroy, the possibility certainly exists that the writer of the story may have concocted his tale to embarrass the general.

36. OR, ser. 1, 25: pt. 1, 110, 118.

37. "Gen. Jones' Thirty Day Scout."

38. A Rough, "Messrs. Editors."

39. OR, ser. 1, 25: pt. 1, 119; "Northwestern Virginia Raid."

40. OR, ser. 1, 25: pt. 1, 104, 120; Summers, *Baltimore and Ohio*, 139.

6. The Gettysburg Campaign

1. OR, ser. 1, 27: pt. 3, 865.

2. "Into 'Em Again," *Rockingham Register*, June 12, 1863; "Affairs in Western Virginia," *Richmond Daily Dispatch*, June 15, 1863. That winter, despite the uproar caused by his harsh treatment of Rebel sympathizers in northwestern Virginia, Milroy was promoted to major general. He now commanded the Second Division, 8th Army Corps, and his headquarters were at Winchester.

3. "Into 'Em Again."

4. "For the Register," *Rockingham Register*, July 31, 1863.

5. Maxwell and Swisher, *History of Hampshire County*, 646–47; Baker, "Diary," 124.

6. OR, ser. 1, 27: pt. 2, 314; Noyalas, *"My Will Is Absolute Law,"* 111–18.

7. "For the Register"; "A Paying Business," *Richmond Daily Dispatch*, June 30, 1863.

8. "For the Register." The federals at Cherry Run that day were refugees from the fighting at either Martinsburg or Winchester. The day before this skirmish, the troops from the 15th (West) Virginia Infantry posted at Cherry Run had been evacuated by rail to Sir John's Run and then on to New Creek. See Egan, *Flying Gray-Haired Yank*, 120–22.

9. "For the Register"; French, *Four Years Along the Tilhance*, 59; Smith, "Diary of James Ripley Smith," 26–27; "Statement of a Refugee from Hancock, Maryland," *Richmond Daily Dispatch*, July 1, 1863; Nesbitt, "Otho Nesbitt Diary," 199. The village of Millstone Point, Maryland, was about five miles downstream from Hancock.

10. "For the Register."

11. Ibid.

12. Smith, "Diary," 26.

13. "For the Register."

14. Ibid.

15. Ibid.

16. Ibid.; "The Rebels Burning Canal Boats," *Civilian and Telegraph*, June 25, 1863; Smith, "Diary," 26.

17. *Thirty-Seventh Annual Report*, 49. The B&O scribe mistakenly noted that McNeill's raid on Sir John's Run and Great Cacapon occurred on June 27. All other accounts confirm June 20 as the date.

18. *Rockingham Register*, July 31, 1863; Sentinel, "Imboden's Command," *Staunton Vindicator*, July 3, 1863. The road over Little Mountain is the same route that Union brigadier general Frederick W. Lander used in his successful February 14, 1862, attack on Virginia militia guarding Bloomery Gap. On April 25, 2013, the author, accompanied by landowners Kenny and Eileen Johnson and friends Rick Snowden and Tommy Swain, hiked a portion of the old trace. See Steve French, "Finding Lander's 1862 Route from Paw Paw to Bloomery Gap," *Morgan Messenger*, May 25, 2013.

19. OR, ser. 1, 27: pt. 3, 905–6.

20. Imboden, *War Diary*, 8; Smith, "Diary," 22; *Rockingham Register*, July 31, 1863.

21. Imboden, "War Diary," WVA, 8; Smith, "Diary," 22; Cordell, *Civil War Damage Claims*, 6–9; French, *Imboden's Brigade*, 36–38.

22. Cordell, *Civil War Damage Claims*, 37–38; Patterson, "Memoirs of D. H. Patterson, 41–42." The Patterson typescript was provided by Will Ford, former owner of the Patterson property at Webster Mills.

23. Patterson, "Memoirs," 42.

24. Ibid., 42–43; Cordell, *Civil War Damage Claims*, 32. The Patterson family later listed their June 24 losses as $2,150 dry goods, $100 notions, $150 groceries, $50 tobacco, $50 hardware, and a $15 saddle. After the raid, William Patterson rented the store to another man and moved the family to Springfield, Ohio.

25. Cordell, *Civil War Damage Claims*, 32; Patterson, "Memoirs," 43. D. H. Patterson wrote his recollections at an advanced age, and some of his statements are erroneous. For example, he claims the incident occurred on June 28, refers to Captain McNeill as "Col. Penz," and claims there were at least 250 rebels at Webster Mills. However, using the records of the postwar Pennsylvania Claims Commission and other primary sources, I have concluded that, for the most part, his story is accurate.

26. Schaff, "Gettysburg Week," 169.

27. *African American Historic Sites*; French, *Imboden's Brigade*, 57.

28. French, *Imboden's Brigade*, 57, 59, 60–61; Thompson, *Horses, Hostages and Apple Cider*, 38–42; Schaff, "Gettysburg Week," 168–69.

29. "The Late Rebel Invasion," *Mercersburg Journal*, July 17, 1863; Schaff, "Gettysburg Week," *Old Mercersburg*, 169.

30. "Late Rebel Invasion"; Delauter, *McNeill's Rangers*, 47; Donehoo, *A History of the Cumberland Valley*, 363.

31. Donehoo, *A History of the Cumberland Valley*, 363.

32. Harbaugh, *Mercersburg in War Times*, 90.

33. Ibid., 90–91; Schaff, "Gettysburg Week," 170.

34. Schaff, "Gettysburg Week," 170.

35. "Late Rebel Invasion"; Edminston, "Civil War Days in Mercersburg," 7–8.

36. "Late Rebel Invasion"; Schaff, "Gettysburg Week," 169–70.

37. Schaff, "Gettysburg Week," 169–70.

38. Ibid.; "Late Rebel Invasion"; Edminston, "Civil War Days," 7–8.

39. Schaff, "Gettysburg Week," 169–70; *Mercersburg Journal*, July 17, 1863.

40. French, *Imboden's Brigade*, 66; Schaff, "Gettysburg Week," 169.

41. OR, ser. 1, 51: pt. 2, 731.

42. *Manor Diary*, 60; Williamson, *Mosby's Rangers*, 79–80.

43. Williamson, *Mosby's Rangers*, 79–80; "Late Rebel Invasion"; *Philadelphia Inquirer*, July 2; "The Invasion of Pennsylvania," *Richmond Whig*, July 7, 1863; Edminston, "Civil War Days in Mercersburg," 8; Nesbitt, "Otho Nesbitt Diary," 190. Williamson writes, on page 79 of *Mosby's Rangers*, that "we crossed the Blue Ridge at Snicker's Gap and thence to the Potomac River near Hancock, where we crossed on the morning of July 1." The ford above Sleepy Creek, Mosby's most likely crossing point, is about four and a half miles downriver from Hancock, the Cherry Run ford approximately ten miles. Crossing at either place would give them time to be in Mercersburg by noon.

44. Fay, "M'Neill's Rangers," *Baltimore Sun*, Aug. 7, 1906.

45. Imboden, "Confederate Retreat," 422–27.

46. Nesbitt, "Otho Nesbitt Diary," 200. Nesbitt is referring to Sergeant Joseph Vandiver. See Delauter, *McNeill's Rangers*, 125.

47. Imboden, "Confederate Retreat," 427–28.

48. Imboden, "War Diary," WVA, 9; Farrar, *Twenty-Second Pennsylvania Cavalry*, 121.

49. Farrar, *Twenty-Second Pennsylvania Cavalry*, 121; Nesbitt, "Otho Nesbitt Diary," 200.

50. Farrar, *Twenty-Second Pennsylvania Cavalry*, 121–22; "Captain Greenfield among the Rebel Trains!" *Washington Reporter*, July 15, 1863; Kitchen, "The Experiences, Sufferings, and Privations of Joseph G. Kitchen of Berkeley County, W.Va., During the Years 1861, 1862, 1863, and 1864," *Xenia Sentinel*, May 17, 1864. Kitchen, son of West Virginia state senator Bethuel M. Kitchen, had served for a time in the 1st Maryland Cavalry (Union) and was a noted local scout and guide. After the Confederates forced Milroy from Winchester, Kitchen hid on North Mountain for a time before escaping by way of Hancock to Pennsylvania.

51. Imboden, "War Diary," WVA, 9.

52. Ibid; Farrar, *Twenty-Second Pennsylvania Cavalry*, 121, 122; Delauter, *McNeill's Rangers*, 48–49.

53. Farrar, *Twenty-Second Pennsylvania Cavalry*, 122; Nesbitt, "Otho Nesbitt Diary," 200.

54. Farrar, *Twenty-Second Pennsylvania Cavalry*, 200; "Captain Greenfield among the Rebel Trains!"

55. Nesbitt, "Otho Nesbitt Diary," 200; Fay, "M'Neill's Rangers."

56. Imboden, "War Diary," WVA, 10; *Rockingham Register*, July 24, 1863.

7. Fight in a Graveyard

1. C. E. W., "Capt McNeill's Last Scout," *Rockingham Register*, Aug. 28, 1863.

2. Harold Garber, "The Hardy Heritage," *Moorefield Examiner*, Jan. 21, 2009. Forsyth's story originally appeared in the June 15, 1925, edition of the Piedmont, West Virginia, *Evening Times*. Forsyth had written a letter to the editor of the paper commenting on a number of Civil War incidents. The old veteran incorrectly stated that Lieutenant Welton was one of the prisoners.

3. Ibid.; John Fay, "M'Neill's Rangers," *Baltimore Sun*, Aug. 7, 1906.

4. OR, ser. 1, 29: pt. 1, 33; Bates, *History of the Pennsylvania Volunteers*, vol. 4, 852. On August 11 Rebecca Van Meter noted in her diary that the first Yankee troopers had arrived in the area on Wednesday, August 5. She added, "Roving in every direction after horses & cattle, they are like Mad men full of venom for what we have been destroying in Pennsylvania and Western V. we have not heard half the destruction in town& all around." See Van Meter, *Old Fields*, 227. Lost River begins near Brock's Gap and flows northward some thirty-one miles until disappearing beneath Sandy Ridge. After flowing two miles underground, it reappears as the Cacapon River. See Voorhees, "Lost River," 435.

5. Oates, *Hanging Rock Rebel*, 214–17. Blue's recollections of his Civil War service first appeared in a series of articles Blue wrote for the *Hampshire Review* between the years 1898 and 1901, using his wartime diary as a guide. On July 1 Herriott had enlisted in the 11th Virginia Cavalry when Jones's brigade was at Greencastle, Pennsylvania. See Armstrong, *11th Virginia Cavalry*, 149.

6. Oates, *Hanging Rock Rebel*, 217, 219. The Branson that Blue refers to was either Ranger Private William Branson or Corporal William F. Branson, 11th Virginia Cavalry. See Delauter, *McNeill's Rangers*, 117; Armstrong, *11th Virginia Cavalry*, 125.

7. Oates, *Hanging Rock Rebel*, 217.

8. Ibid., 218.

9. Ibid., 219–21.

10. Ibid., 218.

11. Ibid, 218–19.

12. Fay, "M'Neill Rangers"; OR, ser. 1, 29: pt. 1, 33; Bates, *History of the Pennsylvania Volunteers*, vol. 4, 852, 866; Van Meter, *Old Fields*, 219; "From the Valley of Virginia," *Richmond Whig*, Aug. 18, 1863; "From the Valley," *Staunton Spectator*, Aug. 11, 1863.

13. Delauter, *McNeill's Rangers*, 51–52; OR, ser. 2, 6: 304–5.

14. OR, ser. 2, 6: 304–5; Oswald "Brilliant Achievements by McNeill's Partisan Rangers," *Mountain City Times*, May 29, 1869.

15. OR, ser. 1, 29: pt. 1, 33; Delauter, *McNeill's Rangers*, 52. According to the August 28, 1863, edition of the *Rockingham Register*, on August 22 some Rangers delivered two "securely ironed" young spies to the provost marshal in Harrisonburg. The Rangers had captured the pair in "Hopkins Gap, an obscure and unfrequented pathway through the mountains near Brock's Gap." One was a Rebel deserter named Bell and the other a federal soldier.

16. Farrar, *Twenty-Second Pennsylvania Cavalry*, 132–33.

17. Ibid., 133.

18. Ibid., 134–35; Haas, *Dear Esther*, 174. Later that day the rebels also captured Hallam. Two of the six men died in prison. While being shipped south to Andersonville, Georgia, Sergeant Hassan jumped from the train and escaped to federal lines.

19. ORS 9: 568–69; Hogbin, "Diary of James Clark Hogbin"; Judy, *History of Grant and Hardy Counties*, 257–58; OR, ser. 1, 29: 102.

20. OR, ser. 1, 29: 102, 105, 106; ORS 9: 568–69; Fay, "With M'Neill in Virginia," 408.

21. Fay, "With M'Neill in Virginia," 408; Farrar, *Twenty-Second Pennsylvania Infantry*, 135; "The Dash on Moorefield," *Richmond Daily Dispatch*, Sept. 19, 1863.

22. Ranger, "Capt. McNeill's Last Capture," *Rockingham Register*, Sept. 25, 1863; Fay, "With M'Neill in Virginia," 408.

23. Fay, "With M'Neill in Virginia," 408–9.

24. Ibid., 409; Ranger, "Capt. McNeill's Last Capture."

25. Fay, "With M'Neill in Virginia," 409; "From General Lee's Army," *Richmond Examiner*, Sept. 17, 1863.

26. Fay, "With M'Neill in Virginia," 409.

27. Ibid.; Farrar, *Twenty-Second Pennsylvania Cavalry*, 136; Ranger, "Capt. McNeill's Last Capture"; "A Successful Dash on the Enemy," *Staunton Spectator*, Sept. 22, 1863.

28. Ranger, "Capt. McNeill's Last Capture"; Fay, "With M'Neill in Virginia," 409–10; "From General Lee's Army."

29. OR, ser. 1, 29: pt. 1, 106; Delauter, *McNeill's Rangers*, 121; Van Meter, *Old Fields*, 229.

30. OR, ser. 1, 29: pt. 2, 755.

8. The Charlestown Raid and a Wagon Train Fight

1. OR, ser. 1, 27: pt. 3, 1032, 1051; Tucker, *Brigadier General John D. Imboden*, 172; Woodward, *Defender of the Valley*, 88–89.

2. Tucker, *Brigadier General John D. Imboden*, 178–79; "The Rebels Attack and Capture of Charlestown, Va.," *Philadelphia Inquirer*, Oct. 20, 1863.

3. Barr and Musick, "They Are Coming," 22, 24; Newcomer, *Cole's Cavalry*, 76.

4. Lieutenant F. Carter Berkeley, "Imboden's Dash into Charlestown," *Baltimore Sun*, Aug. 30, 1903; *Staunton Spectator*, Oct. 27, 1863; Gilmor, *Four Years in the Saddle*, 113.

5. *Staunton Spectator*, Oct. 27, 1863; Berkeley, "Imboden's Dash into Charlestown."

6. Berkeley, "Imboden's Dash into Charlestown"; OR, ser. 1, 29: pt. 1, 489–90; *Staunton Spectator*, Oct. 27, 1863.

7. Gilmor, *Four Years in the Saddle*, 114–15.

8. OR, ser. 1, 29: pt. 1, 485–86; Newcomer, *Cole's Cavalry*, 77.

9. *Staunton Spectator*, Oct. 27, 1863.

10. OR, ser. 1, 29: pt. 1, 488, 491; Barr and Musick, "They Are Coming," 16; Newcomer, *Cole's Cavalry*, 79–80; *Staunton Spectator*, Oct. 27, 1863; Steve French, "Rebels Shatter Union Force in Charlestown Rout," *Washington Times*, Mar. 3, 2001.

11. "Leading Citizen of Galveston Succumbs," *Fort Worth Star-Telegram*, Aug. 20, 1914; Williams, *Rebel Brothers*, 10–11, 177, 181.

12. Van Meter, *Old Fields*, 230–31.

13. *Rockingham Register*, Nov. 27, 1863; "Escape of Rebels From Camp Chase," *Public Ledger*, Sept. 26, 1863. In a postwar letter to author Benjamin F. Van Meter, Lieutenant Welton claimed that "Roosevelt was not the first man who commanded the 'Rough Riders.' Missouri John Cunningham gave this name to McNeill's Rangers during the war." See Benjamin Van Meter, *Genealogies and Sketches*, 175.

14. OR, ser. 1, 29: pt. 1, 650–51. In late April 1862 Union cavalry captain W. S. Fish surveyed the turnpike between Burlington and Petersburg for "the feasibility of transporting trains over it and to examine & observe the facilities of foraging on or near the road." He found the condition of the road "admirable better than any I have seen . . . it . . . shows considerable engineering skill in its building." Capt. W. S. Fish to Maj. J. M. Lyon (private collection of Woodrow Simmons; photocopy courtesy of Woodrow Simmons).

15. OR, ser. 29: pt. 1, 650; Miller, "Capture of a Wagon Train," 20.

16. Miller, "Capture of a Wagon Train," 20; "McNeill's Last Capture," *Rockingham Register*, Nov. 27, 1863. Lieutenant Moomau's last name is sometimes spelled "Mooman" or "Moomaw." Samuel Fleming was a Hampshire County farmer. On February 8, 1864, federal troops captured him and charged him with being a "guerrilla and highway robber," and he served prison stints at Camp Chase and Fort Delaware. See Armstrong, *11th Virginia Cavalry*, 142.

17. "McNeill's Last Capture"; Miller, "Capture of a Wagon Train," 20; OR, ser. 1, 29: pt. 1, 650; Armstrong, *7th Virginia Cavalry*, 209. Captain Enright is possibly E. C. Enright; see Delauter, *McNeill's Rangers*, 119.

18. OR, ser. 1, 29: pt. 1, 650.

19. Ibid.; Miller, "Capture of a Wagon Train," 20.

20. "McNeill's Last Capture."

21. Miller, "Capture of a Wagon Train," 20.

22. Ibid.

23. Ibid.

24. "McNeill's Last Capture"; Delauter, *62nd Virginia Infantry*, 84, 102, 106.

25. "McNeill's Last Capture"; OR, ser. 1, 29: pt. 1, 651.

26. OR, ser. 1, 29: pt. 1, 651.

27. Ibid., 646, 649. Located just south of Medley, the Moorefield-Allegheny Junction was where the Moorefield-Allegheny Turnpike met the Patterson Creek Valley Turnpike.

28. OR, ser. 1, 29: pt. 1, 649.

29. Farrar, *Twenty-Second Pennsylvania Cavalry*, 141.

30. OR, ser. 1, 29: pt 1, 649.

31. OR, ser. 1, 29: pt. 1, 647–48; Van Meter, *Old Fields*, 232.

32. "Yankee Harness for Sale," *Rockingham Register,* Dec. 4, 1863.

33. OR, ser. 1, 29: pt. 1, 644, 646; Lang, *Loyal West Virginia,* 291.

34. Van Meter, *Old Fields,* 234; Thoburn to Boreman, Jan. 14, 1864; Boreman to Harper, Nov. 28, 1863, and Harper to Boreman, Jan. 16, 1864, Civil War Union Militia Collection, box 5, folder 8A, WVA.

35. OR, ser. 2, 6: 862.

36. Stevenson, *Boots and Saddles,* 241–43; Tucker, *Brigadier General John D. Imboden,* 189–90.

37. "A Gallant Confederate," *Rockingham Register,* Jan 8, 1864.

38. "Letter from Senator Carskadon," *Wheeling Intelligencer,* January 6, 1864; "Carskadon House."

9. Trouble with Rosser

1. OR, ser. 1, 33: 7. At this time Rosser was still a colonel, but according to Rosser's biographer, the late Dr. Millard Bushong, "Although Rosser had been commanding a brigade, had been recommended, and been called a general, his promotion languished in the Confederate Senate before it was finally confirmed on February 17, 1864." See Bushong and Bushong, *Fightin' Tom Rosser,* 68.

2. OR, ser. 1, 33: 7; Gilmor, *Four Years in the Saddle,* 138; Fravel, "Between the Lines," 249.

3. OR, ser. 1, 33: 7; S, "Captain McNeill's Last Adventure with the Yankees," *Rockingham Register,* Jan. 29, 1864. The Rangers reached Moorefield on December 31. Private Henry M. Trueheart wrote, "Our arrival in Moorefield was in a heavy snow, very cold, and my first night was spent at Mr. Robert Gilkerson's huddled together with fifteen or twenty other soldiers." See Trueheart, "Memoirs of Henry Martyn Trueheart," TFP, 1904, box 2, F-11, 10.

4. McDonald, *A History of the Laurel Brigade,* 216, "Captured—A Yankee Train and Yankees," *Rockingham Register,* Jan. 8, 1864; *Wheeling Daily Intelligencer,* Jan. 8, 1864; Powell, *Civil War Memoirs of Little Red Cap,* 23; Farrar, *Twenty-Second Pennsylvania Cavalry,* 150.

5. Farrar, *Twenty-Second Pennsylvania Cavalry;* "Captured—A Yankee Train and Yankees"; OR, ser. 1, 33: 5–6.

6. OR, ser. 1, 33: 7–8.

7. Ibid., 8; ORS 59: 721, 739; Gilmor, *Four Years in the Saddle,* 138–39; S, "Captain McNeill's Last Adventure."

8. S, "Captain McNeill's Last Adventure"; Gilmor, *Four Years in the Saddle,* 139.

9. Jones, *Gray Ghosts and Rebel Raiders,* 213. According to a story related by Jones, Rosser was still angry about an earlier confrontation with Captain McNeill. Somewhere along the trail, the old farmer had chastised Rosser for his harsh treatment of horses. OR, ser. 1, 33: 1081.

10. OR, ser. 1, 33: 1081–82.

11. Ibid.

12. Ibid.

13. John Fay, "M'Neill's Rangers," *Baltimore Sun*, Aug. 7, 1906; Farrar, *Twenty-Second Pennsylvania Cavalry*, 153; Delauter, *McNeill's Rangers*, 57.

14. S, "Captain McNeill's Last Adventure."

15. Farrar, *Twenty-Second Pennsylvania Cavalry*, 153–54; S, "Captain McNeill's Last Adventure."

16. S, "Captain McNeill's Last Adventure"; ORS 9: 569, 590.

17. O. P. H., "For the Register," *Rockingham Register*, Feb. 12, 1864; OR, ser. 1, 33: 7, 43.

18. OR, ser. 1, 33: 43.

19. Farrar, *Twenty-Second Pennsylvania Cavalry*, 156–57; OR, ser. 1, 33: 38.

20. OR, ser. 1, 33: 40–41, 43, 45; O. P. H., "For the Register"; L., "Rosser's Raid," *Richmond Examiner*, Feb. 18, 1864.

21. OR, ser. 1, 33: 45.

22. O. P. H., "For the Register."

23. OR, ser. 1, 33: 45; Smith, *Nathan Goff, Jr.*, 38. The following spring Confederate authorities, in retaliation for a federal tribunal sentencing Major Thomas Armsey to fifteen years of hard labor, ordered Goff placed in solitary confinement in a cold, damp basement cell in Libby Prison. Fearing the worst, his family and their influential Republican politicos back home later persuaded President Lincoln to expedite an exchange of the two officers. Upon reaching Washington that September, Goff met with Lincoln and convinced the president to restart the exchange of Confederate and Union prisoners. See French, "Ex-POW talks Lincoln into prisoner deal," *Washington Times*, July 29, 2006.

24. OR, ser. 1, 33: 38–39.

25. Ibid., 43–44.

26. OR, ser. 1, 33: 46, 1139–40.

27. OR, ser. 1, 33: 46; "Confederate Raid on the Baltimore and Ohio Railroad," *Richmond Daily Dispatch*, Feb. 8, 1864.

28. OR, ser. 1, 33: 44, 46, 504; Van Meter, *Old Fields*, 237–38; "The Fight in West Virginia," *New-York Daily Reformer*, Feb. 8, 1864.

29. "The Fight in West Virginia"; OR, ser. 1, 33: 35, 36, 44; Bushong, *Old Jube*, 168.

30. James L. Vallandingham, "In the Virginia Mountains," *Philadelphia Times*, Sept. 6, 1884.

31. Delauter, *McNeill's Rangers*, 63.

32. "City Intelligence—Serenade to Marshal Kane," *Richmond Examiner*, Feb. 24, 1864.

33. "$100 Reward—Overcoat Lost," *Rockingham Register*, Mar. 4, 1864.

34. Farrar, *Twenty-Second Pennsylvania Cavalry*, 167.

35. "Letter from Lieutenant Pearne of the 15th New York Cavalry," *Syracuse Journal*, n.d., 15th Regiment Cavalry, NY Volunteers, Civil War Newspaper Clippings, New York State Military Museum and Veterans Research Center.

36. Farrar, *Twenty-Second Pennsylvania Cavalry*; OR, ser. 1, 33: 228.

37. OR, ser. 1, 33: 228; Delauter, *McNeill's Rangers*, 63; Farrar, *Twenty-Second Pennsylvania Cavalry*, 168; F, "From West Virginia," *Washington Reporter*, Mar. 16, 1864.

38. F, "From West Virginia"; Farrar, *Twenty-Second Pennsylvania Cavalry*, 168.

39. Delauter, *McNeill's Rangers*, 63–64, 120, 122; Fay, "M'Neill's Rangers," *Baltimore Sun*, Aug. 7, 1906; "Capture of Yankees," *Rockingham Register*, Mar. 29, 1864.

40. Farrar, *Twenty-Second Pennsylvania Cavalry*, 168–69; OR, ser. 1, 33: 228.

41. "A Returned Soldier," *Rockingham Register*, April 4, 1864; "Items from the Valley," *Richmond Whig*, April 12, 1864; Delauter, *McNeill's Rangers*, 120.

42. Delauter, *McNeill's Rangers*, 64; OR, ser. 1, 33: 719; Williams, *Rebel Brothers*, 190–91; Henry M. Trueheart to Catharine "Cally" Trueheart, April 14, 1864, TFP (emphasis in the original).

43. John S. Bond to Arthur Boreman, April 29, 1864, WVAGP, Union Militia 1861–1865, box 07, Hardy County, folder 7, WVA.

10. Bloomington and Piedmont

1. Henry M. Trueheart to Charles Trueheart, April 8, 1864, TFP; Henry Trueheart to Catharine "Cally" Trueheart, April 14, 1864, TFP; Williams, *Rebel Brothers*, 188–91.

2. Delauter, *McNeill's Rangers*, 65; Williams, *Rebel Brothers*, 188. McNeill scholar Dr. Robert Keller believes Private Andrew Jackson Bobo, who, on Sept. 2, 1862, deserted from Company B, 1st Virginia Partisan Rangers, may have been the soldier in question. In a letter to the author dated March 10, 2013, he writes, "I included A. Jackson's Bobo's service record. One of the girls hated to think that he had been a deserter and got McNeill in deep trouble with Imboden."

3. Delauter, *McNeill's Rangers*, 65; Gilmor, *Four Years in the Saddle*, 146–47.

4. OR, ser. 1, 33: 1253.

5. Grant, *Personal Memoirs*, 368–69. Grant's original plan called for Sigel to stay in Cumberland while Major General O. C. Ord would lead Sigel's troops up the valley. A personal conflict between the two, however, led to Ord requesting to be relieved from his departmental duties. On April 17 Grant granted his request. See Knight, *Valley Thunder*, 30–32.

6. Farrar, *Twenty-Second Pennsylvania Cavalry*, 195–96; Knight, *Valley Thunder*, 33–34.

7. Bright, "McNeill Rangers," 353. The term "Lincoln's lifeline" denotes the B&O's important wartime role in transporting Union troops, livestock, foodstuffs, and war matériel.

8. Duncan, "Raid on Piedmont," 26; Peerce, "Capture of a Railroad Train," 352.

9. Peerce, "Capture of a Railroad Train," 352.

10. Ibid.; OR, ser. 1, 37: pt. 1, 374; A Delayed Passenger, "New Creek Military Energy," *Baltimore American*, May 9, 1864. Peerce's small command included Charles Watkins, John Lynn, George W. Allen, William Pool, Benjamin Worting, George Little, James Crawford, John Overman, Wayne Cosner, and Pete Deverman.

11. A Delayed Passenger, "New Creek Military Energy"; OR, ser. 1, 37: pt. 1, 382; Duncan, "Raid on Piedmont," 31–32; "The Damage to the Baltimore and Ohio Railroad—What McNeill Captured," *Charleston Mercury*, May 24, 1864; Williams, *Rebel Brothers*, 192.

12. Williams, *Rebel Brothers*, 192; *Thirty-Eighth Annual Report*, 54; OR, ser. 1, 37: pt. 1, 69; Duncan, "Raid on Piedmont," 30–31; Maxwell and Swisher, *History of Hampshire County*, 668; W. H. G., "Piedmont During the War," *Piedmont Times*, Sept. 25, 1895; J. William Hunt, "Across The Desk," *Cumberland Sunday Times*, Aug. 6, 1961.

13. OR, ser. 1, 37: pt. 1, 68; A Delayed Passenger, "New Creek Military Energy"; Leonora Wood, "Capture of Bloomington Bridge Formed Incident in Local History During Civil War," *Moorefield Examiner*, n.d.; "The Raid on the Railroad at Bloomington—Details of the Affair," *Illustrated New Age*, May 7, 1864.

14. A Delayed Passenger, "New Creek Military Energy."

15. Ibid.; Peerce, "Capture of a Railroad Train," *Southern Bivouac*, 354; Wood, "Capture of Bloomington Bridge." Although Union records say that Bagely had only one gun, Hambright remembered two. He said, "We saw Mulligan's Jackass Battery going up Westernport Hill. . . . The battery had a small cannon on the neck of each horse." See OR, ser. 1, 37: pt. 1, 68.

16. Peerce, "Capture of a Railroad Train," 352–53.

17. Ibid., 353.

18. *Thirty-Eighth Annual Report*, 55; "Another Account," *Philadelphia Inquirer*, May 6, 1864; "The Raid on the Railroad at Bloomington"; "Incidents of the Raid on the Railroad," *Evening Star*, May 6, 1864.

19. Peerce, "Capture of a Railroad Train," 353.

20. Ibid., 353–54.

21. Ibid., 354; Confederate Amnesty Papers: Case Files for Applications from Former Confederates for Presidential Pardons, West Virginia—Peerce, John T.,—Pierce, John T., NA.

22. Peerce, "Capture of a Railroad Train," 353; "Raid on the Railroad at Bloomington."

23. W. R. Porter, "A Railroad Man's Battle with Union and Confed—Keeping the Railroad Repaired in War Time was a Task for Hercules," *Baltimore Sun*, Dec. 9, 1906.

24. Wood, "Capture of Bloomington Bridge."

25. Ibid.; Peerce, "Capture of a Railroad Train," 354; *Thirty-Eighth Annual Report*, 54; Porter, "A Railroad Man's Battle"; Grant, "Battle of Bloomington Bridge," 57; Wood, "Capture of Bloomington Bridge"; Hunt, "Across the Desk," Nov. 4, 1945.

26. Hunt, "Across the Desk"; Peerce, "Capture of a Railroad Train," 2, 354; "Damage to the Baltimore and Ohio Railroad."

27. "Damage to the Baltimore and Ohio Railroad"; Trueheart, "Memoirs," TFP, 1904, box 2, F-11, 13. In a May 21, 1864, letter to his brother Charles, Trueheart writes, "We lost three or four horses killed & wounded and a man badly wounded that was coming out with us." See Williams, *Rebel Brothers*, 194. Also, the Ranger who described the raid in an article for the *Rockingham Register*, later reprinted in the *Charleston Mercury*, wrote,

"We had one man and a horse killed and another horse wounded by the explosion of a shell." See "Damage to the Baltimore and Ohio Railroad."

28. Wood, "Capture of Bloomington Bridge"; Wood, "Bloomington Captured by McNeill's Confederate Rangers," 3; Hunt, "Across the Desk," Aug. 27, 1961; Hunt, "Across the Desk," Sept. 3, 1961; "John Thomas Walsh—Obituary," *Piedmont Herald*, June 4, 1936; "A Sad Shot," *Cleveland Leader*, May 20, 1864. According to author Leonora Wood, "The boy, John T. Walsh, of Allegany County, Maryland, taught school in this section for 48 years. He became known as the 'one-armed school teacher.' Mr. Walsh, who was an enthusiastic student of history . . . enjoyed talking of the period following the war and . . . was considered one of the most interesting and accurate authorities on the reconstruction period." In his adult life, Hambright worked for a time as the editor of the *Cumberland Daily News*. See Hunt, "Across the Desk," Nov. 4, 1945.

29. Peerce, "Capture of a Railroad Train," 354–55; OR, ser. 1, 37: pt. 1, 398. In an undated postwar letter sent to President Andrew Johnson, many locals who lived in and around Burlington petitioned the president to refuse Peerce's request for executive clemency. After listing many reasons why Peerce should not receive a presidential pardon, the men closed their letter with this statement: "We therefore pray your Excellency to let the law take its course, as we think there is no man less deserving of Executive Clemency than he." West Virginia governor Arthur I. Boreman also wrote the president and asked that he not pardon Peerce. But the rebel's humane treatment of the passengers and prisoners at Bloomington, and a letter from General George Crook telling how Peerce had treated him kindly after the Rangers captured him in late February 1865, caused Johnson to grant Peerce a full pardon on April 6, 1866. See Confederate Amnesty Papers: Case Files of Applications from Former Confederates for Presidential Pardons, West Virginia—Peerce, John T,—Pierce, John T., NA.

30. Trueheart, "Memoirs," TFP, 1904, box 2, F-11, 13.

31. *Thirty-Eighth Annual Report*, 54–55; "Another Account"; OR, ser. 1, 37: pt. 1, 382.

32. OR, ser. 1, 37: pt. 1, 390, 391, 393, 396; "Another Account"; Brown, "A History of the Sixth Regiment West Virginia," 341–42; Nichols, *A Summer Campaign*, 27.

33. OR, ser. 1, 37: pt. 1, 401; Stevenson, *Boots and Saddles*, 260, 264.

34. Farrar, *Twenty-Second Pennsylvania Cavalry*, 185–86, 199–200.

35. Ibid., 200.

36. Ibid.; Delta, "From the 22nd Penna. Cavalry," *Washington Reporter*, June 8, 1864; Elwood, *Elwood's Stories*, 187.

37. Elwood, *Elwood's Stories*, 187; John Fay, "M'Neill's Rangers," *Baltimore Sun*, Aug. 7, 1906.

38. Fay, "M'Neill's Rangers"; Farrar, *Twenty-Second Pennsylvania Cavalry*, 200–201; Elwood, *Elwood's Stories*, 187–88.

39. Elwood, *Elwood's Stories*, 190; Farrar, *Twenty-Second Pennsylvania Cavalry*, 201; Fay, "M'Neill's Rangers," *Baltimore Sun*, Aug. 7, 1906; Delta, "From the 22nd Penna. Cavalry"; Haas, *Dear Esther*, 209.

40. Haas, *Dear Esther*; Elwood, *Elwood's Stories*, 188; Farrar, *Twenty-Second Pennsylvania Cavalry*, 201.

41. Imboden, "Battle of New Market," 481. Writing many years after the battle, Imboden said that Capt. Bartlett told him the other command rode "eastward through Front Royal, passing through that town and taking the road through Chester Gap." It is the author's opinion that the force Bartlett spotted riding east was probably near Berryville at the time. See Stevenson, *Boots and Saddles*, 260, 264.

42. Imboden, "Battle of New Market," 481; OR, ser. 1, 37: pt. 1, 726. Colonel Smith's foot soldiers garnered a number of horses during the Gettysburg Campaign, and the regiment gradually evolved into mounted infantry. Soldiers in a mounted infantry unit traveled on horseback, but during any fighting they dismounted and fought on foot.

43. Delta, "From the 22nd Pennsylvania Cavalry"; Haas, *Dear Esther*, 209; Elwood, *Elwood's Stories*, 188–89.

44. Elwood, *Elwood's Stories*, 189; Hass, *Dear Esther*, 209; Delta, "From the 22nd Penna. Cavalry"; Farrar, *Twenty-Second Pennsylvania Cavalry*, 201.

45. Farrar, *Twenty-Second Pennsylvania Cavalry*, 201–2; Sam Taylor, "A Ride Into Obscurity," *Moorefield Examiner*, July 13, 1985. According to Taylor, "The rear guard . . . formed in line on or near the hill where the East Hardy High School now stands."

46. Farrar, *Twenty-Second Pennsylvania Cavalry*, 202.

47. Ibid.; Elwood, *Elwood's Stories*, 190; Delta, "From the 22nd Penna. Cavalry."

48. Delta, "From the 22nd Penna. Cavalry;" Farrar, *Twenty-Second Pennsylvania Cavalry*, 202.

49. Williams, *Rebel Brothers*, 193; Elwood, *Elwood's Stories*, 190; Trueheart, "Memoirs," TFP, 1904, box 2, F-11, 13–14.

50. OR, ser. 1, 37: pt. 1, 70.

51. Ibid.

52. Imboden, "Battle of New Market," 481.

11. The Timber Ridge Fight

1. OR, ser. 1, 37: pt. 1, 522–23.

2. Farrar, *Twenty-Second Pennsylvania Cavalry*, 204.

3. Williams, ed., *Rebel Brothers*, 194, 196.

4. OR, ser. 1, 37: pt. 1, 554; T. P., "From the Ringgold," *Washington Reporter*, June 15, 1864.

5. Elwood, *Elwood's Stories*, 205.

6. Ibid., 205–6; Armstrong, *11th Virginia Cavalry*, 147. It appears that Harness led a band of local guerrillas. Recently, Woodrow Simmons discovered prisoner of war records for Private Peter Funkhouser of "Harness Ind. Cav." According to these papers, Funkhouser was captured at Moorefield on August 7, 1864.

7. Elwood, *Elwood's Stories*, 206.

8. Farrar, *Twenty-Second Pennsylvania Cavalry*, 205.

9. Ibid.; Elwood, *Elwood's Stories*, 206; Haas, *Dear Esther*, 214.

10. Farrar, *Twenty-Second Pennsylvania Cavalry*, 206; T. P., "From the Ringgold."

11. T. P., "From the Ringgold"; Elwood, *Elwood's Stories*, 207–8.

12. Elwood, *Elwood's Stories*, 207–8 ; T. P., "From the Ringgold"; Farrar, *Twenty-Second Pennsylvania Cavalry*, 206.

13. Farrar, *Twenty-Second Pennsylvania Cavalry*, 206, 207, 471, 499; T. P., "From the Ringgold"; Elwood, *Elwood's Stories*, 207; Haas, *Dear Esther*, 214.

14. John Fay, "M'Neill's Rangers," *Baltimore Sun*, August 7, 1906.

15. OR, ser. 1, 37: 608, 629–30; ORS 56: 120.

16. Haselberger, *Confederate Retaliation*, 17; Imboden, "Battle of New Market," 485.

17. Williams, *Rebel Brothers*, 194.

18. Ibid., 195; Haselberger, *Confederate Retaliation*, 19–20; "Hunter's Raid 1864," *Richmond Dispatch*, July 8, 1900.

19. "Hunter's Raid 1864." Private Lloyd Clary was the scout mentioned in the article. See Delauter, *McNeill's Rangers*, 118.

20. "Hunter's Raid 1864"; Williams, ed., *Rebel Brothers*, 195.

21. Imboden, "Battle of New Market," 485.

22. Williams, *Rebel Brothers*, 195.

23. Ibid.; Imboden, "Battle of New Market," 485; Fay, "M'Neill's Rangers."

24. Haselberger, *Confederate Retaliation*, 20, 22, 25; Williams, *Rebel Brothers*, 196.

12. Johnson's Run and Springfield

1. John S. Bond to Arthur I. Boreman, June 4, 1864; WVAGP, Union Militia 1861–1865, box 07, Hardy County, folder 7, WVA.

2. "Swamp Dragons," *Rockingham Register*, Jan. 8, 1864; Calhoun, *'Twixt North and South*, 126.

3. Calhoun, *'Twixt North and South*, 15.

4. Ibid., 14–15.

5. Ibid., 15; Steve French, "Swamp Dragons Were Legends During the Civil War," *Morgan Messenger*, Nov. 11, 1998; Steve French, "Two Brothers Lead Rebel Guerrilla Raids," *Washington Times*, July 7, 2007.

6. Calhoun, *'Twixt North and South*, 102–4.

7. Ibid., 108–9; "Swamp Dragons Killed," *Richmond Enquirer*, May 2, 1864; J. G. Ketterman to Arthur Boreman, April 28, 1864, WVAGP, Union Militia, 1861–1865, box 19, Pendleton County, folder 7, WVA; "Terrible State of Affairs," *Daily National Intelligencer*, May 11, 1864.

8. Judy, *History of Grant and Hardy Counties*, 255; Calhoun, *'Twixt North and South*, 126–27; Williams, *Rebel Brothers*, 196–97.

9. Williams, *Rebel Brothers*, 197; Calhoun, *'Twixt North and South*, 126–27; Judy, *History of Grant and Hardy Counties*, 238, 255–56. Judy based his account of the Johnson

Run fight on an interview with Simon E. Riggleman. At the time of their talk, the Home Guard veteran and participant in the fight was eighty-two. Judy's account and Harrison M. Calhoun's writings on the incident differ to some extent on how the fight started. Since Riggleman was there, I decided to rely on his version of events. According to Petersburg historian Bob Mohr, local tradition has it that Barbara Ann Mowry fought on the side of the Rangers. He says, "Who knows how or why she was involved in the fight, but the story is that she carried embers from a nearby fireplace in a stove shovel and attempted to set one or more of the wagons on fire. According to Sonny Mowry, one of her descendants, 'She was a mean woman.'" Interviews with Bob Mohr, Apr. 19, 2015, Dec. 1, 2015.

10. Judy, *History of Grant and Hardy Counties*, 255; Calhoun, *'Twixt North and South*, 127. After the fight, one of the Swamps pulled a gun on a bystander named Christian Bensenhaver and ordered him to "gather up the dead." Helped out by a blacksmith, Bensenhaver loaded the corpses onto his wagon and carted them away. See "Just Between Me and You," *Moorefield Examiner*, Dec. 1, 1937.

11. Calhoun, *'Twixt North and South*, 127; Judy, *History of Grant and Hardy Counties*, 238; Williams, *Rebel Brothers*, 197; OR, ser. 1, 37: pt. 1, 656; "Obituary—William H. Coakley," *Rockingham Register*, n.d.; John Fay, "M'Neill's Rangers," *Baltimore Sun*, Aug. 7, 1906; Delauter, *McNeill's Rangers*, 71.

12. Judy, *History of Grant and Hardy Counties*, 256.

13. Ibid.; Williams, *Rebel Brothers*, 197.

14. *Wheeling Daily Intelligencer*, June 27, 1864; ibid., June 28, 1864.

15. OR, ser. 1, 37: pt. 1, 675–76. See Cale, "General Kelley's Prize Horse 'Philippi,'" 54; Scott, *Civil War Era in Cumberland*, 88. According to Cale, Kelley bought this farm, Swan Meadows, in December 1863. Fort Pendleton was a Union outpost that protected the Northwestern Turnpike Bridge at Gorman, Maryland. See Price, "Fort Pendleton," 27.

16. Nichols, "Fighting Guerrillas," 21.

17. Trueheart, "Memoirs," TFP, 1904, box 2, F-11, 13.

18. Ibid.

19. OR, ser. 1, 37: pt. 1, 356; Fay, "M'Neill's Rangers,"; Maxwell and Swisher, *History of Hampshire County*, 668; ORS 74: pt. 2, 422.

20. Williams, *Rebel Brothers*, 197.

21. OR, ser. 1, 37: pt. 1, 356.

22. Nichols, "Fighting Guerrillas," 21.

23. OR, ser. 1, 37: pt. 1, 681.

24. "Another Exploit of Capt. M'Neill," *Richmond Daily Dispatch*, July 6, 1864.

25. Ibid.

13. To the Gates of Washington

1. Tucker, *Brigadier General John D. Imboden*, 260–61.

2. Williams. *Rebel Brothers*, 200.

3. Price, *Memorials*, 10–11; Curran, "Memory, Myths, and Musty Records," pt. 1, 29–35. Professor Curran notes that Woodson, Scott, and the others went to City Point because at that time Vicksburg, Mississippi, the regular exchange point for that region, was under siege.

4. *Rockingham Register*, Feb. 5, 1864.

5. *Rockingham Register*, April 1, 1864.

6. Price, *Memorials*, 15–16; Curran, "Memory, Myths, and Musty Records," pt. 1, 38–40; Knight, *Valley Thunder*, 159, 294; "Casualties in the 62nd at New Market," *Staunton Vindicator*, May 27, 1864.

7. Delauter, *McNeill's Rangers*, 32–33, 35–37; Early, "Early's March to Washington," 493; Haselberger, *Confederate Retaliation*, 43–45.

8. Haselberger, *Confederate Retaliation*, 45; Price, *Memorials*, 17; Early, "Early's March to Washington," 493–94.

9. OR, ser. 1, 37: pt. 2, 25–28, 42; Hogbin, "Diary," 3; Haselberger, *Confederate Retaliation*, 52.

10. Haselberger, *Confederate Retaliation*, 52–53; Hogbin, "Diary," 3; *Thirty-Eighth Annual Report*, 56; Nichols, "Fighting Guerrillas," 22; Haselberger, "Skirmishes," 265–67; OR, ser. 1, 37: pt. 2, 42. Only one armored cannon, or "Monitor," car, nicknamed after the Union navy's famed ironclad warship, was at the bridge. Author Dan Toomey described an armored train: "The train was state-of-the-art in mechanized warfare. The locomotive and tender were located in the center. Two ironclad rifle cars were positioned in front of the engine and two behind. At either end of the train were cannon cars with artillery pieces mounted on both ends." See Toomey, *War Came by Train*, 217.

11. OR, ser. 1, 37: pt. 2, 47.

12. OR, ser. 1, 37: pt. 2, 42–43; Haselberger, "Skirmishes," 265–66; Nichols, "Fighting Guerrillas," 22–23.

13. Williams, *Rebel Brothers*, 200; OR, ser. 1, 37: pt. 2, 44, 46; OR, ser. 1, 43: pt. 1, 3.

14. Tim Snyder, "Potomac River Fords," 4; Nichols, "Fighting Guerrillas," 22.

15. Nichols. "Fighting Guerrillas," 22; John Fay, "M'Neill Rangers," *Baltimore Sun*, Aug. 7, 1906; Williams, *Rebel Brothers*, 200; Price, *Memorials*, 17; OR, ser. 1, 37: pt. 2, 46.

16. OR, ser. 1, 37: pt. 1, 187.

17. Ibid., 190; Williams, *Rebel Brothers*, 200.

18. Williams, *Rebel Brothers*, 200–201; Tucker, *Brigadier General John D. Imboden*, 264; Hogbin, "Diary," 4; Early, "Early's March to Washington," 495.

19. Denney, *Civil War Years*, 434; Williams, *Rebel Brothers*, 201; "The Invasion of Maryland," *Daily Ohio Statesman*, July 18, 1864.

20. "Invasion of Maryland"; Scott Jones, "A Rebel Stampede," *National Tribune,* April 8, 1886.

21. Jones, "A Rebel Stampede."

22. Ibid.; Fay, "M'Neill's Rangers"; Williams, *Rebel Brothers,* 201.

23. Williams, *Rebel Brothers,* 201; Jones, "A Rebel Stampede"; David H. Wallace, ed., *Frederick Maryland in Peace and War,* 137.

24. "Invasion of Maryland"; Williams, *Rebel Brothers,* 201; Maier, *Leather and Steel,* 189. The Rangers always thought that McNeill had killed McDonald. See Fay, "M'Neill's Rangers."

25. Hogbin, "Diary," 4; Fay, "M'Neill's Rangers"; Williams, *Rebel Brothers,* 201; Delauter, *McNeill's Rangers,* 123.

26. J. W. Duffey, "Interesting Civil War Episode," *Shepherdstown Register,* Jan. 31, 1929.

27. Ibid. Some thirty years after the war, Duffey was at Joseph Shaffer's store in Martinsburg telling some men about his narrow escape. During his tale, George Dowling, a clerk in the store, related that he was the young man who had encouraged Duffey to "hurry."

14. Helping McCausland

1. Williams, *Rebel Brothers,* 200; Price, *Memorials,* 18; OR, ser. 1, 37: pt. 2, 418. Traveling through western Maryland in the wake of the rest of Early's cavalry, the Rangers found slim pickings. Other Confederate raiders had already cleaned out many Washington and Frederick County farms. See "The Raid," *Herald of Freedom and Torch Light,* July 20, 1864.

2. OR, ser. 1, 37: pt. 2, 88–89. Sheets', or Sheetz', Mill is present-day Headsville, West Virginia.

3. OR, ser. 1, 37: pt. 2, 173, 320–21.

4. Ibid., 397.

5. Ibid., 455, 488. Romney attorney and local historian Royce Saville stated to the author that during the summer cattlemen from western Hampshire (now Mineral) County, would drive their stock to the top of the mountain for better grazing. Interview with Royce Saville, June 7, 2014.

6. OR, ser. 1, 37: pt. 2, 516–17; Nichols, "Fighting Guerrillas," 25.

7. Nichols, "Fighting Guerrillas," 25; OR, ser. 1, 37: pt. 2, 516–17.

8. Nichols, "Fighting Guerrillas," 25.

9. Ibid.

10. McCausland, "Burning of Chambersburg, Penn," 267–69; "Remains of Colonel Mulligan at Wheeling," *Philadelphia Inquirer,* Aug. 1, 1864; Haselberger, *Confederate Retaliation,* 77. Located about three miles east of Hedgesville, soldiers of both armies frequently used the fields of Dr. Allen Hammond's plantation and the adjoining Jacob French farm as camping sites.

11. Haselberger, *Confederate Retaliation,* 79, 81, 84–88; Schneck, *Burning of Chambersburg,* 16; McCausland, "Burning of Chambersburg," 269.

12. McCausland, "Burning of Chambersburg," 269–70; Ted Alexander, *Southern Revenge*, 119–20, 122–23, 127; Haselberger, *Confederate Retaliation*, 93–98.

13. Haselberger, *Confederate Retaliation*, 103, 105; Alexander, *Southern Revenge*, 127–29; Glenn Cordell, *Civil War Invasions in Fulton County*, 15–16, 21; interview with Sam Buterbaugh, Aug. 9, 2013.

14. Alexander, *Southern Revenge*, 134–35; OR, ser. 1, 37: pt. 2, 515, 533–34, 542.

15. OR, ser. 1, 37: pt. 2, 535; Haselberger, *Confederate Retaliation*, 106; Smith, "Diary," 30.

16. Ibid; OR, ser. 1, 37: pt. 1, 329–30, 355; Haselberger, *Confederate Retaliation*, 106–8, 110; Alexander, *Southern Revenge*, 129; Gilmor, *Four Years in the Saddle*, 213.

17. Haselberger, *Confederate Retaliation*, 112–14; "Late Fight at Oldtown; Near Cumberland," *Illustrated New Age*, Aug. 12, 1864; "The Fight Near Cumberland, Md.," *Baltimore Sun*, Aug. 19, 1864.

18. "Fight Near Cumberland, Md."; OR, ser. 1, 37: pt. 1, 355; ORS 74: 295; Nichols, *A Summer Campaign*, 133; Gilmor, *Four Years in the Saddle*, 215–16.

19. Gilmor, *Four Years in the Saddle*, 216; Nichols, *A Summer Campaign*, 133; Haselberger, *Confederate Retaliation*, 122.

20. Gilmor, *Four Years in the Saddle*, 216–18; "Late Fight at Oldtown"; OR, ser. 1, 37: pt. 1, 355.

21. OR, ser. 1, 37: pt. 1, 355; Gilmor, *Four Years in the Saddle*, 218; "Late Fight at Oldtown."

22. Gilmor, *Four Years in the Saddle*, 219–20; "Late Fight at Oldtown"; ORS 74, 294; Allen, *Historic Old Town*, 38–39. Allen places McNulty's gun on a hill above the Michael Cresap house. That dwelling, though, is in the eastern end of the town.

23. "Late Fight at Oldtown"; OR, ser. 1, 37: pt. 1, 356; ORS 74, 294.

24. OR, ser. 1, 37: pt. 1, 356; *Thirty-Eighth Annual Report*, 59.

25. OR, ser. 1, 37: pt. 1, 356; OR, ser. 1, 37: pt. 2, 588; Maxwell and Swisher, *History of Hampshire County*, 669.

26. Maxwell and Swisher, *History of Hampshire County*, 669. Washington's diary entry confirms that McNeill destroyed the bridge before McCausland's raiders crossed the South Branch. Also, when McCausland crossed the river on August 3, McNeill was off raiding in the Patterson Creek Valley.

27. *Thirty-Eighth Annual Report*, 59; Haselberger, *Confederate Retaliation*, 132.

28. OR, ser. 1, 37: pt. 2, 588–89.

29. Ibid., 589; Haselberger, *Confederate Retaliation*, 135.

30. Haselberger, *Confederate Retaliation*, 133, 135, 137–38. In a postwar article published by the *Philadelphia Times*, former Ranger James L. Vallandingham mentioned that he was at the New Creek fight. At this time, however, I have not found any evidence that Captain McNeill was there. See Vallandingham, "In the Virginia Mountains."

31. Haselberger, *Confederate Retaliation*, 139–40, 142, 144; ORS 74: 295.

32. Haselberger, *Confederate Retailiation*, 144–45; Elwood, *Elwood's Stories*, 229. Elwood claimed that Jesse McNeill gave McCausland the unheeded advice.

33. Beach, *First New York Lincoln Cavalry*, 403; OR, ser. 1, 43: pt. 1, 493.

34. Ibid., 493–94.

35. Maxwell and Swisher, *History of Hampshire County*, 657; Duffey, *Two Generals Kidnapped*, 5.

36. Haselberger, *Confederate Retaliation*, 153–57, 176–77; Booth, *Personal Reminiscences of a Confederate Soldier*, 139–40.

37. Maxwell and Swisher, *History of Hampshire County*, 658–60.

38. Ibid.

39. Williams, *Rebel Brothers*, 203; Price, *Memorials*, 18.

15. MEEMS BOTTOM

1. Grant, *Personal Memoirs*, 469–70.

2. Ibid., 470; Philip Sheridan, *Civil War Memoirs*, 214–16.

3. Ibid., 214–15.

4. Ibid., 219–21.

5. OR, ser. 1, 43: pt. 1, 806. Kelley's promotion to brevet major general occurred on August 5, 1863.

6. OR, ser. 1, 43: pt. 1, 829, 887–88.

7. Ibid., 950.

8. Ibid., 951.

9. Ibid., 959, 968.

10. Ibid., 968, 972; "Affairs around Cumberland," *New York Herald*, Sept. 1, 1864.

11. John S. Bowman, ed., *The Civil War Almanac*, 224–25.

12. OR, ser. 1, 43: pt. 1, 223; Williams, *Rebel Brothers*, 202; John Boggs to Arthur Boreman, Sept. 11, 1864, WVAGP, Union Militia, box 07, Hardy County, folder 4, WVA.

13. Vandiver, "Two Forgotten Heroes," 408–9.

14. Duffey, *M'Neill's Last Charge*, 6; James L. Vallandingham, "In the Virginia Mountains," *Philadelphia Times*, Sept. 6, 1884.

15. Duffey, *M'Neill's Last Charge*, 6–7.

16. Ibid., 7. The distant sound of cannon fire drifting down the valley came from fighting around Mount Crawford. See Hotchkiss, *Make Me a Map of the Valley*, 234.

17. Duffey, *M'Neill's Last Charge*, 7–8. Whether the Rangers burned the bridge or not remains questionable. On Oct. 5 Colonel Oliver Edwards, commanding the federal post at Winchester, reported that "the bridge at Edenburg has been burned."

18. Duffey, *M'Neill's Last Charge*, 8–9, 11, 13; OR, ser. 1, 43: pt. 1, 415; Vallandingham, "In the Virginia Mountains." In September 1862 McNeill took this same horse from a Knobly Mountain farm, near Ridgeville, on the captain's first partisan raid.

19. Vallandingham, "In the Virginia Mountains"; Duffey, *M'Neill's Last Charge*, 9.

20. *Pocahontas Times*, Mar. 11, 1929; OR, ser. 1, 43: pt. 1, 51; Van Meter, *Genealogies and Sketches*, 175.

21. OR, ser. 1, 43: pt. 1, 51; Vallandingham, "In the Virginia Mountains."

22. Duffey, *M'Neill's Last Charge*, 10–11; Elizabeth Weller, "Captain McNeill," *Moorefield Examiner*, Mar. 28, 1907; Vallandingham, "In the Virginia Mountains"; OR, ser. 1, 43: pt. 1, 185, 415.

23. Weller, "Captain McNeill"; Duffey, *M'Neill's Last Charge*, 11–12; Delauter, *McNeill's Rangers*, 121.

24. Duffey, *M'Neill's Last Charge*, 12–14; OR, ser. 1, 43: pt. 2, 308. Hoping to meet a supply train coming up the valley, the Pennsylvanians traveled to Winchester. Upon reaching the town the evening of October 3, those on horseback reported in to the post commander, Colonel Oliver Edwards. The others came in to camp the next day. A day or two later they all rejoined their regiment at Guard Hill. See OR, ser. 1, 43: pt. 1, 185, 514. Although Duffey wrote that the Rangers paroled all of their captives, at least one, Lieutenant William Wallace Murphy, Company G, remained with them. According to regimental records, Murphy was a prisoner from October 3, 1864, until February 21, 1865. In September 1876 Murphy, then farming in Minnesota, was a leading participant in the capture of outlaws Cole, Jim, and Bob Younger. See Gardner, *Shot All To Hell*, 162–65, and Younger, *Story of Cole Younger*, 88. It appears that the paroled soldiers were sent to Camp Parole in Annapolis, Md., to await exchange. For example, an entry in Private Robert Monahan's pension file reads, "Oct. 31/64 absent in Parole CP, Annapolis, Md." On Nov. 19, 1864, the *Army and Navy Journal* reported, under "Dismissal Confirmed": "Captain James Jackson, 14th Pennsylvania Cavalry, to date October 23, 1864, for allowing himself & party to be disgracefully surprised & captured while on duty guarding a bridge near Mt. Jackson, Va."

25. Weller, "Captain McNeill."

26. Ibid.; OR, ser. 1, 43: pt. 2, 272, 415.

27. Weller, "Captain McNeill"; Duffey, *M'Neill's Last Charge*, 18–19; Vallandingham, "In the Virginia Mountains"; Hotchkiss, *Make Me a Map of the Valley*, 234.

28. Duffey, *McNeill's Last Charge*, 18–19.

29. Ibid., 18; Van Meter, *Genealogies and Sketches*, 174. Duffey also recalled that a few years after the incident, a former federal soldier claimed that he had shot McNeill after "he had been captured and disarmed by one of the Rangers and left standing beside a horse." Then, taking out a pocket pistol he reached over the horse's neck and shot the captain. Duffey, however, rejected the man's assertion, writing, "Conceding that the man was there, his story has the general air of improbability, and is contradicted by the nature of the wound." See Duffey, *M'Neill's Last Charge*, 18.

30. Vallandingham, "In the Virginia Mountains." In an unpublished paper written in 2000, researchers Francis Haselberger and Woodrow Simmons compared five different McNeill Ranger rosters compiled by various individuals. George Valentine's name, however, does not appear on any of them. See Haselberger and Simmons, "Roster of McNeill's Rangers." In a conversation with Civil War author and researcher Clyde Cale Jr., Cale noted that a Private George Valentine served in the 1st Maryland Cavalry Battalion. For more information on this man, see Driver, *First and Second Maryland Cavalry, C.S.A.*, 295.

31. Vallandingham, "In the Virginia Mountains."

32. Ibid.; Delauter, *McNeill's Rangers*, 122; Weller, "Captain McNeill."

33. OR, ser. 1, 43: pt. 1, 308; *Daily National Intelligencer*, Oct. 7, 1864.

34. Duffey, *M'Neill's Last Charge*, 20; "McKinley as a Warrior," *Daily Item*, Mar. 13, 1897. While attending President McKinley's first inauguration, Elizabeth Weller recounted the story of Sheridan stopping at her house to a Washington, D.C., reporter. "In the reviewing stand on inauguration day," wrote the reporter, "an elderly woman, whose youthful beauty had not yet faded, said when McKinley entered his little glass house. [']I haven't seen him since he was Sheridan's aide in the Shenandoah Valley. I was nursing the sick and wounded of the Confederate side at Rude's Hill. My patient at the time was Major McNeill.[']"

35. OR, ser. 1, 43: pt. 1, 308.

36. Weller, "Captain McNeill"; Duffey, *M'Neill's Last Charge*, 20–21. Duffey wrote that after Sheridan left, his men burned the Weller outbuildings. Rebel cavalry arrived in time, though, to stop the flames from engulfing the house. Elizabeth Weller's account, however, does not mention this. There is some question as to when the ambulance arrived to pick up McNeill. Weller claims it was that night, and Duffey indicates it was a few days later. Another account states it was two weeks later after Sheridan defeated Early at the Battle of Cedar Creek. See Delauter, *McNeill's Rangers*, 85.

16. Kelley's Tigers

1. N. M. Burkholder, "The Barn Burners," *Richmond Dispatch*, July 22, 1900; Van Meter, *Genealogies and Sketches*, 175.

2. Keen and Mewborn, *43rd Battalion*, 200–201; OR, ser. 1, 43: pt. 1, 509.

3. OR, ser. 1, 43: pt. 1, 509; Keen and Mewborn, *43rd Battalion*, 201; Evans and Moyer, *Mosby's Confederacy*, 33–34.

4. Elwood, *Elwood's Stories*, 267.

5. Ibid., 268. Based on White's recollection, Elwood's account places Lieutenant Colonel Mosby on the scene. But White may have mistaken another officer for Mosby. After making his decision, it is the author's opinion that it would have been out of character for the hard-fighting "Gray Ghost" to back down. Also, at this time Mosby was suffering from an ankle injury. His foot was heavily bandaged, and he used a cane. Elwood, though, does not mention this fact.

6. Elwood, *Elwood's Stories*, 288; Farrar, *Twenty-Second Pennsylvania Cavalry*, 477.

7. OR, ser. 1, 43: pt. 2, 383; James L. Vallandingham, "In the Virginia Mountains," *Philadelphia Times*, Sept. 6, 1884; *Wheeling Daily Intelligencer*, Oct. 3, 1864; ibid., Nov. 3, 1864.

8. A Soldier, "For the Register," *Rockingham Register*, Nov. 18, 1864; Woodrow Simmons to author, Sept. 1, 2014.

9. A Soldier, "For the Register"; Woodrow Simmons, Pratt's great-great-grandson writes, "I am pretty sure Seymour Baldwin was married to the sister of my gg grand-

mother Susan Bobo Simmons. Susan was married to the Sandford Yoakum Simmons that had their bodies brought back and buried in the Snodgrass Cemetery. After much research, I am pretty sure that this is now called the New House Cem. at Rig." Woodrow Simmons to author, Sept. 1, 2014.

10. Vallandingham, "In the Virginia Mountains."

11. Ibid.

12. Ibid.

13. Ibid.

14. Ibid.

15. Ibid. At the end of his article, Vallandingham recalled that in 1866 he was traveling the road between Petersburg and the ford "when I was joined by two withered-looking old men dressed in linsey-woolsey of the mountain country. They asked me if I had ever heard of the killing of three young men sometime in November or December 1864 before, and if so, whether I knew where they were buried. I told them I had heard of it and also been told where the bodies were laid." Vallandingham then took the men up a glen to a spring near a mountainside, and after digging through a pile of leaves with a stick, produced a hat and a few leg bones. One man shouted out, "Don't that's enough. I know where he is. . . . One of those boys is my son." With that, all three men returned to the road and went their separate ways.

16. Sheridan, *Civil War Memoirs*, 273–84.

17. OR, ser. 1, 43: pt. 1, 467; Norton, "*The red neck ties*," 48, 52, 54–55; SPUR, "Letter from the 15th N.Y. Cavalry," *Syracuse Journal*, Dec. 1864, Newspaper Clippings, New York State Military Museum and Veterans Research Center.

18. OR, ser. 1, 43: pt. 1, 772; ibid., pt. 2, 522; Norton, "*The red neck ties*," 55; "Southern War News," *Illustrated New Age*, Nov. 18, 1864; Trueheart, *Memoirs*, TFP, 1904, box 2, F-11, 14.

19. Trueheart, *Memoirs*, TFP, 1904, box 2, f-11, 14.

20. Norton, "*The red neck ties*," 52, 55; Phisterer, *New York in the War of the Rebellion*, 315; "Southern War News"; Delauter, *McNeill's Rangers*, 117; Jim McGhee to author, Nov. 26, 2014.

21. *Thirty-Ninth Annual Report*, 40; OR, ser. 1, 43: pt. 2, 522.

22. OR, ser. 1, 43: pt. 2, 541, 542, 556.

23. Ibid., pt. 1, 652; Howard, "George Robert Latham," 410–11.

24. OR, ser. 1, 43: pt. 1, 652.

25. Ibid., 652–53; Williams, *Rebel Brothers*, 205.

26. OR, ser. 1, 43, pt. 1: 653; Van Meter, *Old Fields*, 240–41.

27. Van Meter, *Old Fields*, 240; OR, ser. 1, 43: pt. 1, 653.

28. Duffey, *M'Neill's Last Charge*, 21; "Death of Capt. Jno. McNeill," *Rockingham Register*, Nov. 18, 1864; "Tribute of Respect," *Rockingham Register*, Nov. 25, 1864. According to research by Edinburg, Virginia, author Donna Shrum, McNeill was buried in Harrisonburg's Woodbine Cemetery. Shrum to author, Sept. 7, 2014.

17. Old Maid's Lane

1. Duffey, "Daring Capture," 351; William, *Rebel Brothers*, 208.

2. OR, ser. 1, 43: pt. 1, 655. Marlington, West Virginia, author Andrew Price later commented on the caste system the Swamp Dragons faced. He wrote, "The regulars were always ready to put the state troops on the firing line . . . and then never recognized them after the war socially or financially." See Andrew Price, "Confederate Raids," *Moorefield Examiner*, Aug. 15, 1929.

3. OR, ser. 1, 43: pt. 1, 668–69; ibid., pt. 2, 676.

4. OR, ser. 1, 43: pt. 1, 662–63; Wert, "Attacking the Invincible," 12; H, "McNeill's Rangers," *Richmond Whig*, Dec. 16, 1864. Rosser, formerly a colonel, was commanding Major General Fitz Lee's cavalry division. On September 19 Lee had been seriously wounded at the Battle of Third Winchester. See Sifikas, *Who Was Who in the Civil War*, 379, 556.

5. McDonald, *A History of the Laurel Brigade*, 323. It is possible that the man who accompanied Peerce was not James L. Williams but Private Joseph V. Williams. Like Peerce, Joseph Williams lived in the immediate area and served in Company F, 7th Virginia Cavalry. See Armstrong, *Seventh Virginia Cavalry*, 246; McDonald, *A History of the Laurel Brigade*, 321.

6. H, "McNeill's Rangers"; Duffey, "Daring Capture," 350; Williams, *Rebel Brothers*, 206.

7. Williams, *Rebel Brothers*, 206; H, "McNeill's Rangers."

8. H, "McNeill's Rangers"; Williams, *Rebel Brothers*, 207; "A Good Job," *Rockingham Register*, Dec. 2, 1864; H, "McNeill's Rangers"; Duffey, "Daring Capture," 351.

9. Duffey, "Daring Capture," 351; Rev. L. H. Davis, "Personal Incidents," *Moorefield Examiner*, April 2, 1914.

10. Williams, *Rebel Brothers*, 207; Davis, "Personal Incidents."

11. Duffey, "Daring Capture," 351; OR, ser. 1, 43: pt. 1, 663.

12. OR, ser. 1, 43: pt. 1, 663; Van Meter, *Old Fields*, 240.

13. Duffey, "Daring Capture," 351.

14. Van Meter, *Old Fields*, 240; Williams, *Rebel Brothers*, 207.

15. Williams, *Rebel Brothers*, 207; OR, ser. 1, 43, pt. 1: 663; Davis, "Personal Incidents."

16. "A Good Job"; OR, ser. 1, 43: pt. 1, 660, 663.

17. "A Good Job"; Van Meter, *Old Fields*, 280; "McNeill's Rangers," *Moorefield Examiner*, March 4, 1915; John Fay, "M'Neill's Rangers," *Baltimore Sun*, Aug. 7, 1906; Duffey, "Daring Capture," 352.

18. "A Good Job"; Williams, *Rebel Brothers*, 207.

19. Williams, *Rebel Brothers*, 207–8; "A Good Job"; OR, ser. 1, 43: pt. 1, 663; Duffey, "Daring Capture," 352; Price, *Memorials*, 18.

20. OR, ser. 1, 43: pt. 1, 663–64. Potts returned to New Creek with thirteen prisoners. The enemy force that Potts mentioned seeing was Major E. H. McDonald's detachment, which had attacked Piedmont on the afternoon of November 28. See McDonald, "A Rough Sketch," 124.

21. Davis, "Personal Incidents."

22. McDonald, *A History of the Laurel Brigade*, 325–26; Fitzhugh, "Civil War Memoirs," 49.

23. Davis, "Personal Incidents."

24. McDonald, *A History of the Laurel Brigade*, 326; McDonald, "A Rough Sketch," 123; Haselberger, "General Rosser's Raid," 97–98; Fitzhugh, "Civil War Memoirs," 49–50.

25. OR, ser. 1, 43: pt. 1, 660, 665, 658.

26. McDonald, *A History of the Laurel Brigade*, 326, 327; Fitzhugh, "Civil War Memoirs," 50.

27. Fitzhugh, "Civil War Memoirs," 50–51.

28. Ibid., 51; McDonald, *A History of the Laurel Brigade*, 327–28; *Wheeling Daily Intelligencer*, Dec. 2, 1864.

29. *Wheeling Daily Intelligencer*, Dec. 2, 1864.

30. McDonald, "A Rough Sketch," 123; OR, ser. 1, 43: pt. 1, 665.

31. OR, ser. 1, 43: pt. 1, 665; *Thirty-Ninth Annual Report*, 40; McDonald, "A Rough Sketch," 123–24.

32. OR, ser. 1, 43: pt. 1, 657; "The Surprise and Capture of New Creek," *Wheeling Daily Intelligencer*, Dec. 6, 1864; "The Raid on New Creek, Va." *Baltimore Sun*, Dec. 5, 1864; Civil War Damage Claims Filed Before the Southern Claims Commission: Petition of Ellen C. Cox, No. 20334, NA. According to Paschal B. Gentry's recollection, "I met with him in Maryland, and about the first day of October 1864, we were employed by Capt. Harrison of the Military Post at New Creek, W.Va. and on the 28thday of November 1864, he [Cox] was killed by the rebel Gen. Rosser's command at New Creek."

33. "More About the Late New Creek Raid," *Wheeling Daily Intelligencer*, Dec. 7, 1864.

34. OR, ser. 1, 43: pt. 1, 664, 671; OR, ser. 1, 43: pt. 2, 743.

35. OR, ser. 1, 43: pt. 1, 661, 713, 780; Wert, "Attacking the Invincible," 16; Bushong and Bushong, *Fightin' Tom Rosser*, 153.

36. OR, ser. 1, 43: pt. 1, 654.

37. Ibid., 659.

38. H, "McNeill's Rangers."

39. Davis, "Personal Incidents"; Duffey, "McNeill's Rangers," *Moorefield Examiner*, March 9, 1915.

40. Duffey, "Daring Capture," 351.

18. Punishing the Swamp Dragons

1. "The Right Thing At Last," *Journal*, Dec. 28, 1864.

2. Van Meter, *Old Fields*, 241.

3. Williams, *Rebel Brothers*, 209.

4. Myers, *The Comanches*, 346; Calhoun, *'Twixt North and South*, 128.

5. Myers, *Comanches*, 347–48; Crouch, *Rough-Riding Scout*, 1, 9. The infamous Mobberly did not survive the war. On the afternoon of April 5, 1865, he ran out of

luck when a band of three Loudoun Rangers and three civilians hiding in a hayloft ambushed the guerrilla as he rode into the barnyard of a Loudoun County, Virginia, farm. The Unionists then took his body to Harpers Ferry, where post commander Brigadier General John Stevenson put it on public display outside his headquarters. Locals seeking souvenirs cut off most of his clothes (Crouch 29).

6. Myers, *Comanches*, 348.

7. Ibid., 349.

8. Ibid., 349–50; Calhoun, *'Twixt North and South*, 127–28.

9. Calhoun, *'Twixt North and South*, 128; Myers, *Comanches*, 350.

10. Myers, *Comanches*, 350–51; Calhoun, *'Twixt North and South*, 129.

11. Calhoun, *'Twixt North and South*, 129.

12. Ibid; Myer, *Comanches*, 351.

13. Myers, *Comanches*, 351–52: Calhoun, *'Twixt North and South*, 130.

14. Calhoun, *'Twixt North and South*; Myers, *Comanches*, 351–52.

15. Calhoun, *'Twixt North and South*, 126–30.

16. Oswald, "Brilliant Achievement by McNeill's Partisan Rangers," *Mountain City Times*, May 29, 1869; McNeill, "Capture of Generals Kelley and Crook," 410.

17. "From West Virginia—Movements of General Early," *Richmond Daily Dispatch*, Jan. 5, 1865.

18. *Rockingham Register*, Jan 13, 1865; "Capture of Swamp Dragons."

19. Rohrbaugh to Pierpoint, Jan 15, 1865, WVUMC, box 07, Hardy County, folders 1 and 5, WVA.

20. Ibid.

21. Ibid.

22. Ibid.

23. Ibid.

24. "Capture of Swamp Dragons," *Rockingham Register*, Jan. 20, 1865; George Martin to author, Nov. 11, 2014. The article referred to Kelly as a lieutenant, but according to company records, he was only a private.

25. OR, ser. 1, 46: pt. 1, 451.

26. Ibid.

27. Ibid.

19. Capture of a Cavalier

1. Gilmor, *Four Years in the Saddle*, 257, 276–77; OR, ser. 1, 51: pt. 2, 1051.

2. OR, ser. 1, 51: pt. 2, 1051; Gilmor, *Four Years in the Saddle*, 277.

3. OR, ser. 1, 51: pt. 2, 1051.

4. Curran, "Memory, Myths, and Musty Records," pt. 2, 169.

5. Sheridan, *Memoirs*, 288–90; Gilmor, *Four Years in the Saddle*, 277; Joseph E. McCabe, "Capture of Harry Gilmor," *Philadelphia Weekly Times*, July 28, 1883. Union cavalry historian Allan Tischler believes that Rowand's companion was James Campbell. Tischler to author, Dec. 3, 2014.

6. William Gilmore Beymer, *On Hazardous Service: Scouts and Spies of the North and South*, 5, 29; McCabe, "Capture of Harry Gilmor, *Philadelphia Weekly Times*, July 28, 1883.

7. OR, ser. 1, 46: pt. 1, 455–56.

8. Ibid., 456.

9. Ibid.

10. Beymer, *On Hazardous Service*, 29; Moyer, *History of the Seventeenth Regiment*, 226; Duffey, "Blue and the Gray in Reunion," 6.

11. Gilmor, *Four Years in the Saddle*, 277.

12. Ibid.; Moyer, *History of the Seventeenth Regiment*, 226; Joseph E. McCabe Papers, Alderman Library, University of Virginia, MSS 7112, box 7093; "From West Virginia," *Baltimore Sun*, Feb. 9, 1865.

13. "From West Virginia," *Baltimore Sun*, Feb. 9, 1865.

14. Moyer, *History of the Seventeenth Regiment*, 226; Gilmor, *Four Years in the Saddle*, 278; McCabe, "Capture of Harry Gilmor," McCabe Papers.

15. Gilmor, *Four Years in the Saddle*, 278–79; OR, ser. 1, 46: pt. 1, 456.

16. OR, ser. 1, 46: pt. 1, 456; Gilmor, *Four Years in the Saddle*, 279; Casler, *Four Years in the Stonewall Brigade*, 262.

17. Delauter, *McNeill's Rangers*, 117, 119, 121–24; OR, ser. 1, 46: pt. 1, 456.

18. Maxwell and Swisher, *History of Hampshire County*, 470–71.

19. Casler, *Four Years in the Stonewall Brigade*, 260–61, 265; Woodrow G. Simmons, "The Murder of Captain Stump," pts. 1 and 2, *Moorefield Examiner*, April 20, 27, 2005.

20. Moyer, *History of the Seventeenth Regiment*, 227. Mullihan's account is the only primary source that mentions Stump "hanging and cutting the throats of Union prisoners."

21. Moyer, *History of the Seventeenth Regiment*, 228.

22. Ibid. According to author William G. Beymer, "There were verbal orders to hang all those that were proved to be bushwhackers, and Young compiled a 'blacklist' of all such in the vicinity of Winchester—their names and haunts and habits." See Beymer, *On Hazardous Service*, 108.

23. *Boston Evening Transcript*, Feb. 11, 1865. Stump was armed with three LeMat revolvers, an unusual nine-shot sidearm that featured another barrel that fired one round of buckshot. Manufactured in Belgium or France, an English company exported them to the South.

24. M, "Capt. Geo. W. Stump," *Rockingham Register*, Mar. 24, 1865.

25. Ibid. It is the author's opinion that Ranger Manny Bruce wrote the letter to the *Register*. See Casler, *Four Years in the Stonewall Brigade*, 266.

26. Maxwell and Swisher, *History of Hampshire County*, 654.

27. Casler, *Four in the Stonewall Brigade*, 264–65. Captain Stump is buried in the family graveyard just north of Hickory Grove.

28. Casler, *Four Years in the Stonewall Brigade*, 264–65; OR, ser. 1, 46: 456.

29. OR, ser. 1, 46: 456–57; Casler, *Four Years in the Stonewall Brigade*, 267; Gilmor, *Four Years in the Saddle*, 281.

30. Casler, *Four Years in the Stonewall Brigade*, 268.

20. The Kidnapping of the Generals

1. Thomas and Williams, *History of Allegany County,* 389; McNeill, "Capture of Generals Kelley and Crook," 410.

2. McNeill, "Capture of Generals Kelly and Crook"; "Acted as Pilot on Famous Raid at Cumberland," *Winchester Evening Star,* Feb. 3, 1925; Duffey, *Two Generals Kidnapped,* 6.

3. Duffey, *Two Generals Kidnapped,* 6–7; McNeill, "Capture of Generals Kelly and Crook," 410; Thomas and Williams, *History of Allegany County,* 389; Oswald, "Brilliant Achievement by McNeill's Partisan Rangers," *Mountain City Times,* May 29, 1869.

4. Oswald, "Brilliant Achievement"; "McNeill's Raid into Cumberland," 80; Duffey, *Two Generals Kidnapped,* 7–8.

5. Duffey, *Two Generals Kidnapped,* 8; Oswald, "Brilliant Achievement."

6. Oswald, "Brilliant Acheivement."

7. McNeill, "Capture of Generals Kelly and Crook," 410.

8. Ibid., Duffey, *Two Generals Kidnapped,* 21. Although McNeill later wrote that he had sixty-five men, on page 21 of his account Duffey lists the names, including McNeill, of sixty-three officers and men. Casler, however, wrote that both Manny Bruce and Isaac Parsons went along too. See Stegmier, "Kidnapping of Generals Crook and Kelley," 25, 47. Another soldier claimed to have been on the raid. On October 27, 1864, Private Joseph M. Womack, 6th South Carolina Cavalry, escaped from the Elmira, New York, prison camp. In a letter describing his subsequent adventures, he claimed to have joined the Rangers and participated in the capture of the generals. By mid-December, however, Womack was back with his regiment. See Holmes, *Elmira Prison Camp,* 154–58.

9. McNeill, "Capture of Generals Kelly and Crook," 410.

10. "McNeill's Raid into Cumberland," 81; "Oswald, "Brilliant Achievement"; "The True Tale of the Capture of Generals Crook and Kelley," *Wheeling Intelligencer,* Sept. 19, 1877; Duffey, *Two Generals Kidnapped,* 8; Thomas and Williams, *History of Allegany County,* 390; McNeill, "Capture of Generals Kelly and Crook," 411.

11. McNeill, "Capture of Generals Kelly and Crook"; "A Daring Capture," *Clarke Courier,* July 23, 1891; Thomas and Williams, *History of Allegany County,* 390; Duffey, *Two Generals Kidnapped,* 8–9.

12. "Rebel Vandiver," *Shepherdstown Register,* Oct. 26, 1888; McNeill, "Capture of Generals Kelly and Crook," 411.

13. McNeill, "Capture of Generals Kelly and Crook," 411; "A Daring Capture," *Clarke Courier,* July 23, 1891; Thomas and Williams, *History of Allegany County,* 390–91; Scharf, *History of Western Maryland,* 296. The unidentified author of "McNeill's Raid into Cumberland," which appeared in the August 1872 edition of *Lily of the Valley* magazine, stated on page 81 that when "abandonment of the object seemed probable. . . . Fay . . . volunteered to make the attempt with ten men."

14. Haselbarger, "Union Troops in Cumberland," 1.

15. Thomas and Williams, *History of Allegany County,* 391.

16. Ibid.; Oswald, "Brilliant Achievement"; McNeill, "Capture of Generals Kelly and Crook," 411; Crook, *General George Crook*, 135.

17. Crook, *General George Crook*, 135; Duffey, *Two Generals Kidnapped*, 10; McNeill, "Capture of Generals Kelly and Crook," 411; Haselberger, "Union Troops in Cumberland," 1. According to Haselberger, Corporal Burkhard Krebs and Private Frederick Knoedel were two of the three pickets. Trueheart, "Memoirs," TFP, 1904, box 2, F-11, 15.

18. "Rebel Vandiver," *Shepherdstown Register*, Oct. 26, 1888; Thomas and Williams, *History of Allegany County*, 391–92; Oswald, "Brilliant Achievement"; Scharf, *History of Western Maryland*, 296; Duffey, *Two Generals Kidnapped*, 10.

19. Duffey, *Two Generals Kidnapped*, 10–11; Oswald, "Brilliant Achievement"; "The Capture of Gens. Crook and Kelly," *Hardy County News*, Sept. 12, 1901; OR, ser. 1, 46: pt. 2, 626; Scharf, *History of Western Maryland*, 296.

20. Scharf, *History of Western Maryland*, 297; Duffey, *Two Generals Kidnapped*, 11; "Arrival of the Yankee Generals Crook and Kelley—How They Were Captured," *Lynchburg Virginian*, Mar. 1, 1865.

21. "Final Curtain Down in Old Time Playhouse: Cumberland Theater where two Union Generals Attended Prior to Capture by Raiders, Closes," *Washington Star*, Mar. 22, 1929; Armstrong, *7th Virginia Cavalry*, 179.

22. "Lieut. McNeill's Exploit," *Richmond Whig*, Feb. 28, 1865. According to the article, the paper got a firsthand account of the raid from "one of the participants in the gallant affair."

23. "Capture of Gens. Crook and Kelly"; Thomas and Williams, *History of Allegany County*, 393; Trueheart, "Memoirs," TFP, 1904, box 2, F-11, 15; McNeill, "Capture of Generals Kelly and Crook," 411.

24. "Rebel Vandiver"; "A Daring Capture," *Clarke Courier*, July 23, 1891; W. G. McDowell, "How Crook and Kelley Were Kidnapped," *Richmond Times-Dispatch*, Mar. 19, 1911. McNeill had asked Gassman to accompany Fay on his scouting trip into Cumberland. Gassman, however, was still mending from a bullet wound suffered in the November 27 Old Fields fight. Fay took Hallar instead.

25. McDowell, "How Crook and Kelley Were Kidnapped"; "A Bold Rebel Dash," *Herald of Freedom and Torch Light*, Mar. 1, 1865 (reprint of a *Cumberland Civilian* story); Charles to Eddie, Mar. 20, 1865 (private collection of George Fletcher); Trueheart, "Memoirs," TFP, 1904, box 2, F-11, 15. Some accounts say that Cooper's first name was George.

26. McDowell, "How Crook and Kelley Were Kidnapped"; Duffey, *Two Generals Kidnapped*, 12–13; "Capture of Gens. Crook and Kelley: An Attempt to Fix the Historical Facts Connected Therewith," *Springfield Republican*, April 18, 1901. The article printed in the *Springfield Republican* was a letter to the editor written by Baltimore resident Henry P. Goddard. Many years after the war, Mrs. Fannie Dailey Markand, sister of Mary and Jim Dailey, wrote to Goddard that "General Crook became engaged the evening before his capture."

27. Thomas and Williams, *History of Allegany County*, 393.

28. Ibid.; "A Daring Capture," *Clarke Courier*, July 23, 1891; McDowell, "How Crook and Kelley Were Kidnapped," *Richmond Times-Dispatch*, Mar. 19, 1911; *Peninsula Enterprise*, Sept. 9, 1893; "Was Glad to Be Called Liar on One Occasion," *Winchester Evening Star*, June 14, 1922; Duffey, *Two Generals Kidnapped*, 12–13. According to McDowell, "After the war Mr. Gassman got quite a mild scolding from the lady in question for carrying off her missives to her lover."

29. "Arrival of the Yankee Generals Crook and Kelley," *Lynchburg Republican*, Mar. 1, 1865; "The Late Raid on Cumberland," *Baltimore Sun*, Feb. 24, 1865; Duffey, *Two Generals Kidnapped*, 13–14.

30. Thomas and Williams, *History of Allegany County*, 393; "A Bold Rebel Dash," *Herald of Freedom and Torch Light*, Mar. 1, 1865; McNeill, "Capture of Generals Kelly and Crook," 412; Jesse McNeill to Jubal Early, Feb. 22, 1865 (private collection of Woodrow Simmons; photocopy courtesy of Woodrow Simmons); Duffey, *Two Generals Kidnapped*, 14; OR, ser. 1, 46: pt. 2, 626; Cale, "General Kelley's Prize Horse 'Philippi,'" 52–53. The pony was the property of an officer's son. It soon wandered off.

31. McNeill, "Capture of Generals Kelly and Crook," 411; Thomas and Williams, *History of Allegany County*, 393; "A Bold Rebel Dash"; Oswald, "Brilliant Achievement"; "McNeill's Raid into Cumberland," 83; Trueheart, "Memoirs," TFP, 1904, box 2, F-11, 15. On page 45 of the book *184 Miles of Adventure*, J. William Joynes writes, "There was a double guard lock above the canal that served as an entrance and exit for boats between the river and canal basin."

32. Thomas and Williams, *History of Allegany County*, 391; McNeill, "Capture of Generals Kelley and Crook," 412; Duffey, *Two Generals Kidnapped*, 14–15.

33. *Pocahontas Times*, March 11, 1929; "True Tale of the Capture"; Duffey, *Two Generals Kidnapped*, 15–16; Trueheart, "Memoirs," TFP, 1904, box 2, F-11, 15–16.

34. "The Capture of Generals Kelley and Crook," *Fairmont National*, Feb. 25, 1865.

35. "Capture of Gens. Crook and Kelly," *Hardy County News*.

21. The Getaway

1. "West Virginia: The Late Rebel Raid on Cumberland, Md.," *New York Herald*, Feb. 26, 1865; "Summoned Suddenly: General Crook Dies at the Grand Pacific Hotel Chicago," *Cincinnati Commercial Tribune*, Mar. 22, 1890; Farrar, *Twenty-Second Pennsylvania Cavalry*, 452; Haselberger, "Union Troops in Cumberland," 1. Future U.S. president William McKinley's recollections of the kidnapping of General Crook appeared in the Mar. 22, 1890, edition of the *Cincinnati Commercial Tribune*.

2. Duffey, *Two Generals Kidnapped*, 13; "Late Rebel Raid on Cumberland"; "West Virginia: The Late Rebel Raid on Cumberland"; Scott, *Civil War Era in Cumberland*, 211; Farrar, *Twenty-Second Pennsylvania Cavalry*, 452; OR, ser. 1, 46: pt. 1, 447, 469.

3. Farrar, *Twenty-Second Pennsylvania Cavalry*, 452; Van Meter, *Old Fields*, 244; OR, ser. 1, 46: pt. 2, 667.

4. Farrar, *Twenty-Second Pennsylvania Cavalry*, 452–54; OR, ser. 1, 46: pt. 1, 469; "West Virginia: The Late Rebel Raid on Cumberland."

5. "West Virginia: The Late Rebel Raid on Cumberland"; "The Capture of Generals Kelley and Crook, and Captain Thayer Melvin," *Wheeling Daily Intelligencer*, Feb. 22, 1865; "Further Particulars about the Capture of Generals Crook, Kelley and Captain Melvin," *Wheeling Daily Intelligencer*, Feb. 23, 1865; "Local Belle of Sixties Is Dead In Chattanooga," *Winchester Evening Star*, Aug. 8, 1916.

6. "Further Particulars about the Capture."

7. Thomas and Williams, *History of Allegany County*, 394; "Capture of Philippi," *Wheeling Daily Intelligencer*, Feb. 24, 1865; McDonald, *A History of the Laurel Brigade*, 351; Farrar, *Twenty-Second Pennsylvania Cavalry*, 453, "McNeill's Raid into Cumberland."

8. Duffey, *Two General Kidnapped*, 16; "A Raid That Netted Two Generals," *Richmond Times-Dispatch*, Jan. 6, 1935; Casler, *Four Years in the Stonewall Brigade*, 339. On Feb. 5, 1905, Casler was in Dallas and happened upon Bruce's liquor store, went in, and discovered his former comrade was the owner. At their reunion, Bruce told him his version of what had happened at the Stump farm.

9. "A Raid That Netted Two Generals;" Casler, *Four Years in the Stonewall Brigade*, 339.

10. "A Raid That Netted Two Generals."

11. McNeill, "Capture of Generals Kelly and Crook," 412.

12. Duffey, *Two Generals Kidnapped*, 16; Farrar, *Twenty-Second Pennsylvania Cavalry*, 453; Casler, *Four Years in the Stonewall Brigade*, 339. "Robert Moorehead, A McNeill Ranger Dies in Oklahoma," *Winchester Evening Star*, May 26, 1925. As indicated in the text, Moorehead, a private in the 11th Virginia Cavalry, was not a McNeill Ranger. Duffey does not list either Moorehead or Urton as being on the raid, yet it is evident that both were in the Parsons' Hill area. At the time, Urton, who had been seriously wounded on December 3, 1862, was not in active service. Although Farrar states that the skirmish happened "as this party approached Romney," all Ranger accounts refer to it as happening along Trough Road. Moorehead's obituary pinpoints the Parsons' Hill site.

13. "A Raid That Netted Two Generals"; "One of the Crook Kelley Captors," *Wheeling Daily Intelligencer*, Feb. 23, 1865; Casler, *Four Years in the Stonewall Brigade*, 339; Armstrong, *11th Virginia Cavalry*, 176, 184.

14. McNeill, "Capture of Generals Crook and Kelly," 412.

15. Van Meter, *Old Fields*, 244; Farrar, *Twenty-Second Pennsylvania Cavalry*, 453–54; Duffey, *Two Generals Kidnapped*, 17; OR, ser. 1, 46: pt. 2, 667; "McNeill's Raid into Cumberland." At twelve-thirty in the afternoon, Troxel's force was three miles south of Purgitville. There he dispatched a rider back to New Creek with the news that "a small scout is in my front. I hope to catch them before they reach Moorefield. . . . Imboden's command is reported at Moorefield. I am marching as rapidly as possible." Although his scouts just missed catching the raiders, he arrived too late. See Farrar, *Twenty-Second Pennsylvania* Cavalry, 453. According to the diary of Cumberland resident and Southern sympathizer Pricilla McKaig, Capt. T. W. Kelley was in town that evening. She writes,

"About 6 o'clock, Wright Kelley came to our house and insulted us most grossly and outrageously, cursed and abused us and with pistol in hand ran around the house and tried to get in to shoot us. He is a miserably, desperate, degraded wretch." It would have been impossible, however, for Kelley to be there at that hour. Rebecca Van Meter's diary entry definitely puts the young captain in Old Fields that afternoon. It is the author's opinion that either McKaig confused the young captain with one of his brothers or he arrived in Cumberland at a much later hour. See Baldwin, Mudge, and Schlegel, *McKaig Journal*, 97.

16. OR, ser. 1, 46: pt. 1, 471.

17. McNeill, "Capture of Generals Kelly and Crook," 413.

18. "A Little Thing for a Big Man," *Spirit of Jefferson*, Mar. 30, 1869; Cale, "General Kelley's Prize Horse 'Philippi,'" 54. John Arnold eventually gave Philippi to General Rosser. On April 9, 1865, the horse was shot during the fighting at Appomattox Court House. Sometime after the war, Kelley found out that Rosser had given the wounded animal to Colonel Michael Harmon the following winter. Kelley traveled to Harmon's home in Staunton and found that Philippi was still suffering from his wound and unfit for travel. He decided to leave the animal there until it fully recovered. Later, when the horse was better, Kelley moved Philippi to his Swan Meadow farm, near Oakland, Maryland. Kelley also filed a lawsuit against Arnold for damages to his horse. In 1871 Kelley received a judgment of $350 (Cale, 53–54).

19. McNeill, "Capture of Generals Kelly and Crook," 413.

20. Ibid.

21. Jesse McNeill to Jubal Early, Feb. 22, 1865 (private collection of Woodrow Simmons; photocopy courtesy of Woodrow Simmons).

22. Duffey, *Two Generals Kidnapped*, 17–18; McNeill Ranger, "The True Tale of the Capture of Crook and Kelley," *Wheeling Daily Intelligencer*, Sept. 19, 1877; Confederate Amnesty Papers: Case Files of Applications from Former Confederates for Presidential Pardons, West Virginia—Peerce, John T.,—Pierce, John T., NA; Thomas and Williams, *History of Allegany County*, 394–97.

23. Scott, *Civil War in Cumberland*, 213; "Final Curtain Down in Old Time Playhouse," *Washington Star*, Mar. 22, 1929; "The Capture of Generals Kelley and Crook," *Fairmont National*, Feb. 25, 1865; *Mirror and Farmer*, April 8, 1865.

24. Duffey, *Two Generals Kidnapped*, 18; McDowell, "How Crook and Kelley Were Kidnapped," *Richmond Times-Dispatch*, Mar. 19, 1911; *Sandusky Register*, Mar. 22, 1865. According to McDowell, "After the war, this Irishman was appointed postmaster of Harrisonburg."

25. Duffey, *Two Generals Kidnapped*, 18; OR, ser. 1, 46: pt. 1, 471–72.

26. "Arrival of the Yankee Generals Crook and Kelley," *Lynchburg Virginian*, Mar. 1, 1865 (reprint of a *Richmond Enquirer* story). According to author William G. Beymer in *Hazardous Service*, Early's prediction that the federals would now capture him almost came true. Major Henry Young did go on a one-man mission to capture Early. As Beymer wrote, "He could have taken Early; for two nights he stood sentry at his very

door while the faithless Confederate guard—with whom he had changed places—went into town sweethearting! But with nearly sixty miles to travel in an enemy's country, winter-bound and hampered by a prisoner, he realized that sometime in the ensuing pursuit he must either free Early or kill him, and he did not wish to do either—once he had him." Young afterward said to General Edwards, "Had Early been guilty of murdering prisoners or of sanctioning it, I could and would have taken his life, but I did not consider it to be civilized warfare to kill him under the circumstances (123–24)."

27. Felix, "General's Last Story," 5; Gordon, *Reminiscences of the Civil War*, 362; Duffey, *Two Generals Kidnapped*, 18.

28. Duffey, *Two Generals Kidnapped*, 18–19; Keen and Mewborn, *43rd Battalion*, 237–38, 250.

29. Duffey, *Two Generals Kidnapped*, 19–20; McNeill, "Capture of Generals Kelly and Crook," 413.

30. *Sandusky Register*, Mar. 22, 1865; "Capt. Thayer Melvin," *Wheeling Daily Intelligencer*, Mar. 28, 1865.

31. "Release of Crook and Kelley," *Philadelphia Inquirer*, Mar. 16, 1865; "By Telegraph," *Daily Eastern Argus*, Mar. 14, 1865; Hayes, *Diaries and Letters*, 566, 569; "Capture of Gens. Crook and Kelley," *Springfield Republican*, April 18, 1901.

32. "Capture of Gens. Crook and Kelley"; "Baltimore," *Philadelphia Inquirer*, Mar. 17, 1865; "Capt. Thayer Melvin"; OR, ser. 1, 46: pt. 2, 725.

33. Stegmier, "Kidnapping of Generals Crook and Kelley," 43–44; OR, ser. 1, 46: pt. 3, 68, 72, 81.

34. "General Crook," *West Virginia Journal*, Mar. 29, 1865.

35. "Capture of Gens. Crook and Kelley." General Kelley agreed with Melvin's claim that Crook's capture was the Rangers' main objective. In an interview given shortly before his death, he said "that the plan was laid out by Jim Dailey . . . Jim thought it would be a very smart thing to make the capture." See Edson Brace, "Saved by a Boy," *Cleveland Leader*, August 15, 1891.

36. *Rockingham Register*, Mar. 24, 1865.

22. The Baker Place Fight and a Train Robbery

1. Bushong and Bushong, *Fightin' Tom Rosser*, 166; McDonald, *A History of the Laurel Brigade*, 359–60. Since November, Rosser had commanded all cavalry in the Valley District. On February 28, 1865, the Confederate Senate approved Rosser's promotion to major general effective November 4, 1864. That winter, the twenty-eight-year-old Texan's already hard task of defending the area was complicated by his troopers' high absentee rate and the poor physical condition of many horses. See Bushong and Bushong, *Fightin' Tom Rosser*, 145, 165–66.

2. "Early's Defeat in the Valley," *Macon Telegraph*, Mar. 30, 1865; OR, ser. 1, 46: pt. 1, 528.

3. OR, ser. 1, 46: pt. 1, 528.

4. Ibid.; "The War News," *Richmond Examiner*, Mar. 10, 1865.

5. OR, ser. 1, 46: pt. 1, 528; "Two Victories," *Daily Constitutionalists*, Mar. 15, 1865; McDonald, *A History of the Laurel Brigade*, 362.

6. McDonald, *A History of the Laurel Brigade*, 362; "General Sheridan's Victory," *Hartford Daily Courant*, Mar. 11, 1865.

7. OR, ser. 1, 46: pt. 1, 528–29; McDonald, *A History of the Laurel Brigade*, 362–63.

8. McDonald, *A History of the Laurel Brigade*, 362–63; "Mr. D. Murdock's Letter," *Philadelphia Inquirer*, Mar. 17, 1865; OR, ser. 1, 46: pt. 1, 459; "5th New York Cavalry Regiment," *Syracuse Journal*, n.d.

9. OR, ser. 1, 46: pt. 1, 459; McDonald, *A History of the Laurel Brigade*, 363; "Two Victories."

10. Curran, "Memory, Myth, and Musty Records," pt. 2, 170; OR, ser. 1, 46: pt. 2, 985; "An Incident of Guerrilla Warfare," *Wheeling Intelligencer*, April 8, 1865.

11. "Swamps Swamped," *Rockingham Register*, April 7, 1865.

12. Ibid.

13. *Wheeling Daily Intelligencer*, Mar. 22, 1865.

14. OR, ser. 1, 46: pt. 1, 555; Sturm, *From a "whirlpool of death,"* 114, 119, 149.

15. Sturm never identified the girl by her first name; Miss Baker was either twenty-four-year-old Samantha or her sixteen-year-old sister Marcella. See Sturm, *From a "whirlpool of death,"* 119–20; OR, ser. 1, 46: pt. 1, 555.

16. OR, ser. 1, 46: pt. 1, 555; Sturm, *From a "whirlpool of death,"* 120.

17. Sturm, *From a "whirlpool of death,"* 120.

18. Ibid., 123, 132–33; OR, ser. 1, 46: pt. 1, 555.

19. OR, ser. 1, 46: pt. 1, 555; Sturm, *From a "whirlpool of death,"* 124.

20. Sturm, *From a "whirlpool of death,"* 125–26.

21. Ibid., 129; OR, ser. 1, 46: pt. 1. A careful reading of the company roster in Delauter's *McNeill's Rangers* shows that no Rangers were killed in action during this period. If the locals' reports were true, the soldiers were from another company or were guerrillas.

22. Sturm, *From a "whirlpool of death,"* 130–33. Some years after the war, Sturm encountered a Ranger named Johnson, who had been in the fight. He asked the man about the Baker girl, and he told Sturm, "He knew the girl well and told me she got well, and told me who she married" (130).

23. "Swamps Swamped."

24. "Swamp Raid," *Rockingham Register*, Apr. 7, 1865.

25. OR, ser. 1, 46: pt. 1, 538.

26. Ibid., 538–39; "A Daring Rebel Outrage," *Philadelphia Inquirer*, April 1, 1865; "Raid of Rebel Guerrillas on the Baltimore and Ohio Railroad," *Baltimore Sun*, April 1, 1865; "Diabolical Guerrilla Outrage," *Milwaukee Sentinel*, April 7, 1865; "The Recent Raid On The Baltimore and Ohio Railroad," *Baltimore Sun*, April 6, 1865.

27. "Recent Raid"; OR, ser. 1, 46: pt. 1, 538.

28. "General News," *Hartford Daily Courant*, April 3, 1865; "Recent Raid."

29. "Recent Raid"; "Raid of Rebel Guerrillas."

30. OR, ser. 1, 46: pt. 1, 538–39; Farrar, *Twenty-Second Pennsylvania Cavalry*, 458.

31. OR, ser. 1, 46: pt. 1, 538–39; *Thirty-Ninth Annual Report*, 44.

32. OR, ser. 1, 46: pt. 1, 539; Farrar, *Twenty-Second Pennsylvania Cavalry*, 459; Snyder, "Potomac River Fords," 24.

33. "General Orders No. 18."

23. End of the Line

1. Farrar, *Twenty-Second Pennsylvania Cavalry*, 459–60, 462; Curran, "Memory, Myth, and Musty Records," pt. 2, 170; Williams, *Rebel Brothers*, 217; Delauter, *McNeill's Rangers*, 117; Delauter, *18th Virginia Cavalry*, 63–64, 73–74, 84, 88–90. In an April 24, 1865, letter written to his mother, Henry Trueheart noted the meeting with a group of federal officers but did not give the exact date. He wrote, "The Yankees met us a few days since under a flag of truce offering the terms accorded to Lee and also permit us to retain all private horses, arms, and accoutrements." According to author Roger Delauter's research for *18th Virginia Cavalry*, this meeting occurred on April 22 (63–64).

2. Farrar, *Twenty-Second Pennsylvania Cavalry*, 462; OR, ser. 1, 46: pt. 3, 525, 934.

3. OR, ser. 1, 46: pt. 3, 914–15; Farrar, *Twenty-Second Pennsylvania Cavalry*, 462.

4. Farrar, *Twenty-Second Pennsylvania Cavalry*, 462.

5. Williams, *Rebel Brothers*, 218; paroles of Jesse McNeill on May 5 in New Creek and Isaac Judy on May 10 in Romney (photocopies courtesy of Woodrow Simmons); "General McNeil Surrendered," *Alexandria Gazette*, May 10, 1865; "West Virginia," *Wheeling Daily Intelligencer*, May 10, 1865; Delauter, *McNeill's Rangers*, 107–8; Maxwell and Swisher, *History of Hampshire County*, 687–88.

6. Maxwell and Swisher, *History of Hampshire County*, 688–89; Isaac Judy parole (photocopy courtesy of Woodrow Simmons). On May 24 the Federals captured Ranger Private Alex Carlisle. He was paroled before the end of the month. See Delauter, *McNeill's Rangers*, 118.

7. Delauter, *McNeill's Rangers*, 108–9, 119.

8. OR, ser. 1, 46: pt. 3, 1116–17; John Michael to F. P. Pierpoint, May 8, 1865, WVAGP, Union Militia, box 07, Hardy County, folder 7, WVA.

9. Farrar, *Twenty-Second Pennsylvania Cavalry*, 463–64.

10. Haas, *Dear Esther*, 274.

11. Farrar, *Twenty-Second Pennsylvania Cavalry*, 464–66, 471; Elwood, *Elwood's Stories*, 272–73. Elwood and Farrar disagree on the date of Corbitt's death. Relying on regimental records, Farrar lists the sergeant dying on July 20. Corbitt, who had been married to Romney native Gertrude Poling, was buried by his comrades in Romney's Indian Mound Cemetery a few days after his death.

12. Elwood, *Elwood's Stories*, 289; Delauter, *McNeill's Rangers*, 110; Duffey, "Blue and the Gray in Reunion," 6.

13. Duffey, "Blue and the Gray in Reunion," 6; Delauter, *McNeill's Rangers*, 110.

14. "Reunion of the Ringgolds"; *Riverside Daily Press*, Aug. 27, 1902; Elwood, *Elwood's Stories*, 269, 273.

15. Elwood, *Elwood's Stories*, 269–70.

16. Delauter, *McNeill's Rangers*, 111; "Vets Deck Comrades Graves," *Baltimore Sun*, Sept. 1, 1910.

EPILOGUE

1. Pugh, *Capon Valley*, 59, 64–65; Duffey, "Capt. Jesse C. McNeill," CV20528–29; E. E. Meredith, "Bits of History," *Hampshire Review*, December 18, 1918.

2. Delauter, *McNeill's Rangers*, 119.

3. Duffey, "Acted as Pilot on Famous Raid at Cumberland," *Winchester Evening Star*, Feb. 3, 1925.

4. "Virginia Brevities," *Baltimore Sun*, April 9, 1897; Rick Wolfe to author, Aug. 8, 2015.

5. "Death Summons Ranger Who Helped in Daring Deed," *Winchester Evening Star*, Oct. 31, 1927.

6. Williams, *Rebel Brothers*, 218. "Leading Citizen of Galveston Succumbs," *Dallas Morning News*, Aug. 20, 1914.

7. "Rebel Vandiver," *Shepherdstown Register*, Oct. 26, 1888; Delauter, *McNeill's Rangers*, 125.

8. Delauter, McNeill's Rangers, 125; Mohr to author, June 1, 2015.

9. "General Crook Is Called," *Omaha World-Herald*, Mar. 22, 1890; "Summoned Suddenly: General George Crook Dies at the Pacific Hotel in Chicago," *Cincinnati Commercial Traveler*, Mar. 22, 1890; "With Military Honors," *Critic and Record*, Nov. 12, 1890; "Death Of An Estimable Lady," *Baltimore Sun*, Sept. 25, 1895. In its September 9, 1893, issue, the *Peninsula Enterprise* reported that "Capt. Jesse McNeill . . . still has in his possession the sword taken from General Crook. It is his intention to present the sword to the General's widow."

10. Rick Wolfe to author, Aug. 8, 2015.

11. "Death of Maj. James P. Hart," *Washington Evening Star*, Jan. 13, 1908; Elwood, *Elwood's Stories*, 279–80.

12. Edson Brace, "Saved by a Boy," *Cleveland Leader*, Aug. 15, 1891; "Gen. Kelley Dead," *Wheeling Register*, July 17, 1891; Lang, *Loyal West Virginia*, 323.

13. "Col. Gilmor's Death," *Baltimore Sun*, Mar. 5, 1883; Timothy Ackinclose, *Sabres and Pistols*, 174–80, 189.

14. National Park Service, *National Registration of Historic Places*, "Peerce Home Place," Oct. 1990, sect. 6, 2; ibid., sect. 7, 7; ibid., sect. 8, 4–6; John T. Peerce Amnesty Application, NA; Joe Geiger to author, Sept. 15, 2015.

15. Van Meter, *Old Fields*, 253.

16. Curran, "Memory, Myths, and Musty Records," pt. 2, 172.

Appendix

1. Duffey, "Daring Capture," 352. In their examination of five different Rangers rosters, Francis Haselberger and Woodrow Simmons concluded that 257 different men had one time or another served in the company. See Haselberger and Simmons, "Roster of McNeill's Partisan Rangers."

Bibliography

ARCHIVES

Alderman Library, University of Virginia
    Joseph McCabe Papers–Bonnage Collection
Museum of the Confederacy, Richmond, Va., Eleanor Brockenbrough Library
    Thaddeus Fitzhugh, M.D. "Civil War Memoirs of Thaddeus Fitzhugh"
National Archives, Washington, D.C.
    Civil War Damage Claims Filed Before the Southern Claims Commission, 1871–1880
    Compiled Service Records of Confederate Soldiers Who Served in Organizations
        from the State of Missouri
    Confederate Amnesty Paper-Case Files for Applications from former Confederates
        for Presidential Pardons.
Rosenberg Library, Galveston, Tex.
    Trueheart Family Papers
West Virginia Archives, Charleston
    Civil War Union Militia Collection
    Imboden, Francis. "War Diary of Captain Francis Imboden" (typescript)
    West Virginia Adjutant General Papers, Union Militia, 1861–1865

NEWSPAPERS

Alexandria (Va.) *Gazette*
Army and Navy Journal
Augusta Daily Constitutionalist
Baltimore American
Baltimore Sun
Boston Traveler
Charleston Mercury

Cincinnati Commercial Tribune
Civilian and Telegraph (Cumberland, Md.)
Clarke Courier (Berryville, Va.)
Cleveland Leader
Columbia (Mo.) *Daily Tribune*
Columbia Missouri Statesman
Critic and Record (Washington, D.C.)
Cumberland (Md.) *Sunday Times*
Daily Eastern Argus (Portland, Me.)
Daily Illinois Journal (Kankakee, Il.)
Daily Item (Winchester, Va.)
Daily Ohio Statesman (Columbus)
Daily Times Delta (Visalia, La.)
Dallas Morning News
Fairmont (W.Va.) *National*
Fort Worth Star-Telegram
Hampshire Review (Romney, W.Va.)
Hardy County (W.Va.) *News*
Hartford Daily Courant
Herald of Freedom and Torchlight (Hagerstown, Md.)
Illustrated New Age (Philadelphia)
Lynchburg Virginian
Macon (Ga.) *Telegraph*
Mercersburg (Pa.) *Journal*
Milwaukee Sentinel
Mirror and Farmer (Manchester, N.H.)
Moorefield (W.Va.) *Examiner*
Morgan Messenger (Berkeley Springs, W.Va.)
Mountain City (Md.) *Times*
National Tribune (Washington, D.C.)
New-York Daily Reformer
New York Herald
New York Herald-Tribune
Omaha World-Herald
Peninsula Enterprise (Accomac, Va.)
Philadelphia Inquirer
Philadelphia Times
Philadelphia Weekly Times
Piedmont (W.Va.) *Evening Times*
Piedmont (W.Va.) *Times*
Pocahontas (W.Va.) *Times*

Point Pleasant (W.Va.) *Daily Register*
Public Ledger (Philadelphia)

Richmond Daily Dispatch
Richmond Dispatch
Richmond Examiner
Richmond Times-Dispatch
Richmond Whig
Riverside (Calif.) *Daily Press*
Rockford (Ill.) *Republican*
Rockingham (Va.) *Register*
Sandusky (Ohio) *Register*
Shepherdstown (W.Va.) *Register* (West Virginia)
Spirit of Jefferson (Charles Town, W.Va.)
Springfield (Ohio) *Republican*
Staunton (Va.) *Spectator*
Staunton (Va.) *Vindicator*
Syracuse (N.Y.) *Journal*
Urbana (Ill.) *Union*
Washington (D.C.) *Evening Star*
Washington (D.C.) *Times*
Washington (Pa.) *Reporter*
West Virginia Journal (Charleston)
Winchester (Va.) *Evening Star*
Wheeling (W.Va.) *Daily Intelligencer*
Wheeling (W.Va.) *Register*
Xenia (Ohio) *Sentinel*

Primary Sources

Baker, I. Norval. "Diary and Recollections of I. Norval Baker." *Winchester–Frederick County Historical Papers* 3 (1955): 96–128.

Baldwin, Helene, Michael Allen Mudge, and Keith Schlegel, eds. *The McKaig Journal: A Confederate Family of Cumberland.* Cumberland, Md.: Allegany County Historical Society, 1984.

Barr, Paul E., Jr., and Michael P. Musick, eds. "They are Coming, Testimony at the Court of Inquiry on the Capture of Charles Town." *Magazine of the Jefferson County Historical Society* 54 (1989): 15–53.

Bates, Samuel P. *History of the Pennsylvania Volunteers 1861–1865.* Vols. 3 and 4. Harrisburg, Pa.: B. Singerly, State Printer, 1869.

Beach, William H. *The First New York (Lincoln) Cavalry: From April 1861 to July 1865.* Baltimore: Butternut and Blue, 1983.

Beymer, William Gilmore. *On Hazardous Service: Scouts and Spies of the North and South.* New York: Harper and Brothers, 1912.

Booth, George W. *Personal Reminiscences of a Maryland Soldier in the War Between the States.* Baltimore: Press of Fleet, McGinney, 1898.

Casler, John. *Four Years In The Stonewall Brigade.* 2nd ed. Girard, Kans.: Appeal, 1906.

Crook, George. *General George Crook: His Autobiography.* Norman: University of Oklahoma Press, 1946.

Duffey, J. W. "The Blue and the Gray in Reunion." *Confederate Veteran* 35 (1927): 6–7.

———. "Capt. Jesse C. McNeill." *Confederate Veteran.* 20 (1912): 528–29.

———. "Daring Capture by McNeill's Rangers." *Confederate Veteran* 26 (1918): 350–53.

———. *M'Neill's Last Charge.* Harrisonburg, Va.: Old South Institute Press, 2005.

———. *Two Generals Kidnapped.* Harrisonburg, Va.: Old South Institute Press, 2005.

Early, Jubal A. "Early's March to Washington in 1865." In Johnson and Buel, *Battles and Leaders,* vol. 4, 492–99.

Edminston, J. D., ed. "Civil War Days in Mercersburg as Related in the Diary of the Rev. Thomas Creigh, D.D. August 1, 1862–July 20, 1865." In *Papers Read Before the Kittochtinney Historical Society,* vol. 12, 29–40. Chambersburg, Pa.: Repository Printing House, 1950.

Egan, Michael. *The Flying Gray-Haired Yank or The Adventures of a Volunteer.* Philadelphia: Hubbard Brothers, 1888.

Elwood, John. *Elwood's Stories of the Old Ringgold Cavalry 1847–1865.* Coal Center, Pa.: John Elwood, 1912.

Farrar, Samuel Clarke. *The Twenty-Second Pennsylvania Cavalry and the Ringgold Battalion 1861–1865.* Pittsburgh: Twenty-Second Pennsylvania Ringgold Cavalry Association, 1911.

Fay, John. "With M'Neill in Virginia." *Confederate Veteran* 15 (1907): 408–10.

Fravel, Linden, ed. "Between the Lines: Steele Family Diaries" N.d. Unpublished manuscript. Private collection of Linden Fravel.

French, Steve, ed. *Four Years Along the Tilhance: The Civil War Diary of Elisha Manor.* Berkeley Springs, W.Va.: Steve French, 2004.

"General Orders No. 18: Head-Quarters Second Infantry Division, Department West Virginia, Cumberland, Md., April 3, 1865." Photocopy of original document in private collection of George Fletcher.

Gilmor, Harry. *Four Years in the Saddle.* New York: Harper and Brothers, 1866.

Gordon, John B. *Reminiscences of the Civil War.* New York: Charles Scribner, 1901.

Grant, Ulysses, S. *Personal Memoirs of U. S. Grant.* New York: Da Capo Press, 1982.

Haas, Ralph, ed. *The Civil War Letters of Private Aungier Dobbs Centerville, Pennsylvania. . . .* Apollo, Pa.: Clossen Press, 1991.

Harbaugh, James F. Linn. *Mercersburg in War Times: The Complete Series of Articles Published in the Mercersburg Journal, June 20, 1902 to April 24, 1903.* Mercersburg, Pa.: Harry Steiger, 2002.

Haselberger, Francis, and Woodrow Simmons, comps. "Roster of McNeill's Rangers." N.d. Unpublished manuscript. Private collection of Woodrow Simmons.

Hayes, Rutherford B. *Diaries and Letters of Rutherford B. Hayes.* Vol. 2. Columbus: Ohio Archeological and Historical Society, 1922.

Hogbin, James Clark. "Diary of James Clark Hogbin." Typescript of unpublished typescript. N.d. Private collection of Michael Hogbin.

Holmes, Clayton Woods. *The Elmira Prison Camp: A History of the Military Prison at Elmira, N.Y. July 6, 1864, to July 10, 1865.* New York: G. P. Putnam, 1912.

Hotchkiss, Jedediah. *Make Me a Map of the Valley: The Civil War Journals of Stonewall Jackson's Topographer.* Dallas: Southern Methodist University Press, 1973.

Imboden, John D. "The Battle of New Market, Va. May 15, 1864." In Johnson and Buel, *Battles and Leaders,* vol. 4, 480–86.

———. "The Confederate Retreat From Gettysburg." In Johnson and Buel, *Battles and Leaders,* vol. 3, 420–29.

Johnson, Robert U., and C. C. Buel, eds. *Battles and Leaders of the Civil War.* 4 vols. New York: 1887–1888.

Kaler, James Francis, comp. *The Story of American Heroism: Thrilling Narratives of Personal Adventures During the Great Civil War as told by the Medal Winners and Roll of Honor Men.* New Haven, Conn.: Butler and Alger, 1896.

Keyes, C. M., ed. *The Military History of the 123d Regiment of Ohio Volunteer Infantry.* Sandusky: Regiment Steam Press, 1904.

Lang, Theodore F. *Loyal West Virginia, 1861–1865.* Baltimore: Deutsch Publishing Co. 1895.

Maxwell, Hu. *History of Tucker County, West Virginia.* Kingwood, W.Va.: Preston, 1884.

Maxwell, Hu, and H. L. Swisher. *History of Hampshire County, West Virginia.* Morgantown: A. Brown Broughner, 1897.

McCausland, John. "The Burning of Chambersburg." *Southern Historical Society Papers* 31, 266–70.

McDonald, Major Edward H. "A Rough Sketch of the Incidents in the Experience of Major E. H. McDonald as a Confederate Soldier." N.d. Unpublished manuscript. Private collection of Louise McDonald.

McDonald, William N. *A History of the Laurel Brigade: Originally Ashby's Cavalry of the Army of Northern Virginia and Chew's Battery.* Baltimore: Kate S. McDonald, 1907.

McNeill, Jesse C. "Capture of Generals Kelly and Crook." *Confederate Veteran* 14 (1906): 410–12.

"McNeill's Raid into Cumberland." *Lily of the Valley,* August 1872, 78–84.

Miller, Charles M. "Capture of a Wagon Train by M'Neill's Men." *Confederate Veteran* 21 (1913): 20.

Morton, Oren F. *A History of Pendleton County, West Virginia.* Franklin, W.Va.: Owen Morton, 1910.

Moyer, Henry, comp. *History of the Seventeenth Regiment Pennsylvania Volunteer Cavalry.* Lebanon, Pa.: Sowers, 1911.

Mulligan, James A. "The Siege of Lexington." In Johnson and Buel, *Battles and Leaders*, vol. 1, 306–13.

Myers, Frank M. *The Comanches: A History of White's Battalion, Virginia Cavalry.* Baltimore: Kelly, Piet, 1871.

Neese, George M. *Three Years in the Confederate Horse Artillery.* New York: Neale, 1911.

Nesbitt, Otho. "Otho Nesbitt Diary." In *Windmills of Time*, 181–209. Clear Spring, Md.: Clear Spring Alumni Association, 1981.

Newcomer, C. Armour. *Cole's Cavalry or Three Years in the Saddle in the Shenandoah Valley.* Freeport, N.Y.: Books for Library Press, 1970.

Nichols, Clifton M. *A Summer Campaign in the Shenandoah Valley in 1864: "One Hundred Days" (Four Months and Two Days) of Soldier Life with the 152d Regiment Ohio Volunteer Infantry.* Springfield, Ohio: New Era Company 1899.

Nichols, William E. "Fighting Guerrillas in West Virginia." *Civil War Times Illustrated*, April 1967, 20–27.

Norton, Chauncey S. *"The red neck ties;" or History of the Fifteenth New York Volunteer Cavalry.* Ithaca, N.Y.: Journal Book and Job Print House, 1891.

Oates, Dan, ed. *Hanging Rock Rebel: Lieutenant John Blue's War in West Virginia and the Shenandoah Valley.* Shippensburg, Pa.: Burd Street Press, 1994.

Patterson, D. H. "Memoirs of D. H. Patterson." Photocopy of unpublished manuscript. N.d. Private collection of the author.

Peerce, John T. "Capture of a Railroad Train." *Southern Bivouac* 2: 352–55.

Phisterer, Frederick. *New York in the War of the Rebellion.* Vol. 2. Albany: Weed, Parsons, 1890.

Powell, Ransom. *Civil War Memoirs of Little Red Cap: A Drummer Boy at Andersonville Prison.* Cumberland, Md.: Harold Scott, 1997.

Price, William T. *Memorials of Edward Herndon Scott, M.D.* Wytheville, Va.: Jim Presgraves, 1974.

Rawling, C. J. *History of the First Regiment Virginia Infantry.* Philadelphia: J. B. Lippincott, 1887.

Schaff, Phillip, DD. "The Gettysburg Week." In *Old Mercersburg*, 167–75. Mercersburg, Pa.: Women's Club, 1949.

Scharf, J. Thomas. *History of Western Maryland: Being a History of Frederick, Montgomery, Carroll, Washington, Allegany, and Garrett Counties from the Earliest Period to the Present Day.* Vol. 1. Philadelphia: Louis H. Everts, 1882.

Schneck, Benjamin. *The Burning of Chambersburg, Pennsylvania.* Lexington, Ky.: Civil War Classic Library, 2014.

Sheridan, Philip. *Civil War Memoirs.* New York: Bantam Books, 1991.

Smith, James Ripley. "Diary of James Ripley Smith." In *Hancock 1776–1976*, edited by Emily Leatherman, 17–33. Hancock, Md.: Hancock Bicentennial Commission, 1976.

Stevenson, James B. *Boots and Saddles: A History of the First Volunteer Cavalry of the War: Known as the First New York (Lincoln) Cavalry and Also As the Sabre Regiment. Its Organization, Campaigns, and Battles.* Harrisburg, Pa.: Patriot, 1879.

Sturm, Jesse Tyler. *From a "whirlpool of death . . . to victory": Civil War Remembrances of Jesse Tyler Sturm 14th West Virginia Infantry.* Charleston: West Virginia History, 2002.

Summers, Festus, ed. *A Borderland Confederate: The Diary of William L. Wilson.* Pittsburgh: University of Pittsburgh Press, 1962.

Thirty-Seventh Annual Report of the President and Directors to the Stockholders of the Baltimore and Ohio R.R. Co. for the Year Ending September 30, 1863. Baltimore: J. B. Moore, 1865.

Thirty-Eighth Annual Report of the President and Directors to the Stockholders of the Baltimore and Ohio R.R. Co. for the Year Ending September 30, 1864. Baltimore: Printing Office, 1864.

Thirty-Ninth Annual Report of the President and Directors to the Stockholders of the Baltimore and Ohio R.R. Co. for the Year Ending September 30, 1865. Baltimore: John F. Wiley, 1865.

United States War Department. *Atlas to Accompany the Official Records of the Union and Confederate Armies.* Washington, D.C.: Government Printing Office, 1891–1895.

———. *Supplement to the Official Records of the Union and Confederate Armies.* Wilmington, N.C.: Broadfoot, 1994.

———. *The War of the Rebellion: A Compilation of the Official Records of the Union and Confederate Armies.* 128 vols. Washington, D.C.: Government Printing Office, 1880–1881.

Vandiver, W. D. "Two Forgotten Heroes—John Hanson McNeell and His Son Jesse." *Missouri Historical Review* 21, no. 3: 404–19.

Van Meter, Rebecca. *Old Field in Peace and War: Rebecca Van Meter's Diary 1855–1865.* Parsons, W.Va.: McClain, 2012.

Wallace, David H., ed. *Frederick, Maryland in Peace and War: The Diary of Catharine Susannah Thomas Markell.* Frederick, Md.: Frederick County Historical Society, 2006.

Williams, Edward B., ed. *Rebel Brothers: The Civil War Letters of the Truehearts.* College Station: Texas A&M Press, 1995.

Williamson, John J. *Mosby's Rangers: A Record of the Operations of the Forty-Third Battalion of Virginia Cavalry from its Organization to Surrender.* New York: Sturgis and Walton, 1909.

Younger, Cole. *The Story of Cole Younger by Himself.* Provo, Utah: Triton Press. 1988.

SECONDARY SOURCES

Abbot, Haviland. "General John D. Imboden." *West Virginia History* 29 (January 1960): 88–122.

Ackinclose, Timothy. *Sabres and Pistols: The Civil War Career of Colonel Harry Gilmor C.S.A.* Gettysburg, Pa.: Stan Clark Military Books, 1997.

African American Historic Sites of Mercersburg. Mercersburg, Pa.: Mercersburg Historical Architectural Review Board, n.d.

Alexander, Ted. *Southern Revenge*. Shippensburg, Pa.: White Mane, 1989.

Allen, Irwin G. *Historic Old Town*. Parsons, W.Va.: McClain, 1983.

Ambler, C. H. "Romney in the Civil War." *West Virginia History* 5 (April 1944): 151–200.

Armstrong, Richard. *7th Virginia Cavalry*. Lynchburg, Va.: H. E. Howard, 1992.

———. *11th Virginia Cavalry*. Lynchburg, Va.: H. E. Howard, 1989.

Ashby, Iret, and Ruth Ashby. "Jones' Raid." *Glades Star* 5 (June 1961): 84–85.

Bowman, John, ed. *The Civil War Almanac*. New York: Gallery Books, 1983.

Bright, Simon Miller. "McNeill's Rangers: A Study in Confederate Guerrilla Warfare." *West Virginia History* 12 (1951): 338–87.

Brown, Genevieve Gist. "A History of the Sixth Regiment West Virginia." *West Virginia History* 9 (July 1948): 315–68.

Bushong, Millard K. *Old Jube: A Biography of General Jubal A. Early*. Boyce, Va.: Carr, 1955.

Bushong, Millard K., and Dean M. Bushong. *Fightin' Tom Rosser C.S.A.* Shippensburg, Pa.: Beidel, 1983.

Cale, Clyde, Jr. "General Kelley's Prize Horse 'Philippi.'" *Glades Star–Civil War Sesquicentennial Issue*, 2012, 52–53.

———. *Gray Days in Morgantown: The Story of the Great Confederate Raid of April 27 and 28, 1863, Morgantown, Virginia (West Virginia)*. Morgantown: Monongalia Historical Society, 2013.

Calhoun, Harrison M. *'Twixt North and South*, edited by Judge Harlan M. Calhoun. Franklin, W.Va.: McCoy, 1974.

Cordell, Glenn R. *Civil War Damage Claims From Fulton County, Pennsylvania*. McConnellsburg, Pa.: Fulton County Historical Society, 2001.

———. *Civil War Invasions in Fulton County*. McConnellsburg, Pa.: Fulton County Historical Society, 1979.

Crouch, Richard E. *Rough Riding-Scout: The Story of John W. Mobberly Loudoun's Own Civil War Guerrilla Hero*. Arlington, Va.: Elden Editions, 1994.

Curran, Thomas F. "Memory, Myths, and Musty Records: Charles Woodson's Missouri Cavalry in the Army of Northern Virginia," Part 1. *Missouri Historical Review* 9 (October 1999): 25–40.

———. "Memory, Myths, and Musty Records: Charles Woodson's Missouri Cavalry in the Army of Northern Virginia," Part 2. *Missouri Historical Review* 94 (January 2000): 160–75.

Delauter, Roger U., Jr. *18th Virginia Cavalry*. Lynchburg, Va.: H. E. Howard, 1985.

———. *McNeill's Rangers*. Lynchburg, Va.: H. E. Howard, 1988.

———. *62nd Virginia Infantry*. Lynchburg, Va. H. E. Howard, 1988.

Denney, Robert E. *The Civil War Years: A Day-By-Day Chronicle*. New York: Gramercy Books, 1992.

Donehoo, Dr. George F., ed. *A History of the Cumberland Valley in Pennsylvania*. Harrisburg: Susquehanna History Association, 1930.

Driver, Robert J., Jr. *First and Second Maryland Cavalry, C.S.A.* Charlottesville, N.C.: Rockbridge Publishing, 1999.

Duncan, Richard R. "The Raid on Piedmont and the Crippling of Franz Sigel in the Shenandoah Valley." *West Virginia History* 55 (1996): 25–40.

Evans, Thomas J., and James M. Moyer. *Mosby's Confederacy: A Guide to the Roads and Sites of Colonel John Singleton Mosby.* Shippensburg, Pa.: White Mane Publishing, 1991.

French, Steve. *Imboden's Brigade in the Gettysburg Campaign.* Berkeley Springs, W.Va.: Steve French, 2008.

———. *Rebel Chronicles: Raiders, Scouts and Train Robbers of the Upper-Potomac.* Hedgesville, W.Va.: Steve French, 2012.

Gardner, Mark Lee. *Shot All To Hell: Jesse James, The Northfield Minnesota Raid, and the Wild West's Greatest Escape.* New York: William Morrow, 2013.

Grant, John. "Battle of Bloomington Bridge." *Glades Star–Civil War Sesquicentennial Issue.* November 2012, 37.

Grant, Patience. "Episodes of Cavalry Raids of 1863." *Glades Star–Civil War Sesquicentennial Issue*, November 2012, 26–27.

Haselberger, Francis E. *Confederate Retaliation: McCausland's 1864 Raid.* Shippensburg, Pa.: Burd Street Press, 2000.

———. "General Rosser's Raid on New Creek Depot." *West Virginia History* 26 (January 1965): 86–109.

———. "Skirmishes at South Branch and Patterson's Creek, West Virginia." *West Virginia History* 25 (July 1964): 265–69.

———. "Union Troops in Cumberland." Unpublished manuscript. N.d. Private collection of Woodrow Simmons.

Howard, Ken. "George Robert Latham." *West Virginia Encyclopedia.* Charleston: West Virginia Humanities Council, 2006, 410–11.

Hoye, Captain Charles E. "The War in This Section." *Glades Star–Civil War Sesquicentennial Edition*, November 2012, 19–22.

Jones, Virgil Carrington. *Gray Ghosts and Rebel Raiders.* New York: Henry Holt, 1958.

Joynes, J. William, ed. *184 Miles of Adventure: Hiker's Guide to the C&O Canal.* Baltimore: Boy Scouts of America, 1970.

Judy, Elvin Lycurgus. *History of Grant and Hardy Counties, West Virginia.* Charleston: Charleston Print Company, 1951.

Keen, Hugh C., and Horace Mewborn. *43rd Battalion Virginia Cavalry Mosby's Command.* Lynchburg, Va.: H. E. Howard. 1983.

Keller, S. Roger, ed. *Riding with Rosser.* Shippensburg, Pa.: Burd Street Press, 1997.

Knight, Charles M. *Valley Thunder: The Battle of New Market.* New York: Savas Beatie, 2010.

Maier, Larry B., ed. *Leather and Steel: The 12th Pennsylvania Cavalry in the Civil War.* Shippensburg, Pa.: Burd Street Press, 2001.

McClelland, Ross. "We Were Enemies: Pennsylvanians and Virginia Guerrillas." *Civil War Times* 22: December 1983, 40–45.

McElroy, John. "Highly Important But Not Official." *Pearson's Magazine* 17 (June 1907): 654–60.

Noyalas, Jonathan. *"My Will Is Absolute Law": A Biography of Union General Robert H. Milroy.* Jefferson, N.C.: McFarland, 2006.

Pauley, Michael J. *Carskadon House.* Washington, D.C.: National Park Service, 1986. www.wvculture.org/shpp/nr/mineral/87000487.pdf.

Piston, William Garrett, and Richard W. Hatcher. *Wilson's Creek: The Second Battle of the Civil War and the Men Who Fought It.* Chapel Hill: University of North Carolina Press, 2000.

Price, W. W. "Fort Pendleton." *Glades Star–Civil War Sesquicentennial Issue.* November 2012, 27–29.

Pugh, Maud. *Capon Valley: Its Pioneers and Their Descendents, 1698–1940.* Baltimore: Gateway Press, 1948.

Roberts, Charles S. *The West End-Cumberland to Grafton 1849–1991.* Baltimore: Barnard, Roberts, 1991.

Robinson, Felix, ed. "The General's Last Story." *Tableland Trails* 2, no. 2 (Summer 1956).

Roy, Carrie H. *Captain Snyder and His Twelve of West Virginia.* New York: Hearthstone Press, 1977.

Sauers, Richard A. *The Devastating Hand of War: Romney, West Virginia During the Civil War.* Glen Farris, W.Va.: Gauley Mountain Press, 2001.

Scott, Harold, Sr. *The Civil War Era in Cumberland, Maryland and Nearby Keyser, West Virginia.* Cumberland, Md.: Harold Scott, 2000.

Sifikas, Stewart. *Who Was Who in the Civil War.* New York: Facts on File, 1988.

Smith, G. Wayne. *Nathan Goff, Jr.: A Biography.* Charleston, W.Va.: Education Foundation, 1959.

Snyder, Tim. "Potomac River Fords Used by Union and Confederate Armies. 1861–1865." N.d. Unpublished manuscript. Private collection of the author.

Stegmier, Mark Joseph. "The Kidnapping of Generals Crook and Kelley by McNeill's Rangers." *West Virginia History* 29 (1967): 13–43.

Summers, Festus. *The Baltimore and Ohio in the Civil War.* Gettysburg: Stan Clark Military Books, 1993.

Thomas, James W., and Thomas J. C. Williams. *History of Allegany County, Maryland.* Vol. 1. Baltimore: L. R. Titsworth, 1924.

Thompson, John W., IV. *Horses, Hostages and Apple Cider: J.E.B. Stuart's 1862 Pennsylvania Raid.* Mercersburg, Pa.: Mercersburg Printing, 2002.

Toomey, Daniel Carroll. *The War Came By Train: The Baltimore & Ohio Railroad During the Civil War.* Baltimore: Baltimore & Ohio Railroad Museum, 2013.

Tucker, Spencer C. *Brigadier General John D. Imboden: Confederate Commander in the Shenandoah.* Lexington: University Press of Kentucky, 2003.

Van Meter, Benjamin F. *Genealogies and Sketches of Some Old Families.* Louisville: John
    P. Morton, 1901.
Voorhees, Mary. "Lost River." In *West Virginia Encyclopedia,* 435. Charleston: Charles-
    ton, West Virginia Humanities Council, 2006.
Watro, Lonnie. "Forgotten Mountain Men of Freedom." www.wvgenweb.org.
Wert, Jeffrey. "Attacking the Invincible." *Civil War Times Illustrated* 20 (Feb. 1982): 8–17.
———. "George Crook: Sheridan's Second Fiddle." *Civil War Times* 22 (December
    1983): 10–17.
Wiley, S. T. *History of Preston County.* Parsons, W.Va.: McClain, 1990.
Wood, Lenora. "Bloomington Captured by McNeill's Confederate Rangers." *Glades
    Star–Civil War Sesquicentennial Issue,* 2012, 2–3.
———. "Capture of Bloomington Bridge Formed Incident in Local History During
    Civil War." *Moorefield Examiner,* n.d.
Woodward, Harold R., Jr. *Defender of the Valley: Brigadier General John D. Imboden
    C.S.A.* Berryville, Va.: Rockbridge, 1996.

Index

Neill's Rangers in, 217; James Mulligan's command leaving, 26; John D. Imboden's forces march on, 61; McNeill's Rangers in, 126, 154; occupation by Robert H. Milroy's troops, 21, 22, 23; raid by John H. McNeill, 62, 63; rebel advance on, 24, 25; reunion of McNeill's Rangers in, 219; Thomas "Tom" Rosser's Cavalry near, 157; Stephens evacuation of, 61; Union search for Harry Gilmor in, 175, 177, 178; Union troops in, 58, 59, 61, 100, 101, 106, 108, 136, 152, 201

Moorefield-Allegheny Junction, 73, 78, 107

Moorefield and Allegheny Turnpike, 160

Moorehead, Robert, 198

Morgan, John Hunt, 69–70

Morgantown, WV, 38, 39, 40

Morrow, James E., 62, 63–64

Morton, Samuel W., 91

Mosby, John S., 53, 80, 91, 148, 202, 207–8

Mosby's Rangers, 99, 147, 148

Mount Crawford, 205

Mount Jackson, 104, 141, 144, 153, 207

Mount Storm, 38

Mulligan, James, 5, 25, 26, 36, 41, 62, 63, 74, 78, 85, 86; alert to attack on Moorefield, WV, 61; attack by Sterling Price, 3–4; death of, 128; guarding of railroad, 108; occupation of Petersburg, WV, 61; plan to capture rebel camp, 62, 64; and surrender to Sterling Price, 4; wintering in Petersburg, WV, 69; wounding of, 4

Mulligan, Marian, 4

Mullihan, George D., 177, 178, 179, 180

Myers, Frank, 167

Myers, Henry A., 20, 25, 34–35, 100, 101, 102, 103

Myrtle Street Prison, 5. *See also* Bernard Lynch's Slave Market

National Pike, 45, 130

Neismith, John H., 141

Nesbitt, Otho, 54, 56

New Creek, WV, 20, 36, 57, 99, 113, 126, 127, 134, 138, 164; attack by Thomas "Tom" Rosser, 155, 160, 162, 163, 166, 167; attack by John McClausland, 134; attack by McNeill's Rangers, 92, 93, 94; Confederate soldiers surrendering at, 214, 216, 217;

James Mulligan's command returning to, 26; Pendleton County Scouts in, 112; Robert E. Lee's decision to attack, 78; Union soldiers in, 11, 16, 33, 95, 111, 148, 152, 153

Newhard, Edward, 14

New Market, Battle of, 104, 119

New Market, VA, 82, 104, 108; Confederate camps at, 167

New York Herald, 180, 181

newspapers. *See individual newspapers*

Nichols, Charles, 189

Nichols, Clifton, 132

Nichols, Clinton, 99

Nichols, William D., 114, 115, 120, 122, 127

9th Maryland Infantry, 67, 119

Norton, Chauncey, 151

North Branch Potomac River, 134, 162, 163

North Branch Bridge, 121, 126

North Branch Turnpike, 21

North Fork, 140, 207

North River, 12, 205

North River Mountain, 12

Northwestern Hotel, 12

Northwestern Turnpike, 21, 28, 33, 38, 92, 98

Northwestern Virginia Brigade, 28, 47, 66

Northwestern Virginia Railroad, 32, 41, 42

Norton, Chauncey, 151

Oakland, MD, 31, 33, 38, 39, 60

Ohio National Guard, 99, 138

Ohio River, 33

Old Fields, WV, 21, 22, 34, 35, 36, 37, 69, 74, 84, 135; battles in, 164; Confederate soldiers in, 136, 141; McNeill's Rangers in, 92, 167; Union soldiers in, 106, 153

Old Town, MD, 122, 127, 130, 132

Oley, John S., 171

Olivet Cemetery, 62, 114, 171, 218, 219; burial of John H. McNeill, 82; McNeill's Rangers buried in, 108, 114; reburial of John H. McNeill in, 171

154th Ohio National Guard, 106

152nd Ohio National Guard, 99, 121, 132, 133

153rd Ohio National Guard, 114, 120, 121, 130, 138

116th Ohio Infantry, 24

123rd Ohio Infantry, 24, 26, 29

Orange Court House, VA, 69